A George P. Elliott Reader

The Bread Loaf Series of Contemporary Writers

GEORGE P. ELLIOTT

A George P. Elliott
READER

SELECTED

POETRY AND PROSE

Middlebury College Press
Published by University Press of New England
Hanover and London

MIDDLEBURY COLLEGE PRESS
Published by University Press of New England,
Hanover, NH 03755
© 1992 by the Estate of George P. Elliott
All rights reserved
Printed in the United States of America   5   4   3   2   1

CIP data appear at the end of the book

Contents

A Bread Loaf Contemporary

A T A T I M E when the literary world is increasingly dominated by commercial formulas and concentrated financial power, there is a clear need to restore the simple pleasures of reading: the experience of opening a book by an author you know and being delighted by a completely new dimension of her or his art, the joy of seeing an author break free of any formula to reveal the power of the well-written word. The best writing, many authors affirm, comes as a gift; the best reading comes when the author passes that gift to the reader, a gift the author could imagine only by taking risks in a variety of genres including short stories, poetry, and essays.

As editors of The Bread Loaf Series of Contemporary Writers we subscribe to no single viewpoint. Our singular goal is to publish writing that moves the reader: by the beauty and lucidity of its language, by its underlying argument, by its force of vision. These values are celebrated each summer at the Writers' Conference on Bread Loaf Mountain in Vermont and in each of these books.

We offer you the Bread Loaf Contemporary Writers series and the treasures with which these authors have surprised us.

Robert Pack
Jay Parini

About the Author

GEORGE P. ELLIOTT was born on June 16, 1918, in Knightstown, Indiana, and grew up on a plantation in the southern California desert near Riverside. In 1941 he married Mary Emma Jeffress, who later became an editor for the *Hudson Review,* and they had a daughter, Nora. He worked as a shipfitter, translating blueprints into directions for shipbuilders; as a junior analyst for the War Labor Board during World War II; as a reporter with the American Federation of Labor *News* for the San Francisco Bay area; as a business agent for the Technical Engineers, Architects and Draftsmen labor union; and for six months as a real estate broker in Berkeley. Educated at the University of California, Berkeley (B.A. 1939, M.A. 1941), he began teaching in 1947 at St. Mary's College of California. He stayed at St. Mary's through 1955, when he left to teach at Cornell University. He later taught at Barnard College in New York City, at the State University of Iowa at Ames, at Berkeley, and again at St. Mary's before going to Syracuse University, where he spent seventeen years, serving as coordinator of the graduate writing program from 1978 until the time of his death on May 3, 1980.

He was the recipient of two fellowships, in 1961 and 1970, from the Guggenheim Foundation; a Ford Foundation grant in 1965; an award for literary distinction from the National Institute of Arts and Letters (1969); two D. H. Lawrence fellowships; and fellowships from the Fund for the Advancement of Education (1953) and from the *Hudson Review* (1956). In 1971 he received an honorary Doctor of Humane Letters from St. Lawrence University. As a guest of the Rockefeller Foundation he twice spent a month, once in 1967 and again in 1977, at the Villa Serbelloni, Bellagio, Como, Italy.

His collection of short stories *Among the Dangs* was nominated for the 1962 National Book Awards, given by the American Institute of Arts and Letters. In 1977 he served as one of three judges in the fiction category for those awards. Elliott also served as a judge for the Guggenheim Foundation, four years for fiction and five for poetry; once for the National Endowment for the Arts; once for the New York Council of the Arts; twice for the Brandeis literary awards; twice for the Hopwood awards; and once for the University of Iowa Press short story collection contest. He was on the Supervising Committee of the English Institute (1967–70), and he served as outside reader several times for university presses—the University of Georgia Press, L.S.U. Press, the University of Chicago Press, Oxford University Press, B.Y.U. Press, and Cornell University Press. He was a member of the Corporation of Yaddo from 1965 to 1980, for which he served on the Executive and Admissions Committees, and he taught several summers at the Bread Loaf Writers' Conference. In 1978 he served as a member of the Board of Directors of the Associated Writing Programs.

George Elliott's career as a teacher and a man of letters included his participation at many writers' conferences, including those of Bread Loaf, the University of Utah, Northwestern University, the University of Colorado, the University of Florida, the University of Santa Clara, Green Mountains, the University of Rochester, and Olivet College. He taught classes and conducted writing workshops around the country and abroad and from 1962 to 1977 gave 118 lectures and readings. Many of his lectures were printed as essays. These ranged in subject from Chekhov (presented as the first in a series on Chekhov given by writers at Cornell University in the fall of 1976 and printed in the *Cornell Review*) to the nature of beauty (*Snarls of Beauty,* given as a lecture at the University of Virginia and published in 1978 in the *Virginia Quarterly Review*). He taught graduate and undergraduate writing workshops and literature courses (on Henry James, Shakespeare, and Dante), directed doctoral dissertations, served on doctoral committees, directed master's theses in fiction and poetry, and served on master's theses committees in other disciplines—art, fine arts, religion, philosophy, and visual communications.

His publications are as follows: *Poems,* Porpoise Books, 1954; *Fifteen Modern American Poets* (editor), Holt, Rinehart & Winston, 1956; *Parktilden Village* (novel), Beacon, 1958; *Among the Dangs* (short stories), Holt, Rinehart & Winston, 1961; *Fever and Chills* (narrative poem), Stone Wall Press, 1961; *David Knudsen* (novel), Random House, 1962; *A Piece of Lettuce* (essays), Random House, 1964; *Fourteen Poems,* Goosetree Press, 1964; *Types of Prose Fiction* (editor), Random House, 1964; *In the World* (novel), Viking, 1965; *Dorothea Lange* (essay), Museum of Modern Art, distributed by Doubleday & Co., 1966; *From the Berkeley Hills* (poems), Harper & Row, 1968; *An Hour of Last Things* (short stories), Harper & Row, 1968; *Conversions* (essays), Dutton, 1971; *Muriel* (novel), Dutton, 1972; *Young Woman's Song* (poetry), Red Hanrahan Press, 1972; *Themes in World Literature* (editor), Houghton Mifflin, 1975; and *Reaching* (poems), Santa Susana Press, California State University, Northridge Libraries, 1979.

R. P.

J. P.

S T O R I E S

Faq'

D U R I N G the war my geographer was a lieutenant in the Air Corps. On one of his trips to North Africa his plane flew over the lower edge of the Atlas Mountains, where they meet the Sahara. For long stretches the range was a desolation, as he had expected, relieved only by a few ribbons of green. No doubt rivers from melting snows came down these valleys and squandered themselves in the desert, supplying just enough water to keep a strip of trees and grasses alive on their banks. All this was what he had learned in his studies. But he had also been taught that no one lived on the south side of the mountains, and yet he was quite certain that in one of the valleys he had seen a cluster of huts and some smoke weaving up through the trees. The smoke could have been mist—though it was a hot clear day—but the huts were certainly human dwellings. His curiosity was aroused. He resolved to satisfy it as soon as he was able.

After the war, when he was able to investigate, he discovered only two references to anything that could possibly be identified as his special valley. The first was in a book written in 1837 by one Benjamin Huntley, *Exploring the Atlas Mountains*. Huntley mentions hearing of the existence of a village somewhere south of Mount Tizi, but he says he doubts if his informants were reliable. The other reference was in a twelfth-century Arabic manuscript now in the Royal Library in Madrid, a report on revenues from slave trading in Spain and northwest Africa. On a map in this manuscript a spot considerably south and west of Mount Tizi is identified as Faq'. There is nothing in the text to explain Faq'; there was nothing but the word itself on the old parchment map. There was nothing else at all anywhere. What was he to do?

If he sought the assistance of one of the learned societies, he would certainly lose much or all of the credit for the discovery—if discovery there was to be. But the expenses would probably come to more than his purse could bear, unless he risked making the explorations quite alone and with no further reconnaissance by air. And it was a risk— the region was a true wilderness, mountainous, arid, huge, and inhospitable even to plants. But he was young and a good mountaineer and he could speak Arabic, and for years he had been risking his life for a lesser cause—to him—than this. His is the sort that wants every place to be given its right name; for him the words terra incognita signify an admission of defeat or a region of impenetrable cold; error is his evil. It was clear what he must do: discover Faq'.

I will not tell you much about the adventures he had before he reached his goal, the delays caused by the suspicion and incredulity of small officials, the hostility of the hill people, the grandeur of that wilderness in which he wandered for weeks not even sure of the existence of his goal, the privation and fatigue and load of bad doubt which only his pride could support, the great good fortune by which he was saved from starvation by a wounded eagle dropping from the skies near to him—too weak to kill it outright, he had to suck its blood. But finally he stood at the brink of a fertile valley, a valley flat and broad for these mountains, but inaccessible from above because of the sheer rise of the range and from the sides because of the steep cliffs and, as he found, uninviting from below because it narrowed to a gorge that emptied the river out precipitously; but people lived here—it was Faq'. It took him three days to discover the tortuous route of access into the valley, and one whole day to get to the floor. Among rushes at the edge of the river he collapsed, one hand trailing in the water, flat on his belly, sunk at last into that weariness which his pride no longer needed to deny. He lay there for at least one day and perhaps two, he had no way of knowing. When he awoke he could scarcely roll over, and the hand which had fallen into the water was wrinkled white and seemed to be paralyzed. It was lucky for him that he was not discovered, for the women of Faq' would have killed him if they had found him asleep.

He finally rolled onto his back, and lay wondering whether he would ever be able to get up. But as he lay there in the soft rushes in the warmth of afternoon he began to notice, as though for the first time, that vast clean sky under which he had so long labored; and in his fatigue he could not resist the sudden fancy that the sky was not *over* him—he was not *below* its perfection, but rather he was a part of it. "For is not the blueness of the sky," he said to himself, "achieved only by the refraction of light on innumerable particles, which are about me here as well as out there, and maybe in me for all I know?" The longer he lay, looking not up but out, into, among, the more it seemed to him that the sky was not so absolute a blue as it had been on the days before. Yet there could be no mist, not here on this side of these mountains. He lay wondering whether so much blandness had deceived his senses, but he was swimming in that perfection all the same; and then suddenly an explanation for the seeming mistiness occurred to him. It was a light smoke haze. He remembered the curls of smoke he had seen from the airplane, and he observed that there was no wind. No doubt a nearly imperceptible film of smoke obscured his perfect vision. This saddened him for a moment, but then he thought, "Why is it not as absolute a perfection, the sky with this faint and even haze in it, as a clean sky? These smoke particles have been added, but thinly like the blue particles, perfectly distributed. They are not an adulteration, but a version of that other perfection, a part of it, distributed differently now than before; if it hadn't been for that tiny difference I would never have noticed the whole, huge sublimity, and who can say that one of these versions is truer than the other?" Full of these reflections he arose and went down the riverside in search of friends.

He had not gone far when he heard children's laughter in the woods across the river. The stream was neither very wide nor fast-flowing, and at its deepest it did not come over his chest; yet he thought he would never get across it alive. When he was ten yards from the opposite shore he fell in exhaustion into the stream, and floated on the current more dead than alive. But he was caught in an eddy where he lay with his nose and eyes just sticking above water, slowly revolving under the green shade of an hospitable tree like a log in the pool. All he had to do to save himself was to crawl up under the tree onto a pleasant bank. But it didn't seem worth the trouble. It was too lovely there to move, looking up into the twining imperfections of this tree, cool and still and spread out and wet, slowly going about in the eddy, finally without will, only a thing that once had been able to think and now was at peace in the enveloping water, in one complete embrace happy. He does not yet understand why he ever climbed out of the water. He was not conscious of making a decision. All of a sudden it came to him that the sun had gone down and it was time to come home; before he could reflect on this odd notion (where was home?) he found himself climbing out on the bank, a live man again. Never since then has he felt anything out of the ordinary about floating in a river or looking at the sky, and he doesn't know exactly how to explain the experiences of that day— his fatigue perhaps, or the special air and water there, or his relief at finding his goal. What he is sure of is this: while he didn't know what to expect from the people of Faq', he was prepared for it when it came.

It was dusk when he approached the huts. They were long and thin, and all of them pointed up the valley toward the mountains. There were no windows in them. They were interspersed among trees. At some distance he could see a large hut in which there were fire, cooking, noise, children. He crept up to the closest hut, and crouched on the dark side of it listening to the mutter coming from within. The muttering was fast and monotonous, in a man's voice. It seemed to be a praying in some Arabic dialect. He could make out some of the words, or thought he could; they seemed to be numerals. As he listened to that unflagging drone it occurred to him that this must be a machine, no man could do it; but then he heard a clearing of the throat and a slight pause, and he realized it was a man all right, but a man imitating a machine. A praying machine. He thought of hermits.

Footsteps approached. He glued himself to the wall. He heard a woman murmuring, a slight altercation, a moment of laughter, stirring sounds, and then footsteps going away. He looked carefully around the edge of the building and saw a well-built young man, not an old one as he had expected, and a young woman. Side by side they were approaching the building of light and noise. Others were coming to it also. There were no dogs around; at least none had smelled him out, none were barking. He crept nearer the communal house. The odor of cooking food nearly made him faint it was so pleasant. Nevertheless, he lay low a while, trying to understand what was going on. Everything about the scene appeared to be unexceptional and happy. There were several men and many more women and a good many children. Three old women came out into the darkness and on the way to their hut began singing quietly a song the like of which he had never heard. He saw a young man catch and embrace a struggling young woman at the door to the hut, to the general merriment, all with an openness which he had never so much as heard of among Mohammedans. He had no idea what would be best for him to do.

What he finally did was to walk straight toward the doorway crying as loud as he could, which was not very loud, "Food in the name of Allah!"

Well, they took care of him, fed him, and nursed him back to strength again. He learned later that he was the only outsider who had ever been allowed to live in Faq'—to stay alive, I mean, not just abide there. I think it was more than a matter of whim that he was allowed to stay. He was completely at their mercy and they could understand something of what he said, so much was in his favor; but mostly he helped himself with his own honest pride.

After he had eaten some of the vegetable stew which is their chief food, watched intently by a hundred dark, silent faces, the chief, Alfaleen, asked him in their dialect who he was. Now my geographer had noticed that no one had mentioned Allah and that the chief's style was very plain for Arabic, with none of those honorific courtesies universal among Mohammedans. He had noticed this, but hadn't known what to make of it. He answered, "Destroyer of boundaries." There was no response. Either they had not understood his accent or else they were not at all impressed. "Foe of all ignorance," he said. No response. "Seeker of truth."

Then Alfaleen said to him, "What must be?"

"What has always been will always be."

Alfaleen repeated, "What must be?"

"So long as there are hills the rain will flow down them in streams."

Alfaleen repeated, "What must be?"

"Each number will always have two neighbors."

But Alfaleen asked again, "What must be?"

And this time he gave the answer he would never before in his life have given: "Nothing." It saved him.

He has wondered a thousand times why he gave that unlikely answer. He had of course heard of the indeterminacy principle; he had heard, with fascination, that law is a matter of statistical probability and that truth is finally a matter of whichever of the many geometries best suits your needs. But since he had never been able to imagine such things he had not believed in them, and he certainly had never asked himself whether or not a stone *must* fall, two plus two *must* equal four. Yet he had said to Alfaleen, that black, cool, impersonal man, that nothing must be. He attributes this answer of his to the power of Alfaleen's mind. He was concentrating hard on understanding what was being said to him and on choosing the correct Arabic words for his answers, he was weak with fatigue, he sensed that much depended upon his answer, and he was alerted by the very strangeness of the question. Even so, he thinks it was the power of that other mind which put the answer into his mouth. He learned to respect that power.

For a week he convalesced. The women and children, among whom he stayed, treated him with all the friendliness in the world. Alfaleen had commanded him to tell them nothing about the place from which he had come, and had also commanded them not to ask him about it. He had nothing to do but to lie about listening to them, learning what their customs were and how they thought and what they were afraid of—not learning it so much as taking it in like the food and water and bright air. He observed that none of the mature men did any of the ordinary tasks, like gathering fuel, fishing, repairing the huts, irrigating the fields; they seemed to have some other work. The women did not resent this state of affairs; it had not occurred to them, apparently, that things could be otherwise arranged. The children were amazingly unrestricted and happy. There were at least twice as many girls as boys for some reason, but the women did not seem to treat the boys with any great reverence. The children were not allowed to go near the huts at the other end of the village (where he had heard the man praying like a machine). Every morning Alfaleen would take the boys over five off to school. The girls learned from the women. Boys were punished for being too rough, too "manly"; girls were punished for using a number over one hundred. The children had a game which they loved to play, with innumerable variations: a boy would sit in a special position and begin to count in a low regular voice, and a girl or perhaps two or three of them would try to distract him. They would use every means imaginable except hurting: shout in his ear, caress him, throw cold water on him, count backwards in his same rhythm, put food in his mouth. Some of the boys had developed amazing powers of concentration, but the wiles of the girls were irresistible. No boy could hold out for more than a quarter of an hour—but no ordinary boy

8

would have held out against those girls for two minutes, whatever he was doing. One little girl, about eight or nine, who was particularly attached to him—a quiet thing with a clumsy, strong body, rather deliberate, rather grave—told him one morning that she had had a nightmare about the end of the world. She had dreamed, she said, that "they came to the end of the counting and I was one of the ones left over." A little boy who got angry with him once called him a "slow counter." From the awed silence and snickers with which the other children greeted this, he concluded that it was a serious insult. The women and children were the happiest he had ever seen; yet there was nothing intense about what they did. They seemed never to have suffered. He was too feeble, too contented to feel any strangeness about all this; while it lasted it seemed exactly the way things should be. But when he was strong again at the end of a week and Alfaleen removed him from his idyl he was glad it was over.

At first Alfaleen asked him questions about the world from which he had come. "Which men are most revered? Which have the greatest power? For what is a man put to death? What is God nowadays?" But the questioning did not go on for long. Alfaleen was feeling him out, determining just how to introduce him to the life which he was entering. To one who lives with beauty hourly, as to a man in love, the various semblances of beauty to which he may be exposed are all imperfect and not in the least interesting; he wants to be with the true beauty. Alfaleen's was the beauty of truth, and he wanted to share it. He tried tricks and deceptions in his questioning, but he was hopelessly honest; it was clear that no one had lied in Faq' for a long time.

Well, the upshot of it all was that he was deemed worthy to become a bearer of the mystery of the truth, a participant in it. He was taken to a hut of his own in the men's section of the village—a bare, dark, quiet hut—and there taught to count. One sat in a certain manner—the way the boys had sat in their game—weaved in a certain rhythm, closed one's senses to the outside world, thought only of the perfection of one's technique, and counted in a steady voice. He was given a block of numbers very high in the series, told certain permissible abbreviations and short cuts, and left each morning to his counting. Alfaleen instructed him each afternoon in the history and aims of Faq'. He understood it all in a way. He was quite good at counting. But then he had to be; anyone who fell below a certain monthly quota was put to death. So was any cheater. Alfaleen would prowl about outside the huts listening to the voices of the counters—two or three times a day he came by, so keen and trained that he could tell by the very cadences of the murmuring count whether the counter was in danger of falling behind. There were no cheaters.

In the tenth century, when the Arabs were conquerors of north Africa and Spain and were also developing advanced mathematical theories, a nobleman-mathematician named Alfaleen stopped in the province of Maraq' while en route to Spain to enter the faculty of the new college of mathematics. But he fell out with the theologians of Maraq' and was condemned for his heresy. Alfaleen had maintained that pure reason, and only pure reason, could ever achieve the truth, and that since thought was the greatest power in the universe then Allah must be thought. According to the theologians this was as much as to say that the Koran wasn't worth a couple of quadratic equations and that if God is idea then idea is God. To rescue the youth of Spain from such notions they recommended to the governor of Maraq' that he execute Alfaleen. But the governor was an old friend of Alfaleen's father; instead of executing him, he had him and all his party driven off into the granite wilderness to perish for heresy. And that would have been that; but by some hook or crook they fell in with a band of native blacks, founded Faq', and established a colony. Their descendants have lived there in peace ever since. They had no animals or tools, but none were needed. The outside world forgot they were there, and any stranger who happened to come to Faq' was put to death.

So far as their traditions tell, the constitution of Faq' has remained unaltered since its founding—the laws of reason are ageless. There is Alfaleen, the chief, the philosopher, the king; there are the men, who count; and there are the women, who do the work and tend to the men. The original Alfaleen, to whose genius Faq' owes its peace and its purpose, had by the exercise of pure reason seen the folly of racial distinctions; blacks and Arabs had intermingled as they desired, the third Alfaleen was himself pure black, and by now the blend of races is complete. He had seen the problem of keeping down the population; defectives, women who can no longer work, innovators, are all put to death. The ratio of women to men had been kept fairly constant at three to one. Though the women, having no souls, cannot be entrusted with the high mission of Faq', yet the actual survival of the colony has come more and more to rest upon them—they weed out the unfit, they maintain everyone physically, and they keep watch on the men. Indeed, though Alfaleen is the governor, it is the women who actually make and execute all the rules and customs—except, of course, those having to do with the only thing that matters, the exercise of pure reason, the counting.

For Alfaleen had set his people reason's purest problem: number. And each Alfaleen, chosen solely for his ability, spends his life in the contemplation of number and the attributes of number in the confidence that the penetration of this mystery, the final conquering of it, will lay bare the secret to all power. But not many men are capable of such true and ultimate endeavor; hence, as soon as the colony had stabilized itself, Alfaleen, like a good philosopher-king, had set his subjects to the accomplishment of a communal task, one which in its very nature surpasses any other that men have set themselves: counting. By hypothesis the highest nameable number is as far from the end as one is, and there is no end to counting. It is the function of Faq' to test this hypothesis in the only statistically verifiable fashion, actually by counting forever.

The women may not use a number greater than one hundred; the life of Faq' does not make larger numbers necessary and woman's reason would sully truth. Originally there was much defection from the strict regime, and at one time had the insurrectionists banded together they could have overthrown the rule of this godless theocracy, but Alfaleen won out. They have reached a very high number; they expect in our lifetime to reach the number beyond which numbers have no name. Into that darkness Alfaleen will shed the light of reason.

More and more in the past few centuries Alfaleen has come to believe that the core of the problem of number lies in its oneness-endlessness and that the original impulse which set the men of Faq' to telling the rosary of reason's mystery was by no means an expedient but rather an attempt to mechanize the mystery itself. For this, says Alfaleen, is not only the activity of reason, it is reason pure, this counting, because only incidentally does it correspond to anything outside man's mind. It becomes clearer and clearer that without this endless and exact demonstration of reason's truth all reason would be subverted and mankind go back to what it had been before.

Alfaleen said, and certainly he believes it, that there is a sense in which man's destiny hangs upon those counters in Faq', for that they do not reach the end of counting is the demonstration of all hypothesis. If they should reach the end, reason would have done what is impossible to it and the rest would be chess, for then they would have proved that reason too has its law—absolute positive correlation. But if they should quit counting—weary, exhausted, rebellious, defeated—then would you and I have succumbed at last to our weariness and rebellion and defeat, and the women would take over.

At first he was exhilarated by the novelty of the life and what seemed to be the importance of the counting. At the outset boredom was the dread at the back of his mind, but in fact he was never bored. The counting seemed to hypnotize him into a state of strange tranquility. He was tranced, as it were, into reason's realm. So much so, indeed, that it was not many weeks before he quite lost interest in exercise and food and the evening conviviality. Then girls taunted and seduced him, with an innocent artfulness and a voluptuous naïveté which he found (as had the boys in the game) irresistible. One night he counted in his sleep, and all the next day he was required to play with children and make love to young women and lie in the sun. Everything was communal in Faq', property and love as well as the great task. It was a world of reason and sense and trance, and he found it far happier than the world of mystery and strong feeling from which he had come. But eventually he began to think.

Or perhaps not to think so much as to remember. He remembered the anxiety and injustice and despair and the huge splendors of this world—the poverty, the right and wrong, the power, the pain. Especially the pain. He told himself again and again that ten thousand sink that one may rise, that whole cities stink in ugliness that fifty men may make and enjoy only a little beauty. But not all the reasonableness he could muster, nor horror at his memories, nor the truth and high pleasantness of Faq' could drive the thought of pain from his mind. For it was pain, suffering, moral agony, that his memories revolved about. It became clearer and clearer to him that he could not live without pain, not even thus participating in the great task of man's noblest faculty. He tried hurting himself physically; he had a large rock balanced precariously once, ready to roll onto his arm and smash it. But the absurdity of such an act here in this equable valley stopped him from doing it. And afterwards the indignity he felt at not having been able to prepare a greater pain for himself than this which any accident might provide, not having been able to go through with even this little thing made him resolve to leave Faq' as soon as he could. For a long time he had been dissembling at his counting, with great anxiety and guiltiness. Now that he had resolved to leave, all this counting suddenly seemed silly to him, and he dissembled without a qualm.

He sat day after day in his hut making the sounds of counting, and often actually tranced into it—it had its own power. But most of the time he was planning his escape. It was necessarily an escape too, for anyone guilty of any defection, from bad health to rebelliousness, was without mercy or remorse killed. He collected food and water and made himself a substitute for shoes. He walked on rocky ground till his feet were horny. He played and swam very hard till he was strong and supple. He had no human ties to break; four of the women were pregnant at the time, one perhaps with his child, perhaps all four, perhaps none, he did not care. He would miss Alfaleen's cold, pure speculations, but never, he knew, so much as he now missed the pain of this world of ours. He lay in the sun till he was nearly as black as they, and in the middle of one stormy night he left. He was not pursued.

He returned to us after much difficulty. He is suffering with us now, and looking back at the bland perfection of Faq' with a sometimes acute nostalgia. But my geographer is determined never to go there again, for he is sure that though he does not know what is right, for men ordered perfection is wrong, and that though suffering is bad, the lack of suffering is much worse.

Miss Cudahy of Stowes Landing

BINGHAM COULD NOT KNOCK at a strange door without a sense of adventure; to greet and win if he could whatever smiling or screw-eyed or blank stranger the door opened on made his heart beat a little faster, his breath come shorter. In the course of his duties with the Superior Court, he met very few new people, aside from lawyers or their secretaries; he liked the fact that in the manner of their official dealings lawyers still wear wigs, but he made no friends among them. He had a few acquaintances and family friends, and another friend, a woman, whom he might have married several years before but did not. Nearly every door he knocked at he had knocked at a hundred times before, except for the doors of old houses, which held his happiness.

So when one Saturday in early summer he knocked at Miss Cudahy's house in Stowes Landing and no one answered, he gratefully set about inspecting the exterior of the house with the attention it deserved. The telephone operator—in one of these small towns the central intelligence—had given him Miss Cudahy's name and had volunteered the information that she was old, suffered from rheumatism, and was very much the lady. He could see from the outside of the house that the operator had been right—only a lady would befit this grandest house in town; only a lady would have maintained it so handsomely against the sea weather of northern California; only a lady would have kept a marble birdbath in the garden, a Latin sundial under that usually overcast sky, a bronze, stark-naked, well-patinaed faun in a Concord arbor.

For although he was not sure of the rose window over the door, yet the dormer windows, the overhang, the complication of the roof, and the five gables meant to him New England on a hostile coast.

Stowes Landing had been built seventy years ago on the flats back from a three-hundred-foot cliff, north above a logging stream; the meadows stretched freely back for a mile to the line of forest and descending hills; nothing protected the houses from the sea breeze but a hedge for those that planted one. Yet Miss Cudahy's house stood two-and-a-half stories tall and massive, like some determined New Englanders bunched together, suspicious and prepared, resisting whatever the Indians, Spaniards, Mexicans, Russians, Southerners, Middle-Westerners, Chinese, Filipinos, Japanese, Africans, Italians, Armenians, of this dangerous land might have settled among themselves heathenishly to do. That was all right, what one expected, for 1880; but to find it so purely preserved, still yellow with green shutters, in these provinces of light stucco or stained wood, to be able to walk up to it behind its hedge in a legitimate—because pure—curiosity, this affected Bingham as strongly as some people are affected by shaking the hand that shook the hand of Lincoln. He was more excited, as he began his tour, than was altogether reasonable.

On the southern side of the house, the side where the hedge was only twenty feet tall, he found a grizzled little man leaning on the handle of a shovel. His stance and dull stare bespoke one who has worked hard and learned how to rest like a horse standing up; but there was no new-turned bed, no deep hole, only a small cleared space where he was probably going to plant a fuchsia, there being already sixty or seventy of them about the garden.

"Hello," said Bingham. The man did not respond, people frequently didn't. "The lady of the house is not home?"

"Happen Phoebe's out buying," he said in a British dialect so heavy Bingham could hardly understand him.

"I see. I hope you don't mind my looking around till she returns."

He had always made it a point not to start small talk in a situation like this; but that unresponsive gaze said to him, birth, marriage, death may be sizable enough to talk about mister but they are none too large. The man rubbed his chin on the end of the handle.

"I'm only interested in the house," Bingham went on, embarrassed to be introducing a subject so fugitive. "Miss Cudahy—could you tell me . . ."

But he heard, for the second time he realized, a sharp sound behind and above him, a sound as of a gem rapped against glass; when he felt the hairs stand up on the back of his hand he knew that he was being watched from behind the curtains by the eyes of one who had heard but had not answered his knock at the door. He left his sentence to dangle as it would and went on with his inspection; the man began to dig.

In the rear there was a pile of wood far more orderly than most of the garden, a vegetable patch, and a clothesline. And in the corner beyond the clothesline, half-hidden by an arc of delphiniums, there was a garden to itself, earth scratched and leveled, scarcely a dead petal on the blossoms, no rows but a wandering intermixed variety of plants and shrubs, stepping stones for paths; there were single roses and single geraniums, three tulips, Indian paintbrush, and succulents from the sea cliffs (most of them with small bright flowers, for June is spring in Mendocino) and a rolling fringe of yellow oxalis. He stood in a sort of wonder at the sweetness of that garden, at how dainty and feminine and itself it seemed down between the still-too-vigorous huge old house and the hedge which here was more than thirty feet in height. He wondered who Phoebe was.

That hedge—there were a number of such hedges along that part of the coast, but Miss Cudahy's was as dense and perfectly trimmed as any he had seen and much the highest. These hedges were dark green and thick and not very noisy even in the wind; very dark green, they were kept trimmed smooth as moss, with rounded edges, and this one which had ascents and dips in it for no reason that he could make out, at one point rose taller than the house; dark, impermeable cypress green, for though it kept out the wind it kept out everything else as well. He could not imagine how Chin-on-Shovel did the job of trimming, and he did not even want to imagine what it was like to live out a life with a prospect of gray skies, unkept fuchsias, and the dark of the green.

One at the front and the other at the rear, two arches ran through the hedge like the mouse runs that pierced the vast walls of Muscovite palaces. Through the rear gate as he was standing there a young woman entered, with a basket of groceries in one hand, a bonnet on her head—more a bonnet than a hat—and a spring to her step. "Hello," he said, but she did not look at him. He stepped forward between two delphiniums and called again. She stopped, her lips a little open with surprise, and looked at him with a directness, a lack of demure withdrawal, which rather surprised him. "Could you tell me, please," he began, but she turned from him and ran up the stairs and into the house. He could think of no better course than to wait for a few discreet minutes and go knock at the front door. This he did, though not without trepidation.

She answered, with lowered eyes. He apologized for having startled her and handed her his card. Without a word she walked back into the house. She appeared, at closer sight, a plain young woman, her hair drawn severely back to a bun, her face devoid of make-up yet not sallow, her clothes undistinguished for their color or grace; yet there was a certain tone to her body that set her off from an ordinary maid or housekeeper, a vigor to her step and a flirt, a fillip perhaps, to her skirts when she turned that charmed him. She returned and opened the door wide to him; he thanked her and stepped into the hall; she smiled, not just politely but as though she were suppressing some private amusement, and ushered him into the parlor.

There, swathed in pastel chiffons, lay a huge old woman on a chaise longue.

"Mr. Bingham!" she called forth like the captain of one brig to the captain of another. "Come in, sir. Sit down." And she made what seemed to be some sort of complicated hailing motions with her hands.

"Thank you, Miss Cudahy," he said, and sat in a pale oak horsehair chair near her. When he looked around the girl had disappeared. "I'm afraid I rather startled Phoebe out in the garden a few minutes ago."

"Did you?" she cried. "She did not inform me of that. And how do you know her name?"

"Your gardener, I gathered it from him."

"Ah yes, of course." And he saw how, with a loll of her great head and a flick of her left hand, heavy with rings, she peered out between the curtains invisibly. Then she, with a suddenness that surprised him, turned back and said to him sharply, "You're from the FBI."

He had seen witnesses caught off-balance, and had pitied them for their slowness and dullness; now here he was thrown by an old woman's judo.

"Who, me?" he said. "Oh no, gracious no. I'm only . . ."

"Very well," she waved his stuttering aside. "One of the other investigators. Which?"

"No, I assure you, I am interested in old houses. I enjoy them very much, and I . . ."

"I see." She paused, the sort of pause that did not permit him to speak. He sat watching her fill a curved pipe with tobacco, tamp it, and light up. "You may smoke," she said, and docilely he lit a cigarette. "You traced me through the California Historical Society."

"No," he said, "I am merely traveling, alone, along the Mendocino coast, looking for houses of the New England captains that settled here. And I found yours simply by driving down the street looking for it."

"How did you discover me behind this hedge?"

"By getting out of my automobile and looking through the gate."

"I see." She stared with a concentration as great as Phoebe's; it had an altogether different effect on him. "Well, you've seen the outside and you're in the parlor. What do you think?"

He began to exclaim over it, and rising asked her permission to investigate the parlor more closely.

"In good time," she said. "Sit down, Mr. Bingham. We will have tea."

She pulled a tasseled cord behind her head, and Phoebe appeared. She waved her hands at Phoebe with a mixture of fluttering and grace and indolence, and threw her head back onto the pillows. "Pardon me," she murmured; her mouth fell a little ajar. "One has to rest a good deal. More than one would have chosen."

He could look at her closely now. It was a heavy, pale, sensual face with dark pouches under the deep eyes; she was not so old as he had originally thought, not over sixty. Her arms were bare and fleshy; day was, he imagined, when those white arms had excited at least the admiration of men. He could see that one of her legs, extended on the chaise longue, was bound in some sort of rubber legging reaching halfway down the calf; the other, foot on the floor, would have served well on a duke in the days of knee breeches. She breathed heavily, nearly wheezing. "Asthma," she muttered, "damned nuisance." He sat straight in his slick, hard chair.

At the sound of Phoebe with the tea tray at the door, he turned in pleased expectation. "Don't bother to speak to her," said Miss Cudahy scarcely moving her gray lips; he realized that she must have been watching him from under her lids. "Phoebe is deaf and dumb."

He blushed and did not know where to look.

II

He did not see them again for a month and would not have gone back at all, even to see the rest of the house, had it not been for the newel, which he had only glanced at as he had been leaving the house; there was not another in California to compare to it. The month was workaday and legal, marked only by his failure to persuade an owner in North Oakland not to redecorate a Victorian specimen with mourning veil eaves, and by a rather curious invitation to speak. He received a telephone call and then a visit from a cultivated, charming, shrewd little woman named Pickman-Ellsworth, who wanted him to speak to the Alameda Fuchsia Society about the use of fuchsias in New England. He had to explain to her that he knew little about the subject and nothing at first hand. She received his refusal without protest, yet she continued talking, about one thing and another; she said that she had read some of his articles in the magazine *Golden West*; she kept throwing him subjects, visibly trying to "draw him out." He did not quite understand her purpose. She had black, quick eyes and sat very erect in her chair. She spoke to her chauffeur as she left with precisely that combination of dryness, condescension, and politeness with which she had addressed Bingham.

The newel at the foot of the stairs drew him back, that exquisitely carved, white newel with its promise of fine interiors on the second floor; the fluted newel, and, he had to confess it to himself, a curiosity about Miss Cudahy's household stronger than his repugnance for her herself.

He opened the gate, went through the hedge tunnel and walked up the stairs to the porch without seeing the English gardener. He knocked the grand knocker—Miss Cudahy had no doorbell, indeed he felt that the electric lights in the old gas fixtures had advanced progress enough for her—and he stood waiting for Phoebe to open to him. He had calculated to himself what expression and gesture would best let Phoebe know the friendliness and pity he felt for her, what smile would blend recognition and warmth and yet least intrude upon her intimacy; the deference of the superior to the afflicted seemed to Bingham one of the few courtesies surviving from that high and better-mannered world lost to us to our diminution. This he had calculated—or, rather, had hoped to achieve—but he reckoned without Phoebe. How could he have known her? A glimpse of her, brown-dressed in the garden, scurrying like a quail for cover; as maid in the hall, eyes downcast, smiling; a tea through which she had sat like a little girl, knees tightly pressed together, watching with a twinkle in her eye everything they did. How could he have known that the moment she opened the door now and saw him her eyes would light up, her cheeks would flush rosy red, her poor voice would crack a little, her hands would open out to him? Open so warmly and impetuously that he, smiling, would clasp them warmly in his, to the distress of all courtesy but to his most grateful pleasure. He did not touch people with casual affection, but rather shrank from it; he preferred words of congratulation to a slap on the back, the smile of privacy to a cocktail-party kiss. Fastidiousness entails its dangers; he accepted them knowingly. But Phoebe's hands, rough-skinned and strong with work yet smaller than his, feminine in his, did not presume any intimacy or force any warmth of response: they extended him her words of greeting, inflection of her pleasure, her affection even, yet with hand's immediacy, touch's conviction. He smiled at her, foolish with sudden pleasure; his condescension snapped in her hands like a twig. He did not even feel embarrassed. It was as though he had known her a long time.

She took his hat and coat—it was a windy afternoon—and when she returned from hanging them up and found him admiring the newel she pointed out to him something he had not yet noticed: the baseboard running along below the banisters, fretted beautifully and out of pure exuberance, uselessly, obscurely. She clasped her hands in pleasure at his pleasure.

He started to his feet at Miss Cudahy's large voice, "Mr. Bingham, is that you?"

He pointed, and Phoebe led him by the hand to the parlor door; as she opened the door she let go his hand; after he had gone in she withdrew from them like a maid.

"Mr. Bingham," said Miss Cudahy, frowning as he advanced, "what delayed you in the hall?"

"The newel," he said. "And Phoebe drew my attention to the fretted baseboard on the staircase."

"Did she?" said Miss Cudahy. "I hope you are well." And she took his hand.

"Very well," he answered, and it was all he could do to out-squeeze the gray-faced, lame old woman. "I hope in turn that your health has improved."

"How could it?" she said; she lolled back and pulled the rope. "At my age, in a climate like this, with no one to talk to?"

"It is hard," he said; he could scarcely have said less.

"Do you know how hard?" she replied scornfully. Phoebe appeared and Miss Cudahy waved some message at her. "Mr. Bingham, are you intending to buy my house? What do you want of me?"

"Believe me, I am interested only in the beauty of your house. I study old houses as an avocation."

"Beauty comes high on the market these days," she said fixing him with her eye. "Some kinds of beauty. Does this kind?"

"No," he answered flatly. "It does not."

"Are you just here for the day again, Mr. Bingham?"

"No, I am spending part of my vacation exploring these parts."

"How much of it, do you think?"

"That depends upon many considerations."

"One of which is me, I take it?"

"Indeed," he said in the manner of a gallant, "how could it be otherwise?"

"The *Golden West* said you were a lawyer."

"Not exactly a lawyer. I am in legal work."

"Not a lawyer but in legal work," she repeated. "Slippery."

"Miss Cudahy," he said, arising, with all the dignity he could muster, "I would very much appreciate your permission to explore the rest of this house. I will take no photographs of it and write nothing about it for publication without your signed permission." This was more than she had let him get out during his entire first visit; only his anger had broken him through her complex defense so that he could now confront her simply with what he wanted.

"Ho," she shouted, "I've offended you, have I? I offend people. It usually takes longer with others. You are different. Sit down, young man, you've seen only this room and the hall, and there's more here worth the seeing you may be sure."

He sat down, gritting his teeth behind his smile. "The newel, Miss Cudahy, is worthy of McIntyre himself."

"Yes," she said quizzically, "worthy of him. In the master bedroom"—she knew how to play her mouse—"on the second floor, Mr. Bingham, where I have not been for three years—my damned joints," she said banging the knee of her left leg—"in the master bed-room, when you get to it, you will notice the mantel. McIntyre, is it? I must tell you about that someday."

"Why not tell me now?" he said with the last of his anger.

Phoebe came in bearing the tea things; neither of them turned toward her.

"Because, Mr. Bingham, it is not my pleasure."

They had tea.

III

For the twentieth time he looked at the note she had slipped into his hand: "Meet me outside the rear gate at 4:30." Already he had waited a quarter of an hour; a cold wind was blowing in from the sea; every fantasy of waiting afflicted him, wrong time, wrong place, accident, change of heart; he shivered back into his car. He did not happen to be looking when she came through the hedge and ran around the back of his car. Suddenly there she was, opening the door and slipping in beside him smiling. The ruefulness, the trace of anxiety vanished from her face when she saw how gladly he forgave her, her forehead smoothed, she squeezed his arm. What could he do but take her hands in his? The good humor and affection of her smile became a sort of radiance which warmed him, as he would not have believed possible three hours before.

What did she want? He started to draw out a pencil and paper, but she gently restrained his hands. With perfect good humor and seriousness, in a few quick gestures, she suggested driving some-where, getting out, and walking. He started the car; she directed. On the cliff above a turbulent, rocky surf she stopped them and led him down a path. He heard a bell buoy offshore busy in its melan-choly; he had never stood close to rough weather on the sea before. Phoebe sprang up onto a rock beside him and leaned her hand on his shoulder; her hair glistened with blown spray, there were tiny drops on her eyelashes; she kept looking from the surf back at his face expectantly; he did not disappoint her. She clapped her hands and occasionally her voice emitted some of its pathetic, ugly symp-toms of excitement. She led him to a sort of overhang where they could squat protected from the wind; he noticed that Phoebe's free hand pressed feelingly against the rock, and he imagined her delicate excitement from the waves' crashing on the outside of the rocks of their cave. He knew that later he would worry about the propriety of his behavior with Phoebe, wonder what he should have done instead, speculate on what she was thinking, what his actions meant to her; but for the time that they huddled together there his affection for her, pure and unamorous as though she were a child, dissolved all questions of motive, propriety, consequence, and left only a residue of unalloyed content. Squatting in a cold cave with a view of lashing breakers under a heavy sky, damp, feet cold, holding hands with a deaf-mute girl he had met only once before, truly he thought himself seven sorts of fool, but he grinned at the thought.

She peered out of the cave at the sky, looked at him ruefully, and made some sign gestures; then, remembering he could not understand them, she put hands gently on his arm with a look of apology. Phoebe's gestures and the movements of her features expressed, with the economy and delicacy of a trout swimming in a clear pool, a range of ideas and emotions. Yet physically she was not delicate, but rather blunt and unsymmetrical; not pretty but, Bingham thought, one of the beautiful opposites of pretty. Then and there in the cave she taught him a dozen ordinary words in sign language: I, you, car, home, day, like, go, sea, be together, mama, not, must. They laughed a great deal as his fingers blundered some sentences together: I you together like go sea. When he asked her how to say happy she showed him, and house, and door, but when he wrote love on the sand with a twig she shook her head. She made the gestures of liking and being together, but pointed at love and looked at him reprovingly. He saw that she had more tact than he—and very likely more honesty. She told him then she had to go home to Mama. Mama? he asked her, and she nodded. Who? he said with his lips. Miss Cudahy, she wrote on the sand, sprang up, and ran off toward the path. For a few moments he watched her, incredulous and frustrated; he felt very fond of her. He watched her climb the path, not thinking, but only looking at the slight figure quick and graceful in its brown, practical, shapeless clothes; not feeling even, only wishing he knew her well. Just before he got up to follow her he remembered Miss Cudahy's hard look when Phoebe had spilled some tea on the table, and he shuddered to feel cold little feet creeping about his back as they would when, lying in bed on the way to sleep, he chanced to think about the latest advances in bomb-making.

Next morning, arriving just after the postman, he carried Miss Cudahy's mail up to the front door with him. He saw an envelope from Mrs. Pickman-Ellsworth. He was feeling grim when Phoebe let him into the parlor.

"Oh ho," cried Miss Cudahy after the civilities; she waved an envelope at him. "Let's see what Nell has to say about you. Just step into the dining room till I call you, Mr. Bingham, if you don't mind. You'll find Phoebe polishing the silver."

He fumbled among his unsorted emotions, unable to find the one that would suit his response; what he did was simply to thank her and do what she said. After all, he reflected, he had not yet seen the dining room.

Phoebe did not stop polishing, but whenever, in his inspection of the room, he passed near her she would rub against him a little like a cat. Miss Cudahy shouted him back.

"She says you're respectable," she said, and puffed on her pipe a few times gazing at him. "Good reputation, good family. I want you to stay with me, Mr. Bingham, for as long as you're going to be in this vicinity. I like you. You may have the master bedroom; someday I'll tell you who it was made for. Phoebe needs the society of a cultivated man. Poor creature. Do you like her?"

"Very much." But he did not want to talk about her to Miss Cudahy. "Thank you for the invitation. I do not want to intrude. . . ."

"Nonsense, that's my concern, not yours. There are not many literate people hereabouts—Mrs. Townson in Mendocino City, the Chiversers in Fort Bragg, who else? You ask me why I continue to live in Stowes Landing. My answer to you is, I don't. I live in this house."

"You have good taste in houses."

"Because it is your taste? Well, I like to be flattered, Mr. Bingham, but don't try to flatter me about my knowledge of New England houses. Between us we could write a good book on the old houses of this county." She puffed reflectively, gazing at him. "Mine's the best of course. Think it over. You could live here while we were at it. I want to look at my mail now. Would you be so good as to step into the garden and tell Japheth to spray the roses?"

He looked at the appointments of the parlor and hall with a new eye as he walked out; they were his to use, and she would tell him all she knew. On the front steps he imagined a roseate fantasy: a month, even six weeks of solid research and photographing, then one of the major contributions to the history of California architecture would be his. He even looked with a benevolent eye at Japheth, whom he found standing with some cuttings in one hand and clippers in

the other, staring at a rose. He delivered his message with positive
friendliness; Japheth winked at him, touched his cap with the clip-
pers, and then, leering, pulled off a rose branch so that it half-split
the cane. "It wasn't so in the old country," he whispered. Bingham
left hurriedly. Walking away, he rummaged about in his mind for his
fantasy, but he could not find it again.

Half from plan and half because it was the nearest entrance he ran
up the back stairs and into the kitchen. Glistening copper pots and
pans hung on the walls; the old wood stove took up far more room
than it needed to by the standards of modern efficiency; there was
a hatchet in the box with the kindling; three comfortable, mended
kitchen chairs, envy of snobs, sat about the stove; the worn lino-
leum, black-and-white checkered, was as clean with scrubbing as a
boy's ears; the kitchen smelled of apples and coffee. Some sort of
odd combination of flag-arms, as in a railroad signal, was attached
to the wall over the pantry door; even as he was wondering what
it was for one of the flags, the white one, fell out at right angles—
obviously a signal for Phoebe. It jiggled up and down; he stepped
through the pantry into the dining room and went with Phoebe into
the parlor again.

"Do you approve of my kitchen, Mr. Bingham?"

"I do. Phoebe keeps it in admirable order."

"It's a pleasant place to spend the supper hours in the winter, let
me tell you. You must visit us in the winter."

"I should be delighted." He felt constrained to say something
more. "Your garden must have been a prize at one time."

"It was."

"A great pity it has fallen into neglect."

"Do you have ideas for it, Mr. Bingham?" She was full of anima-
tion.

"Only the obvious ideas for the circumstances."

"The very thing!" she cried. "It would give you some exercise
as we worked on our book. I can see by your figure you don't get
enough exercise. Splendid, sir, a splendid addition."

He smiled painfully. "I don't enjoy gardening."

"Nonsense. You need it." She saw that she had gone too far. "Of
course, of course," she went on heavily, "there would be no necessity.
Japheth keeps the fuchsias from dying out. Phoebe would work with
you in the garden. She likes it. She likes being with you."

Phoebe, having lip read the gist of the conversation, smiled up at Bingham so sweetly that he, in relief from the old woman, half reached out his hand to her in response; propriety halted him. Phoebe, seeing his broken gesture, stepped beside him and took his hand; all three laughed at his blush.

"Well," said Miss Cudahy, shifting her bulk about, "everything is working out handsomely. Phoebe must show you your room. You must fetch your things and install yourself. We shall take an outing one day soon, Mr. Bingham. Zenobia Dobbs has a house in Greenwood you should see the inside of before you leave here, and I doubt if you went alone that she would be so hospitable to you as I have been."

He did not thank her for her hospitality, as she apparently wanted him to do, because he did not think she had been moved by hospitality to do what she was doing. He said he should like to see the house in Greenwood.

"But where is this town?" he asked. "I don't recognize the name."

"They took to calling it Elk a few years ago. There are not many like you, Mr. Bingham, who cherish the old things. The world rots and we rot with it." She tossed some keys to Phoebe, fluttered her hand, and shifted herself back on her chair. Among her pale violet clothes, in that light that cast no shadow, her face seemed nearly ethereal. Yet her body was huge.

Upstairs Phoebe showed him the master bedroom; she kept looking from his face to the mantel or the bedstead or the molding, pleased yet puzzled by the great impression the room was making on him, trying to see it with his eyes. She showed him the bathroom, Japheth's room, a dark cupboard, and her own room facing west, austere this side of barrenness, feminine only in the lace curtains. Then, with sparkling eyes, dancing a little in excitement, taking both his hands in one of hers, she opened the door to the last bedroom. His impression was one of darkness, scent, frills, musty old letters. She threw open the shutters; they were in a boudoir, among a luxury which had made feminine and intimate the stern woodwork, the right-angled room. There was a satin quilt on the low bed; at the sight of it he made a mock gesture of indolence, and in an instant Phoebe was lying there. She took some pins out of her hair and shook it free, brown, fine hair. She laid her head at a certain angle on the pillows, curved one arm up over her head and the other onto her stomach, and turned her body in the fashion of all experience and luxuriation. It was only a moment until she bounced up smiling and clasping his hand, simple and young again.

He heard a clicking in the hall, and Miss Cudahy shouting that she wanted Phoebe. He told her; she put up her hair in a second. On their way down she flipped the hall flag back up into place. On the landing of the stairs, yielding to what impulse he did not know, he stopped Phoebe just to look at her intently. Her face was cheery and flushed; when she saw his expression she pressed herself against him, her head bowed onto his shoulder; he held her tightly a moment and kissed the top of her head. Miss Cudahy called again and they went on down.

She looked thunderous. "Mr. Bingham," she said. "I heard the springs squeak."

He was very angry. "I dare say you did. I pressed the mattress to see what it was like, and Phoebe sat on the bed in the south room."

"Sat on it!" cried Miss Cudahy and motioned to Phoebe to go stand beside her. "Sat on it indeed! She jumped on it."

"Yes and lay on it," he said, thin-lipped. "It is more luxury than she is used to."

"That was my room and my mother's before me. I have restored it. I intended that you should look at the architecture and not the décor. I am displeased."

"Indeed. As though the one were not a part of the other."

"Well," she said, and suddenly she smiled and put her arm around Phoebe's legs, stroking her thigh. "One cannot be too careful. What is your opinion of what you saw upstairs?"

"It all but equals the newel in excellence."

"Quite so. Now then, Mr. Bingham," she said affably, "I think we can manage a way of working together. There are problems, of course, not insuperable ones I trust. How soon will you be able to come?"

"Why . . . I am not sure. I would have to arrange for a leave of absence beyond my usual vacation allowance."

"Rather. It will take us months at least, by my plan."

"Oh, I don't . . ."

"You have no sentimental ties in Oakland? No, and Phoebe will be with us. You will be kind to Phoebe, Mr. Bingham? She has suffered from the lack of suitable male acquaintance."

"Why," he stammered, not knowing how to avoid indelicacy, "to be sure, I am fond of Phoebe, I will be kind, there is no problem."

"She means much to me, sir. Perhaps I try, as they say, to relive my youth through her. What does it matter? I mean her to be happy." She pressed her cheek against Phoebe's hip. "Did you ever see finer legs, sir?" Phoebe smoothed indulgently the iron-gray hair, smiling at Bingham. "We must handle Phoebe with care, must we not?"

IV

On his fourth morning at Miss Cudahy's he left at dawn to drive up the coast as far as Fort Bragg. The ragged coastline, the somber landscape illuminated by spring flowers, the old barns patched with moss, the sheep, the small towns all pleased him greatly, but he found no architectural points of interest to him, nothing he had not seen the like of before. He was not concentrating well, to be sure. He rubbered along, the amateur tourist; he said to himself that he had exhausted the district, but in truth he had left his thoughts disassembled behind. He returned to Stowes Landing not long after lunch, having intended to stay away until dark.

He knocked at the door, which was kept always locked; he had not been entrusted with a key. Finally the old woman herself answered.

"Ho," she said and pounded her cane on the floor in her pleasure. "I was wanting you. It's too fine a day to waste in old houses. We're going for an outing down to Greenwood. Good. Good. Give me ten minutes in my room and I'll be ready."

"Fifteen," he said. "I want to clean up before going out again."

"Very well," she answered and stalked down the hall toward her room. "That's a fine sun they've got out there. Damn the hedge on a day like this."

There was not a sound upstairs as he washed and changed. There seldom was. He wished he knew whether Phoebe was in her room.

Miss Cudahy clumped back into the hall again and called him down. She was in front of the hall mirror arranging on her head a wide-brimmed, violet hat with a fringe of tiny tassels.

"We're off!" she cried. "Zenobia Dobbs, you must see her house. I haven't been in it for years. So you like my newel, Mr. Bingham." He exclaimed again that he did. "It's never been photographed." He said what she wanted him to say. "Well, help me down the stairs."

"I did not realize you could go down steps, Miss Cudahy."

"Down I can make it. It's up that breaks my back. You'll have to get Japheth to help you get me up."

She leaned heavily on his shoulder, taking the steps one at a time, and at the bottom she paused to snort like a horse.

"Where is Phoebe?" he asked.

"In the kitchen, I suppose. Where she belongs at any rate."

"She is coming with us?" he asked, just barely polite.

"I had not planned that she should."

"She would enjoy it," he said. "I will fetch her."

"Zenobia and she do not hit it off."

"Then I shall take Phoebe for a walk while you have tea with Mrs. Dobbs."

She did not answer him but started off toward the south side of the house.

Phoebe was not in the kitchen, not anywhere downstairs. He had to open the door to her room to see if she was in it. She was lying crosswise on her bed, like a child, her head and bare arms bright in the sunshine that poured through her window. She had taken off her shoes and stockings; her legs were stretched up the side of the wall, one foot rubbing the other. He shook his head to clear it, and told her—he had learned more of her sign language—to put on her bathing suit and come for a trip. She clapped her hands with joy, leaped up, and pushed him out of her room playfully.

They found Miss Cudahy waving her cane at glowering Japheth and threatening to beat him. Bingham led her to the car.

"Hmph," she snorted as the three of them drove away. "They said he was hopeless but I knew I could handle him. The fools, they decided he needed love and kindness, but he took it for weakness. I've had him for years, and I give him unbuttered bread and a whip. And liquor on Saturday night."

"Miss Cudahy," he said, "have you ever considered having Phoebe taught to speak? I believe there are people who . . ."

"I have considered it, Mr. Bingham, but I shall not have it done. She is happy. At Mrs. Dobbs' you will return for me at five o'clock, and she will show you the house. You might leave Phoebe in the car."

"I would hate to leave Phoebe in the car," he said, and he told himself that only if the house were very attractive would he do it.

Phoebe, seeing their angry heads, leaned forward from the back seat and laid a restraining hand on each of them.

"In the eyes of God, Mr. Bingham, she may be worth ten of us. Meanwhile she does what I tell her to do and I'd thank you to remember it." He just managed to swallow his anger. As it were in payment she said, "My grandfather, of whom I was telling you yesterday, brought the newel and the two mantels around the Horn on his own ship. They cost him a fortune."

He touched Phoebe's hand with his and so did Miss Cudahy. They smiled at her and fell silent. There was brilliant sunlight all the way to Elk.

They spent two hours on the beach alone. There was a tunnel through a tall rock island a few yards offshore through which the ocean drove, frothing and soughing; once, the tide coming in, a great wave made a whistling noise in the tunnel. A northbound ship near the horizon spent the two hours going out of sight. They found some crabs in a pool and scared them back into their ledge and laughed at their anger and clicking. The water was too cold for swimming but they waded in it a little; most of the time they lay on the sand. Bingham thought her legs to be in the lovely hinterland between trim and heavy, and from the way she took off her skirt, from the way she displayed them and drew his head once down into her lap, he knew she wanted him to admire them, to touch them with his fingers. There was scarcely a moment when they were not touching.

He asked her if she wanted to learn to speak. She smiled rather wistfully and nodded, but told him she was happy anyway. He told her it was a shame that Miss Cudahy would not do it. She shook her head and put a finger on his lips. He told her there was a school in Oakland where she could learn to speak. She closed her eyes, smiling, till he promised not to continue with the subject, and she kissed the tip of his nose. They were half an hour late for Miss Cudahy. He did not think the Dobbs house worth enough to abandon Phoebe in the car just to see it.

Miss Cudahy did not seem to mind their being late; she seemed mellow. Several times on the way home she motioned for Phoebe's hand, pressed it against her cheek, nipped at her finger with her lips. "You are keeping our bargain, Mr. Bingham," she said. "I have never known Phoebe to be happier. Tomorrow may be a good day for you to commence your photography."

Japheth and he together got her up the front steps; the problem was to transport her in such a way as to let her think they were only helping her. Japheth did not even try, and she was furious with him.

Once she beat Bingham on the neck. "I'm so sorry," she trumpeted. "Mistake, mistake." And she beat Japheth the harder for her error. He spat on the steps as he went back to work in the garden.

At dinner Bingham found it just possible to be civil. Miss Cudahy was wheezing a good deal and did not make much demand upon him; he was able to brood inward upon his own thoughts. They were not even thoughts, just two strong sensations about which his mind prowled and peered with no result: Miss Cudahy's mistaken blow on his neck and, quite as vivid though smaller and softer, the warm light kiss Phoebe had put there as soon as she could to make up for the blow. He had not been struck in anger since he was a child, nor kissed so tenderly. He did not know what to make of such strong experience. He felt neither anger nor gratitude, felt nothing that deserved so differentiated a name as resentment, say, or affection; indeed, so far as he knew he felt nothing except, on the skin and down into the muscles of his neck, the two touches of the two women. Yet, when at the end of the meal, staring at a crumb like a yogi, he did not hear Miss Cudahy ask him a question and she rapped on her tumbler with her ring, barking out, "Mr. Bingham," he started from his chair and glared at her wildly a moment, leaned on the edge of the table, and whispered intently, "No! No!"

"No coffee?" she said, a little taken aback.

He subsided under Phoebe's restraining hand. "Sorry," he mumbled, "I was thinking of something else. Yes, coffee please." He had been feeling more than touches on the neck, and with that feudal rap on the glass some of it began turmoiling up and out.

He did not even assist Miss Cudahy from her chair, but bolted into the kitchen where he wiped dishes for Phoebe as she washed. She kept her eyes downcast on her business, even when he patted her arm for attention or physically turned her head about she did not look at his eyes, but only at his lips or at his hands stumbling and tripping in their rush like lips stuttering from anger; once she caught the frustrated things and kissed each palm gently, then turned back to her suds. He stood beside her, the kisses warm in his hands, just staring at her; feeling his chin begin to quiver he bustled back to his job. But his anger was gone, and all he felt now was that Phoebe was altogether delicate and alive and pitiable and needing to be saved. He understood now, without hatred, how Miss Cudahy would want to hold her; but Phoebe must be saved, more, she must want to be saved.

As she was hanging up the dishcloth, finished, he held her waist with a gentleness she immediately recognized, for she looked back over her shoulder up into his eyes; he kissed her; scarcely moving, she yielded against him. There were tears in their eyes when they drew apart, and at that instant Bingham felt that he might have fetched her coat and hat and driven her off to Oakland without an objection from her. But she must freely desire to leave Miss Cudahy, she must not be swayed from that old woman's will only to become subject to his, though better, will. He sat her by the oven, poured a cup of coffee for each of them, sat in front of her so that their knees touched, and asked her, "Will you come to Oakland with me?" It would have been coy of her, gazing against his earnest gaze, to treat his question playfully, to pretend she didn't take him seriously—the leap of eagerness that brightened her eyes and pressed her hands together meant to him only that she wanted to come to Oakland, yet she did not sign the answer in return. "I can take you with me when I go. I have friends you can stay with till we find a permanent arrangement for you. Don't worry, I will make it a point to see you often." It would have been weak of her, under his insistence, to have begun crying in order to avoid meeting his challenge, yet he saw tears come to her eyes after his last pressing. He would have relented—must she not choose freely—but that she answered him then: I owe Miss Cudahy so much.

"Of course," he answered, "and you can return to her if you want, but you owe it to yourself to go to the school."

She needs me, Phoebe pleaded, what would she do without me?

And with that he pounded the table, but not too loud, for fear Miss Cudahy would hear him.

It would be like a betrayal, Phoebe told him.

"You must leave her sooner or later," he responded—No, her head shook—"you owe it to yourself to go now." She buried her face in her hands, but in a heat of compelling he pulled them away and clutching her wrists hard said with his lips, "You must come with me."

She wilted then, as though he had uttered a magic formula, composed of common words perhaps but nonetheless magic. She would come if he would get Miss Cudahy's permission.

"But no, but no! You must come of your own free will."

Shaking her head, miserable, she sat on his lap and hid her face against his neck, so that all he could do, imagining how the old woman would greet such a proposal, was to hold Phoebe as though she were crying, in need of comforting; yet he was conscious of her warm breathing, of her lips half-kissing the soft joining of his shoulder and neck, of her woman's body which his hands were embarrassed now to hold.

Old Japheth came in for coffee and at the sight of them muttered, "Bitch! Bitch!"

In a desperation of confusion, Bingham pushed Phoebe off his lap and, flapping his hands, went up to his room.

But there was no peace for him there. To rescue her became, as he writhed on the bed in that handsome, alien room, his obsession and immediate need. His pain was purer and stronger than it could have been had he suspected for a second that there was more causing it than the desire to liberate an oppressed, afflicted person he knew. But as it was that pain was so great that he had to creep back downstairs again hoping to find Phoebe in the kitchen alone where he could bring matters to a head, for he did not know what he would do if she did not assert herself tonight. The afterwards would work itself out, and if Miss Cudahy should suffer then she should suffer.

As he reached, silently, the bottom step he saw through the half-open door to the parlor Phoebe sitting beside Miss Cudahy, who was lolling back in the chaise longue looking at her from under her eyelids and fondling her arm. For a long time he froze on that step; all he felt for that painful time was the gracefully curving, worn, smooth old wood of the rail in his hand. Quivering with emotions he did not understand and no longer cared about controlling he went into the room. As he spoke, but not until then, he realized from the suspicion of quaver in his voice that he would not be able to stand up to the old woman.

"Miss Cudahy," he said as evenly as he could manage, "I thank you for your hospitality, but I am leaving."

"What?" she cried, altogether surprised. "You are just becoming one of us."

"I am not. I am leaving immediately."

"You have not taken your photograph yet."

"No," he said; he had thought he would be adamant. "I am obliged to leave suddenly." He would make no excuse, only get out. But his eye was drawn by the exquisite proportions of the frame around the window behind the two women. "Perhaps when I come back up later this summer I shall be able to complete my study."

"*Our* book, Mr. Bingham?"

"Of course, of course, complete our study."

"Perhaps. We shall see." She thrust unhappy Phoebe from the chair. "I shall get to the bottom of this."

He packed in five minutes. Phoebe was waiting for him in the hall, tears in her eyes. He wrote down the name of the motel where he was going to stay the night and told her to come there first thing in the morning. She nodded, and looked at him in bewilderment, longingly.

At the front door he was touching her hands good-bye and telling her she must come as soon as she could, when Miss Cudahy shouted, "Send Phoebe to me at once!" He kissed her quickly on the cheek and left.

v

Waking in that alien, ugly motel, he could not remain alone but neither did he want to go near the surge of the sea. He walked toward the hills through a pleasant pasture, and as he was walking he heard bleating sheep on the other side of a fence—he watched them in the light of the high moon. They stared at him for a moment like citizens in a bus, and when he rattled the top rail of the fence they stared at him again and shied away. He played with them off and on for an hour or more, an hour of relief; their stares were simple and sufficient, they left him alone.

He lay in bed feeling as though he were floating. He put his hands under his head and gazed at the moon, not thinking so much as watching thoughts dance through his mind. The moon had wheeled into the western sky by the time he had fallen asleep.

A rattle at the door awakened him. The moon had set. He sat up and called, "Who is it?" There was another rattle and a low, amorphous cry. He opened the door to Phoebe. She grasped both his hands in hers, hard, and threw herself face down on the bed, crying, turned away from him. He closed the windows and built a fire in the stove, and then for fifteen minutes or so sat on the bed beside her, stroking her hair and arms, shuddering a little with alarm, ready to weep himself that he could say nothing to her.

At last she turned her face toward him, and gradually her crying subsided. Her mouth, now that he came to watch her face so closely, lost the contours of grief and reassumed its usual expression; hers was somehow softer than most mouths, less revealing of character, more innocent. She ceased to make those hard, inchoate cries that disturbed him. She became Phoebe again. He was astonished in a new way at how tenderly he felt toward her, thinking of what she must be suffering now partly for his sake.

"Did she scold you?" he asked, and her answer was only the most rueful smile in the world. "What is this?" He bent down to look at three fresh bruises on the back of Phoebe's leg, just above the knee. "Did she hurt you?" he said to her. She shrugged; what difference did it make? "Pinch?" She shrugged: yes, but it was the least of my pain. "Vicious," he muttered to himself, pounding the fist of one hand into the palm of the other, "damned, cruel, vicious old bitch."

Phoebe made him sit beside her and asked him if he would ever come back to the house. He told her no. Her lip quivered, she threw her arms around him as though to hold him forever and pulled him down beside her. When he could he freed himself and told her she must go with him. When are you leaving? Tomorrow, he answered, and she turned from him again to cry. He was trembling with anger so hard that Phoebe finally turned over and smiled as best she could. He gave her his handkerchief to use for her tears.

He lay down facing her and put his arm over her waist; their legs were touching. They lay looking at each other peacefully, touching gently. But it seemed to him after a time that something was required of him; the simplest, easiest thing to do would be to kiss her, but just because it was so easy he distrusted it, and besides it would be taking advantage of her as he had sworn to himself not to do; perhaps he should renew his offer to take her to the school in Oakland, assuring her again that he had meant it.

But when she saw what he was starting to tell her she stopped him, tenderly but certainly. Her hand, still and yet alive, lay curled against his throat, warm and other and loving, and seemed to him to reproach him for some lack. It was all he could do to support her unflinching gaze; in no way did she actually reproach him yet he could not respond to that gaze with a smile or in fact with any expression at all. It was not a response her gaze sought, but somehow him himself; an unpitying, devouring, utterly unmalicious gaze, it did not demand, it took. As the uneasy night wore on, lying half-embraced on his left side awkwardly, he gradually suffocated with the knowledge that Phoebe had the unopposable rights of one who, in a way he was appalled to imagine, loved.

At the first evidences of dawn he leaped up and dressed, telling her that for the sake of her reputation she must leave the motel immediately. She lay, watching his bustle with her steady, innocent, direct gaze. He stood before her, urging her to rise. Is this the last time I shall ever see you? He could not bear her directness.

"No, no, of course not, it's all settled. How could you say such a thing? You are going with me to Oakland, today, now, as soon as you've packed your bags. We're going to Miss Cudahy's now." He was frenetic and pressed too hard. "I'll be waiting for you in the car outside the hedge at nine o'clock. It's all settled?"

She smiled into tears, into the tears, he thought, of joy, and nodded. She pulled him down on top of her and held him so hard and kissed him so ardently that he was alarmed. They left the motel. For a moment, parking outside the hedge, kissing her again, he had the wild notion of driving off with Phoebe then and there, however it might look. But before he had time either to act on the impulse or to reject it, with a cry that startled him she had opened the door of the car and run in.

At nine o'clock she had not emerged from that tunnel in the hedge, nor at quarter past. At nine-thirty he got out of the car and went in the front gate. At the window of her room on the second floor Phoebe was standing, wearing her bathrobe, evidently crying. She kept shaking her head. She made a gesture, from her heart to her lips to him, that could have meant only one thing. His heart throbbing in his throat with the pity and the loss, he made the signs "Together, we must go together." If there had been any way for him to get her free from that house he would have used it at that moment; he blamed himself for having let her come back at all; he could scarcely bear to think of her life locked in as it would be and had been. She buried her face in her hands and turned slowly from the window.

He ran to the front door and pounded the knocker; there was no response. He knocked till the great door reverberated; he would have shouted had he not been afraid of alarming the neighbors. Finally there was the sound of a cane and of coughing at the end of the hallway. He trembled; his lips were tense with the recriminations with which he would greet Miss Cudahy.

She opened the door, wide, and stood staring at him. "Yes?"
Instantly he became aware of his dishevelled appearance. "As you
know, my work, it is. . . ."

"Go get your Kodak, Mr. Bingham," she said, guttural with scorn.
She pointed with her cane, holding her arm out full length, the gar-
ments trailing. "You may photograph my newel if you're quick about
it." His mouth opened, but he did not say anything. "Mind you don't
go upstairs," said Miss Cudahy, and went back down the hall.

He turned, went down the steps, and ran to his car. On his
way back in, burdened with his camera and lighting equipment, he
glanced furtively up, and was grateful to see that Phoebe had drawn
the curtains to her room. He had to run out again for his tripod
because he could not hold the camera steady. There was not another
sound in the house as he worked. In fifteen minutes he had finished
and left.

The NRACP

THE NATIONAL RELOCATION AUTHORITY: COLORED PERSONS

Office of Public Relations   *Colored Persons Reserve*
                                                              Nevada

Dear Herb,

Pardon the letterhead. I seem to have brought no stationery of my own, it's a dull walk to the commissary, and I found this paper already in the desk drawer.

Your first letter meant more to me than I can say, and the one I received yesterday has at last aroused me from my depression. I will try to answer both of them at once. You sensed my state of mind, I could tell it from little phrases in your letter—"open your heart, though it be only to a sunset"; "try reading *Finnegans Wake;* if you ever get *into* it you won't be able to fight your way out again for months." I cherish your drolleries. They are little oases of half-light and quiet in this rasping, blinding landscape.

How I hate it! Nothing but the salary keeps me here—nothing. I have been driven into myself in a very unhealthy way. Long hours, communal eating, the choice between a badly lighted reading room full of people and my own cell with one cot and two chairs and a table, a swim in a chlorinated pool, walks in this violent, seasonless, arid land—what is there? There seem to be only two varieties of people here: those who "have culture," talk about the latest *New Yorker* cartoons, listen to imitation folk songs and subscribe to one of the less popular book clubs; and those who play poker, talk sports and sex, and drink too much. I prefer the latter type as people, but unfortunately I do not enjoy any of their activities except drinking. Since I know the language and mores of the former type, and have more inclination toward them, I am thrown with people whom I dislike intensely. In this muddle I find myself wishing, selfishly, that you were here; your companionship would mean so much to me now. But you knew better than I what the Colored Persons Reserve would mean—you were most wise to stay in Washington, most wise. You will be missing something by staying there, but I assure you it is something well worth missing.

I must mention the two universal topics of conversation. From the filing clerks to my division chief I know of no one, including myself, who does not talk absorbedly about mystery stories. A few watered-down eclectics say they haven't much preference in mysteries, but the folk songers to a man prefer the tony, phony Dorothy Sayers-S.S. Van Dine type of pseudo-literary snobbish product, and the horsy folk prefer the Dashiell Hammett romantic cum violent realism. There is one fellow—a big domed Irishman named O'Doone who wears those heavy rimmed, owlish glasses that came into style a couple of years ago just after the war—who does nothing but read and reread Sherlock Holmes, and he has won everyone's respect in some strange fashion by this quaint loyalty. He's quite shy, in a talkative, brittle way, but I think I could grow fond of him.

Everyone finds a strong need to read the damnable things, so strong that we prefer the absolute nausea of reading three in one day—I did it once myself for three days on end—to not reading any. What is it actually that we prefer not to do? I can only think of Auden's lines, "The situation of our time Surrounds us like a baffling crime." Of our time and of this job.

What are we doing here? That is the other subject none of us can let alone. We are paid fantastic salaries (the secretary whom I share with another writer gets four hundred dollars a month, tell Mary *that* one), and for one whole month we have done nothing while on the job except to read all the provisions and addenda to the Relocation Act as interpreted by the Authority or to browse at will in the large library of literature by and about Negroes, from sociological studies to newspaper poetry in dialect. You know the Act generally of course, but I hope you are never for any reason subjected to this Ph.D.-candidate torture of reading to exhaustion about a subject in which you have only a general interest. But the *why* of this strange and expensive indoctrination is totally beyond me. I thought that I was going to do much the same sort of public relations work here on the spot as we had been doing in the State Department; I thought the salary differential was just a compensation for living in this hellhole. That's what everyone here had thought too. It appears, however, that there is something more important brewing. In the whole month I have been here I have turned out only a couple of articles describing the physical charms of this desiccated cesspool; they appeared in Negro publications which I hope you have not even heard of. Beyond that I have done nothing but bore myself to death by reading Negro novels and poetry.

They are a different tribe altogether; I would be the last to deny that their primeval culture is wonderful enough to merit study—but not by me. I have enough trouble trying to understand the rudiments of my own culture without having this one pushed off onto me.

I have been stifled and confused for so long that all my pent-up emotions have found their worthiest outlet in this letter to you, my dear friend. I have been vowing (as we used to vow to quit smoking, remember?) to stop reading mysteries, but my vows seldom survive the day. Now I do solemnly swear and proclaim that each time I have the urge to read a mystery I will instead write a letter to you. If these epistles become dull and repetitious just throw them away without reading them. I'll put a mark—say an M—on the envelope of these counter-mystery letters, so you needn't even open them if you wish. I'm sure there will be a lot of them.

Does this sound silly? I suppose it does. But I am in a strange state of mind. There's too much sunlight and the countryside frightens me and I don't understand anything.

Bless you,
Andy

March 14

Dear Herb,

It wasn't as bad as I had feared, being without mysteries. We get up at seven and go to work at eight. Between five and six in the afternoon there's time for a couple of highballs. From seven or so, when dinner is over, till ten or eleven—that's the time to watch out for. After you have seen the movie of the week and read *Time* and the *New Yorker* you discover yourself, with that autonomic gesture with which one reaches for a cigarette, wandering toward the mystery shelf and trying to choose between Carter Dickson and John

Dickson Carr (two names for the same writer, as I hope you don't know). On Sundays there's tennis in the early morning and bowling in the afternoon. But those gaping rents in each tightly woven, just tolerable day remain, no matter what you do. At first I thought I should have to tell myself bedtime stories. One evening I got half-drunk in the club rooms and absolutely potted alone in my own room afterward. First time in my life. Another time O'Doone and I sat up till midnight composing an "Epitaph for a Mongoose." I can't tell you how dreary some of our endeavors were; O'Doone still quotes one of mine occasionally. He's a strange fellow. I can't exactly figure him out but I like him in an oblique sort of way. Neither of us fits into any of three or four possible schemes of things here, and we share a good deal in general outlook. But he can amuse himself with a cerebral horseplay which only makes me uneasy. O'Doone has a French book—God knows where he got it—on Senegalese dialects; he goes around slapping stuffy people on the back and mumbling, "Your grandmother on your father's side was a pig-faced gorilla" or else a phrase which in Senegalese has something to do with transplanting date trees but which in English sounds obscene, and then he laughs uproariously. In any event, he's better off than I, who am amused by almost nothing.

Now that you have been spared the threatened dejection of my counter-mystery letters I must confess to the secret vice which I have taken up in the past week. It grows upon me too; it promises to become a habit which only age and infirmity will break. I had thought it a vice of middle age (and perhaps it is—are we not thirty-eight, Herb? When does middle age commence?). I *take walks*. I take long walks alone. If I cannot say that I enjoy them I do look forward to them with the eagerness with which an adolescent will sometimes go to bed in order to continue the dream which waking has interrupted.

Not that my walks are in any way dreamlike. They are perfectly real. But they take place in a context so different from any of the social or intellectual contexts of the CPR day and they afford such a strong emotional relief to it that I think they may be justly compared to a continued dream. My walks, however, have a worth of their own such as dreams can never have. Instead of taking me from an ugly world to a realm of unexplained symbols they have driven me toward two realities, about which I must confess I have had a certain ignorance: myself and the natural world. And standing, as I feel I do, at the starting point of high adventure I feel the explorer's excitement and awe, and no self-pity at all.

I have recaptured—and I am not embarrassed to say it—the childhood delight in stars. That's a great thing to happen to a man, Herb: to be able to leave the smoke-and-spite-laden atmosphere of bureaucracy, walk a few miles out into the huge, silent desert, and look at the stars with a delight whose purity needs no apology and whose expansiveness need find no words for description. I am astonished by the sight of a Joshua tree against the light blue twilight sky, I am entranced by the vicious innocence of one of the kinds of cactus that abound hereabouts. I enjoy these garish sunsets with a fervor that I once considered indecent. I cannot say that I like this desert—certainly not enough to live in it permanently—but it has affected me very deeply. I think that much of my trouble during my first month here was resisting the force of the desert. Now I no longer resist it, yet I have not submitted to it; rather I have developed a largeness of spirit, a feeling of calm and magnificence. Which I am sure is in part lightheadedness at having such a weight of nasty care removed all at once, but which is wonderful while it lasts.

But it's not *just* lightheadedness. Some obstruction of spirit, an obstruction of whose existence I was not even aware, has been removed within me, so that now I can and dare observe the complexities of that catalogued, indifferent, unaccountable natural world which I had always shrugged at. One saw it from train windows, one dealt with it on picnics, one admired the nasturtiums and peonies of one's more domesticated friends, one approved of lawns and shade trees. What then? What did one know of the rigidity of nature's order or of the prodigality with which she wastes and destroys and errs? I came here furnished only with the ordinary generic names of things— snake, lizard, toad, rabbit, bug, cactus, sagebrush, flower, weed— but already I have watched a road runner kill a rattlesnake and I am proud that I know how rabbits drink. Do you know how rabbits drink? I you ask what difference it makes to know this I can happily reply, "None at all, but it gives me pleasure." A pleasure which does not attempt to deny mortality, but accepts it and doesn't care—a true pleasure and one worth cherishing.

11 P.M.

I owe it to you, I know, to give a somewhat less personal, less inward account of this place. But a calculated, itemized description of anything, much less of so monstrous a thing as a desert, is beyond me. Instead I'll try to give you an idea of what effect such physical bigness can have upon the people in it.

Our buildings are situated at the head of a very long valley—the Tehuala River Valley—which is partially arable and which is good for grazing purposes in both the upper and lower regions. The highway into the valley (that is, the highway that leads to the east, as well as the railroad) runs not far from our settlement. Being public relations, we are located just within the fence, a huge, barbarous fence with guards. We have had a rather surprising number of visitors already, and hundreds more are expected during the summer. Our eight buildings are flat-roofed, gray, of a horizontal design, and air-conditioned. But our view of the valley is cut off by a sharp bend about four or five miles below us. The tourists, in other words, can see almost nothing of the valley or of the Reserve stretching for eight hundred miles to the southwest, for this is the only public entrance to the Reserve and no airplanes are permitted over any part of it. Around the turn in the upper valley is yet another even more barbarous, even better guarded fence, past which no one goes except certain Congressmen, the top officials (four, I believe) in the NRACP, and SSE (Special Service Employees, who, once they have gone past that gate, do not return and do not communicate with the outside world even by letter). All this secrecy—you can fill in details to suit yourself—is probably unnecessary, but it does succeed in arousing an acute sense of mystery and speculation about the Reserve.

Well, being no more than human I walked the five miles to the bend the other day, climbed a considerable hill nearby, and looked out over the main sweep of the valley for the first time. I was hot and tired when I reached the foot of the hill so I sat down—it was around 5:30—and ate the snack I had brought. When I reached the top of the hill the sun was about to set; the long shadows of the western hills lay over the floor of the valley and in some places extended halfway up the hills to the east. Far, far to the west, just to the north of the setting sun, was a snow-capped mountain, and immediately in front of me, a mile and a half or so away, stretched the longest building I have ever seen in my life. It had a shed roof rising away from me and there were no windows on my side of the building. Nothing whatsoever broke the line of its continuous gray back. It was at least a mile long, probably longer. Beyond it lay dozens of buildings exactly like this one except for their length; some of them ran, as the long one did, east and west, some ran north and south, some aslant. I could not estimate to my satisfaction how large most of them were; they seemed to be roughly the size of small factories. The effect which their planner had deliberately calculated and achieved was that of a rigidly patterned, unsymmetrical (useless?) articulation of a restricted flat area. Nothing broke the effect, and for a reason which I cannot define these buildings in the foreground gave such a focus and order to the widening scene that lay before me that I stood for the better part of an hour experiencing a pure joy— a joy only heightened by my grateful knowledge that these Intake buildings were designed to introduce an entire people to the new and better world beyond. The fine farms and ranches and industries and communities which would arise from these undeveloped regions took shape in the twilight scene before me, shimmering in the heat waves rising from the earth.

But presently it was quite dark—the twilights are very brief here— and I was awakened from my reverie by the lights going on in one of the buildings before me. I returned to the PR settlement and to my solitary room in a state of exaltation which has not yet deserted me.

For an hour, the Universe and History co-extended before me and they did not exclude me. For while I am but a grain on the shore of event only within my consciousness did this co-extending take place and have any meaning. For that long moment mine was the power.

I will write again soon.

Andy

March 20

Dear Herb,

You complain that I didn't say anything directly about my voyage of discovery into myself as I had promised in my last letter. And that the internal high pressures of urban life are blowing me up like a balloon in this rarefied atmosphere.

Maybe so. I'll try to explain what has been going on. But I forgot to take a cartographer on my voyage, so that my account may resemble, in crudeness, that of an Elizabethan freebooter in Caribbean waters. (If I had the energy I'd try to synthesize these balloon voyage metaphors, but I haven't.)

It all began when I asked myself on one of my walks why I was here, why I had taken this job. $8,000 a year—yes. The social importance of the project—maybe (but not my personal importance to the project). Excitement at being in on the beginning of a great experiment in planning—yes. The hope of escaping from the pressures of Washington life—yes. These are valid reasons all of them, but on the other side—why I should want *not* to come here—are better reasons altogether. An utter absence of urban life. No friends. No chance of seeing Betty. The loss of permanent position (this one you pointed out most forcefully) in State for a better paid but temporary job here. Too inadequate a knowledge of my duties, or of the whole NRACP for that matter, to permit me to have made a decision wisely. And an overpowering hatred of restrictions. (Never once, Herb, for three years to be allowed to leave this Reserve! I've been sweating here for seven weeks, but 156 weeks! Christ!) Now I had known, more or less, all these factors before I came here, all these nice rational, statistical factors. But when I asked myself the other night in the false clarity of the desert moonlight why I had chosen to come, why really, I still could not answer myself satisfactorily. For I was still certain of one thing: that none of the logical reasons, none of my recognized impulses would have brought me here singly or combined.

Being in the mood I also asked myself why I had continued to live with Clarice for five years after I had known quite consciously that I did not love her but felt a positive contempt for her. Betty accounted for part of it, and the usual fear of casting out again on one's own. But I would not have been on my own in any obvious sense; I am sure you know of my love affairs during those five years; I could have married any of three or four worthy women. I asked myself why it was that from the moment Clarice decided once and for all to divorce me (she did the deciding, not me; I don't think you knew that) I lost my taste for my current inamorata and have not had a real affair since.

These questions I was unable to answer, but at least I was seriously asking them of myself. I was willing and able to face the answers. The key to the answer came from my long-limbed, mildly pretty, efficient, but (I had orginally thought) frivolous and banal secretary,

Ruth. She is one of those women who because they do not have an "intellectual" idea in their noodles are too frequently dismissed as conveniently decorative but not very valuable. Perhaps Ruth really is that, but she has made two or three remarks recently which seem to me to display an intuitive intelligence of a considerable order. Yet they may be merely aptly chosen, conventional observations; it is hard to tell. She interests me. She has a maxim which I resent but cannot refute: "There are those who get it and those who dish it out; I intend to be on the side of the dishers." (Is this the post-Christian golden rule? It has its own power, you know.) In any case, the other day I was sitting in my cubicle of an office, in front of which Ruth's desk is placed—she services two of us. I had my feet up on the desk in a rather indecorous fashion, and I had laid the book I was reading on my lap while I smoked a cigarette. I suppose I was daydreaming a little. Suddenly Ruth opened the door and entered. I started, picked up the book, and took my feet off the table top.

Ruth cocked an eye at me and said, "You like to feel guilty, don't you? All I wanted to know was whether you could spare time for a cup of coffee."

So we went to the café and had coffee and didn't even mention her statement or its cause.

But it set me thinking; the longer I thought about it the better I liked it. I had always discounted wild, Dostoevskian notions like that as being too perverse to be true, but now I am not at all sure that frivolous, red-nailed Ruth wasn't right. So long as Clarice had been there to reprove me for my infidelities I had indulged in them. When her censorship was removed, the infidelities or any love affairs at all lost their spice, the spice being the guilt that she made me feel about them. Then, having divorced Clarice, I took this job. The job is a sop to my sense of guilt at being white and middle-class (that is to say, one of Ruth's "dishers"), a sop because I am participating in an enterprise whose purpose is social justice. At the same time it is a punishment because of the deprivations I am undergoing; yet the actual luxury of my life and my actual status in the bureaucracy, high but not orthodox, privileged yet not normally restricted, nourishes the guilt which supports it. I suppose Freud could tell me what it is that causes the sense of guilt in the first place, but I am not going to bother to find out. There are certain indecencies about which one ought not to inquire unless one has to. Social guilt—that is to say a sense of responsibility toward society—is a good thing to have, and I intend to exploit it in myself. I intend to satisfy it by doing as fine a job as I possibly can; furthermore I intend to find a worthy European family, Italian perhaps, who are impoverished and to support them out of my salary. I must confess that the CARE packages we sent to Europe immediately after the war made me feel better than all the fine sentiments I ever gave words to.

I am grateful that I came here. I have been thrown back upon myself in a way that has only benefited me.

We begin work soon. The first trainload of Negroes arrived today, five hundred of them. They are going through Intake (the buildings I described in my last letter) and our work, we are told, will commence within a few days. Exactly what we are to do we will be briefed on tomorrow. I look forward to it eagerly.

Andy

I read this letter over before putting it in the envelope. That was a mistake. All the excitement about myself which I had felt so keenly sounds rather flat as I have put it. There must be a great deal for me yet to discover. As you know, I have never spent much of my energy in intimacies, either with myself or with other people. One gets a facsimile of it when talking about the universal stereotypes of love with a woman. But this desert has thrown me back upon myself, and from your letter I take it you find my explorations of interest. However, you must not expect many more letters in so tiresome a vein. I will seal and mail this one tonight lest I repent in the morning.

April 10

Dear Herb,

I have not known how to write this letter, though I've tried two or three times in the past week to do it. I'm going to put it in the form of a homily with illustrations. The text: "There are those who get it and those who dish it out; I intend to be on the side of the dishers."

First, in what context did it occur? It is the motto of a charming young woman (any doubts I may have expressed about her are withdrawn as of now; she is all one could ask for) who is not malicious and who does not in the least want to impose her beliefs or herself upon other people. She sends one hundred dollars a month to her mother, who is dying of cancer in a county hospital in Pennsylvania. When she told me she was sending the money I asked her why.

47

"Why?" said Ruth. "I'm disappointed in you to ask me such a thing."

"All right be disappointed, but tell me why."

She shrugged in a humorous way. "She's my mother. And anyway," she added, "we're all dying, aren't we?"

The important thing to note about Ruth is that she means it but she doesn't care. Just as she doesn't really care whether you like her clothes or her lovely hair; she does and you should—the loss is yours if you don't. She was reared in a perfectly usual American city, and she has chosen from its unconscious culture the best in custom and attitude.

But she said it here in the public relations division of the Colored Persons Reserve, here where there is as much getting and dishing out as anywhere in the world, where the most important Negro in the Reserve, its president, may be in a very real sense considered inferior to a white window washer. The first time O'Doone heard her say it (he had dropped by to talk awhile and Ruth had joined us) he made the sign of the cross in the air between himself and Ruth and backed clear out of the room. He didn't return either. I'm sure he's not religious. I don't know why he did that.

What does the statement imply? Primarily it makes no judgment and does not urge to action. It is unmoral. "There is a condition such that some people must inflict pain and others must receive it; since it is impossible to be neutral in this regard and since I like neither to give nor to take injury I shall choose the path of least resistance. I shall ally myself with the inflictors not because I like their side and certainly not because I dislike the other side but only because in that way I myself am least interfered with." No regret, no self-deception (*it is impossible to be neutral*), only true resignation. This circumstance is as it is, and it will not and should not be otherwise. There is a certain intensity of joy possible after resignation of this order greater than we frustrated hopers know. (Where do I fit into this scheme? I think I have discovered one thing about myself from contemplating Ruth's maxim: I want profoundly to be a disher, but my training has been such, or perhaps I am only so weak, that I am incapable of being one with a clear conscience. Consequently I find myself in a halfway position: dishing it out, yes, but at the behest of people I have never seen, and to people I will never know.) Ruth took a job with the NRACP for the only right reason: not for any of my complicated ones nor for the general greed but because she saw quite clearly that here was one of the very pure instances of getting it and of dishing it out. She left a job as secretary to an executive in General Electric for this. I think she gets a certain pleasure from seeing her philosophy so exquisitely borne out by event. Ruth is twenty-seven. I think I am in love with her. I am sure she is not in love with me.

Tell me, Herb, does not this maxim ring a bell in you? This girl has had the courage to put into deliberate words her sense of the inevitable. Do you not admire her for it? And is she not right? She is right enough. If you doubt it let me tell you what our job here is.

The authorities consider the situation potentially explosive enough to warrant the most elaborate system of censorship I have ever heard of. To begin with there is a rule that during his first week in the Reserve every Negro may write three letters to persons on the outside. After that period is over only one letter a month is permitted. Now all letters leaving here during the first week are sent to PR where they are censored and typed in the correct form (on NRACP letter-head); the typed copies are sent on and the originals are filed. The reason for this elaborate system is interesting enough and probably sound; every endeavor is to be made to discourage any leaking out of adverse reports on conditions in the CPR. There are some fourteen million Negroes in the nation not all of whom are entirely pleased with the prospect of being relocated, and there are an indeterminate number of Caucasian sympathizers—civil liberties fanatics for the most part—who could cause trouble if any confirmation of their suspicions about the CPR should leak out. We have put out a staggering amount of data on the climatic, agricultural, power production, and mining conditions of the region, and we have propagandized with every device in the book. Yet we know well enough how long it takes for propaganda to counteract prejudice, and sometimes how deceptive an apparent propaganda success can be. We are more than grateful that almost the entire news outlet system of the nation is on our side.

Well, after the three letters of the first week have been typed and sent the writer's job begins. Every effort is made to discourage the interned Negroes from writing to the outside. For one thing we keep in our files all personal letters incoming during the first month. Anyone who continues to write to an internee after this month needs to be answered. The filing clerks keep track of the dates, and forward all personal letters to us. (The clerks think we send the letters on to the internees.) We then write appropriate responses to the letters in the style of the internee as we estimate it from his three letters. We try to be as impersonal as possible, conveying the idea that everything is fine. Why do we not forward the letters to the internees to answer? First of all we do, if the internees request it. They are told that they will receive letters only from those persons whose letters they request to see, and such a request involves yards of red tape. Very few are expected to use the cumbersome mechanism at all. Secondly we write the letters for them simply to save ourselves time and trouble. We would have a lot of rewriting to do anyway; this method assures us of complete control and an efficient modus operandi. Any Negro outside who writes too many insistent letters will be, at our request, relocated within a month; we do not want any unnecessary unhappiness to result from the necessarily painful program. Friends and relatives are to be reunited as fast as possible. Whole communities are to be relocated together to avoid whatever wrenches in personal relationships we can avoid.

Is not this getting it and dishing it out on a fine scale? All for very good reasons I know, but then is it not conceivable that there are always good reasons for the old crapperoo? Sometimes I feel absolutistic enough to say, *if it's this bad for any ultimate reason whatsoever then to hell with it.* After which sentiment comes the gun at the head. But then reason reinstates my sense of the relativity of values, and on I go writing a letter to Hector Jackson of South Carolina explaining that I've been so busy putting up a chicken house and plowing that I haven't had a chance to write but I hope to see you soon. (I doubt if I will.)

Andy

I forgot to mention—I have a special job, which is to censor the letters of all the clerical personnel in PR. One of my duties is to censor any reference to the censorship! A strange state of affairs. None of them know that this job is mine; most think the censor must be some Mail Department employee. I must say one looks at some people with new eyes after reading their correspondence.

I need hardly say—but in case there is any doubt I will say—that this letter is absolutely confidential. How much of our system will become publicly known I cannot guess but naturally I don't want to jump the official gun in this regard.

April 12

Dear Herb,

Let me tell you about the strange adventure I had last evening. I am still not quite sure what to make of it.

Immediately after work I picked up a few sandwiches and a pint of whiskey and walked out into the desert on one of my hikes. One more meal with the jabber of the café and one more of those good but always good in the same way dinners and I felt I should come apart at the seams. (Another thing I have learned about myself: I am ill-adapted to prison life.) I had no goal in view; I intended to stroll.

But I found myself heading generally in the direction of the hill from which I had looked over the Tehuala Valley and the city of CPR Intake buildings. I came across nothing particularly interesting in a natural history way so that by early dusk I was near to the hill. I decided to climb it again and see what I could see.

The first thing I saw, in the difficult light of dusk, was a soldier with a gun standing at the foot of the hill. I came around a large clump of cactus and there he was, leaning on his rifle. He immediately pointed it at me and told me to go back where I belonged. I objected that I had climbed this hill before and that I could see no reason why I shouldn't do it again. He replied that he didn't see any reason either, but I couldn't just the same; they were going to put up another fence to keep people like me away. I cursed at the whole situation; if I had dared I would have cursed him too, for he had been rude as only a guard with a gun can be. But before I left I pulled out my pint and took a slug of it. The guard was a changed man.

"Christ," he said, "give me a pull."

"I should give you a pull."

"Come on," he said, "I ain't had a drop since I came to this hole. They won't even give us beer."

"All right, if you'll tell me what the hell's going on around here."

He made me crouch behind a Joshua tree, and he himself would not look at me while he talked. I asked him the reason for all the precautions.

"They got a searchlight up top the hill with machine guns. They sweep the whole hill all the time. They can see plain as day in the dark. They keep an eye on us fellows down here. I know. I used to run the light."

"I haven't seen any light," I said.

51

He glanced at me with scorn.

"It's black," he said. "They cut down all the bushes all around the top part of that hill. Anybody comes up in the bare place—pttt! *Any*body. Even a guard."

"I still don't see any light."

"Man, it's black light. You wear glasses and shine this thing and you can see better than you can with a regular light searchlight. It's the stuff. We used to shoot rabbits with it. The little bastards never knew what hit them!"

I didn't want to appear simple so I didn't ask any more questions about the black light. He was an irascible fellow, with a gun and a knife, and he had drunk most of the bottle already.

"Why do you let me stay at all?" I asked.

"Can't see good in the dusk. Not even them can't."

I couldn't think of anything more to say.

"I used to be guard on the railroad they got inside. Say, have they got a system! Trains from the outside go through an automatic gate. All the trainmen get on the engine and drive out. Then we come up through another automatic gate and hook on and drag it in. Always in the daytime. Anybody tried to hop train, inside or out—pttt! Air-conditioned box cars made out of steel. Two deep they come. Never come in at night."

"Are you married?"

"Ain't nobody married up front, huh?"

I didn't answer.

"Well, is there?"

"No, but there could be if anybody felt like it."

"Well, there ain't even a woman inside. Not a damn one. They let us have all the nigger women we want. Some ain't so bad. Most of them fight a lot."

He smashed the pint bottle on a rock nearby. "Why didn't you bring some real liquor, God damn you?" he said in a low voice full of violence. "Get the hell back home where you belong. Get out of here. It's getting dark. I'll shoot the guts out of you too. Bring me something I can use next time, huh? Get going."

"Stay under cover," he shouted after me. "They're likely to get you if they spot you. They can't miss if it's dark enough."

The last I heard of him he was coughing and spitting and swearing. I was as disgusted as scared, and I must confess I was scared stiff.

I walked homeward, slowly recovering my emotional balance, trying to understand what had happened to me with that guard, the meaning of what he had told me. For some absurd reason the tune *In the Gloaming* kept running through my head in the idiotic way tunes will; I was unable to concentrate intelligently upon the situation.

I heard a sound at some distance to my left. I stopped, suddenly and inexplicably alarmed to the point of throbbing temples and clenched fists. A slim figure in brown came through the cactus; as it approached I could see that it was a young woman. She did not see me, but her path brought her directly to where I was standing. I did not know whether to accost her at a distance or to let her come upon me where I stood. By the time I had decided not to accost her I could see that it was Ruth.

"Why Ruth!" I cried with all the emotion of relief and gratified surprise in my voice and perhaps something more. "What are you doing here?"

She started badly, then seeing who it was she hurried up to me and to my surprise took my arms and put them around her body. "Andy, I am so glad to see you. Some good angel must have put you here for me."

I squeezed her, we kissed, a friendly kiss, then she drew away and shook herself. She had almost always called me Mr. Dixon before; there was a real affection in her "Andy."

"What's the matter?" I asked her. "Where have you been?"

"I didn't know you took walks too."

"Oh yes. It's one way to keep from going nuts."

She laughed a little and squeezed my arm. I could not refrain from kissing her again, and this time it was not just a friendly kiss.

"Where did you go?" I asked again.

"To that hill. I went up there a couple of times before. There was a guard there who wanted to lay me."

We didn't speak for a few moments.

"I think he almost shot me for giving him the brushoff. I didn't look back when I left, but I heard him click his gun. You don't know how glad I was to see you."

So we kissed again and this time it was serious.

"Wait a minute," she said, "wait a minute."

She unlocked her arm from mine, and we continued on our way not touching.

"I had some trouble with a guard too," I said. "I wonder why they're so damned careful to keep us away."

"Mine told me they didn't want us to get any funny ideas. He said things aren't what they seem to be in there."

"Didn't you ask him what he meant?"

"Sure. That's when he said I'd better shut up and let him lay me or else he'd shoot me. So I walked off. I'm not going to call on *him* again."

I put my arm around her. I can't tell you how fond I was of her at that moment, of her trim, poised body, her courage, her good humor, her delightful rich voice and laughter. But she only kissed me gently and withdrew.

"I want to keep my head for a while, darling," she said.

I knew what she meant. We walked on in silence, hand in hand. It was moonlight. If I was lightheaded now I knew why.

When we were about half a mile from our buildings we came across O'Doone also returning from a walk.

"Well," he said brightly, "it *is* a nice moon, isn't it?"

It wouldn't do to say that we had met by accident; I was embarrassed, but Ruth's fine laugh cleared the air for me.

"Nicest I ever saw," she said.

"Did you ever walk up that hill," I asked him, "where you can see out over the valley?"

"Once," he said in a surprisingly harsh voice. "I'd rather play chess."

We went into one of the recreation rooms and O'Doone beat me at three games of chess. Ruth sat by, knitting—a sweater for a cousin's baby. We talked little, but comfortably. It would have been a domestic scene if it had not been for the fifty or sixty other people in the room.

Herb, what does it all mean?

Andy

April 20

Dear Herb,

[If all goes well you will receive the following letter from Ruth's cousin, who will be informed by O'Doone's sister to forward it to you. O'Doone's sister will also send you instructions on how to make the invisible ink visible. I first wrote the letter in visible ink, intending to mail it in the usual way, I was prepared to take all the certainly drastic consequences that would come from its being read by someone of authority. But O'Doone's invisible ink (what a strange fellow to have brought a quart of it here! He said he had brought it only to play mysterious letter games with his nephew. I wonder.) and Ruth's baby sweater, upon the wrapping of which I write this, combined to save me. If the authorities catch *this* I don't care what happens. It takes so long to write lightly enough in invisible ink for no pen mark to show on the paper that I doubt if I will have the patience to use it often. Most of my letters will be innocuous in regular ink. I may add an invisible note or two, between the lines, in the margin, or at the end. O'Doone says it's not any of the ordinary kinds and if we're careful the authorities are not likely to catch us. O'Doone is strange. He refused to take this whole ink matter for anything more than a big joke, as though we were digging a tunnel under a house, O'Doone pretending we are just tunneling in a strawstack to hide our marbles, myself trying to protest (but being laughed at for my lapse in taste) that we are really undermining a house in order to blow it up. Which perhaps we are. In any event I don't have the energy left to rewrite this letter, I'll merely copy it off invisibly.]

I cannot tell you how shocked I was to discover the familiar, black censor's ink over five lines in your last letter. The censor censored! I had not thought of that. In my innocence I had thought that we writers in the higher brackets could be trusted to be discreet. One would think I was still a loyal subscriber to the *Nation* I was so naïve. But no—I am trusted to censor the letters of inferiors (I suspect my censorship is sample-checked by someone), but my own letters are themselves inspected and their dangerous sentiments excised. And, irony of ironies, your own references to the fact that my letters were censored were themselves blacked out.

Who is it that does this? The head of PR here? That's a strange way to make him waste his time. One of his assistants? Then the head must censor the assistant's letters. And the chief board of the NRACP censors the head's letters? And the President theirs? And God his? And . . . ?

Which is the more imprisoned: the jailer who thinks he is free and is not, or the prisoner who knows the precise boundaries of his liberty and accepting them explores and uses all the world he has? I am a jailer who knows he is not free. I am a prisoner who does not know the limits of his freedom. All this I voluntarily submitted to in the name of a higher freedom. Ever since my adolescence, when the New Deal was a faith, liberty has been one of the always repeated, never examined articles of my creed. Well, I have been examining liberty recently, and she's a pure fraud.

One thing I have learned: you don't just quietly put yourself on the side of Ruth's dishers, you become one of them yourself. A disher *has* to dish it out, he cannot help it at all, and he pays for it. Or maybe I am only paying for my guilt-making desire to be a more important disher than I am.

Ruth was surprised at my distress upon receiving your censored letter. She only shrugged. What had I expected, after all? It was inevitable, it was a necessity. That's the key word, Herb, *necessity*. Not liberty, *necessity*. True liberty is what the prisoner has, because he accepts *necessity*. That's the great thing, to recognize and accept *necessity*.

I've been working slowly toward a realization of this. I think my decision to work in the NRACP came from recognizing the social necessity of it. The Negro problem in America was acute and it was insoluble by any liberal formula. This solution gives dignity and independence to the Negroes. It staves off the depression by the huge demand for manufactured products, for transportation, for the operations of the NRACP itself; but perhaps most important of all, it establishes irrevocably in the American people's mind the wisdom and rightness of the government, for if capitalism must go (as it must) it should be replaced peaceably by a strong and wise-planned state. Such a state we are proving ourselves to be. Very well. I accepted this. But what I forgot was that I, I the individual, I Andrew Dixon, must personally submit to the stringencies of necessity. The relics of the New Deal faith remained to clutter up my new attitude. This experience, coming when and as it did, particularly coming when Ruth's courageous wisdom was nearby to support me, has liberated me (I hope) into the greater freedom of the prisoner of necessity.

At least such are my pious prayers. I cannot say I am sure I fully understand all the strictures of necessity. I *can* say I do not enjoy those I understand. But pious I will remain.

Remember the days when we thought we could *change* necessity? Democracy and all that? How much older I feel!

Andy

May 1

Mary my dear,

Please let me apologize—sincerely too, Mary—for having neglected you so cruelly for the past months. Herb tells me you are quite put out, and well you might be. I can find no excuses for it, but I will stoutly maintain that it was not a question of hostility or indifference to you, my dear. Actually I have been going through something of a crisis, as Herb may have been telling you. It has something to do with the desert, and something to do with the NRACP, and a lot to do with the charming young woman whose picture I enclose. She is Ruth Cone. We are getting married in a couple of Sundays—Mother's Day. Why Mother's Day I really don't know, but she wants it so there's no help. The details of our plighting troth might amuse you.

A couple of evenings ago I was playing chess in the recreation room with a man named O'Doone, my only friend here. Ruth was sitting beside us knitting some rompers for a cousin's baby. From time to time we would chat a little; it was all very comfortable and unromantic. O'Doone, between games, went to the toilet. When he had left Ruth said to me with a twinkle in her eye, "Andy darling, don't you see what I am doing?" I replied, "Why yes, my sweet, knitting tiny garments. Is it . . . ?" And we both laughed heartily. It was a joke, you see, a mild comfortable little joke, and no one would have thought of it a second time except that when we had finished laughing it was no longer a joke. Her face became very sober and I am sure mine did too. I said, "Do you want children, Ruth?" "Yes," she replied. "Do you want to have my children?" "Yes," she said again, without looking at me. Then with the most charming conquest of modesty that you can imagine she turned her serious little face to me, and we very lightly kissed. O'Doone had returned by then. "Well," he said in a bright way, "do I interrupt?" "Not at all," I answered, "we have just decided to get married." He burbled a little, in caricature of the overwhelmed, congratulating friend, pumped our hands, and asked us when we were marrying. "I don't know," I said. "Why not

57

tomorrow?" "Oh no," said Ruth severely, "how can I assemble my trousseau?" At which O'Doone went off into a braying laugh, and we set up the chess pieces. "Bet you five to one," he said, "I win this game in less than sixty moves." I wouldn't take his bet. It took him about forty moves to beat me. Thus did Dixon and Cone solemnly vow to share their fortunes.

It's the first marriage in PR. Everybody will attend. The chief promised me Monday off and temporary quarters in one of the guest suites. We are to get a two-room apartment in the new dormitory that is nearly completed. Such privacy and spaciousness will make us the envy of the whole community. I'm sure there will be a spate of marriages as soon as the dormitory is completed. We will not be married by a holy man, partly because neither of us believes in it and partly because there isn't one of any kind on the premises. (I wonder why there were those detailed questions about religious beliefs on our application forms.) There was a little trouble at first about who was authorized to marry people here. The PR chief, as the only person permitted to leave the place, went out and got himself authorized to do it legally. I think he rather fancies himself in the capacity of marrier. He runs to paternalism.

Ruth urges me—she assumes quite rightly that I have not done it already—to tell you some of the homely details of life here. Of our sleeping rooms the less said the better. The beds are comfortable, period. We live quite communally, but very well. There's a fine gymnasium with swimming pool and play fields attached—tennis, baseball, squash, fencing, everything but golf. There's the best library (surely the best!) in the world on American Negro affairs, and a reasonably good one of modern literature. We have comfortable working quarters and a long working day. There is a fine desert for us to walk around in, and I have come to need an occasional stroll in the desert for spiritual refreshment. And we eat handsomely, except for vegetables. In fact, the only complaint that I have of the cooking is the monotony of its excellence: roast, steak, chop, stew. Almost never liver and kidneys and omelettes and casseroles, and always frozen vegetables. Well, probably the Negroes will be producing plenty of vegetables within a few weeks. There's lots of liquor of every kind. There is a sort of department store where one can buy everything one needs and most of the luxuries one could want in this restricted life. There's a movie a week—a double-feature with news and cartoon—and bridge or poker every day. A microcosmic plenitude.

As for the rest of our routine life here I can think of nothing interesting enough to mention. We work and avoid work, backbite, confide, suspect. It's a bureaucratic existence, no doubt of that.

Will this epistle persuade you to forgive me?

Now you must write to me—soon.

Devotedly yours,

Andy

(*In invisible ink, between the lines of the preceding letter*)

O'Doone, who sometimes gives his opinions very obliquely, came to me today with some disturbing figures. He wasn't in the least jaunty about them and I must confess that I am not either.

According to *Time*, which seems to know more about the CPR than we do, there have been about 50,000 Negroes interned already, and these 50,000 comprise nearly all the wealthy and politically powerful Negroes in the nation (including an objectionable white-supremacy Senator one of whose great-great-grandmothers turns out to have been black). The leaders were interned first, reasonably enough, to provide the skeleton of government and system in the new state which they are to erect. *But*, O'Doone points out, we have yet to receive from them a request for letters from an outsider, and if any Negroes at all are going to make such requests it must surely be these, the most important, the least afraid of red tape. (He also pointed out that not one of the entertainers or athletes of prominence has been interned. That, I'm afraid, is all too easily explained.) You see, says O'Doone, you see? But he didn't say, Why? to me, and I'm glad he didn't, for I can't even guess why.

Another statistic he had concerned the CPR itself. We all know that the figures on natural resources in the CPR are exaggerated. Grossly. Fourteen million people cannot possibly live well in this area, and O'Doone demonstrated that fact to me most convincingly. Economically, the Negro problem in the U.S. has been that they provided a larger cheap-labor market than consumer market. Now the false stimulus of capitalizing their beginnings here will keep American industry on an even keel for years and years, but after that what? O'Doone bowed out at that point, but I think I can press the point a little further. They will provide a market for surplus commodities

59

great enough to keep the pressures of capitalism from blowing us
sky high, meanwhile permitting the transition to a planned state to
take place. Very astute, I think, very astute indeed.

June 12

Dear Herb,

Why I have not written, you ought to be able to guess. I will not
pretend to any false ardors about Ruth. She is wise and winning as a
woman, and everything one could ask for as a wife. I love her dearly.
She has not read very widely or profoundly, but I think she is going to
do something about that soon. We are happy together and I think we
shall continue to be happy during the difficult years to come. What
more can I say?

Why are happiness and contentment and the sense of fulfillment
so hard to write about? I can think of nothing to say, and besides
Ruth is just coming in from tennis (it's 9:30 Sunday morning).

10 P.M.

Ruth has gone to bed so I will continue in another vein.

I have been discovering that the wells of pity, which have lain
so long locked and frozen in my eyes, are thawed in me now. I am
enclosing a letter which came in from a Negress in Chicago to her
lover in the CPR, and his response. It is the first letter from inside
except for the usual three during the first week that I have read. Ap-
parently a few have been coming out now and then, but this is my
first one. I cannot tell you how I pitied both these unhappy people.
When Ruth read them she said, "My, what a mean man! I hope he
has to collect garbage all his life." I cannot agree with her. I think
his little note betrays an unhappiness as great as the woman's, and
even more pitiable for being unrecognized, unappreciated. Judge for
yourself. I can think of nothing to add.

Andy

Honey, dear child, why don't you write to me? Don't you even remember
all those things you told me you'd do no matter what? And you're not even
in jail, you just in that place where we all going to go to sooner or later. O I
sure hope they take me there with you. I can't live without you. But I don't
even know who to ask to go there with you. I went to the policeman and
they said they didn't know nothing about it. I don't know what to do. You
don't know how I ache for you honey. It's just like I got a tooth pulled out
but it ain't no tooth it's worse, and there is no dentist for it neither. There's

a fellow at the store keeps bothering me now and again, but I assure him I don't want him, I got a man. I thought I had a man, you, but I don't hear nothing from you. Maybe you got something there, I don't see how you could do it not after those things you said, but if you have tell me so I can go off in some hole and die. I don't want this Lee Lawson, he's no good, it's you I want, sweetheart, you tell me it's all right. I *got* to hear from you or I'll just die.

Dear ———,
I've been so busy baby, you wouldn't believe how busy I've been. You'll be coming here pretty soon and then you'll feel better too. It's nice here. We'll get along fine then. You tell that guy to leave you be. You're my gal. Tell him I said so.

Yours truly,

———

(*In invisible ink*)
I didn't include these letters because I thought they were in the Héloïse-Abélard class, but because I wanted to say something about them and also because they gave me more invisible space.

The man's response came to us already typed. That very much astonished me, and O'Doone, when I told him, let fly a nasty one. "I suppose," he said, "they have a couple of writers in there writing a few letters in place of the Negroes, which we then relay. Complicated, isn't it?" Not complicated, upsetting. Devastating. What if it were true? (And I must say this letter has an air more like the PR rewrite formula than like a real letter. Then *none* of the Negroes would have even filtered connection with the outside world.) Why? Why fool even us? Is there no end to the deception and doubt of this place?

O'Doone posed another of his puzzles yesterday. He read in the current PR weekly bulletin that the CPR has been shipping whole trainloads of leather goods and canned meats to China and Europe for relief purposes, under the government's supervision, of course. O'Doone came into my office at once, waving the bulletin and chortling. "How do you like it?" he cried. "Before we get a carrot out of them the Chinese get tons of meat." Then a sudden light seemed to dawn on his face. "Where did all the cattle come from?"

A strange thing happened: O'Doone's intelligent, sensitive face collapsed. The great domed forehead remained almost unwrinkled, but his features looked somehow like one of those children's rubber faces which collapse when you squeeze them. No anguish, no anxiety, only collapse. He left without a word. I wish he had never come here with that news.

Last night I lay awake till three or four o'clock. I could hear trucks and trains rumbling occasionally throughout the night, entering and leaving the Reserve. But that guard I met at the foot of the hill told me that they only bring internees in the daytime. Are those shipments? How can it be? Sometimes I am sick at heart with doubt and uncertainty.

I dreamt last night that I was a Gulliver, lying unbound and unresisting on the ground while a thousand Lilliputians, all of them black, ate at me. I would not write the details of that dream even in invisible ink. Not even in plain water.

July 4

Dear Herb,

Hail Independence Day! Some of the overgrown kids around here are shooting off firecrackers. No one is working. It is all very pleasant. I suppose March 20th will be the Independence Day of the new Negro nation—the day when the first trainload arrived. How long ago that seems already. I do not think I have ever been through so much in so short a time.

Now for the real news. Ruth is pregnant! Amazing woman, she remains outwardly as humorous and self-contained as ever. No one else knows her condition because she wants to avoid as much as possible of the female chatter that goes with pregnancy. She insists upon playing tennis still. Yet she is not all calmness and coolness; when we are lying in bed together before going to sleep she croons little nonsense hymns to pregnancy in my ear, and yesterday afternoon at the office she walked into my cubicle and placed my hand over her womb. Then she kissed me with an unviolent passion that I have never known before in my life. I tell you, she's a wonderful woman.

How miraculous is conception and growth! I no more understand such things than I really understand about the stars and their rushings. One event follows another, but I'm sure I don't know why. If you permit yourself to, you get back to an archaic awe realizing that you have started off a chain of miracles. I never had a sense of littleness when observing the naked heavens, of man's puniness, of my own nothingness. Perhaps it was a fear of that feeling which for so long prevented me from looking upward at all. I mentioned my reaction to O'Doone on one of the first occasions of our meeting. He nodded and said, "But is not a man more complex than a star, and in every way but one that we know of more valuable?" What he said remains with me yet, and when I am presented with the vastness of the stars and the forces which operate within them I am impressed and excited but not depressed by the imagined spectacle. Their bigness does not make me little. My own complexity does not make them simple. Perhaps man is no longer the center of the universe, but neither is anything else. That I have learned.

But when I am presented with the proof of the powers that men (and myself) possess, I still feel a little off balance. When Clarice was pregnant with Betty I had no such feeling. I felt annoyed chiefly. But now, in this desert, in the CPR, I have been sent back at last to fundamentals, to the sources of things; I realize fully how unaccountable is birth of life. Ruth, who never departed far from the sources, is less embarrassed in admitting her sense of mystery.

One thing I am going to teach this child if it can be taught anything: that the humane tradition has been tried and found wanting. It's over, finished, kaput. A new era of civilization commences. Once kindness and freedom were good for something, but no more. *Put yourself in his place*—never. Rather, fight to stay where you are. I think we are entering upon an age of reason and mystery. Reason which accepts and understands the uttermost heights and depths of human power, man's depravity, and his nobility—and, understanding these, dares use them toward a great and future goal, the goal of that stern order which is indispensable to the fullest development of man. Mystery toward all that is not explainable, which is a very great deal. Rationalism failed, for it asserted that everything was ultimately explainable. We know better. We know that to destroy a man's sense of mystery is to cut him off from one of the sources of life. Awe, acceptance, and faith are wonderful sources of power and fulfillment. I have discovered them. My child shall never forget them.

Andy

(In invisible ink)

I have put the gun to my temple, Herb, I have pointed the knife at my heart. But my nerve failed me. There were a few days when I was nearly distracted. My division chief told me to stay home till I looked better, but I dared not. I think it was only Ruth's pregnancy

63

that saved me. My newly awakened sense of mystery plus my powers of reason have saved me. This is the third letter I have written you in a week, but I threw the others away. I knew they were wild and broken, and I was not sure at all that I was physically able to write in such a manner as to avoid detection.

It came to a head two weeks ago. O'Doone entered my office, his face looking bright and blasted. He dropped a booklet on my desk and left after a few comments of no importance. The booklet was an anthropologist's preliminary report on certain taboos among American Negroes; the fellow had been interviewing them in Intake. There was nothing of special interest about it that I could see except that it was written in the past tense.

I expected O'Doone to reclaim the booklet any day. For some reason he had always done the visiting to me, not I to him. He was very restless and I am slothful. But a week passed and no O'Doone. I did not meet him in the café nor in the recreation room. I went to his own room, but he did not answer. The next day I went to his office and his secretary told me he had not shown up for two days. I returned to his room. It was locked. The janitor unlocked it for me. When I entered I saw him lying dead on his bed. "Well, old boy," I said to drive the janitor away, I don't know why, "feeling poorly?" He had drunk something. There was a glass on the table by his bed. There was no note. His face was repulsive. (That is a mystery I have learned to respect, how hideous death is.) He was cold and somehow a little sticky to the touch. I covered his face with a towel and sat down. I knew I should call someone, but I did not want to. I knew the janitor would remember letting me in and my staying too long. Yet I felt that was something I must do. What it was I could not remember, something important. It took me an eternity to remember: the invisible ink. I knew where he had kept it; it was not there. I looked throughout his room and it was simply gone. I left.

I still did not notify anyone of his suicide. I was not asking myself why he had done it. Or perhaps I was only shouting, Where's the ink? in a loud voice to cover up the little question, Why? I went to our rooms and straight to the liquor shelf, took down the Scotch, poured myself a stiff one, and drank. It was horrible; I spat it out, cursing. Then I recognized the odor; O'Doone had come over, poured out the Scotch (I hope he enjoyed it himself), and filled the bottle with the invisible ink. At that I broke down in the most womanish way and cried on the bed (never ask, Why? Why? Why?).

Ruth found me there some time later. I told her everything that had happened, and she immediately pulled me together. She had the sense to know I had been acting more oddly than was wise. She notified the right people and O'Doone was disposed of. No one asked me any embarrassing questions, and no official mention of O'Doone's end was made anywhere.

I must continue this on a birthday card.

(*In invisible ink on a large, plain Happy Birthday card to Mary*)

I had still not allowed myself to ask why he had done it, but Ruth put the thing in a short sentence. "He was too soft-hearted to stand it here." She was right; he was a Christian relic. He knew more than he could bear. I resolved to go that very evening again to the hill where the black searchlight threatened the night.

Some sandwiches. Four half-pints of whiskey. A hunting knife (a foolish gesture, I know). Plain drab clothes. The long walk in the still hot, late-afternoon sun. Sunset. The huge, sudden twilight. Then I was within sight of a guard (not the same one I had seen before) standing by the new fence at the foot of the hill.

I crept up toward him under cover of brush and cactus till I was close enough to toss a half-pint of whiskey in his direction. His bored, stupid face immediately became animated by the most savage emotions. He leveled his gun and pointed it in my general direction. He could not see me, however, and rather than look for me he crouched, eyes still searching the underbrush, to reach for the bottle. He drained it in five minutes.

"Throw me some more," he whispered loudly.

"Put the gun down."

I aimed my voice away from him, hoping that he would not spot me. I was lying flat beneath a large clump of sagebrush. There was a Joshua tree nearby and several cactus plants. He pointed the gun at one of the stalks of cactus and crept up toward it. Then he suddenly stopped, I don't know why, and walked back to his post.

"What yer want?" he asked.

I tossed out another bottle. He jumped again, then got it and drank it.

"What's going on in there?"

65

"They're fixing up the niggers," he said. "You know as much about it as I do."

He began to sing *Oh! Susannah* in a sentimental voice. It was beginning to get too dark for my safety. I was desperate.

I tossed out another bottle, only not so far this time. When he leaned for it I said very clearly, "You look like a butcher."

He deliberately opened the bottle and drank off half of it. "Butcher, huh? Butcher?" He laid down his gun and took his villainous knife out. "I'm no butcher. I won't have nothing to do with the whole slimy mess. I won't eat them, no sir, you can do that for me. But I can do a little carving, I think. No butcher, you son of a bitch. You dirty, prying, nigger-eating son of a bitch. I'll learn you to call me a butcher."

He was stalking the cactus again. He lunged forward at it and with much monotonous cursing and grunting dealt with it murderously. Meanwhile I crawled out on the other side of the sagebrush and ran for it. He never shot at me. Nothing happened except that I too ran full tilt into a cactus and had to walk hours in agony of flesh as well as of spirit. I vomited and retched till I thought I would be unable to walk further.

I must continue this letter some other way.

Andy

(*In invisible ink on the papers wrapping another sweater for Ruth's cousin's baby*)

I told Ruth nothing of what I had learned; not even *her* great sense of the inevitable could survive such a shock, I think. Yet sometimes it seems to me that she must surely know it all. I do not want to know whether she knows. Could I support it if she did?

It was more painful pulling the cactus needles out than it had been acquiring them. But she removed them all, bathed the little wounds with alcohol, and put me to bed. The next morning I awoke at seven and insisted upon going to work. I sat all day in my office, eating crackers and drinking milk. I didn't accomplish a thing. It was then that my chief told me to take it easy for a while. I was in a sort of stupor for a couple of days; yet to everyone's consternation I insisted on going to work. I accomplished nothing and I intended to accomplish nothing, it was just that I could not tolerate being alone. In fact today was the first day I have been alone for more than five minutes since I returned from the walk. But today I have regained a kind of composure, or a semblance of composure, which for a time I despaired of ever possessing again. And I know that by the time I have given shape enough to my thoughts to put them on this paper for you to read I shall have gained again a peace of mind. To have you to write to, Herb, that is the great thing at this point. Without you I do not know what I would have done.

So much for my emotions. My thinking, my personal philosophy, has gone through at least as profound an upheaval as they. In the chaos of my mind, in which huge invisible chunks of horror hit me unexpectedly from unexpected angles again and again, my first coherent and sensible idea came in the form of a question. "Why did they make it possible for me to find out what has been going on?" (For I finally realized that it was no fluke that I had discovered it, or O'Doone either, or anyone with the suspicions and the courage for it. When the atom bombs were being produced, the whole vast undertaking was carried off without a single leak to the outside. So if I had been able in so simple a way to find out what had been going on in the CPR it was only because they didn't care. They could have stopped me.)

Then I thought, invisible ink is scarcely new in the history of things. Perhaps they have been reading my correspondence with you all along and will smile at this letter as they have smiled at others. Or perhaps they haven't taken the trouble to read it because they simply don't care.

Perhaps the authorities not only did not care if we gradually found out, but wanted us to. Why should they want us to? Why, if that were true, should they have put up so formidable a system—double fences, censorship, lies, etc., etc.—of apparent preventatives?

The only answer that makes sense is that they want the news to sift out gradually and surreptitiously to the general population—illegally, in the form of hideous rumors to which people can begin to accustom themselves. After all, many knew generally that something like the atom bomb was being manufactured. Hiroshima was not the profound and absolute shock in 1945 that it would have been in 1935, and a good deal of the preparation for its general acceptance was rumor. It is in the people's interest that the CPR function as it does function, and especially so that they can pretend that they have nothing to do with it. The experience of the Germans in the Jewextermination camps demonstrated that clearly enough. It would do no good for me to go around crying out the truth about NRACP, because few would believe me in the first place and my suppression would only give strength to the rumors—which are required and planned for anyhow.

But I still had to set myself the task of answering, Why? What drove them (whoever *they* are) to the decision to embark upon a course which was not only revolutionary but dangerous? I accepted the NRACP as inevitable, as *necessity;* there remained only the task of trying to understand wherein lay the mystery of the *necessity* and of adjusting myself to the situation. The individual, even the leader, has no significant choice to make in the current of event. That current is part of natural law; it is unmoral, cruel, wasteful, useless, and mysterious. The leader is he who sees and points out the course of history so that we may pursue that course with least pain. It is odd that we Americans have no such leader; what we have is committees and boards and bureau heads who collectively possess leadership and who direct our way almost impersonally. There is nothing whatsoever that I myself would like so much as to be one of those wise, courageous, anonymous planners. I think I possess the wisdom. But in place of courage I have a set of moral scruples dating from an era when man was supposed to have a soul and when disease took care of overpopulation. The old vestigial values of Christianity must be excised in the people as they are being excised in me. The good and the lucky are assisting at the birth of a new age; the weak and unfit are perishing in the death of an old. Which shall it be for us?

For my own part I think I am in a state of transition from being one of the unfit to being one of the fit. I feel it. I will it. There are certain external evidences of it. For example, I was face to face with the truth at the end of April, but instead of acknowledging what I saw I turned to my love for Ruth. Yet that refusal to recognize the truth did not long survive the urgings of my sense of necessity. And I remember when being confronted with piecemeal evidences of truth that I was unable to explain a number of them. You know, Herb, how accomplished a rationalizer I can be, yet this time I did not even *try* to rationalize many of the facts.

It is dawn outside. I cannot read this letter over, so I am not entirely sure how incoherent it is. I feel that I have said most of what I wanted to say. I am not very happy. I think I shall sleep the better for having written this. I eat nothing but bread and fruit and milk. A bird is singing outside; he is making the only sound in the world. I can see the hill which separates us from the Intake buildings. It's a pleasant hill, rather like an arm extending out from the valley sides, and I am glad it is there. I am cold now, but in three hours it will be warm and in five hours hot. I am rambling I know. But suddenly all my energy has leaked out. I walk to the door to see Ruth so happily sleeping, mysteriously replenishing life from this nightly portion of death, and I think of that baby that she is bearing and will give birth to. If it were not for her and the baby I am sure I should have gone mad. Is not that a mystery, Herb? Our child shall be fortunate; it is the first conscious generation of each new order in whom the greatest energy is released. There are splendid things ahead for our child.

It is not my fault. I did not know what I was doing. How could I have known? What can I do now?

I stare at the lightening sky. Exhausted, I do not know why I do not say farewell and go to bed. Perhaps it is because I do not want to hear that little lullaby that sings in my ears whenever I stop: I have eaten human flesh, my wife is going to have a baby; I have eaten human flesh, my wife is going to have a baby.

Remember back in the simple days of the Spanish Civil War when Guernica was bombed how we speculated all one evening what the worst thing in the world could be? This is the worst thing in the world, Herb. I tell you, the worst. After this, nothing.

Perhaps if I lay my head against Ruth's breast and put her hands over my ears I can go to sleep. Last night I recited Housman's "Loveliest of trees, the cherry now" over and over till I went to sleep, not because I like it particularly but because I could think of nothing else to recite.

My wife is going to have a baby, my wife is going to have a baby, my wife is going to have a baby.

Bless you,
Andy

69

Among the Dangs

I G R A D U A T E D from Sansom University in 1937 with honors in history, having intended to study law, but I had no money and nowhere to get any; by good fortune the anthropology department, which had just been given a grant for research, decided that I could do a job for them. In idle curiosity I had taken a course in anthro, to see what I would have been like had history not catapulted my people a couple of centuries ago up into civilization, but I had not been inclined to enlarge on the sketchy knowledge I got from that course; even yet, when I think about it, I feel like a fraud teaching anthropology. What chiefly recommended me to the department, aside from a friend, was a combination of three attributes: I was a good mimic, a long-distance runner, and black.

The Dangs live in a forested valley in the eastern foothills of the Andes. The only white man to report on them (and, it was loosely gossiped, the only one to return from them alive), Sir Bewley Morehead, owed his escape in 1910 to the consternation caused by Halley's comet. Otherwise, he reported, they would certainly have sacrificed him as they were preparing to do; as it was they killed the priest who was to have killed him and then burned the temple down. However, Dr. Sorish, our most distinguished Sansom man, in the early thirties developed an interest in the Dangs which led to my research grant; he had introduced a tribe of Amazonian head-shrinkers to the idea of planting grain instead of just harvesting it, as a result of which they had fattened, taken to drinking brew by the tubful, and elevated Sorish to the rank of new god. The last time he had descended among them—it is Sansom policy to follow through on any primitives we "do"—he had found his worshipers holding a couple of young Dang men captive and preparing them for ceremonies which would end only with the processing of their heads; his godhood gave him sufficient power to defer these ceremonies while he made half-a-dozen transcriptions of the men's conversations and learned their language well enough to arouse the curiosity of his colleagues. The Dangs were handy with blowpipes; no one knew what pleased them; Halley's comet wasn't due till 1986. But among the recordings Sorish brought back was a legend strangely chanted by one of these young men, whose very head perhaps you can buy today from a natural science company for $150 to $200, and the same youth had given Sorish a sufficient demonstration of the Dang prophetic trance, previously described by Morehead, to whet his appetite.

I was black, true; but as Sorish pointed out, I looked as though I had been rolled in granite dust and the Dangs as though they had been rolled in brick dust; my hair was short and kinky, theirs long and straight; my lips were thick, theirs thin. It's like dressing a Greek up in reindeer skins, I said, and telling him to go pass himself off as a Lapp in Lapland. Maybe, they countered, but wouldn't he be more likely to get by than a naked Swahili with bones in his nose? I was a long-distance runner, true, but as I pointed out with a good deal of feeling I didn't know the principles of jungle escape and had no desire to learn them in, as they put it, the field. They would teach me to throw the javelin and wield a machete, they would teach me the elements of judo, and as for poisoned darts and sacrifices they would insure my life—that is, my return within three years—for five thousand dollars. I was a good mimic, true; I would be able to reproduce the Dang speech and especially the trance of the Dang prophets for the observation of science—"make a genuine contribution to learning." In the Sansom concept the researcher's experience is an inextricable part of anthropological study, and a good mimic provides the object for others' study as well as for his own. For doing this job I would be given round-trip transportation, an M.S. if I wrote a thesis on the material I gathered, the temporary insurance on my life, and one hundred dollars a month for the year I was expected to be gone. After I'd got them to throw in a fellowship of some sort for the following year, I agreed. It would pay for filling the forty cavities in my brothers' and sisters' teeth.

Dr. Sorish and I had to wait at the nearest outstation for a thunderstorm; when it finally blew up I took off all my clothes, put on a breechcloth and leather apron, put a box of equipment on my head, and trotted after him; his people were holed in from the thunder and we were in their settlement before they saw us. They were taller than I, they no doubt found my white teeth as disagreeable as I found their stained, filed teeth, but when Sorish spoke to me in English (telling me to pretend indifference to them while they sniffed me over) and in the accents of American acquaintances rather than in the harsh tones of divinity their eyes filled with awe of me. Their taboo against touching Sorish extended itself to me; when a baby ran up to me and I lifted him up to play with him, his mother crawled, beating her head on the ground till I freed him.

The next day was devoted chiefly to selecting the man to fulfill Sorish's formidable command to guide me to the edge of the Dang country. As for running—if those characters could be got to the next Olympics, Ecuador would take every long-distance medal on the board. I knew I had reached the brow of my valley only because I discovered that my guide, whom I had been lagging behind by fifty feet, at a turn in the path had disappeared into the brush.

Exhaustion allayed my terror; as I lay in the meager shade recuperating I remembered to execute the advice I had given myself before coming: to act always as though I were not afraid. What would a brave man do next? Pay no attention to his aching feet, reconnoiter, and cautiously proceed. I climbed a jutting of rock and peered about. It was a wide, scrubby valley; on the banks of the river running down the valley I thought I saw a dozen mounds too regular for stones. I touched the handle of the hunting knife sheathed at my side, and trotted down the trackless hill.

The village was deserted, but the huts, though miserable, were clean and in good repair. This meant, according to the movies I had seen, that hostile eyes were watching my every gesture. I had to keep moving in order to avoid trembling. The river was clear and not deep. The corpse of a man floated by. I felt like going downstream, but my hypothesized courage drove me up.

In half a mile I came upon a toothless old woman squatting by the track. She did not stop munching when I appeared, nor did she scream, or even stand up. I greeted her in Dang according to the formula I had learned, whereupon she cackled and smiled and nodded as gleefully as though I had just passed a test. She reminded me of my grandmother, rolled in brick dust, minus a corncob pipe between her gums. Presently I heard voices ahead of me. I saw five women carrying branches and walking very slowly. I lurked behind them until they came to a small village, and watched from a bush while they set to work. They stripped the leaves off, carefully did something to them with their fingers, and then dropped them in small-throated pots. Children scrabbled around, and once a couple of them ran up and suckled at one of the women. There remained about an hour till sunset. I prowled, undetected. The women stood, like fashion models, with pelvis abnormally rocked forward; they were wiry, without fat even on their breasts; not even their thighs and hips afforded clean sweeping lines undisturbed by bunched muscles. I saw no men.

Before I began to get into a lather about the right tack to take I stepped into the clearing and uttered their word of salutation. If a strange man should walk in your wife's front door and say "How do you do" in an accent she did not recognize, simultaneously poking his middle finger at her, her consternation would be something like that of those Dang women, for unthinkingly I had nodded my head when speaking and turned my palm up as one does in the United States; to them this was a gesture of intimacy, signifying desire. They disappeared into huts, clutching children.

I went to the central clearing and sat with my back to a log, knowing they would scrutinize me. I wondered where the men were. I could think of no excuse for having my knife in my hand except to clean my toenails. So astonishing an act was unknown to the Dangs; the women and children gradually approached in silence, watching; I cleaned my fingernails. I said the word for food; no one reacted, but presently a little girl ran up to me holding a fruit in both hands. I took it, snibbed her nose between my fingers, and with a pat on the bottom sent her back to her mother. Upon this there were hostile glances, audible intakes of breath, and a huddling about the baby who did not understand any more than I did why she was being consoled. While I ate the fruit I determined to leave the next move up to them. I sheathed my knife and squatted on my hunkers, waiting. To disguise my nervousness I fixed my eyes on the ground between my feet, and grasped my ankles from behind in such a way—right ankle with right hand, left with left—as to expose the inner sides of my forearms. Now this was, as I later learned, pretty close to the initial posture taken for the prophetic trance; also I had a blue flower tattooed on my inner right arm and a blue serpent on my left (from the summer I'd gone to sea), the like of which had never been seen in this place.

At sundown I heard the men approach; they were anything but stealthy about it; I had the greatest difficulty in suppressing the shivers. In simple fear of showing my fear I did not look up when the men gathered around, I could understand just enough of what the women were telling the men to realize that they were afraid of me. Even though I was pelted with pebbles and twigs till I was angry I still did not respond, because I could not think what to do. Then something clammy was plopped onto my back from above and I leaped high, howling. Their spears were poised before I landed.

"Strangers!" I cried, my speech composed. "Far kinsmen! I come from the mountains!" I had intended to say *from the river lands*, but the excitement tangled my tongue. Their faces remained expressionless but no spears drove at me, and then to be doing something I shoved the guts under the log with my feet.

And saved my life by doing so. That I seemed to have taken, though awkwardly, the prophetic squat; that I bore visible marvels on my arm; that I was fearless and inwardly absorbed; that I came from the mountains (their enemies lived toward the river lands); that I wore their apron and spoke their language, albeit poorly, all these disposed them to wonder at this mysterious outlander. Even so they might very well have captured me, marvelous though I was, possibly useful to them, dangerous to antagonize, had I not been unblemished, which meant that I was supernaturally guarded. Finally, my scrutinizing the fish guts, daring to smile as I did so, could mean only that I was prophetic; my leap when they had been dropped onto my back was prodigious, "far higher than a man's head," and my howl had been vatic; and my deliberately kicking the guts aside, though an inscrutable act, demonstrated at least that I could touch the entrails of an eel and live.

So I was accepted to the Dangs. The trouble was they had no ceremony for naturalizing me. For them every act had a significance, and here they were faced with a reverse problem for which nothing had prepared them. They could not possibly just assimilate me without marking the event with an act (that is, a ceremony) signifying my entrance. For them nothing *just happened*, certainly nothing that men did. Meanwhile, I was kept in a sort of quarantine while they deliberated. I did not, to be sure, understand why I was being isolated in a hut by myself, never spoken to except efficiently, watched but not restrained. I swam, slept, scratched, watched, swatted, ate; I was not really alarmed because they had not restrained me forcibly and they gave me food. I began making friends with some of the small children, especially while swimming, and there were two girls of fifteen or so who found me terribly funny. I wished I had some magic, but I knew only card tricks. The sixth day, swimming, I thought I was being enticed around a point in the river by the two girls, but when I began to chase them they threw good-sized stones at me, missing me only because they were such poor shots. A corpse floated by; when they saw it they immediately placed the sole of their right foot on the side of their left knee and stood thus on one leg till the corpse floated out of sight; I followed the girls' example, teetering. I gathered from what they said that some illness was devastating their people; I hoped it was one of the diseases I had been inoculated against. The girls' mothers found them talking with me and cuffed them away.

I did not see them for two days, but the night of my eighth day there the bolder of them hissed me awake at the door of my hut in a way that meant "no danger." I recognized her when she giggled. I was not sure what their customs were in these matters, but while I was deliberating what my course of wisdom should be she crawled into the hut and lay on the mat beside me. She liked me, she was utterly devoid of reticence, I was twenty-one and far from home; even a scabbly little knotty-legged fashion model is hard to resist under such circumstances. I learned before falling asleep that there was a three-way debate among the men over what to do with me: initiate me according to the prophet-initiation rites, invent a new ceremony, or sacrifice me as propitiation to the disease among them as was usually done with captives. Each had its advantages and drawbacks; even the news that some of the Dangs wanted to sacrifice me did not excite me as it would have done a week before; now, I half-sympathized with their trouble. I was awakened at dawn by the outraged howl of a man at my door; he was the girl's father. The village men gathered and the girl cowered behind me. They talked for hours outside my hut, men arrived from other villages up and down the valley, and finally they agreed upon a solution to all the problems: they proposed that I should be made one of the tribe by marriage on the same night that I should be initiated into the rites of prophecy.

The new-rite men were satisfied by this arrangement because of the novelty of having a man married and initiated on the same day, but the sacrifice party was visibly unmollified. Noticing this and reflecting that the proposed arrangement would permit me to do all my trance research under optimum conditions and to accumulate a great deal of sexual data as well I agreed to it. I would of course only be going through the forms of marriage, not meaning them; as for the girl, I took this vow to myself (meaning without ceremony): "So long as I am a Dang I shall be formally a correct husband to her." More's a pity.

Fortunately a youth from down the valley already had been chosen as a novice (at least a third of the Dang men enter the novitiate at one time or another, though few make the grade), so that I had not only a companion during the four-month preparation for the vatic rites but also a control upon whom I might check my experience of the stages of the novitiate. My mimetic powers stood me in good stead; I was presumed to have a special prophetic gift and my readiness at assuming the proper stances and properly performing the ritual acts confirmed the Dangs' impressions of my gift; but also, since I was required to proceed no faster than the ritual pace in my learning, I had plenty of leisure in which to observe in the smallest detail what I did and how I, and to some extent my fellow novice, felt. If I had not had this self-observing to relieve the tedium I think I should have been unable to get through that mindless holding of the same position hour after hour, that mindless repeating of the same act day after day. The Dangs *appear* to be bored much of the time, and my early experience with them was certainly that of ennui, though never again ennui so acute as during this novitiate. Yet I doubt that it would be accurate to say they actually are bored, and I am sure that the other novice was not, as a fisherman waiting hours for a strike cannot be said to be bored. The Dangs do not sate themselves on food; the experience which they consider most worth seeking, vision, is one which cannot glut either the prophet or his auditors; they cannot imagine an alternative to living as they live or, more instantly, to preparing a novice as I was being prepared. The people endure; the prophets, as I have learned, wait for the time to come again, and though they are bitten and stung by ten thousand fears, about this they have no anxiety— the time will surely come again. Boredom implies either satiety, and they were poor and not interested in enriching themselves, or the frustration of impulse, and they were without alternatives and diver-

sions. The intense boredom which is really a controlled anxiety, they
are protected from by never doubting the worth of their vision or
their power to achieve it.

I was assisted through these difficult months during which I was
supposed to do nothing but train by Redadu, my betrothed. As a nov-
ice I was strictly to abstain from sexual intercourse, but as betrothed
we were supposed to make sure before marriage that we satisfied
one another, for adultery by either husband or wife was punishable
by maiming. Naturally the theologians were much exercised by this
impasse, but while they were arguing Redadu and I took the obvious
course—we met more or less surreptitiously. Since my vatic training
could not take place between sunrise and sundown I assumed that
we could meet in the afternoon when I woke up, but when I began
making plans to this effect I discovered that she did not know what
I was talking about. It makes as much sense in Dang to say, "Let's
blow poisoned darts at the loss of the moon," as to say, "Let's make
love in broad daylight." Redadu dissolved in giggles at the absurdity.
What to do? She found us a cave. Everyone must have known what I
was up to, but we were respectable (the Dang term for it was harsher,
deed-liar) so we were never disturbed. Redadu's friends would not
believe her stories of my luxurious love ways, especially my biting
with lips instead of teeth. At one time or another she sent four of
them to the cave for me to demonstrate my prowess upon; I was glad
that none of them pleased me as much as she did for I was beginning
to be fond of her. My son has told me that lip-biting has become if
not a customary at any rate a possible caress.

As the night of the double rite approached, a night of full moon,
a new conflict became evident: the marriage must be consummated
exactly at sundown, but the initiation must begin at moonrise, less
than two hours later. For some reason that was not clear to me,
preparing for the initiation would incapacitate me for the consum-
mation. I refrained from pointing out that it was only technically
that this marriage needed consummating and even from asking why I
would not be able to do it. The solution, which displeased everyone,
was to defer the rites for three nights, when the moon, though no
longer perfectly round, would rise sufficiently late so that I would, by
hurrying, be able to perform both of my functions. Redadu's father,
who had been of the sacrifice party, waived ahead of time his claim
against me; legally he was entitled to annul the marriage if I should

leave the marriage hut during the bridal night. And although I in turn could legally annul it if she left the hut I waived my claim as well so that she might attend my initiation.

The wedding consisted chiefly of our being bound back to back by the elbows and being sung to and danced about all day. At sunset we were bound face to face by the elbows (most awkward) and sent into our hut. Outside the two mothers waited—a high prophet's wife took the place of my mother (my Methodist mother!)—until our orgastic cries indicated that the marriage had been consummated, and then came in to sever our bonds and bring us the bridal foods of cold stewed eel and parched seeds. We fed each other bite for bite and gave the scraps to our mothers, who by the formula with which they thanked us pronounced themselves satisfied with us. Then a falsetto voice called me to hurry to the altar. A man in the mask of a moon slave was standing outside my hut on his left leg with the right foot against his left knee, and he continued to shake his rattle so long as I was within earshot.

The men were masked. Their voices were all disguised. I wondered whether I was supposed to speak in an altered voice; I knew every stance and gesture I was to make, but nothing of what I was to say; yet surely a prophet must employ words. I had seen some of the masks before—being repaired, being carried from one place to another—but now, faced with them alive in the failing twilight, I was impressed by them in no scientific or aesthetic way—they terrified and exalted me. I wondered if I would be given a mask. I began trying to identify such men as I could by their scars and missing fingers and crooked arms, and noticed to my distress that they too were all standing one-legged in my presence. I had thought that was the stance to be assumed in the presence of the dead! We were at the entrance to The Cleft, a dead-end ravine in one of the cliffs along the valley; my fellow novice and I were each given a gourdful of some vile-tasting drink and were then taken up to the end of The Cleft, instructed to assume the first position, and left alone. We squatted as I had been squatting by the log on my first day, except that my head was cocked in a certain way and my hands clasped my ankles from the front. The excitements of the day seemed to have addled my wits, I could concentrate on nothing and lost my impulse to observe coolly what was going on; I kept humming *St. James Infirmary* to myself, and though at first I had been thinking the words, after awhile I realized that I had nothing but the tune left in my head. At moonrise we were brought another gourd of the liquor to drink, and were then taken to the mouth of The Cleft again. I did, easily, whatever I was told. The last thing I remember seeing before taking the second position was the semicircle of masked men facing us and chanting, and behind them the women and children—all standing on the left leg. I lay on my back with my left ankle on my right and my hands crossed over my navel, rolled my eyeballs up and held the lids open without blinking, and breathed in the necessary rhythm, each breath taking four heartbeats, with an interval of ten heartbeats between each exhalation and the next inspiration. Then the drug took over. At dawn when a called command awakened me, I found myself on an islet in the river dancing with my companion a leaping dance I had not known or even seen before, and brandishing over my head a magnificent red and blue, new-made mask of my own. The shores of the river were lined with the people chanting as we leaped, and all of them were either sitting or else standing on both feet. If we had been dead the night before we were alive now.

After I had slept and returned to myself, Redadu told me that my vision was splendid, but of course she was no more permitted to tell me what I had said than I was able to remember it. The Dangs' sense of rhythm is as subtle as their ear for melody is monotonous, and for weeks I kept hearing rhythmic snatches of "St. James Infirmary" scratched on calabash drums and tapped on blocks.

Sorish honored me by rewriting my master's thesis and adding my name as co-author of the resultant essay, which he published in *JAFA* (*The Journal of American Field Anthropology*): "Techniques of Vatic Hallucinosis among the Dangs." And the twenty-minute movie I made of a streamlined performance of the rites is still widely used as an audio-visual aid.

By 1939 when I had been cured of the skin disease I had brought back with me and had finished the work for my M.S. I still had no money. I had been working as the assistant curator of the University's Pre-Columbian Museum and had developed a powerful aversion to devoting my life to cataloguing, displaying, restoring, warehousing. But my chances of getting a research job, slight enough with a Ph.D., were nil with only an M.S. The girl I was going with said (I had not told her about Redadu) that if we married she would work as a nurse to support me while I went through law school; I was tempted by the opportunity to fulfill my original ambition, and probably I would have done it had she not pressed too hard; she wanted me to leave anthropology, she wanted me to become a lawyer, she wanted to support me, but what she did not want was to make my intentions, whatever they might be, her own. So when a new grant gave me the chance to return to the Dangs I gladly seized it; not only would I be asserting myself against Velma, but also I would be paid for doing the research for my Ph.D. thesis; besides, I was curious to see the Congo-Maryland-Dang bastard I had left in Redadu's belly.

My assignment was to make a general cultural survey but especially to discover the *content* of the vatic experience—not just the technique, not even the hallucinations and stories, but the qualities of the experience itself. The former would get me a routine degree, but the latter would, if I did it, make me a name and get me a job. After much consultation I decided against taking with me any form of magic, including medicine; the antibiotics had not been invented yet, and even if there had been a simple way to eradicate the fever endemic among the Dangs, my advisers persuaded me that it would be an error to introduce it since the Dangs were able to procure barely enough food for themselves as it was and since they might worship me for doing it, thereby making it impossible for me to do my research with the proper empathy. I arrived the second time provided only with my knife (which had not seemed to impress these stone-agers), salve to soothe my sores, and the knowledge of how to preserve fish against a lean season, innovation enough but not one likely to divinize me.

I was only slightly worried how I would be received on my return, because of the circumstances under which I had disappeared. I had become a fairly decent hunter—the women gathered grain and fruit—and I had learned to respect the Dangs' tracking abilities enough to have been nervous about getting away safely. While hunting with a companion in the hills south of our valley I had run into a couple of hunters from an enemy tribe which seldom foraged so far north as this. They probably were as surprised as I and probably would have been glad to leave me unmolested; however, outnumbered and not knowing how many more were with them, I whooped for my companion; one of the hunters in turn, not knowing how many were with me, threw his spear at me. I side-stepped it and reached for my darts, and though I was not very accurate with a blowpipe I hit him in the thigh; within a minute he was writhing on the ground, for in my haste I had blown a venomous dart at him, and my comrade took his comrade prisoner by surprise. As soon as the man I had hit was dead I withdrew my dart and cut off his ear for trophy, and we returned with our captive. He told our war chief in sign language that the young man I had killed was the son and heir of their king and that my having mutilated him meant their tribe surely would seek to avenge his death. The next morning a Dang search party was sent out to recover the body so that it might be destroyed and trouble averted, but it had disappeared; war threatened. The day after that I chose to vanish; they would not think of looking for me in the direction of Sorish's tribe, north, but would assume that I had been captured by the southern tribe in retribution for their prince's death. My concern now, two years later, was how to account for not having been maimed or executed; the least I could do was to cut a finger off, but when it came to the point I could not even bring myself to have a surgeon do it, much less do it myself; I had adequate lies prepared for their other questions, but about this I was a bit nervous.

I got there at sundown. Spying, I did not see Redadu about the village. On the chance, I slipped into our hut when no one was looking; she was there, playing with our child. He was as cute a little preliterate as you ever saw suck a thumb, and it made me chuckle to think he would never be literate either. Redadu's screams when she saw me fetched the women, but when they heard a man's voice they could not intrude. In her joy she lacerated me with her fingernails (the furrows across my shoulder festered for a long time); I could do no less than bite her arm till she bled; the primal scene we treated our son to presumably scarred him for life—though I must say the scars haven't shown up yet. I can't deny I was glad to see her too, for, though I felt for her none of the tender, complex emotions I had been feeling for Velma, emotions which I more or less identified as being love, yet I was so secure with her sexually, knew so well what to do and what to expect from her in every important matter that it was an enormous, if cool, comfort to me to be with her. *Comfort* is a dangerous approximation to what I mean; being with her provided, as it were, the condition for doing; in Sansom I did not consider her my wife and here I did not recognize in myself the American emotions of love or marriage, yet it seemed to me right to be with her and our son was no bastard. *Cool*—I cannot guarantee that mine was the usual Dang emotion, for it is hard for the cool to gauge the warmth of others (in my reports I have denied any personal experience of love among the Dangs for this reason). When we emerged from the hut there was amazement and relief among the women: amazement that I had returned and relief that it had not been one of their husbands pleasuring the widow. But the men were more ambiguously pleased to see me. Redadu's scratches were not enough and they doubted my story that the enemy king had made me his personal slave who must be bodily perfect. They wanted to hear me prophesy.

Redadu told me afterward, hiding her face in my arms for fear of being judged insolent, that I surpassed myself that night, that only the three high prophets had ever been so inspired. And it was true that even the men most hostile to me did not oppose my reentry into the tribe after they had heard me prophesy; they could have swallowed the story I fed them about my two-year absence only because they believed in me the prophet. Dangs make no separation between fact and fantasy, apparent reality and visionary reality, truth and beauty. I once saw a young would-be prophet shudder away from a stick on the ground saying it was a snake, and none of the others except the impressionable was afraid of the stick; it was said of him that he was a beginner. Another time I saw a prophet scatter the whole congregation, myself included, when he screamed at the sight of a beast which he called a cougar; when sober dawn found the speared creature to be a cur it was said of the prophet that he was strong, and he was honored with an epithet, Cougar-Dog. My prophesying the first night of my return must have been of this caliber, though to my disappointment I was given no epithet, not even the nickname I'd sometimes heard before, Bush-Hair.

I knew there was a third kind of prophesying, the highest, performed only on the most important occasions in the Cave-Temple where I had never been. No such occasion had presented itself during my stay before, and when I asked one of the other prophets about that ceremony he put me off with the term Wind-Haired Child of the Sun; from another I learned that the name of this sort of prophesying was Stone is Stone. Obviously I was going to have to stay until I could make sense of these mysteries.

There was a war party that wanted my support; my slavery was presumed to have given me knowledge which would make a raid highly successful; because of this as well as because I had instigated the conflict by killing the king's son I would be made chief of the raiding party. I was uneasy about the fever, which had got rather worse among them during the previous two years, without risking my neck against savages who were said always to eat a portion of their slain enemy's liver raw and whose habitat I knew nothing of. I persuaded the Dangs, therefore, that they should not consider attacking before the rains came, because their enemies were now the stronger, having on their side their protector, the sun. They listened to me and waited. Fortunately it was a long dry season, during which I had time to find a salt deposit and to teach a few women the rudiments of drying and salting fish; and during the first week of the rains every night there were showers of falling stars to be seen in the sky; to defend against them absorbed all energies for weeks, including the warriors'. Even so, even though I was a prophet, a journeyman prophet as it were, I was never in on these rites in the Cave-Temple. I dared not ask many questions. Sir Bewley Morehead had described a temple surrounded by seventy-six poles, each topped by a human head; he could hardly have failed to mention that it was in a cave, yet he made no such mention, and I knew of no temple like the one he had described. At a time of rains and peace in the sky the war party would importune me. I did not know what to do but wait.

The rains became violent, swamping the villages in the lower valley and destroying a number of huts, yet the rainy season ended abruptly two months before its usual time. Preparations for war had already begun, and day by day as the sun's strength increased and the earth dried the war party became more impatient. The preparations in themselves lulled my objections to the raid, even to my leading the raid, and stimulated my desire to make war. But the whole project was canceled a couple of days before we were to attack because of the sudden fever of one of the high prophets; the day after he came down five others of the tribe fell sick, among them Redadu. There was nothing I could do but sit by her, fanning her and sponging her till she died. Her next older sister took our son to rear. I would allow no one to prepare her body but myself, though her mother was supposed to help; I washed it with the proper infusions of herbs, and at dawn, in the presence of her clan, I laid her body on the river. Thank heaven it floated or I should have had to spend another night preparing it further. I felt like killing someone now; I recklessly called for war now, even though the high prophet had not yet died; I was restrained, not without admiration. I went up into the eastern hills by myself and returned after a week bearing the hide of a cougar; I had left the head and claws on my trophy in a way the Dangs had never seen; when I put the skin on in play by daylight and bounded and snarled only the bravest did not run in terror. They called me Cougar-Man. Redadu's younger sister came to sleep with me; I did not want her, but she so stubbornly refused to be expelled that I kept her for the night, for the next night, for the next; it was not improper.

The high prophet did not die, but lay comatose most of the time. The Dangs have ten master prophets, of whom the specially gifted, whether one or all ten, usually two or three, are high prophets. Fifteen days after Redadu had died, well into the abnormal dry spell, nearly all the large fish seemed to disappear from the river. A sacrifice was necessary. It was only because the old man was so sick that a high prophet was used for this occasion, otherwise a captive or a woman would have served the purpose. A new master prophet must replace him, to keep the complement up to ten. I was chosen.

The exultation I felt when I learned that the master prophets had co-opted me among them was by no means cool and anthropological, for now that I had got what I had come to get I no longer wanted it for Sansom reasons. *If the conditions of my being elevated,* I said to myself, *are the suffering of the people, Redadu's death, and the sacrifice of an old man, then I must make myself worthy of the great price. Worthy*—a value word, not a scientific one. Of course, my emotions were not the simple pride and fear of a Dang. I can't say what sort they were, but they were fierce.

At sundown all the Dangs of all the clans were assembled about the entrance to The Cleft. All the prophets, masked, emerged from The Cleft and began the dance in a great wheel. Within this wheel, rotating against it, was the smaller wheel of the nine able-bodied master prophets. At the center, facing the point at which the full moon would rise, I hopped on one leg, then the other. I had been given none of the vatic liquor, that brew which the women, when I had first come among the Dangs, had been preparing in the small-throated pots, and I hoped I should be able to remain conscious throughout the rites. However, at moonrise a moon slave brought me a gourdful to drink without ceasing to dance. I managed to allow a good deal of it to spill unnoticed down with the sweat streaming off me, so that later I was able to remember what had happened, right up to the prophesying itself. The dance continued for at least two more hours, then the drums suddenly stopped and the prophets began to file up The Cleft with me last dancing after the high prophets. We danced into an opening in the cliff from which a disguising stone had been rolled away. The people were not allowed to follow us. We entered a great cavern illuminated by ten smoking torches and circled a palisade of stakes; the only sound was the shuffle of our feet and the snorts of our breathing. There were seventy-six stakes, as Morehead had seen, but only on twenty-eight of them were heads impaled, the last few with flesh on them still, not yet skulls cleaned of all but hair. In the center was a huge stone under the middle of which a now dry stream had tunneled a narrow passage; on one side of the stone, above the passage, were two breastlike protuberances, one of which had a recognizable nipple in the suitable place. Presently the dancing file reversed so that I was the leader. I had not been taught what to do; I wove the file through the round of stakes, and spiraled inward till we were three deep about The Stone; I straddled the channel, raised my hands till they were touching the breasts, and gave a great cry. I was, for reasons I do not understand, shuddering all over; though I was conscious and though I had not been instructed, I was not worried that I might do the wrong thing next. When I touched The Stone a dread shook me without affecting my exaltation. Two moon slaves seized my arms, took off my mask, and wrapped and bound me—arms at my side and legs pressed together in a deer hide—and then laid me on my back in the channel under The Stone with my head only half out, so that I was staring up the sheer side of rock. The dancers continued, though the master prophets had disappeared. My excitement, the new unused position, being mummied tightly, the weakness of the drug, my will to observe, all kept me conscious for a long time. Gradually, however, my eyes began to roll up into my head, I strained less powerfully against the thongs that bound me, and I felt my breathing approach the vatic rhythm. At this point I seemed to break out in a new sweat, on my forehead, my throat, in my hair; I could hear a splash, groggily I licked my chin—an odd taste—I wondered if I was bleeding. Of course, it was the blood of the sick old high prophet, who had just been sacrificed on The Stone above me; well, his blood would give me strength. Wondering remotely whether his fever could be transmitted by drinking his blood I entered the trance. At dawn I emerged into consciousness while I was still prophesying; I was on a ledge in the valley above all the people, in my mask again. I listened to myself finish the story I was telling. "He was afraid. A third time a man said to him: 'You are a friend of the most high prophet.' He answered: 'Not me. I do not know that man they are sacrificing.' Then he went into a dark corner, he put his hands over his face all day." When I came to the Resurrection a sigh blew across the people. It was the best story they had ever heard. Of course. But I was not really a Christian. For several weeks I fretted over my confusion, this new, unsuspected confusion.

I was miserable without Redadu; I let her sister substitute only until I had been elevated, and then I cast her off, promising her however that she and only she might wear an anklet made of my teeth when I should die. Now that I was a master prophet I could not be a warrior; I had enough of hunting and fishing and tedious ceremonies. Hunger from the shortage of fish drove the hunters high into the foothills; there was not enough; they ate my preserved fish, suspiciously, but they ate them. When I left it was not famine that I was escaping but my confusion; I was fleeing to the classrooms and the cool museums where I should be neither a leftover Christian nor a mimic of a Dang.

My academic peace lasted for just two years, during which time I wrote five articles on my researches, publishing them this time under my name only, did some of the work for my doctorate, and married Velma. Then came World War II, in which my right hand was severed above the wrist; I was provided with an artificial hand and given enough money so that I could afford to finish my degree in style. We had two daughters and I was given a job at Sansom. There was no longer a question of my returning to the Dangs. I would become a settled anthropologist, teach, and quarrel with my colleagues in the learned journals. But by the time the Korean War came along and robbed us of a lot of our students, my situation at the university had changed considerably. Few of my theoretical and disputatious articles were printed in the journals, and I hated writing them; I was not given tenure and there were some hints to the effect that I was considered a one-shot man, a flash-in-the-pan; Velma nagged for more money and higher rank. My only recourse was further research, and when I thought of starting all over again with some other tribe—in northern Australia, along the Zambesi, on an African island—my heart sank. The gossip was not far from the mark—I was not a one hundred percent scientist and never would be. I had just enough reputation and influential recommendations to be awarded a Guggenheim Fellowship; supplemented by a travel grant from the university this made it possible for me to leave my family comfortably provided for and to return to the Dangs.

A former student now in Standard Oil in Venezuela arranged to have me parachuted among them from an SO plane. There was the real danger that they would kill me before they recognized me, but if I arrived in a less spectacular fashion I was pretty sure they would sacrifice me for their safety's sake. This time, being middle-aged, I left my hunting knife and brought instead at my belt a pouch filled with penicillin and salves. I had a hard time identifying the valley from the air; it took me so long that it was sunset before I jumped. I knew how the Dangs were enraged by airplanes, especially by the winking lights of night fliers, and I knew they would come for me if they saw me billowing down. Fortunately I landed in the river, for though I was nearly drowned before I disentangled my parachute harness I was also out of range of the blowpipes. I finally identified myself to the warriors brandishing their spears along the shore; they had not quite dared to swim out after so prodigious a being; even after they knew who I said I was and allowed me to swim to shore they saw me less as myself than as a supernatural being. I was recognized by newcomers who had not seen me so closely swinging from the parachute (the cloud); on the spot my epithet became, and remained, Sky-Cougar. Even so no one dared touch me till the high prophet—there was only one now—had arrived and talked with me; my artificial hand seemed to him an extension of the snake tattooed onto my skin, he would not touch it; I suddenly struck him with it and pinched his arm. "Pinchers," I said using the word for a crayfish claw, and he laughed. He said there was no way of telling whether I was what I seemed to be until he had heard me prophesy; if I prophesied as I had done before I had disappeared I must be what I seemed to be; meanwhile, for the three weeks till full moon I was to be kept in the hut for captives.

At first I was furious at being imprisoned, and when mothers brought children from miles about to peek through the stakes at the man with the snake hand I snarled or sulked like a caged wolf. But I became conscious that one youth, squatting in a quiet place, had been watching me for hours. I demanded of him who he was. He said, "I am your son," but he did not treat me as his father. To be sure, he could not have remembered what I looked like; my very identity was doubted; even if I were myself, I was legendary, a stranger who had become a Dang and had been held by an enemy as captive slave for two years and had then become a master prophet with the most wonderful vision anyone knew. Yet he came to me every day and answered all the questions I put to him. It was, I believe, my artificial hand that finally kept him aloof from me; no amount of acquaintance could accustom him to that. By the end of the first week it was clear to me that if I wanted to survive—not to be accepted as I once had been, just to survive—I would have to prophesy the Passion again. And how could I determine what I would say when under the vatic drug? I imagined a dozen schemes for substituting colored water for the drug, but I would need an accomplice for that and I knew that not even my own son would serve me in so forbidden an act.

I called for the high prophet. I announced to him in tones all the more arrogant because of my trepidations that I would prophesy without the vatic liquor. His response to my announcement astonished me: he fell upon his knees, bowed his head, and rubbed dust into his hair. He was the most powerful man among the Dangs, except in time of war when the war chief took over, and furthermore he was an old man of personal dignity, yet here he was abasing himself before me and, worse, rubbing dust into his hair as was proper in the presence of the very sick to help them in their dying. He told me why: prophesying successfully from a voluntary trance was the test which I must pass to become a high prophet; normally a master prophet was forced to this, for the penalty for failing it was death. I dismissed him with a wave of my claw.

I had five days to wait until full moon. The thought of the risk I was running was more than I could handle consciously; to avoid the jitters I performed over and over all the techniques of preparing for the trance, though I carefully avoided entering it. I was not sure I would be able to enter it alone, but whether I could or not I knew I wanted to conserve my forces for the great test. At first during those five days I would remind myself once in a while of my scientific purpose in going into the trance consciously; at other times

I would assure myself that it was for the good of the Dangs that I was doing it, since it was not wise or safe for them to have only one high prophet. Both of these reasons were true enough, but not very important. As scientist I should tell them some new myth, say the story of Abraham and Isaac or of Oedipus, so that I could compare its effect on them with that of the Passion; as master prophet I should ennoble my people if I could. However, thinking these matters over as I held my vatic squat hour after hour, visited and poked at by prying eyes, I could find no myth to satisfy me; either, as in the case of Abraham, it involved a concept of God which the Dangs could not reach, or else, as with Oedipus, it necessitated more drastic changes than I trusted myself to keep straight while prophesying— that Oedipus should mutilate himself was unthinkable to the Dangs and that the gods should be represented as able to forgive him for it was impious. Furthermore, I did not think, basically, that any story I could tell them would in fact ennoble them. I was out to save my own skin.

The story of Christ I knew by heart; it had worked for me once, perhaps more than once; it would work again. I rehearsed it over and over, from the Immaculate Conception to the Ascension. But such was the force of that story on me that by the fifth day my cynicism had disappeared along with my scientism, and I believed, not that the myth itself was true, but that relating it to my people was the best thing it was possible for me to do for them. I remember telling myself that this story would help raise them toward monotheism, a necessary stage in the evolution toward freedom. I felt a certain satisfaction in the thought that some of the skulls on the stakes in the Cave-Temple were very likely those of missionaries who had failed to convert these heathen.

At sundown of the fifth day I was taken by moon slaves to a cave near The Cleft, where I was left in peace. I fell into a troubled sleep from which I awoke in a sweat. "Where am I? What am I about to do?" It seemed to me dreadfully wrong that I should be telling these, my people, a myth in whose power, but not in whose truth, I believed. Why should I want to free them from superstition into monotheism and then into my total freedom, when I myself was half-returning, voluntarily, down the layers again? The energy for these sweating questions came, no doubt, from my anxiety about how I was going to perform that night, but I did not recognize this fact at

the time. Then I thought it was my conscience speaking, and that I
had no right to open to the Dangs a freedom I myself was rejecting. It
was too late to alter my course; honesty required me, and I resolved
courageously, not to prophesy at all.

When I was fetched out the people were in assembly at The Cleft
and the wheel of master prophets was revolving against the greater
wheel of dancers. I was given my cougar skin. Hung from a stake, in
the center where I was to hop, was a huge, terrific mask I had never
seen before. As the moon rose her slaves hung this mask on me; the
thong cut into the back of my neck cruelly, and at the bottom the
mask came to a point that pressed my belly; it was so wide my arms
could only move laterally. It had no eye holes; I broke into a sweat
wondering how I should be able to follow the prophets into the Cave-
Temple. It turned out to be no problem; the two moon slaves, one on
each side, guided me by prodding spears in my ribs. Once in the cave
they guided me to the back side of The Stone and drove me to climb
it, my feet groping for steps I could not see; once, when I lost my
balance, the spears' pressure kept me from falling backward. By the
time I reached the top of The Stone I was bleeding and dizzy. With
one arm I kept the mask from gouging my belly while with the other
I helped my aching neck support the mask. I did not know what
to do next. Tears of pain and anger poured from my eyes. I began
hopping. I should have been moving my arms in counterpoint to the
rhythm of my hop, but I could not bear the thought of letting the
mask cut into me more. I kept hopping in the same place for fear of
falling off; I had not been noticing the sounds of the other prophets,
but suddenly I was aware they were making no sounds at all. In my
alarm I lurched to the side and cut my foot on a sharp break in the
rock. Pain converted my panic to rage.

I lifted the mask and held it flat above my head. I threw my head
back and howled as I had never howled in my life, through a con-
stricted, gradually opening throat, until at the end I was roaring;
when I gasped in my breath I made a barking noise. I leaped and
leaped, relieved of pain, confident. I punched my knee desecratingly
through the brittle hide of the mask, and threw it behind me off The
Stone. I tore off my cougar skin, and holding it with my claw by
the tip of its tail I whirled it around my head. The prophets, massed
below me, fell onto their knees. I felt their fear. Howling, I soared
the skin out over them; one of those on whom it landed screamed

hideously. A commotion started; I could not see very well what was happening. I barked and they turned toward me again. I leaped three times and then, howling, jumped wide-armed off The Stone. The twelve-foot drop hurt severely my already cut foot. I rolled exhausted into the channel in the cave floor.

Moon slaves with trembling hands mummied me in the deerskin and shoved me under The Stone with only my head sticking out. They brought two spears with darts tied to the points; rolling my head to watch them do this I saw that the prophets were kneeling over and rubbing dirt into their hair. Then the slaves laid the spears alongside the base of The Stone with the poisoned pricks pointed at my temples; exactly how close they were I could not be sure, but close enough so that I dared not move my head. In all my preparations I had, as I had been trained to do, rocked and weaved at least my head; now, rigidity, live rigidity. A movement would scratch me and a scratch would kill me.

I pressed my hook into my thigh, curled my toes, and pressed my tongue against my teeth till my throat ached. I did not dare relieve myself even with a howl, for I might toss my head fatally. I strained against my thongs to the verge of apoplexy. For a while I was unable to see, for sheer rage. Fatigue collapsed me. Yet I dared not relax my vigilance over my movements. My consciousness sealed me off. Those stone protuberances up between which I had to stare in the flickering light were merely chance processes on a boulder, similes to breasts. The one thing I might not become unconscious of was the pair of darts waiting for me to err. For a long time I thought of piercing my head against them, for relief, for spite. Hours passed. I was carefully watched.

I do not know what wild scheme I had had in mind when I had earlier resolved not to prophesy, what confrontation or escape; it had had the pure magnificence of a fantasy resolution. But the reality, which I had not seriously tried to evade, was that I must prophesy or die. I kept lapsing from English into a delirium of Dang. By the greatest effort of will I looked about me rationally. I wondered whether the return of Halley's comet, at which time all the stakes should be mounted by skulls, would make the Dangs destroy the Cave-Temple and erect a new one. I observed the straight, indented seam of sandstone running slantwise up the boulder over me and wondered how many eons this rotting piece of granite had been tumbled about by water. I reflected that I was unworthy both as a Christian and as a Dang to prophesy the life of Jesus. But I convinced myself that it was a trivial matter, since to the Christians it was the telling more than the teller that counted and to the Dangs this myth would serve as a civilizing force they needed. Surely, I thought, my hypocrisy could be forgiven me, especially since I resolved to punish myself for it by leaving the Dangs forever as soon as I could. Having reached this rational solution I smiled and gestured to the high prophet with my eyes; he did not move a muscle. When I realized that nothing to do with hypocrisy would unbind me desperation swarmed in my guts and mounted toward my brain; with this question it took me over: *How can I make myself believe it is true?* I needed to catch hold of myself again. I dug my hook so hard into my leg—it was the only action I was able to take—that I gasped with pain; the pain I wanted. I did not speculate on the consequences of gouging my leg, tearing a furrow in my thigh muscle, hurting by the same act the stump of my arm to which the hook was attached; just as I knew that the prophets, the torches, the poisoned darts were there in the cave, so also I knew that far far back in my mind I had good enough reasons to be hurting myself, reasons which I could find out if I wanted to, but which it was not worth my trouble to discover; I even allowed the knowledge that I myself was causing the pain to drift back in my mind. The pain itself, only the pain, became my consciousness, purging all else. Then, as the pain subsided leaving me free and equi-poised, awareness of the stone arched over me flooded my mind. Because it had been invested by the people with a great mystery, it was an incarnation; the power of their faith made it the moon, who was female; at the same time it was only a boulder. I understood Stone is Stone, and that became my consciousness.

My muscles ceased straining against the bonds, nor did they slump; they ceased aching, they were at ease, they were ready. I said nothing, I did not change the upward direction of my glance, I did not smile, yet at this moment the high prophet removed the spears and had the moon slaves unbind me. I did not feel stiff nor did my wounds bother me, and when I put on my cougar skin and leaped, pulled the head over my face and roared, all the prophets fell onto their faces before me. I began chanting and I knew I was doing it all the better for knowing what I was about; I led them back out to the waiting people, and until dawn I chanted the story of the birth, prophesying, betrayal, sacrifice, and victory of the most high prophet. I am a good mimic, I was thoroughly trained, the story is the best; what I gave them was, for them, as good as a vision. I did not know the difference myself.

But the next evening I knew the difference. While I performed my ablutions and the routine ceremonies to the full moon I thought with increasing horror of my state of mind during my conscious trance. What my state of mind actually had been I cannot with confidence now represent, for what I know of it is colored by my reaction against it the next day. I had remained conscious, in that I could recall what happened, yet that observer and commentator in myself of whose existence I had scarcely been aware, but whom I had always taken for my consciousness, had vanished. I no longer had been thinking, but had lost control so that my consciousness had become what I was doing; almost worse, when I had told the story of Christ I had done it not because I had wanted to or believed in it but because, in some obscure sense, I had had to. Thinking about it afterward I did not understand or want to understand what I was drifting toward, but I knew it was something that I feared. And I got out of there as soon as I was physically able.

Here in Sansom what I have learned has provided me with material for an honorable contribution to knowledge, has given me a tenure to a professorship—thereby pleasing my wife—whereas if I had stayed there among the Dangs much longer I would have reverted until I had become one of them, might not have minded when the time came to die under the sacrificial knife, would have taken in all ways the risk of prophecy—as my Dang son intends to do—until I had lost myself utterly.

Hymn of the Angels

S I D N E Y did not much like the old-fashioned facade of the Hilton-Sansom, but once inside he found the lobby had been brought as far up-to-date as wall-to-wall gray could bring it and he was satisfied. Two telephone messages were waiting for him: one, marked urgent, he stared at a moment then crumpled up and threw away— let the little fish catch him if they could, they'd appreciate him the more for their trouble—the other, from a Father Hilary at Mount Mary, he took with him to his room.

Even though this new room was so Hilton-familiar Sidney studiously set about clearing it of its hotel welcome and advice and warning, then spread out on the dresser a local paper and read as he wandered about undressing; he moved a chair, flipped on the TV set and saw that its three channels were reasonably clear, scanned the movie ads, brushed his teeth as though he had just got up, scratched his back, glanced over a coast-to-coast columnist—it made the room his own. His eyes were caught by an advertisement for the Club Continentale, from nine to one Sharon Vee and the Happy Hipsters. Sidney perked up immediately, made a grimace at the message from Mount Mary, and put in a call for Sharon.

"Siddy!" She was putting on her little girl voice, which probably meant she wasn't sure yet how glad she was to hear from him.

"How are you, baby?"

"What are you doing in a hamlet like this?"

"Business," he began.

"Naturally business!" she squawked. "You dope, I mean what're you doing?"

"Right now I'm inviting you to dinner tomorrow night."

She purred. "Siddy, you're sweet. Only I can't tomorrow. There's a reason. Couldn't you tonight? How long're you going to be in town?"

"Tonight I'm supposed to go to a monastery for dinner."

She giggled.

"Business," he snapped, "business. Look, you can't make it tomorrow?"

She purred downward. "Let's just have an early dinner now. Can't we, sweetie? I really have been missing you."

He liked to be missed. "Okay honey. Seven at your place?"

"Make it six at yours?"

It was already 4:30, and he'd eaten a large lunch on the plane. He clicked his teeth in annoyance. "Where's the best restaurant?"

"The Hilton."

"Good, that's where I am already. Get here by six."

"Aw honey, come and get me? I'll have to wear my costume for the show tonight. Please? I may have trouble getting in and out or something. It's so tight."

His mouth twitched in irritation. He thought she was making him jump just to show that she could still do it. Then he chuckled. "I get it. You've got a wolf at your heels. Right?"

Her purr arched in acquiescence and gratitude, curled up in his lap, and went to sleep.

He called Mount Mary and left a message for Father Hilary that he would be unable to go out to dinner; showered, shaved, and dressed with care. He hadn't felt better in months.

With his two hundred dollar, light gray suit cut to the minute, his onyx cuff links, his blue Sulka tie, Sidney felt up to her, even though she was two inches taller than he.

She squealed when she opened the door to him, hugged him, gave him five warm kisses all around his mouth, and told him he'd lost weight; she asked him which earrings he preferred. He chose the silver-wire mobiles with amethysts. She wore a floor-length, light blue sheath that ruffled out just above the knees; it came up to her throat, where it was held by a necklace, but it left her arms and back bare. Her bosom was more pin-up than Sidney had ever seen it before; he knew just how falsy this was, but she was right to fill it out, she had hips to go with it, and she knew how to carry herself. Her hair had a wild look, as though she'd just got out of bed; he appreciated how much it cost to produce that look and keep it in place. When they left her hotel and again when they entered the lobby of the Hilton they looked good. Sidney loved it. "We're the best in town, baby," he said, and she cuddled his arm and wrinkled her nose at him.

He half-turned with annoyance at a tap on his shoulder. At first glance he did not recognize the knobby, big, pale face looking down at him; the man wore a black suit, an ecclesiastical collar, and an odd sort of black beret that did not flop, and he had a gap-toothed smile.

"Mr. Goldfarb," he said and stuck out his hand, "I'm Brother Patrick."

Sidney clicked his fingernails in irritation. "Of course." He wanted to punish him for showing up like this. "Sorry. I phoned your place an hour ago. I can't come."

Brother Patrick's face fell. "Sure," he said. "A man like you, in New York and all, meets so many. It's nothing, sir, and of course I'd remember you." His bland forehead puckered. "You could come out to us tomorrow then for sure? The thing is, Mr. Goldfarb, we can't always be sure of Brother Dennis."

He did not look properly off-balance. Sidney introduced him to Sharon, but the only sign of confusion he saw in Brother Patrick was a slight wavering of the eyes when they shook hands. Sharon, how-ever, who had been raised a Catholic, pulled her blue gauze scarf about her shoulders in embarrassment.

"Tomorrow at five," Sidney said. "Can you come for me?"

"Sure," said Brother Patrick. He obviously did not know it was time for him to go, or else he did not know how to; he had taken root like the Irish potato he resembled.

"We have an appointment," said Sidney; he took Sharon's arm and they walked off.

"What on earth!" she whispered.

"The monastery I was telling you about. A record in it maybe."

"You mean they got something *good* buried around here?"

"Look, baby," he said firmly, "anything I got anything to do with is first-class." Sidney gestured about the dining room, and looked Sharon up and down with approval. "First-class."

When they were seated, Sharon looked at him with a tinge of worry in her eyes. "And you're just here to make a record of monks?"

"Not just."

"What I mean is, what're we having dinner for—old-times sake?"

"As a matter of fact, yes."

As a matter of fact he wanted to see if she had some information he could use. But it was so clear she was feeling sentimental that he wanted to make her feel good. Besides, he liked an obstacle such as this for its own sake.

He began to reminisce. He said he had recently had lunch with Henry, Sharon's former husband, and she softened even more.

"What a sweet guy. How is he?"

"Say," Sidney went on, "what's his niece's name? You know, Lily's daughter."

"Linda. What about her?"

"Nothing. I just haven't heard about her for a long time. It's funny—you know how things keep tying together. Here I'm going to see some musical monks and Linda's father became one. What's his name?"

"Is he out here, Siddy?" she cried.

"Not so far as I know," said Sidney, who knew that he was the Brother Dennis in the monastery. "What was his name back when?"

"Fred Stauffer. Isn't it all funny?" She was looking at him suspiciously.

"He was a good clarinetist too," said Sidney. Having got what he wanted he set about sweetening her again. "It's really funny the way people drift in and out of each other's lives." He took one of her hands in both of his. "You know what, honey?"

"What, Siddy?"

"I liked smooching with you more than any other woman I can remember."

She blushed and lowered her eyes. "You shouldn't say things like that. You're sweet though. Now let's change the subject."

"I was soft on you, honey. You knew that."

"Aw sure," she said and patted his hand. "We were consoling each other on the rebound, and it was good too. Now," she declared and went back to her steak, "that's enough of that. It's a good thing you don't have anything to do with Fred Stauffer. He'd be impossible to handle."

"Eh," said Sidney flourishing his fork, "handling people is my business." He was pleased with himself. He had handled her without her even knowing it, and he was telling her so without her even getting it. His virtuosity was partly due to his having nothing much at stake with Sharon. He had not expected her to have any important information for him, but had just probed about in case something usable turned up.

The way jerked through industrial suburbs and dragged through acres of stucco shacks and finally eased out among fields of stubble the color of honey.

"How d'you like our car, Mr. Goldfarb?" said Brother Patrick settling down in his seat and taking off his beret.

Sidney said it was a fine car.

"Sure," said Brother Patrick, "all blue inside—dashboard, upholstery, steering wheel. Snappy, huh?"

"I wasn't going to say anything—not tactful—but I was thinking this is a pretty sporty car for monks. You know?"

Brother Patrick rocked with laughter and the car weaved on the road. "Tactful!" he snorted. "Jesus bless us, tactful!"

"What's the matter?" Sidney snapped. "Don't you think I got tact?"

"Sure, Mr. Goldfarb, sure you have," said Brother Patrick and flapped a hand at him. "It's the tact you'll need for Brother Dennis, that's all."

"Look," said Sidney, "what I am is a recording engineer, not an impresario. Is that clearly understood?" Brother Patrick looked at him slack-jawed. "We can do as good a job technically as any firm in the industry. But the prima donnas, even if they're monks— no. Okay?"

"Sure, Mr. Goldfarb," said Brother Patrick, "I had no idea otherwise." He did not talk again for a good while, and Sidney was pleasantly conscious of his occasional, worried glances.

The buildings of the Seminary of Mount Mary, in Spanish mission style with thick white walls and arched passageways and red-tile roofs, described a great horseshoe on the upper slopes of a mountain looking out over miles of hills and dim vineyards; up the slope two wings extended, and the main building where Sidney was shown into a room formed the base of the horseshoe. In the large enclosed area onto which his windows looked he saw graveled paths, trimmed hedges, rose bushes and beds of low flowers, an arbor, a statue, small lawns, and a trickling fountain. Despite his hurry to freshen up for cocktails Sidney first allowed himself a sip of this quiet. He liked it, it was alien, he was not sure how much of it he wanted.

Father Hilary, the director, was standing by the fireplace in the attitude of one a good six feet tall; in fact Sidney and he were much of a height, five feet five, though Sidney was fatter. From the hearty unction of his greeting and his way of offering the old-fashioneds and from his baby face and bland voice Sidney sized him up as one who thinks he knows how to handle city slickers. So what? He'd show him. The table was set for three, and it was obvious from Brother Patrick's big eyes for the table service that he was staying.

"No Brother Dennis?" said Sidney not concealing his annoyance.

"I hope," said Father Hilary dropping his eyes, "you may meet him after dinner."

"You *hope?*"

"Soup is served," said Father Hilary.

After they were seated and the Brother-waiter had withdrawn, Sidney persisted, "I don't get it. Doesn't he live here?"

"To be sure. But I have given him permission to reside in a building somewhat apart. You may have noticed the small dwelling up the hill above the grotto?"

"No," said Sidney, who was not entirely sure what a grotto was, "I didn't."

"After dinner, if you would like, we will stroll around the grounds."

He started to go into the history of Mount Mary, but Sidney, as soon as the *coq au vin* had been served, came back to Brother Dennis.

"Let me get something straight, Father. Pardon me, but I don't have all the time in the world. How come you can't just say to him, 'Come on down and meet a man on business?' I thought he had to take orders. What is he, a hermit?"

"I could, of course," said Father Hilary. "Brother, will you pour the wine please? This is our Cabernet Sauvignon, Mr. Goldfarb. We are proud of it."

"Great," said Sidney to whom it tasted like any other red wine, "it's really great." More was needed. "Fine bouquet." This seemed to have been the right thing to say.

"Of course Brother Dennis performs his religious duties with the rest of the community, Mr. Goldfarb, but he has set himself a severe discipline in which music, as you can imagine, plays a decisive role. For this reason he is permitted a seclusion greater than normal."

Brother Patrick leaned over, a conspirator again. "He's a genius."

"Well," said Father Hilary deprecatorily.

"That's what it boils down to," said Brother Patrick.

"Brother," said the director, "we don't want to overdo the matter." He turned, formally, bodily, from Brother Patrick and toward Sidney. "I feel as did my predecessor in this office, Father Albert . . ."

"May he rest in peace," said Brother Patrick, and Father Hilary flicked a frown at him.

". . . that Brother Dennis's devotion to his work is of such an order as to exempt him from many of the inessential aspects of our daily routine. For this reason and also for the reason that his performance of his duties has been examplary I hesitate to interfere with his music in any way."

"But you're the boss," said Sidney.

"Mr. Goldfarb, in your company you are the vice-president in charge of operations?" Sidney nodded. "You must have a number of employees under you, some highly trained?" Sidney nodded again. "Do you give them no latitude? Do you order them to do this or that without consulting their wishes and abilities and needs and temperament?"

"Am I a fool? you're asking. If I try to shove a good man around he'll quit on me."

"There's that," said Father Hilary. "Brother, more wine for our guest. Mr. Goldfarb, we approached you, of all the men in the field . . ."

"That reminds me, how did you ever get onto my trail?"

"Brother Patrick was visiting his mother in New York and he has a cousin on the Cardinal's staff." Father Hilary cocked an eyebrow and Sidney nodded. "I was saying, we approached you as the one most likely to handle this matter successfully."

"You mean on the technical end? You know, all I am is a glorified recording engineer. Don't let that vice-president jazz fool you."

"Ah?" said Father Hilary, "we were thinking of more than mere technicalities. We had been given to understand you were—well, tactful."

Brother Patrick caught Sidney's eye and they both laughed.

"I gather, gentlemen, that you have discussed the question?"

Sidney did not want to go into it. "As a matter of fact, Father, I do know something about the type of music from a job I had for a highbrow outfit right after the war. But there's another angle to it." He bared his teeth and watched for reactions. When he punched with a fact he liked the fact blunt. "You see, I'm personally acquainted with Brother Dennis's illegitimate daughter Linda." As a matter of fact he had met Linda only once.

Brother Patrick's mouth fell open, but Father Hilary only cocked his head. "Indeed?"

"A friend of mine over in CBS is her uncle—I'd just as soon not mention him by name if you don't mind—and I got to know Linda through him. He roomed with Brother Dennis when he was still Fred Stauffer, when they were in college."

The table was cleared and charlotte russe was served. Over coffee and brandy they sat sidewise to the table, carefully slipped the foil off cigars which Father Hilary passed out, and lighted them from the urn-shaped, silver-plated lighter on the table.

"I should judge, Mr. Goldfarb, it might be prudent not to bring up the subject of Brother Dennis's earlier life in your discussion with him."

"If it's all the same to you, Father, I think I'll just play this whole thing by ear." Through the French windows he watched a covey of cowled seminarians in dark brown robes twitter along the road. "You know, tact? Technique?"

Brother Patrick coughed and belched smoke. For a long time, while watching the dusk condensing in the valley, Sidney enjoyed the feel of Father Hilary's speculative gaze resting on him.

Gardens to Sidney meant public parks or things that exterior decorators installed in the suburbs. Nor was he used to strolling. For half an hour or more the three of them strolled along the garden paths, inhaling the evening scents; passing the grotto in which he made out a statue of the Madonna; pausing to talk by a statue of Diana in flight, her head turned over her shoulder; circling the fountain, which he learned was fed by a spring—and he enjoyed it. He no longer particularly cared whether anything came of this visit; he was just enjoying it for its own sake in a way he was not used to.

A tall seminarian with folded hands came up to the director. "The practicing has begun, Father."

"In the minor chape?"

"No, Father, in the choir loft. Father Bede is on the organ."

"We will be there shortly, Brother. You may go along." He turned. "We are fortunate. The acoustics may be better for your purposes, Mr. Goldfarb."

The main chapel, dimly lighted, struck Sidney as ordinary, and furthermore it had a bad echo. He prowled about in search of a spot suitable for placing a microphone and found none; he could not see the singers well. In ten minutes he left the building followed by the other two.

"I'm sorry, too much echo. The room's impossible."

"We've got other rooms," said Brother Patrick anxiously.

"Sure," said Sidney, "but you know they were just doing straight Gregorian chant. The market's saturated with it from the best European monasteries."

"Perhaps," said Father Hilary, "we do not have so much to offer."

"Oh, but," said Brother Patrick, "what about the manuscripts?"

They were still on the steps of the chapel; Father Hilary was standing below the other two, half-turned as though expecting them to be following. Sidney got a certain satisfaction in looking down at him in the faint light.

"They have yet to prove their full worth. I'm afraid, Mr. Goldfarb, we may have brought you on a wild goose chase. Won't you come back to the library with me? I should like you to meet some of the others of our community."

Sidney stepped down to go, but Brother Patrick caught his arm and leaned down at him beseechingly.

"You've got to hear our countertenor," he said. "You could stay overnight."

"Brother!" said the director sharply.

"But Father, he can't go without at least hearing Jerome. What an organ he's got, Mr. Goldfarb. Brother Dennis says it's one in millions. You can hear him in the morning."

"If you wish, Mr. Goldfarb? But no, Brother, I think our guest has had all he wants."

"Not yet." But Sidney's interruption was ignored.

"You may go to the brothers' common room, Brother Patrick."

Sidney, not wanting to interfere with discipline, watched till Brother Patrick, head low, was out of earshot. But Father Hilary spoke first.

"Shall we go, Mr. Goldfarb?"

"Is this countertenor, Jerome, in there now?"

"No, Brother Dennis is saving him."

"For what?"

"I thought," said Father Hilary, "you had been briefed on all this?"

Sidney had been. "Here's what I want, Father. I have to be in Sansom by 12:30 tomorrow and I want to hear this Jerome."

"I shall do what is possible. Shall we go now?"

Father Hilary's new tone of voice implied that he was not going to find it possible to do much. The slippery bastard, Sidney thought to himself.

A little after ten, pleading fatigue, he asked if he might take the local paper with him and retire. In truth he was irked by the priests, none of whom he liked any better than Father Hilary; they lounged in leather-upholstered chairs, legs crossed, cowls crumpled at the back of their necks, and pumped him for anecdotes about the famous.

He had not yet established himself in this monastery room but was still puzzling at a cuff link, glancing from it to the newspaper, when he heard a knock. As he was saying, "Come in," the door opened enough to admit Brother Patrick's flat, grinning face.

"Mr. Goldfarb," he said in a stage whisper, "you can see Brother Dennis right away if you'd like to. He's walking."

"Bring him in."

"Oh," said Brother Patrick, "I couldn't do that, sir. He's walking."

"Where?"

"Out in the garden of course, where we were before." Brother Patrick anxiously withdrew his head and looked back down the hall. "Are you coming?"

It was trouble and it was beneath him, but he liked Brother Patrick, who was now in his robe and who, Sidney was sure, was disobeying orders by being here at all.

"I'll come."

"Then I'll just step in here till you're ready."

Sidney pointed at the glamour-puss picture of Sharon Vee in the paper. "She was married for a while to that CBS guy I mentioned,

Linda's uncle." Sidney had nothing to gain from punching Brother Patrick with this fact but the pleasure of seeing his eyes pop. He liked him. "Small world, huh Brother? I met Sharon in the Music and Art high school."

"I didn't know," said Brother Patrick seizing the new subject eagerly, "that you were a trained musician too."

Sidney made a wry gesture. "I got an ear, Brother. I got a grade-A performing ear."

The Madonna was illuminated from below by a small spot concealed in the ground cover surrounding her grotto; otherwise what light the garden received came from the windows of the buildings and by now there were only a handful still shining; the moon was new and faint. At the place where the path turned toward the grotto Brother Patrick caught his arm; when Sidney looked at him questioningly he put a finger to his lips and pointed. Peering, Sidney made out a very short figure on the path before the grotto, bare head inclined, motionless, stiff. They just stood there watching; as Sidney's eyes adjusted to the dark he could make out Brother Dennis's head more clearly; it seemed enormous for a man of such shortness. The Madonna in her artificial cave looked pretty. He heard the puddling sound of the fountain, he heard an owl. After several minutes Brother Dennis pulled his cowl over his head, abruptly grew by two feet, and Sidney, who had not realized Brother Dennis had been kneeling, fell back a pace in astonishment. Brother Patrick plucked at his sleeve and they hurried up to the shadowed figure. By reflected light from the Madonna Sidney could make out something of his features: his cheeks were sunken, his brows jutted like cliff weeds, his neck was scrawny. He stood at least six feet four inches tall.

"Who is it?" he said disagreeably. "Oh it's you, Pat." He lowered his brows at Sidney, and his large mouth fell into a sardonic contour, higher on one side than the other. "Who's this?"

After his initial astonishment, in which there had been a streak of fear, Sidney was inclined to dislike Brother Dennis, if only because of his voice; Sidney distrusted big men with small voices. But he believed in giving a man a chance.

Brother Patrick spoke. "This is Mr. Goldfarb of Imperial-Lighthouse Records, Brother Dennis."

"I don't want any records."

"No, Brother. You know, I told you already. The Cardinal's office?"

"He is not my Cardinal."

"What harm would it do if Mr. Goldfarb listened to the practice tomorrow morning?"

Brother Dennis shrugged. "What good would it do?"

"I might enjoy it," said Sidney with dignity.

Brother Patrick pleaded. "You ought to let him at least hear Jerome once."

"He is by no means well enough trained to appeal to Mr. Goldfarb's presumably expert ear." Brother Patrick slumped. "Excuse me," Brother Dennis added in his thin voice, and started to walk off.

"So," said Sidney, angry but controlled, "so working for the greater glory of God gives you the right to be unkind to a stranger."

Brother Dennis stopped dead in the path, and then with great labor turned around, and came back to them. "Why should I make a record, Mr. Goldfarb?"

"Look, Brother, there's nothing I can tell you about why anybody should or shouldn't make a record. In addition to which I want to be open and aboveboard with you—I'm not sold on the idea myself. I was more or less roped in on this. It's strictly a business feeler on my part, and from what I heard in the church there this evening I'm not enthusiastic. Countertenors, there's a market opening up for them. How big I don't know. It makes a difference what they sing, naturally. So you see, I'm flying blind as yet. All I can tell you about that you don't know already is money. Royalties. Depending on what we think of the item, what we price it at, how big a pressing, you should get fifty cents a record, somewhere in that neighborhood. So—money. Okay, Brother?"

"Money," said Brother Dennis with a scorn worthy of the heavy, dark lines of his face. "Half a dollar a record to titillate aesthetes."

"Who you titillate is your own business." Sidney saw the big hands clench. Having got even he felt generous; besides he was a little scared. "Excuse me. I didn't mean that the way it sounded."

There was a leaden silence.

"Well," said Brother Patrick tentatively.

"Incidentally," said Sidney, "as long as I'm here—your daughter Linda told me to say hello for her."

"Linda!" cried Brother Dennis and stuck his head forward on its long neck.

"Certainly. She's a very fine young lady."

"*You* know *Linda?*"

This time the silence was bronze and rang like a gong.

"Look," said Sidney, angry at the insult but satisfied at having got Brother Dennis so far off-balance, "as long as I've come this far I might as well listen to the rehearsal tomorrow morning. Probably nothing will come of it, but I'd just as soon. Where and when?"

Brother Dennis smacked his lips; when they closed again they made a sour and melancholy line. His large, shaggy head swung toward Brother Patrick. "Eight o'clock in the minor chapel," he said in a voice not only quiet but defeated. "We will go through the Palestrina for Mr. Goldfarb." He started to leave, then turned. "Good night," he said and they answered him.

"Good!" whispered Brother Patrick squeezing Sidney's arm.

"What's good about it?"

"Oh ho, as long as he's let you go this far maybe you'll get to the manuscript hymns. They are what we're after all along."

"*He* doesn't do any of the singing, I hope?"

"Brother Dennis? Oh no sir."

"With that voice of his he'd better not."

"So tell me, Shary, you're here in Sansom alone?"

She looked huffy. "What do you think I'd be stepping out with you for if I wasn't?"

"You know what Henry said about you?"

"What do you mean, he *said?*"

"I mean he told me once in the strictest confidence. He said he trusted you, the limit, up to the hilt. He said as long as you were his you weren't anybody else's and he knew it."

"Aw," she said, "did he say that?" She stared out over the other tables. "We just didn't make a go of it," she said mostly to herself.

Sidney took the opportunity to glance about; he was gratified to see two men leaning toward one another, whispering and side-longing at Sharon.

"Well," she said resuming her public smile, "tell me about the monks."

"I don't know. It was pretty dull as a matter of fact—routine.

They've got a countertenor who may be terrific. They think so anyhow."

"A what?"

"A countertenor, a man with a voice like a contralto, only different. Very nice."

"You mean queer?"

"With a monk who asks? He don't act queer. Anyway it was probably a waste of time." He shrugged.

She stuck her tongue out a little at him, meaning for him not to worry about it. He was not sure what he wanted from her—he was not even sure she had anything more for him—but it was always worthwhile exploring. First stir her up.

"So what happened to the guy with the patch over his eye?"

"Turk," she said.

"Yes," said Sidney, "the pusher."

"Pusher! Who ever said Turk was a pusher?"

"Never mind."

"I do mind. He was no pusher. He was on it maybe—anyway he was hooked for awhile—but anybody said he was a pusher lied."

"Okay baby, I believe you. I was just asking."

"You never met him?" He shook his head. "Well he caught me when I was in Las Vegas getting a divorce from Henry. See, we both had engagements at The Beachcombers."

He watched her tell him all about Turk, watched more than listened, listened more to the tones of her voice than to her words. He was careful not to look into her eyes any more than he could help; they appealed too much, he was not sure for what, but the appeal itself made him uneasy. There was some very soothing mood music being piped into the dining room; so long as she was talking about herself it wouldn't matter whether he paid much attention to what she said. He allowed himself to drift back into the emotions he had felt for her two years before.

"You know, Shary," he said when he could, "I was just waiting for you to come back from Nevada. I was and you never came back."

"Come on, Sid," she said rather harshly, "let's don't start down that route again. Okay?" He shrugged. She winked. "For my own information," she said, "I'm just curious, that's all, who'd you ever hear say Turk was a pusher?"

"Forget it. Maybe it was Tommy Gunn, how can I remember every little detail?"

She looked satisfied. "That creep."

"Shary," he said as she settled back in her seat, "I heard you were in New York this spring."

"As a matter of fact I spent Easter with Henry. I was in town and I just felt like seeing him. He's *too* sweet, that's the thing." She began to drift off again, but he wanted her and patted her hand a little more than sympathetically. She smiled. "Linda was there."

"I haven't seen her since she still had braces on her teeth."

"Well," said Sharon, "she's not going to turn the world upside down on her looks, you understand, but Henry says she's smart. She's an oddball if you ask me—no make-up, talks deep like a man, dirty fingernails."

"Maybe she should see an analyst."

"Analyst!" Sharon cried. "What do you think? At that college of hers they all have analysts, Henry says."

"So she's going to an analyst already?"

"Look," she said clutching his arm, "this is private. These are people's lives we're hashing over. You understand, Sid? She's a good girl and she adores Henry and she keeps her troubles to herself. That's something these days."

"Sure it is."

"And she likes it that way and so does Henry and I'm sorry I breathed a word of it."

"Okay," said Sidney with irritation, "what do you take me for, I write for *Confidential* or something? So what does she want to do with herself? Music?"

"No," said Sharon leaning forward, frowning, beseeching, "she wants to be a social worker."

"Sure," said Sidney. The monks had made him edgy and she was no better; besides it didn't look as though she had anything he could use. He glanced at his watch. "Who could blame her? Say, I hate to do this, but you said you had to get there early."

"She's got her heart set on it, Siddy, you know? A plain-Jane social worker? She wants it?"

"All right, all right," said Sidney, "so the analysis is taking hold. Good."

"What the hell," said Sharon slumping in her chair, "with a father and mother like she has it's a wonder she isn't any goofier than she is."

"What's the matter with Lily?" said Sidney perking up.

"You know." But he did not know. "She's in. She's been in for a couple of years. Henry doesn't talk about it."

"That's terrible, it really is. What's she in?"

"I don't remember the name of it. Up in Connecticut somewhere."

"But what *is* it? A bughouse?"

"Aw," she said, "a mental hospital. Not too much hope." Then she glared at him. "Here I am running off at the mouth to you again. Now forget it, see? Just forget the whole thing."

"That's really terrible about Lily," said Sidney and meant it. "You think I got no respect for her? You never said a word to me, okay?" He had what he wanted. He was feeling jumpy as a cat. "Damn it all, baby, it's tough. Now come on, we got work to do—you got yours and I got mine. It's been good seeing you. I mean it, it really has."

She was angry and there were tears in her eyes, but he was too edgy to smooth her down again.

At six in the morning the phone rang. He let it ring three times while he lay collecting his wits, wondering who it could be.

"Goldfarb speaking."

"Mr. Goldfarb, I'm sorry to bother you, sir, but there's a Brother Patrick here to see you and he says it's important."

"What the hell does *he* want?" Sidney roared, but when he heard the desk clerk's distant voice begin to repeat a polite version of the question he said with resignation, "Tell him to come on up."

He was there in a minute, the gaps between his teeth wider than ever. "I know it's early sir, but they're running through the hymns this morning. I have it from Brother Jerome himself. At eight-fifteen and God knows when you'll get the chance again. I hope you haven't got any appointments you can't break today, Mr. Goldfarb. I cut Mass and drove all the way in on purpose to get you. This is it."

"Does Father Hilary know you're here?"

Brother Patrick's face fell. "Why shouldn't he?"

"And Brother Dennis?"

"No, but he's expecting you back sometime or other."

"You sure are going to a lot of trouble, Brother, and you don't even sing." Brother Patrick just gazed at him. "All right," Sidney said, "you win." Sighing, he lifted the phone from its cradle and ordered breakfast. "I have a luncheon appointment at twelve sharp."

Brother Patrick winced. "I'm pretty sure I could get you back in time."

The trouble was that the Cardinal's office had contacted the chairman of the Board of Directors, who was both Catholic and the biggest stockholder. Sidney had hoped to get out of Sansom without seeing Mount Mary again, and do the rest of the negotiating if there should be any by long-distance telephone. But no, from Brother Patrick to the boss was a direct pipe line.

Brother Patrick steered him toward the minor chapel and then rushed off to his work, reluctantly waving good-bye from the corner. Finding himself alone in the chapel Sidney inspected it with a care he had not had time for the day before. It was severely undecorated except for the marble-topped altar and the stained-glass windows; the proportions of the room, long and narrow with a high ceiling, added to the impression of severity. The windows confused him; saints and ribbons of Latin, as one would expect, but all in modern designs and in color combinations much too striking to seem religious.

"Mr. Goldfarb." It was Brother Dennis alone. "I had not expected to see you again." Or, his voice implied, wanted to see you either.

"Well you know, Brother, I was impressed in spite of myself. I really was. And the longer I thought about it the better I liked it. You know?" Brother Dennis just looked at him. "As for Brother Jerome," Sidney added, "I haven't made up my mind yet."

"The lad needs far more training. It would take an order from the Pope himself to make me expose the lad to the public as he is now."

"I didn't know you ever had voice training," said Sidney blandly. "I thought you were a clarinetist."

"I was," said Brother Dennis, in his voice a new quality that sounded to Sidney like defensiveness, "but for the music we are working on conventional voice training is inappropriate. I don't know what else I can do."

"Would you mind telling me about these hymns?"

Brother Dennis looked at him heavily, then sighed. "Father Bernard discovered the manuscripts in Rome four years ago. The notation has caused us trouble. They are believed to be pre-Gregorian."

"Really?" said Sidney with animation. "There could be a story in this, how he found them in a forgotten monastery maybe? Research?"

"You will find a full account of the manuscripts and their musical significance in a journal of liturgical music or perhaps of musicology, I have not decided which, within a year or two. It is being written now."

"Sure, but I meant the human story. There could be something good." He was thinking of the record slipcover: THE MONKS OF MOUNT MARY PRESENT LOST TREASURES.

"There will be no such story."

"No? Why not?"

"Because Father Bernard is dying of cancer and I will tell you nothing."

Five fresh-faced, smiling student Brothers came in, indiscriminately young.

Sidney retired to the back of the chapel, where he spent the next half-hour simmering down. The singers were facing the altar, and Brother Dennis, though he was facing the body of the church, did not glance at Sidney. They were working on a song the like of which he had never heard; he had to admit that Brother Dennis had got the right four singers to support Brother Jerome's strange and beautiful voice; there was a ruggedness to their timbres which kept each separate from the others, and yet his wholly different-sounding voice gave the four a unity by way of contrast. The hymn had neither harmony nor counterpoint, and its melodic line no tune; the phrasing was causing them trouble, all the more because Brother Dennis himself was not sure what he was after. Sidney could not withhold his respect for the man, who was giving himself to this creative interpretation totally, and when suddenly he caught the long, subtle rhythms already mastered by these five boys his respect became ungrudging.

At 9:45 they took a half-hour break. "Brother," said Sidney catching him on the way out, "I'm impressed. This is a different caliber of singing from the Palestrina."

"We have a long way to go yet," said Brother Dennis. "You might not believe it but I'm glad I know jazz, it helps me with this music."

"So the wild man is tamed," said Sidney. Brother Dennis surprised him with a smile. "Say, Brother, you might be interested to know it—Henry has settled down too, in a different way naturally. And he's crazy about Linda, he really is."

"I have renounced all claims to my past," said Brother Dennis.

Sidney knew this was a delicate situation because he had never heard Henry so much as mention Brother Dennis, and whenever he had referred to Fred Stauffer it had been briefly and with embarrassment. Even so, because of his own desire and because of a certain quaver in Brother Dennis's voice, Sidney decided to go on needling; all he had to lose was a prestige record.

"She's going to be a social worker, you know, that's what she wants to do. Well anyway, Henry's got himself a stable marriage this time, I'm confident. His present wife is an old friend of mine—that's how they met incidentally—and you can rest assured they're doing all right. Henry's grown up a lot in the last few years. He never told me too much about those wild years, just a word now and then. I gather he was heavy on the hooch and you favored the ladies?"

"Ladies!" said Brother Dennis. Sidney nodded watchfully. "That is absolutely not true."

"Oh? That's what people say. I've heard it elsewhere too, that you were keen on the girls."

"I was a voluptuary," said Brother Dennis with blazing eyes, "but I was never promiscuous. Sometimes, God forgive me, we used to stay in bed from the time we woke up till dinnertime, making love, slowly, five and six times, and talking about our bodies. We could spend hours . . . I was luxurious, yes. But Lily was the only one. There was no other. You know Lily?"

"I've met her," said Sidney in a voice diminished with shock.

Brother Dennis wet his lips; the cowl obscured all but the boldest of his features, the deep-set eyes, the heavy brows, the gaunt cheeks, the full and shiny lips. "How is she?"

"Sick. Seriously, so I heard. It's mental. She's in an institution."

"It has come to that," said Brother Dennis, and walked away from him.

If Sidney had come here in his own car he would have driven away at that moment and not returned. Brother Dennis disturbed him in a way and to an extent he could not handle. But having to ferret out Brother Patrick and make up excuses for leaving was more than he felt up to. He settled himself in the last row of pews. There was nothing to look at but the windows. He developed an acute dislike of one in which the colors were dominantly green and yellow—a yellow sheep, a green shepherd. What kind of Catholics were these? He was dreadfully offended by Brother Dennis's confession of sensuality; it had not been a confession even, just a declaration, an explanation, with perhaps a tinge of pleasure mixed in. Sidney could never have said such a thing to anyone of any woman, even if he had done it, which God forbid; a roll in the hay, yes, he had hinted at things like that plenty of times, a conquest, part of the game; but to dwell on it, to say he'd spent all day in bed with a woman who was *named* yet, and to say he'd relished it, five or six times . . . even to do it . . . and for a monk to say so, without so much as lowering his voice, in fact raising it, right in the vestibule of his own church. . . .

The young men returned and clustered in the front of the chapel, chirping in quiet voices, glancing back at him from time to time, giggling. Brother Dennis came in ten minutes late, and said "angelorum" to the singers, who made gestures of surprise. Brother Jerome took a position at the east wall and the other four faced him at the west wall. As Brother Dennis gave his recorder an experimental toot his eye came to rest on Sidney; he frowned, then fumbled inside his robe and fetched out a piece of slate gray paper. As he walked down the aisle Sidney was surprised to see him smiling. He rested one knee on the seat in front of Sidney and leaned against the back of the pew, like a friend.

"This hymn is the only one I'm anything like satisfied with. Here's a photostat of the original manuscript to give you an idea of what we had to work with." He went back.

Sidney tried to study the photostat, but he could not make head or tail of it; he did not know what quantities the signs indicated, nor was he sure that he could make out the one melodic line accompanying the Latin text; there was nothing on the paper but words in a script whose first word, *angelorum,* he could decipher only because he had heard it and odd musical notations hit or miss above the words. The recorder began and after a bar the five voices joined it.

Brother Dennis had pushed back his cowl as the singers had done, and Sidney was amazed to see that his hair was nearly white and stood out on every side; it looked splendid above the dark brown cloth. He swayed his head as he played, but he beat his right foot to another rhythm entirely. The recorder, the quartet, Brother Jerome, all were following the same line, yet there were subtle variations of intensity and phrasing which gave the effect of a complexity far beyond anything Sidney could analyze. Suddenly the recorder stopped and the four rough voices fell to half-volume; Brother Jerome tilted his head back and opened his mouth like a bird, and the sweet tones soared out with a beauty that made Sidney catch his breath. On the last word, *fidelibus*, Brother Jerome was alone; yet he filled the room. His singing seemed to Sidney to be perfectly voluptuous, an essence of voluptuousness, only safe.

Sidney did not know what to do; a solitary audience could not clap and besides he was in a church. Brother Dennis walked back to him, eyes aglow. Sidney nodded at him and smiled as best he could; he regretted all his unkind thoughts about Brother Dennis.

"We're going through it again; the phrasing was off in a few places. Listen to the suspense in those last vowels, *i, e, i,* and the sense of completion in that last *u*." He made the sound with his lips and half-sang it; he was no singer and his voice was weak, yet Sidney got a glimpse of what he meant.

"Brother, I never heard anything like it."

Brother Dennis went back to the singers and began talking to them.

Sidney heard a *psst* from the chapel door; Brother Patrick's face was peeking in. Sidney made a circle of his thumb and forefinger and closed his eyes as though in rapture; Brother Patrick grinned and grinned and blinked his eyes several times and disappeared.

They went through the hymn again. Brother Dennis ghost-sang every syllable with Brother Jerome, floated him with his gestures, leaned toward him, watched his mouth as though his life depended on every sound. To Sidney the gesture with which Brother Dennis rounded off the last note seemed that of a man caressing a woman's hip.

The five young men pulled their cowls up and came down the aisle; Sidney smiled and nodded at them, and they glanced at him several times and smiled as they passed. Brother Dennis came up to him.

"It's the best," said Sidney. "I don't care whether there's a market for it or not it's got to be heard."

"You understand, Mr. Goldfarb, we're a long way from mastering all of them. This is the only one I'm satisfied with."

"That's all right."

"It may be years."

"You're the doctor, we'll be waiting."

"As for the acoustics . . ."

"Don't worry," said Sidney, "we have a few tricks up our sleeve."

"I was in the wine caves recently."

"Where?"

"In the caves where the storage vats are kept, for the wine to age in. I heard one of the working men singing in a vat he was cleaning out. It made an interesting effect. I have hopes we may be able to work something out in the caves."

"Anything you say, Brother."

"There is a different kind of silence in the caves. And the sound of airplanes does not penetrate."

"Planes!" Sidney cried and held his nose. "Especially the jets!"

"And it is possible, not certain in any sense, just conjecture on my part, but it is possible that these hymns were sung in the catacombs."

"Oh?" said Sidney and shivered a little.

"In the catacombs," Brother Dennis said raising his arms, "when we were being persecuted by the Romans—to sing a hymn of the angels in God's heaven. . . ."

"It's really wonderful," said Sidney remembering that his mother's parents had been killed by the Cossacks. "It really is."

"The important thing," said Brother Dennis his arms descending, "is that I mustn't arrange too much, modernize in any way I can help. Everything about it has to be perfect."

"Sure, Brother, I'm prepared to go along with you on anything you say. I'll put every modern facility at your disposal."

"No!" said Brother Dennis. "At the disposal of the hymns!"

"That's it, that's what I meant to say. It's the hymns."

Back at his hotel by 2:30 Sidney felt at a loss; he had a half-hour appointment at five for business cocktails and a business dinner at seven and his plane left at ten; meanwhile he found he could neither rest nor read. He told the hotel operator to put in a call to New York, but as soon as he replaced the phone in its cradle he lifted it again and canceled the call; long-distance business would not ease his mind.

He wanted to think about the music and his experience of hearing it, which still glowed inside him. But both the music and his experience listening to it had been so different from any he knew that he had no words to talk about them with. He could not even talk to himself about them. Intensity, strangeness, and loss of words—he shook himself and set his attention on business.

From the way Brother Dennis had not reacted at the mention of a royalty of maybe fifty cents a record Sidney was reasonably sure he could bring it down ten or twenty cents. It was obvious that the order was prosperous but not greedy, and that Brother Dennis personally did not care about such things as royalties. Even as he was thinking this Sidney lost interest in the business part of it. Dealing was a habit which at the moment he was not pleased to have. He forced his attention back to the royalty; it occurred to him that Father Hilary might very well be shrewd enough to hire a lawyer who would be tough about money. All right, all right. Fifty cents was the top, he'd said it and that was the limit; a prestige record they'd be lucky to sell five thousand copies of—hymn of the angels yet.

At the thought of the song the tiny belligerence he had begun to work up dissolved. Instead he felt hurt. Here he loved the music like nothing he'd ever heard, he was ready to give them sixty, even sixty-five cents a record, and they go hire a watchdog to worry him. The thought of their not trusting him made him not angry but unhappy. Couldn't they tell how much that record meant to him?

On the chance he telephoned Sharon's hotel. Her line was busy. He left his number for her to call him back. Thinking of her, he remembered the afternoon two years before when he had nearly proposed to her. He'd taken her up to his apartment after a recording session and told her he enjoyed being with her more than with any other woman he'd ever known. She told him he was sweet, he really was. They'd necked on the sofa for awhile, but she said she couldn't do it with a man unless she was married to him. Then he'd said something—he was no longer sure exactly what—about loneliness and old friends and both parties living their own lives. If she'd wanted him to propose he would have done it, but somehow, though he was sure she liked him, he hadn't quite got the words said.

The telephone rang. "Hi, Siddy baby."

As soon as he heard her voice—its bold facsimile of affection, its vague suspicion, its publicness made harsher by the instrument—he changed his mind. "I just wanted to say good-bye."

She sounded sorry and wanted to see him, wanted to just enough, sounded just sorry enough.

He started to tell her about the hymn and the Brothers, but instead switched over to telling her about the record he was going to get from them and how he planned to exploit it. "I mean it, Shary, I really do." He did not know exactly what he meant, but he knew he meant something.

"It's been wonderful seeing you, Siddy. Thanks for everything."
He thought that he felt sympathy underneath the hardness of her voice. "Keep in touch," he said. In the comfortable, friendly seeming, old shoe of a phrase he felt like himself. She did her purr job on him and he liked it. "I got to hang up now. I got a crowded calendar for the rest of the day." Saying it, though it was not true, made him feel normal again. "Bye now, baby. Keep in touch."

An Hour of Last Things

I

BETTY HOLLANDER, a tall, lean, pale woman, found herself widowed at the age of thirty-eight by an automobile accident which killed both her husband and his father. Her husband, Winton, was a designer of rest homes, and his father was a retired optometrist with heart trouble. The father and son had been driving to Baltimore, where Winton was to look over three houses which a client of his planned to remodel as rest homes; Mr. Hollander had gone for the outing. It was raining and traffic was heavy. Winton was pressing to make an eleven o'clock appointment. On the outskirts of a town in Delaware a car swerved against him, whereupon he slammed on the brakes and skidded head-on into a furniture van. Mr. Hollander died in the ambulance. Winton lay in the hospital for five days, his liver ruptured, his forehead crushed, and his right eye penetrated by a sliver of glass. All three drivers had been somewhat at fault in the accident: the first driver had swerved to avoid hitting a dog, Winton had been going too fast for the condition of the highway, the truck driver might have turned aside in time had he not been lighting a cigarette at the moment Winton's car had slid at his left headlight. Betty was relieved to put blame and revenge out of her mind by delegating them to the insurance company.

She went into Winton's room at the hospital three times every day, except the day of Mr. Hollander's funeral, when she visited Winton only in the evening. He did not respond to her voice or the touch of her hand. Once he was mumbling fretfully, but she could not make out one syllable. His head was swathed except for his nostrils, mouth, and chin, so that he could not open his jaw enough to get out any words which he might otherwise have been capable of making. The noise he produced was more like whimpering than like speech. The last time she saw him his fingers were plucking at the bedclothes.

In the evening of the fifth day, well after visiting hours, Betty was sitting in the hospital waiting room with a popular magazine right side up in her hands. She had been glancing at a picture story of costumed dogs that had been trained by a boy in Minnesota to dance mostly on their hind legs but also on their front legs. From time to time she tried to understand what the pictures represented, but she could not make it out. A few pages further in the magazine, there was a picture of a gaunt woman, a Protestant missionary's wife, who had just been released from a Chinese Communist prison; the caption read RELEASED AFTER YEARS OF TORMENT; she could not understand that either. On the couch opposite her two shabby young women with blotched skin and miserable eyes sat not even looking at a magazine. The larger one looked as though she wanted to cry. Betty smiled sternly the two times they caught her eye. Confronted with them, she was grateful that she had troubled in the hotel room that afternoon to smooth out her gabardine suit with her traveling iron and that she was wearing shoes with heels instead of the flats she usually wore. The smaller woman kept glancing about, though her lips were moving and her fingers were telling the beads of a rosary. The larger kept wringing her handkerchief, and when a Puerto Rican nurse stepped in and glanced at each of the three, she stuffed her handkerchief into her mouth and cringed.

"Mrs. Hollander?"

Betty nodded, closed the magazine, and set it on the table beside her chair, put her flat purse under her arm, and stood up.

"Would you step this way please?"

The nurse took her behind a partition where there were two straight chairs and a small table and told her that Winton had died five minutes before. Betty had been afraid she would break down at this point, but she did not even feel like crying. She asked the nurse in a businesslike way whether there were any arrangements she should make. The nurse said they would wait till morning and asked her if she wanted a sleeping pill. Betty said certainly not. She would sit there behind the partition having a cigarette—if the nurse would be so good as to bring her an ashtray—and then walk back to the hotel.

As the nurse was leaving, Betty heard one of the other two women murmur to her and the nurse murmur in response. Betty suspected that the nurse was telling them that Betty's husband had just died. There was nothing to look at. She kept forgetting to draw on the cigarette. She became aware of sobs from the other side of the partition; then also of a muttering. She ground out the cigarette and set her mouth. When she strode out from behind the partition, she glanced at the two women on the couch. The larger ceased her sobbing and pressed the knuckles of her hand against her teeth; the smaller dropped her rosary and pressed her companion's right hand in both of hers. They kept that position, seeming to hold their breath, while Betty left the room.

2

Because Mr. Hollander had died before Winton, his only son, Betty inherited Mr. Hollander's property as well as Winton's. Mrs. Hollander, who had divorced Winton's father twenty years before and had lived in Florida since then, wrote Betty a letter condoling with her and congratulating her at once. Betty had inherited enough in insurance and stocks to live without having to work, and she knew that Mrs. Hollander, who had never remarried, was not well off. Betty offered to give her mother-in-law, whom she had known for one week nine years before, half of what Mr. Hollander had left. In the letter accepting this gift, Mrs. Hollander implied that Betty was to be congratulated for getting rid of half her guilt.

Mr. Hollander had lived in the same house in Staten Island for thirty years. After his wife and son had left, he lived there alone for a while, but in the ten years Betty had known him he had had a colored housekeeper who lived in and who came and went quite as she pleased. She had moved out of the house the day after Mr. Hollander's funeral, despite Betty's pleading with her to stay and take care of the house until Betty had decided what to do with it. The housekeeper, who had wept noisily at the funeral, refused, saying it would make her heart too heavy to stay on, for Mr. Hollander had been a good man.

Betty had had Mr. Hollander's body brought back to Staten Island for the funeral service and buried in a perpetual-care grave for which he had already paid. Winton's body, however, in accordance with both his and her own wishes, she had a local undertaker cremate without ceremony; the ashes she had disposed of inexpensively and without fuss. She had found Mr. Hollander's funeral parlor *cum*

Methodist service repulsive. She more or less closed her ears to the words, so that the organ music stayed in the background; but the flowers obtruded upon her. She never wore flowers, and she and Winton had only occasionally permitted flowers in their severe apartment; they preferred a jagged branch with berries on it, or three plumes of grass against a bare wall. Despite these matters of taste, the loud grief of Mr. Hollander's housekeeper and her irrational determination to leave his house troubled Betty. She knew they were not meant as a reproach; nevertheless, she felt reproached; she thought of herself as being rational in her decisions and too emotionally repressed. Since the accident she had wept once, stranglingly, alone in the hotel room the evening after she had first visited Winton in the hospital. None of their friends or acquaintances blamed her by the least inflection or hesitation for the way in which she had disposed of Winton's body; on the contrary, those who mentioned the matter applauded her. After the Goodwill had taken away his clothes, she felt no reluctance, even when she would return late at night, to unlock the door and enter. Though there was a chair he had customarily sat in when he read, she had no impulse to move it, for its position was the most suitable one for the arrangement of the room. All the same, when she thought of Mr. Hollander's housekeeper she felt deficient. She could not relieve her sorrow by putting on noisy ways, and though she knew she was suffering intensely, she had no external signs to prove it, as the housekeeper had. She was half-consciously afraid she was not suffering enough. She felt vaguely that it would be better for her if she moved out of that apartment, in which she had lived with Winton for the nine years of their marriage, and even out of Brooklyn Heights, though many of her friends lived in that neighborhood.

She supposed that she would not be at such loose ends if she had had a child, but then reproached herself for her selfishness. She would have been leaning on someone whom, she agreed with Winton, they had no right to bring into so dreadful a world as this. Mrs. Hollander had made the gift of half of Mr. Hollander's money unsatisfying, so that Betty felt that to have given her the entire estate would have been no more noteworthy than giving ten dollars to the Community Chest. Betty thought of giving the other half of what she had inherited from Mr. Hollander to some such cause as the American

Friends Service Committee; but she knew such a gift would not be a satisfying action to her at that time. Moreover, she began to want to quit her job, having worked in the same social welfare agency for seven years, and she feared that, because of her pervasive, unrelenting malaise, she might need money for further psychoanalysis.

After two weeks of perplexity and indecision, she decided to have another interview with the analyst to whom she had gone for four years but whom she had not needed to see for the past three years. She learned that he had recently moved to St. Louis. Because she had been raised in a town not far from there, she obscurely felt that his leaving New York for St. Louis was a retrogression as her doing so would have been and that he might have betrayed her. All the same, she wrote him asking if she might talk to him over the telephone. He replied immediately, setting a day and hour. She put in the call, expecting little but not knowing what else to do. He astonished her by the open friendliness of his voice. He seemed sympathetic with her for her loss and unimpressed by her symptoms, and they talked for nearly an hour. She had expected him to be elaborately cautious on the subject of Mrs. Hollander; instead, he asked for the practical details and then said she sounded as bad as ever. At that point Betty decided to communicate thereafter with her mother-in-law only through lawyers. She also decided, during that telephone conversation, to quit her job, move into her father-in-law's house, and see how she liked living there; if she did not like it, she would take a trip to Europe. As she suggested these plans over the telephone, she became aware of their ordinariness and apologized for it. The doctor, however, laughed at her apologetic embarrassment in such an indulgent way, telling her like a friend not to be silly, that gratitude warmed her. He also told her that her most threatening problem now was having too much free time on her hands.

When she had picked up the receiver to place the call, she had been sitting stiffly sidewise to the table, on which cigarettes, ashtray, and a cup of coffee were arranged, and the toe of her crossed foot had been pressing hard against a table leg. When she hung up, her shoulders were sagging and one bare foot was tucked under her on the chair. She shoved back the things on the table and laid her head sideways on her arms. The grief had worked its way out into her muscles. She could feel its pain coming up behind her eyes. Her relief at feeling in her very body manifestations of intense sorrow was so great that she did not resist it but let it shake her and course through her.

3

It was the custom at Betty's agency for the colleagues of a departing worker to give a going-away present. Since Betty now had much more money than the others and since they knew how "fussy" her taste was, they decided to give her a farewell dinner instead in the banquet room of a moderately good restaurant, one which the director of the agency seemed to have his heart set on.

The banquet was not as stiff as Betty had anticipated. Most of the three bottles of Scotch on the sideboard had been emptied by the time everyone sat down to eat, and at dinner the director's half case of champagne was matched out of a kitty taken up among the others on the spur of the moment. The food was good; the director's long toast was stuffy, but it was also sentimental. He even made a little joke about how "we are going to miss our Wasp, she kept us on the *qui vive*." (Betty was the only White Anglo-Saxon Protestant in the agency.) Several others were emboldened to make speeches too.

At first Betty feared that she was supposed to respond in kind, but presently she realized that those who spoke were not speaking to or even about her so much as they were using the opportunity to enjoy themselves. She drank all the champagne she wanted, sank back in her chair, and smiled and blinked at people.

The party did not break up till midnight. Everyone agreed that the director was an amiable fellow when he let himself unbend and that the banquet had been a great success. Some of the women wept a little when they said good-bye to Betty, assuring her that they could not stand to think she was going to move out of town and never come back to the agency. She reminded them, eagerly, that she would still be in New York City, but they said—what she knew—that going to Staten Island was quite a trip, only two out of seven of them had ever done it except to go across on the ferry for the ride.

Francy Rugero, her department head for the past year, had maintained an official distance with Betty on the job and had not said much during the evening. However, in the hubbub of farewells, she suddenly loomed in front of Betty and grasped her at arm's length, a hand on each shoulder. She was even taller than Betty, and she was beefy; she was in her forties, and so far as Betty knew she had never been married. Her ebony, lumpy forehead was scowling. Betty, who was blurry with champagne and affection, smiled at her and patted her shaftlike arms. Francy kept staring into Betty's eyes as though searching for something, then hugged her close and kissed her on the cheek. "Good-bye, Betty, damn it," she said in a flat, furious voice, put on her trench coat, and strode out by herself.

4

That morning Betty's possessions, most of which had been selected by Winton, had been moved from the severe apartment to the Victorian house. She had been looking forward uneasily to that first night alone in the house, which she had not yet been able to think of as hers; but the mellow effects of the dinner stayed with her as she wove her little, upright foreign car among the pressures of Flatbush Avenue, across the Brooklyn Bridge, and to the tip of Manhattan. On the ferry, she stood outside so as to be alone and was conscious of the cool air in her nostrils and of the three-quarter moon. She drove along the streets of Staten Island, imagining that their quietness was an invitation and smiling at the silliness of her fancy. She parked her car in her garage and let herself into her house, which for some reason smelled good to her. She stood at the front windows for a few minutes, gazing out over lights which were all the prettier because she could not identify any of them. The weeding out, painting, and rearranging to be done had been preying on her mind, but they now appeared to her as agreeable offices. Doing them would make this house, which she felt awkward and comfortable in, so familiar to her that it would become an expression of herself. At first she had intended to get rid of nearly all of Mr. Hollander's furniture but now she decided to keep a good deal of it; taste or no taste, she liked it. The movers had put her bed, a single mattress on box springs to which legs were attached, in the cluttered guest room; it looked uninviting to her. The housekeeper had left Mr. Hollander's ornate double bed made up, with a fresh counterpane and ironed sheets. Betty did not much like the patterned wallpaper in the master bedroom. Nevertheless she decided to sleep there. Once in the bed, she liked having the headboard there to touch when she stretched out her arms, and the four spooled posts, which had seemed disproportionately tall when the lamps were on, towered about her in the diffuse moonlight both elegant and protecting. Through the open window the sound of crickets came in louder than the noise of the city.

5

At eleven thirty the telephone rang. She sat bolt upright in bed, startled and confused. By the time she had put on her slippers, cleared her throat, and gone into the hall, the line was dead. It seemed to her a bad omen not to have answered the first person to call her in her new house. She was eager for new possibilities. What opportunity had she just missed?

She arranged the garden furniture on the south side of the house, put some Mozart sonatas for violin and piano on her old record player, opened the windows, and took her coffee and toast out in the hot sun. She watched a squirrel in her elm tree. Four little boys in chaps went shooting across her lawn, paying no attention to her. Two cardinals were pecking orange-colored berries in a bush. Her neighbor to the west, a barefoot old woman wearing dark glasses, shorts, and a halter, invited her across the hedge to "come take a dip in our swimming pool any time." Betty thanked her but regretted that she did not swim. It was true that she did not swim, but it was not true that she regretted it at that moment. In her opinion, no one was less worth knowing than a false-young old woman, and nothing more vulgar than a blue cement swimming pool in the back yard of an eighty-year-old house in Staten Island. Her telephone's ringing again abridged this unwanted neighborliness.

It was Francy Rugero saying that she had an extra ticket to the Juilliard School of Music Recital Hall for the next Thursday night. "My cousin is singing there—she's a contralto—making her debut. How would you like to go with me?" Betty said she would like to. "You know, babe, her friends are sort of papering the house for the poor child. I understand she's not bad. I hardly know her even if she is my cousin. Actually, she's my mother's sister's daughter's daughter."

"My God, aren't there any men in your family?"

"Men! In my family we got parthenogenesis down to a science. The only use we got for men is to pleasure ourselves with them from time to time."

They joked awhile longer and then made arrangements to eat together before the recital. Betty was still sitting by the telephone, wondering whether there was something behind Francy's sudden friendliness, when it rang again.

This time it was Harold Garrett. He lived across the hall from Winton's friend Cedric in a dingy apartment house east of Green-

wich Village. She had met Harold two or three times at Cedric's
parties, without much liking him. Harold had told her once that he
made a living by buying blocks of theater tickets and reselling them
to groups but that he "also had a few other little things going on the
side." He spoke breathlessly, like a gossip with a fresh tidbit.

He wanted to come see Betty right away because he knew she
adored music so much she would be wanting a new hi-fi set tailored
for her present needs. She was annoyed that he presumed to know
anything about her taste.

"Are you selling hi-fi equipment?"

The sharpness in her voice halted him. "Not exactly."

"Because I'm not interested in any one brand. If I get one, I'll get
the best and only the best."

He assured her that was all he had in mind.

She announced that she would drop by and see him Thursday
afternoon at five, and hung up.

Her decisiveness with Harold, her all-but rudeness, made her feel
good. It indicated to her that she had accepted these first two phone
calls as omens and had already begun to act on them. She remem-
bered the analyst's warning about too much free time, and realized
that a weight of unconscious worry had disappeared from her mind,
about how she should occupy herself in the unaccustomed leisure
yawning before her. She would turn—with these actions she seemed
already to be turning—to music. For many years she had not bought
a new record and had not gone to as many concerts as she would
have liked to. Winton's indifference to music had prevented her from
satisfying her hunger for it. He had urged her to go to concerts alone
and he had always spoken with genuine regret of what he called his
"tone deafness." Nevertheless, when the time came for her to go to a
concert, it had usually seemed "too much trouble" and she had, re-
sentfully, stayed home with him. When she stayed home like this, he
had not looked pleased so much as puzzled. Even so, she had blamed
him for depriving her of music or at least of causing her to deprive
herself of it.

Now she realized how badly she was treating him in her thoughts,
and was ashamed of herself; she began thinking of the good things
about him. He had been unfailingly courteous and considerate; she
had learned good taste from him; he had rescued her (she always
thought of it as a rescuing) from loneliness. But the main thing was

her inexpressible gratitude to him for having found her eyes beautiful—nothing else, just her eyes, the only part of herself she could believe to be not drab or plain. All her life she had automatically rejected as flattery any man's praise of herself. But Winton had looked into her eyes in a special way the first time they had met—at the house of a mutual acquaintance for dinner—and again and again he had told her she had the most wonderful eyes he had ever seen. She had believed him.

All the same, she looked forward now to going to as many concerts as she wanted to.

6

As she breezed through the door pulling off her gloves, she said, "Hello, Harold." He called her Mrs. Hollander in a deferential voice. She had not recalled that she was quite a bit taller than he. Because she knew he was preying on her, his thin nose appeared to jut from his round fat face like an owl's beak.

He began a circuitous story about advances in electronics and getting things wholesale.

"You're a contact man, right?"

He said you could put it that way.

"On a commission basis?"

He began eagerly to explain that his "associate" was interested only in building the best set the customer could afford, brand was no consideration.

"You get five percent?"

He hunched into himself and nodded.

He began tentatively to tell her about the hi-fi equipment, and in fifteen minutes he had worked himself back up again. She rose, told him she wanted two thousand dollars' worth of equipment installed right away, watched him thank her, and left.

She had not expected money to afford her this sort of pleasure.

7

They strolled in Riverside Park before the recital.

"Her real name," said Francy, "is Delilah. Delilah Strong. So when she got a scholarship to Juilliard, this night-club cousin of ours said she had to change her name to something that would look more dignified in the public eye; you know, some name that didn't mean a thing about Strong. Rosetta, that was our grandmother's name and everybody thought that's what she was going to be, but when she came to register at Juilliard she just up and made it Julia without so much as how-d'you-do to anybody. Gratitude, she said. It's not too bad of a name, but her mother hasn't forgiven her, she says she reached right out of the family. She won't call her anything but Lila to this day, except once in a while when she gets mad she'll call her Juilliard to be mean. I wouldn't be too surprised if Rose-of-Sharon did not come tonight. She's a vengeful woman. She's a day worker, you know, cleans people's houses, and she certainly doesn't have to any longer. She does it out of spite. And she's a Witness."

"What? What? Go slower. I'm all confused."

"A Witness, a Jehovah's Witness. Rose-of-Sharon's a Jehovah's Witness. Humble and bleak, you know, and devastating. Well anyway, Julia—I don't know her so well but what 'Julia' comes easy to me—at least she don't have a father to contend with."

"Where is he?"

"He was funeralized," said Francy, modulating from a standard American into a Southern Negro accent, "in nineteen forty-three, courtesy of the United States Army. He died for his country in upstate New York. They stuck an unsterilized needle in him and he got the jaundice bad."

"Wait!" Betty held her hands over her ears and laughed. "Take it easy."

"I just wanted you to be prepared, babe." Francy chuckled. "Don't be too surprised if she don't do full justice to the Nazis' sugarplum composer."

"What? Dear God, Francy, take it easy on the turns. Who?"

"Richard Strauss. I just want you to realize she wasn't to the manner born. I understand she's going to sing something by him and I didn't want you to hold the results against her too much."

Francy laughed largely. Betty would have understood a constricted laughter, ironic or bitter, but she was troubled by Francy's because it sounded expansive and free.

"Another thing," Betty said abruptly, "the tickets are free, so what did you mean the house was papered?"

"Why, it's counterfeit paper, babe." Francy staggered with laughter against a bench.

Out of contagion, Betty joined in. Her laughter sounded open in her own ears. However, she wondered if even Francy knew what they were laughing about.

Julia walked onto the platform rigidly easy, a slender, pretty, walnut-colored girl with a long neck. She wore a knitted, blue-white, sleeveless dress that made her thighs look thick as a mature woman's, but her shoulders narrow. The way she held her hands seemed to Betty at once artificially studied and naturally graceful. She nodded glacially at her accompanist, a pink girl in a black dress.

She sang three Schubert songs. The first two, out of nervousness and wrong expectation, Betty was unable really to listen to, though she knew the tones were rich and the control firm. The third, "To Be Sung on the Water," was familiar enough so that Betty, now confident of Julia's ability, heard it. Its loveliness infused her till she ached. She wanted to cherish her feeling inwardly awhile, not to behave like just another member of the audience. But to prevent questions or glances from Francy, who was clapping politely, she applauded and smiled like everybody else.

After a trio sonata and an intermission, Julia returned to sing Strauss's "Four Last Songs," which Betty had not known. The music took her over, and filled her with yearning feelings of tolerable despair and love. Because of Francy, she restrained her tears and shouted *Brava!* with a few others. Julia bowed like a queen-to-be.

Despite Francy's reluctance, they sought Julia out in the corridor. They stood to one side with Mrs. Strong, watching Julia. She was surrounded by congratulating friends; she kept clapping her hands and squealing and sometimes she hopped from one leg to the other like a little girl. When only a few remained, she broke away and came up to her mother, who kissed her dourly. Francy introduced Betty, who congratulated her, and then rushed the four of them out to a taxi and to a restaurant away from Julia's school friends. Mrs. Strong said little and watched like a badger. Betty promised to introduce Julia to some influential friends and said she believed in her. When Francy coolly asked who some of these friends were, Betty just smiled. Julia wore a bemused and dazzling smile.

Betty awoke at dawn from a dream of Julia singing. The tones of that dream voice faded so fast that in a minute or two Betty could no longer hear the lovely tune it sang but only a faint continuous chime. When even that had receded out of hearing, she shook herself severely and began to look for meaning in her dream. Finding none, she allowed memories of Julia's actual recital to rise in her mind, and indulged herself in a sensuous ease she had not felt for years.

She decided to give a housewarming party.

8

Harold showed up at five Saturday afternoon to see if the workmen had done a satisfactory job of installing the hi-fi set. He was eager to respond to whatever she said. He seemed to her without corners.

He had not been there ten minutes when Francy telephoned. Her brother-in-law and his wife had tickets to the Desegregation Benefit Ball at Delmonico's that night and they had both come down with the flu. Did Betty have some man she'd like to bring? It would cost nothing but the drinks.

"You can get to my place about nine fifteen and we can all four go from here together. Paul likes to get places not too late."

"Paul?"

"My husband."

Betty, who had been suspicious of Francy for calling again so soon, repeated "husband" with more relief than tact.

"Sure, he hates a big do like this but he has to go to two or three a year. He's a state senator, you know."

"No, I didn't know. An escort. Let me think."

She had worked all day; her hair hadn't been done for weeks; she didn't much like to dance.

"Formal, I suppose?"

"The best you've got."

The only man she could think of was Winton's college roommate, Cedric, and if she felt the slightest obligation to go to this ball, she would have called him up. She did not have to go if she didn't want to, she owed Francy nothing and wanted nothing from her. She realized that, not only did she not want Cedric, she had never much liked him and did not care whether she ever saw him again.

"Harold?" she called. He came to the doorway. She beckoned him over her head. "Do you have a tuxedo?"

He did. She told him about the ball and told him she'd like him to take her if he wasn't busy that night. He blinked; after he said sure, okay, he remembered to smile.

9

There were three hundred people, more or less, at the ball, most of them Negroes, few of them black. Betty had not felt so oppressed by good manners since her high-school graduation dance in a gymnasium lined with mothers. Paul was a man of frigid affability. At first Harold had made small talk, but after a prolonged laugh from Paul froze one of Harold's jokes to death, Harold said little. Couple after couple came up to their table to pay their respects to Paul, and it gave Betty a little amusement to watch Harold's eyes thrum. The main relief she found from the respectability was in observing the subtle pride of body with which some of the people, especially as they were dancing, moved about in their clothes.

After a while, the boredom, the two highballs she drank, the dancers, and the saxophones set up in her a sexual clitter-clatter. She deplored, but did not restrain, the erotic thoughts about Harold which rose into her consciousness. When Paul finally took Francy off to dance, Harold sighed, said what an impressive man Paul was, and invited Betty to dance. They danced together better than she expected, despite his belly and the difference in their height, which her highest heels increased. After one number, Paul and Francy returned to their table; Betty could see Harold yearning to rejoin them, but she was enjoying the dancing too much to want to stop. She enjoyed almost as much keeping him dancing till he was sweating. Three years before, she had had her left breast amputated for cancer. Now, she took a certain satisfaction in observing Harold's uneasiness when, from time to time, she pressed against him the mound of foam rubber which he would naturally take for that breast.

At the next orchestra break when they joined the Rugeros, they found at the table a man whom Paul introduced as Bob Flanders, a writer. Betty remembered that he had written a profile of Bartók in the *New Yorker* and several other pieces on musical subjects. With an animation she had lacked all evening, she took over the conversation, made herself pleasant, and invited everyone to her housewarming party, which she impromptu set for the first Saturday in August. She made Staten Island sound exotic and her house a curiosity worth traveling to see. They were to come any time from midafternoon on; it was quite a trip getting there; she had croquet and badminton. They were to plan on staying for supper. Paul declined; the *New*

Yorker writer hoped he could make it; Harold of course was happy to come; Francy said she would be there with bells on. Betty urged everyone to bring a friend, she was sure everyone would have a good time. She casually mentioned to Francy that she hoped Julia could come, and Francy said she'd bring her.

Presently, to Betty's relief, she felt the erotic nonsense melt away. For the rest of the evening, her thoughts turned, whenever she wished, to Julia: not to the silly girl in the school corridor or the clumsily shy one in the restaurant, but to the young woman on the platform singing Schubert and Strauss. She especially enjoyed imagining Julia dressed in attractive gowns, and began closely observing the best-dressed young women in the hall. She imagined buying Julia an elegant, strapless gown which would set her off well. She had no reason to suppose that Julia could be especially graceful in her bodily movements, since in fact the evening of the recital Julia had walked with something of the gaucherie of a little girl wearing her older sister's shoes. Nevertheless, Betty put her doubts aside and imagined Julia the most graceful of the dancers, her body secretly free inside a stiff, bright gown.

10

Six days later the installation of the hi-fi set was complete; a wall had been taken out and the wound plastered over.

Next morning Betty went to a record outlet. There were thousands of records on the shelves; the catalogue listed thousands more. The aisles in the store were narrow and milling with customers and clerks. The clerk she kept bothering, a squat, pasty-faced man with an uptilted cigar in his mouth, finally stopped to look at her.

"Lady, how much you want to spend?"

"Up to a thousand dollars." She was sure of that much.

He nodded. "How many records you got already?"

"None, really. I've just had a hi-fi set put in."

"Come on."

She followed him across the street to the shipping room. He sat her in a corner, pulled up a chair beside her, and put his notebook and pen on a packing box. They paid no attention to the workers about them, tearing paper and shouting jokes.

"Now," he said riffling the catalogue, "all the ones you were asking about were classical. Do you want some popular too?"

"All classical."

"How about parties? Nothing light?"

"Well, yes, jazz."

"Uh huh. Half a dozen progressive, three or four Dixieland."

"No! Nothing but Dixieland. I know what ones I'd like to have too."

His ball point pen was cocked. There was a lack of responsiveness in his pale eyes waiting for her to speak. For a while she knew what she wanted.

He gave her clear choices, from a one-disc sampling of Gregorian chant or the full Easter liturgy, to *Wozzek* or *The Rake's Progress*. Usually when she said she didn't know, he would go on, but occasionally he would say such and such a recording was too good to pass up and write it down. In two hours she made and let him make a thousand dollars' worth of choices. She would have spent weeks thinking about the task, had she not relied on him. He sounded sure of himself, he was a stranger and cynical, he did it only for money.

"I paid him for the right to blame him for any shortcomings in my choices." She formulated this on the ferry returning to Staten Island, and with the thought she strode about the deck, as happy as though her conscience would be long appeased by her intellect's having made this obscure motive clear.

As soon as she had eaten a dish of cottage cheese, she put on the one record she had paid for in cash and brought home, a long-playing pressing of some old Muggsy Spanier pieces she remembered from her college days. She had brought that one along because Muggsy's had been the only good jazz band she had heard live; the term of praise for his playing had been "really dirty." The afternoon was soft; the windows were open to the sounds of birds and lawnmowers; her neighbor to the east, a gray-haired man with whom she occasionally smiled and nodded, was out weeding. When she put on the record, she expected it to revive memories of the dance hall in East St. Louis where she had been taken on a blind date to listen to Muggsy. Instead, the music left her right in her new large room which needed paint and curtains, slouched in an easy chair, her glasses off, a cup of coffee on the stand beside her, and recreated in her the special, sustained, "cool" excitement which she had cultivated in college for listening to low-down recorded jazz, one foot tapping time, eyes locked on a spot on the rug. Jazz somehow evened up sides within

her and made the dirty combatants embrace in a struggle so taut that
when the music stopped they fell apart exhausted and she dared to
look at them for a while or even to play with them.

11

At four thirty a carload of five women social workers from the
agency arrived. They wore dark glasses with outrageous rims, and
even the one with fat pale legs wore Bermuda shorts and sandals.
After they had exclaimed over the house, four of them went out to
play badminton barefoot on the lawn. The fifth went with Betty into
the kitchen and talked while Betty finished deviling the eggs.

There was a ham in the oven and a large beef roast ready to
go in as soon as the ham came out. There were two green salads
with different dressings; slices of avocado, carrot strips, celery, frilly
radishes, and three kinds of olives; a potato salad, deviled eggs, and a
tomato aspic, with mayonnaise she had made herself; sweet and salt
butter, three kinds of rye bread, and rolls with hard crusts; smoked
salmon and smoked oysters, four spiced sausages, and a hillock of
black caviar and cream cheese; pickles and relishes of every kind;
oranges, cherries, strawberries and powdered sugar, pineapple in
kirsch, peaches; five kinds of cheese; two kinds of wine, ale, Scotch,
and cognac. There were fresh flowers in every room.

By six thirty, over twenty people had come, including a man
who worked with disturbed children in the Staten Island schools; he
turned out to be a killer on the croquet court. By seven thirty, she
counted everyone she remembered having invited but Francy. She felt
the party could not really begin till Francy arrived. Perhaps Francy
would bring Julia? She hovered within sight of the front door. At
eight, Francy arrived with Julia, who was smiling eagerly but at the
same time glancing around nervously.

Rather to Betty's surprise, Bob Flanders, the *New Yorker* writer,
had shown up, though he announced that he had to leave by nine
thirty. She rushed Julia into the dining room, where he had been
ensconced for some time near the caviar. He lounged in an open
window with a bottle of white wine precariously beside him on
the sill, passing pleasantries with whoever came by inside or out-
side, kibitzing on the croquet game, whistling to the music from the
record player. She introduced them and remained in their vicinity,
getting tidbits for Julia to eat. She overheard enough to regret her

arrangement-making. Flanders was asking Julia proper questions about her singing and she was properly answering. He kept tapping his foot and glancing out the window; she was the grande dame in a high-school play who knew nothing about the part but her lines. Betty cringed and fled.

She decided the party was ready for a Handel concerto grosso. The swarthy Staten Island school man came by with a can of ale in his hand and sparkling eyes. She asked him to keep an eye on the record player. He urged her to take a job in his department. She said she would think about it, and went to see how the food was holding out.

The beef roast was done. Francy wanted to carve it, but Betty brushed her aside, telling her that a man must do it. None of the men in the vicinity wanted to. She went outdoors. The older of the two men Harold had brought, a leathery painter named Ronald Turner, said he liked to carve. He made a little production of it, tying an apron high under his armpits, sharpening the knife till it cut a hair, dancing about the table for just the right position to carve in. Francy stood by watching, ready to carp at anything he did wrong, but his slices were thin, even, and straight against the grain.

Wherever Betty found herself, the faces told her that everybody was having a good time.

When she stood gazing out a window or when she went outdoors to watch the vociferous croquet game, she was aware of the curtains of her neighbors, who were home.

"Come on, kid, quit being a hostess," said Francy. "The party will take care of itself. Let yourself go."

Twice Betty came to herself leaning in a doorway staring at Julia, who liked to stand with one hip thrown out and back. Sometimes she would throw her head back in laughter, emphasizing her rather prominent Adam's apple; only the laughter was sensual and open, not her motions.

Both times when Betty caught herself trying to find more physical grace in Julia than was there to be found, she glanced about anxiously. No one had noticed her unseemly stares. She began looking for a dark corner from which she could give herself over to watching Julia as she ached to do. But she could not go far without being reminded of her duties as hostess, which would not permit her to disappear for long.

12

The croquet players came in and stood about in the dining room bragging in the guise of Scotch-and-soda toasts to one another. The next time Betty saw them they were seated around the kitchen table playing bridge.

Outside, she came upon Harold and five or six others seated on the grass at Turner's feet. He was in a lawn chair half-facing the light and was doing the talking.

"Betty Hollander! You must quit wandering around and begin enjoying a most relaxed and enjoyable party. Do sit here."

He stood and urged the chair toward her, but she disposed herself on the grass at the edge of the group.

"I was just trying to explain," he said, settling on the grass too, leaving the chair empty, "to some of these incorrigibly provincial natives of the five boroughs the only reason I ever come to New York is business. I'm here on a straight business trip—to see my gallery about my show this November."

"Ah," said Betty, "I noticed your boots."

He extended his legs and gazed at them. They were short cowboy boots made of soft dust-colored leather with a serpent design carved around the top.

"Hopi," he said with a note of deprecation, flicking the silver tips of his string tie. "I live on a ranch in Arizona, you know."

"All right," said Betty, making her voice sound pleasant, "I don't have any trouble seeing what's so good about Arizona. Just tell me what's so awful about New York."

"The hippopotami." His inflection, and his smile at the little stir of expectancy in his audience, seemed to her rehearsed. "I think of every man," he addressed himself to her, "as having a hippopotamus in him. A gross, hideous beast with a monstrous big maw. And when he defecates . . . Have you ever seen one defecate?" She said she had not. "There's one I know in the San Francisco zoo that likes to bellow, and scrape his tusks on the wall, and blow in his pool awhile, till he gets a good crowd at the fence gawking at him. Then he turns his rear end toward them and lets 'er fly. His tail goes like a little fan and sprays water and dung for yards in every direction, clear out onto the spectators. There, my friends," he said, leaning back on his arms, "you have the ego incarnate." There was a general stir of laughter, during which Betty, watching him, nodded sardonically. He no longer addressed himself to her directly. "In a civilized community, the hippos are seemly about keeping themselves under water. About all you see of them are nostrils, eyes, ears, once in a while the maw. But here, in New York, in Gehenna, they're on the sidewalks, they ride elevators, they buy and sell, a cocktail party is a congress of nude hippos." The last phrase he threw away. He cued his audience with a chuckle.

Betty laughed politely, though she thought him a show-off, and went back to the house.

Someone had put on a Bach suite for unaccompanied cello. Betty came to the doorway to make sure nothing else so demanding was put on, and found Francy alone in the room, listening. When the music ended, instead of relaxing back into her chair, Francy leaned forward into herself.

"The face of one who listens to the space between the stars."

At the sound of Turner's voice at her ear, Betty turned, prepared to jump on him for fanciness. No one else was near, yet he seemed to have been addressing not her but himself. He went away.

She was looking at his ornate phrase to see if it meant something, when Julia came strolling along with downcast eyes.

"Honey," said Betty and blushed at saying the word. "Honey, do you ever listen to the space between the stars?"

Julia frowned and shrugged impatiently. "Not so's you'd notice," she said over her shoulder as she turned around and left.

Betty took this to be a reproof for the phoniness of her own question. She started after Julia to apologize, but before she had gone three steps she stopped, not knowing what to say.

13

Toward eleven Cedric yodeled to her from the open front door. His complexion was albinistic; one eye was pale green and the other pale blue. She had forgotten having invited him. She had forgotten he existed. He brought with him a dapper friend named René Stern, whom Betty had heard about for years; René was a gay seducer and a reporter for the UP. Cedric apologized for being late and presented her with two records for a housewarming present. She offered to make the introductions; they said they'd rather just circulate.

René, who had been peering about, put his fingers on Betty's forearm in a manner that looked friendly but felt intimate. "What a delightful surprise, Mrs. Hollander. It's been some time since I've been in a gathering of new people where I don't have to pass if I don't want to." He was olive-skinned and hazel-eyed, and his accent had Main Line in it. Before she could speak, he directed her attention out the front door. Julia and Bob Flanders were coming up the path. "Who's the chick with Bob?"

"Julia Strong. She is a promising young contralto."

"Fabulous."

She moved ahead of him and spoke to Bob. "I thought you had to leave at nine thirty?" The voice in which she uttered this rudeness was friendly enough. "Well, it's nice you could stay after all." She took Julia's hand and patted it, paying no attention to whatever Bob was saying.

As René closed in, she started to draw Julia aside.

"You know," said Julia, "I got to go to the little girls' room and put some of that cherry-red on my lips."

Betty winced at the gross coyness of this and at the vamp swagger with which Julia walked away; but when Betty glanced at the three men, she was surprised to see that not even Cedric looked disgusted and that the other two were ogling Julia up the steps. With intense relief she felt that she had been wrong to see Julia as vulgar and gauche; Julia really was as desirable as she had found her to be.

The corner of her mouth twitched when she looked at the labels of the records Cedric had brought, sweet tunes played by a conventional band. She would have put the discs away with a thank you, had René not taken them from her and gone to put one on the turntable.

She turned to Cedric. "Is he part Negro?"

His eyes sparkled. "Why do you ask?" He laid his boneless finger on her wrist. "Did he hint?"

"He said he didn't have to pass unless he wanted to. Not that I care. But why did he bring the subject up?"

"Darling," said Cedric, almost breathing into her ear, his eyes flicking about as though for eavesdroppers, "everything about him is so deliciously louche." He lingered over the *sh* sounds.

She restrained her impulse to back away from Cedric. "You know him well?"

"How old is he? Has he ever been married? Is he part Negro? Does he publish poetry under a pseudonym?" Cedric leaned back, his eyes became liquid, his voice lowered in pitch. "He is my closest friend since Winton."

René came up, rescuing her from Cedric's complicitous smile, invited her to dance, and would not accept her refusal. She had disliked him on sight, mostly for the calculation in his gonadotropic glances. She knew she did not dance well, and she intended not to enjoy dancing with him. He did not exactly lead, yet he did not let her lead. Somehow, in a way as blurry yet steady as the music, he managed to make her dance better than she could ever remember having danced.

14

As she approached the door of the laundry room, which was a sort of lean-to added on the rear of the house proper, she saw Julia and René not quite touching noses, their heads moving gently up and down. She stood at the screen door watching.

"See?" he said in his smooth ironic voice. "It's much better than kissing. What did I tell you?"

"Oh, go on." Julia began laughing again.

"I'll prove it."

He held her close and kissed her a long time.

They were dimly illuminated by reflected light, and Betty was close enough to be able to see every detail of their embrace. She thought of going away, but decided that it would be rude of her to do so, for the noise of her moving might interrupt the kiss. After all, it was just young people kissing at a party. As long as chance had stationed her there, she would watch. She could not help watching. When René's hand moved lower down Julia's back and pressed her body hard against his and when their joined mouths opened to one another, Betty experienced an erotic excitement more intense than she had ever felt when she herself had been embraced by a man. Even as she gave herself over to their kiss, she felt a terrible resentment that no man had ever excited her like this.

The kiss slowly ceased. Without letting go of one another, René and Julia began not quite rubbing noses again.

"What did I tell you?" said René. "This is much better than kissing, Julia baby. No? Or shall we do it again till you are really convinced?"

His words struck Betty as being utterly insincere and Julia's laugh mere flirting.

Julia turned in her laughter, saw Betty, and pulled guiltily away from René.

"What gives?" He glanced over his shoulder. "Ah, Betty Hollander, the cause of all this joy. I was just demonstrating the power of nose-rubbing *à la Chinoise*."

Glancing in embarrassment, Julia hurried past Betty into the kitchen and then out of sight.

"Mr. Stern," Betty said. She was set to attack, without having decided where to attack him.

"Yes?"

She noticed the crow's feet at the corners of his eyes and recalled what Cedric had said about his age.

"How old are you?"

"Twenty-seven."

"In a pig's eye you're twenty-seven."

"What gives?" he was saying as she left him there. "What gives around here?"

She poured whiskey into a tumbler, drank it down, shuddered hard, put on the Muggsy Spanier record, and went up to her bedroom. She lay on the bed in the half-dark alone, come what would.

At first the images of caressing Julia that rose in her mind were erotic, but without emotion. "This is wrong" kept ringing in her ears. She clenched her jaws and set out to insult tomorrow's conscience. She tried to make the images deliberately lewd, but they all melted into a kiss. They had no emotional power over her until they became a kiss. She gave up trying to insult her desire, and lay on the bed, dry of throat and rigid from head to toe, imagining herself and Julia embracing in a dark place, kissing and being kissed.

15

She found Julia and René outside in the lawn chairs, leaning toward one another, their feet touching.

"There are only two ways to prevent the destitution of overpopulation," René was saying, "more war or less love. I don't mean less sex. I mean sterile sex, fewer and smaller families, and loveless institutions."

She made the two acknowledge her presence by asking if they needed a drink. Julia pushed her question aside.

"You know, René, you sound like a Witness," said Julia.

"Oh?"

"Except you're more intellectual. You know, they believe the world came to an end in nineteen fourteen."

"Yes?" he said. "They were just one war off, and this is hell nor are we out of it."

Betty could not keep from looking at him, though she thought him insincere in every word he said.

Julia put her hand on his arm. "My mama's a Witness. Tomorrow there's a big rally."

"In Yankee Stadium."

"Well, the main part is, but we live near the Polo Grounds so we're going there with the overflow. Mama doesn't care too much about seeing. As a matter of fact, she'd just as soon stay home and listen to things on the radio, only she's got it in her head she wants to sit in the stands right back of first base. She says she'll never get another chance to sit at first base in the Polo Grounds, so she's going to sit there in a five-dollar seat free and enjoy the word. Why don't you come with us?"

He grinned. "Oh, I'll come. I'll be there observing and observing. I spy for UP. Want to come up to the press box with me?"

"Mama," she complained.

Cedric called René from the living room window. René waved dismissively, but Betty gave him a little shove.

"Go on and see what he wants." Her heart thumped. "I've got something to tell Julia. Go on."

He smiled at her ambiguously, kissed both their hands, and left.

Julia was frowning a little.

"You know the 'Four Last Songs'?" Betty said urgently and stepped close to Julia. "I have a record of them you must hear." She began chattering without following her own words. "It's a wonderful version. You must listen. It would mean so much."

"Yeh? I know the Della Casa record." Julia moved toward the house. "She's great. Why don't we go inside? It's starting to get chilly."

It was nearly three o'clock. Some were dancing again.

16

Betty sat in one of the chairs, tears streaming from her eyes, racked by an enormous wanting.

Harold came by. Because she was sitting with her back to the dim light, she did not bother to wipe her face. Nevertheless, by the double glance he cast at her, she saw that he was aware something was wrong. She was setting herself to hate him.

He spoke of Turner. "He's one of us," Harold kept repeating. "He's a great artist and a great man, yet he's one of us."

This awe struck Betty as soggy and she doubted, without evidence, that Turner could be much of an artist. Yet what Harold said, and a quality in his voice, got to her.

She realized that she did not believe it possible for anyone to be like her and yet wonderful. Harold, whom she thought less than herself, was more than she if only because he believed in the possibility of being more. She squeezed his hand without minding its pudginess. He went away.

Thoughts of Julia returned and fell to wrenching her insides so cruelly she could hardly sit still. Her grief at Winton's death had been purer, but this yearning engulfed it. She longed to have him back, for if he had been alive, he would have safeguarded her from these passions that were boiling up in her, threatening to burst out into actions.

But a surge of the other sorrow made her longing for Winton fade and left her with one desolate thought: having lost her protection from wanting, she could not keep from wanting Julia, whom she did not really like.

17

When the record was being changed, she heard splashing sounds from her neighbor's pool, then a man's voice and a woman's giggle. She clapped her hands to her jaws at the thought of the pool lights going on and disclosing Julia and René swimming naked. Even while she bulged with this image, she recognized a low anxiety: let the swimmers be whites. She stalked the pool.

There were a man and two women swimming, all three whites. When she hissed at them, they came out, goose-pimply in the breeze and slapping themselves, their underwear sticking to their flanks. They were the Staten Island school man and two of the social workers from her former agency. They were amiably drunk, and kept whispering to Betty, as they dressed in the bushes between the two houses, that this was the best party they had been to in years.

As she went into the empty kitchen, she smelled smoke. One of the curtains at the window above the sink was blazing and the other was starting to burn. She gave a little scream and stared at the flames without moving. René was the first to run in; he filled a pan of water and doused the fire in a moment. The wall and ceiling were stained with smoke but not even the curtain rods were injured. Nevertheless, she felt shaken, especially at herself for not having stirred to put out the fire.

There was much talk. No one could imagine what had started the fire. No one admitted to having been in the kitchen for a long time. Betty was uneasily aware of Francy's watching her. Two-thirds of the party had gone home. Betty did not look at anybody. She found herself staring at Julia's yellow shoes.

"Come on," Francy said in a loud clear voice. "It's past three o'clock. We've had enough fun and done enough damage. Now let's go home—everybody."

People looked at Betty, and she looked at Francy with open gratitude.

Once they had assembled their things and stood relaxed in the hall, reluctant to say good-bye, Betty felt better disposed toward them. René cracked a little joke about a fireman, and Turner had something to say about swimming holes. People became aware of Julia's voice; she was telling Bob about her recital at Juilliard.

Julia addressed herself in turn to each of the men and to Francy and Betty. Betty, seeing the others smile with unabashed pleasure at Julia's languid flirtatiousness, felt such a pleasure stir in herself. Julia was confident and humorous; she made fun of herself for having been so scared and stiff, and she spoke of her singing teacher with admiration. When two or three of the other women social workers, as agitated as though they were wives, began to rush about emptying ashtrays and making sotto voce remarks about gaudy little bitches, Betty enjoyed their spite as proving Julia's power. Julia kept up her little star-performance for three or four minutes. At the first sign of masculine defection, she turned everything into thanks to Betty for the party, and the others joined in.

18

When Betty got into bed she shivered for a while. She did not want to sleep off her melancholy; though it pained her, it was intense.

Her consciousness went out like a light.

She was agitating a pan full of cherry jelly. As soon as the liquid was no longer turbulent, it would set, and she must avert this. There were thirty-eight wasps flying about, making a melodious violalike drone. One of them dived into the liquid jelly. She was worried about him, but he seemed to swim about happily, most of the time under the surface. She kept agitating the pan with one hand and fishing for him with the forefinger of the other hand. When she got him out she held him on her finger while he flapped the liquid off his wings. Close up, she saw that he was a tiny hippopotamus with wings. He opened his mouth, uttered a high-pitched bellow, and flew off thrumming as though nothing had happened. Then all thirty-eight flying hippos hovered over the jelly, formed the word FREE in the air, and, holding the formation, flew away from her very fast, till presently all she saw was the tiny word receding, though the viola sounds remained as clear and loud as ever. She awoke in tears, for she had not kept the liquid sufficiently agitated and the jelly had set; no little flying hippos would ever be able to bathe in it again; hereafter they would have to walk on the tough, sticky surface.

Her consciousness clicked back on.

If the hippo was the ego, the jelly would be the id. And then? How dull. She lay in bed listening to the birds and thinking of the party. She writhed under a pang of sadness sharp as a stab of pleurisy, and breathed irregularly through her mouth.

Her mind was taken over by an image of Winton in the hospital bed as she had last seen him. She wanted him back. She could hardly bear not having him. She writhed, and chewed the pillow.

19

She put on brown walking shoes, a beige skirt, and a white blouse, and carried a flat brown purse and a black umbrella. She went by bus, ferry, and subway, because she wanted to be with ordinary people; also, she did not trust herself to drive.

Twenty minutes before the announced starting time, she emerged from the subway west of the Polo Grounds. As she hurried down the hillside she caught a glimpse of part of the shadeless temporary bleachers out beyond left center field; they appeared to be more than half filled already. A helicopter hovered over the stadium.

On the path leading to the grandstand she was paced by a stout colored woman who waddled stiffly and who was closing a tasseled violet umbrella as she went. Two Negro and two white smiling men in badges and arm bands blocked the ramp to the stands. One of the men wore a straw hat on the black band of which was printed in phosphorescent pink letters: PRAYER WORKS. The woman just ahead of Betty waggled her parasol and cried in a well-controlled shout: "Glory, brothers! I've had the spirit all day! First thing I got up this morning, I felt the spirit and it's just been getting stronger as the hours roll by! It's in my heart." Betty saw she was wearing a badge; the men waited till Betty had gone on a way down toward the field and then let the woman, who was steadily shouting, through to the stands.

On the descending ramp a young white woman and two small girls lay in the shade with their heads against the wall in the postures and with the unresponsive eyes of those who are being allowed to die in public places. The three were in pink frocks with white bobby socks and black leatherette shoes. The mother had a large costume-jewelry diamond clipped onto the top of her left ear. By each chewing child stood a box of Crackerjack.

Betty emerged onto the field intending to go straight for the grand-stand behind first base, but the sight of the vast crowd stunned her. An usher asked her in a kindly voice if she didn't want to sit, there were still some seats down front. She let him seat her, so that she might have time to take her bearings. She was on a folding chair in the sixth row, in the full sun, slightly infield from third base.

On the field beyond the rope were batteries of loudspeakers trained on the congregation. From them came blurred music of the kind which gets housewives in supermarkets to buy more than they want of things they do not need. When the helicopter went away, music and crackle from the speakers pained her ears. In the clearing were sprays of flowers, upright palm branches, electronic equipment, persons bustling, and a cluster of Witnesses dressed in costumes of other nations. The music stopped, and a little man went up to the microphone on the speaker's stand out beyond second base. In a Scandinavian accent he introduced visitors from other countries, especially a long grinning man from Ghana in bright robes. The little man announced the next number, which turned out to be an ar-ranged hymn. Betty could not decide whether the singing came from a record or from Yankee Stadium. The Polo Grounds did not join in.

She tried to recall when she had last sung a song with any group on any occasion. The most recent one she could think of was "Auld Lang Syne" at a New Year's Eve party the year before she had met Winton. She did not remember that a couple of times she and Winton and Cedric had spent part of New Year's Eve in front of a television set watching the celebrators in Times Square. On those occasions she had joined the two men in shaking her head at all that grim fun, though secretly she had liked it a little for those others to sing "Auld Lang Syne" for her. Now she looked contemptuously at these who were having their hymns sung for them.

Far over in right field she saw a white-sweatered figure leaping before a section of the grandstands and waving its arms. She got up and started to move in that direction, circling in front of the grandstands, in order to see what it might be doing. On the way she was distracted by a sign up in the stands: DEAF AND DUMB—HARD OF HEARING. From where she stood, there seemed nothing odd about the people in the vicinity of the sign. She stared up into the packed stands in which, even if she had access to them, she scarcely had the heart to go looking for Julia. She felt like crying. She had never seen so many people in one place.

Another hymn started up. The white sweater out in right field was flipping again. She moved toward it. It was a blond athletic young man cheerleading a couple of busloads of white and Negro young men and women strung out behind a streamer which identified them as the Jesus Ralliers of the Ozarks. They wore white sweaters with red JR's on the chest. Betty could not make out what their cheers said. They accompanied every stressed cry with a short hard punch held close to the belly, left, right, left, right. People in the vicinity beamed at the Ralliers.

She became aware of a different sort of motion. A tall man looking down into a reflex camera backed into her.

"Watch where you're going," she said.

He apologized. Then, seeing that she was not a Witness either, he said, "I'm trying to find some place to stand where I can get them all in."

20

In a flat reasonable voice the loudspeakers greeted the multitudes and announced that the government of the United States, like every other government, had failed to do God's bidding but was doing the devil's work by hastening Armageddon. A ripple of applause started in Yankee Stadium but died out before it got far into the Polo Grounds.

It excited Betty to hear the obvious wickedness of governments spoken of in public to scores of thousands of ordinary people, even in the language of stale apocalypse. She had not heard words of such a kind mass-spoken since before the war; but that message, which had seemed so fierce then and now seemed so tame, had been no more than that one government did better or worse than another. The rule of nations was ordained by Jehovah-God not to succeed and Jehovah-God's kingdom had already come, beginning in the fall of 1914. If you'd read your Bible correctly, especially Ezekiel and Revelations, you would see how affairs were fulfilling God's world-scheme. The H-bomb fitted in; it was the devil's invention. Each announcement was greeted with applause.

If the speech had been reasonable, Betty would have argued against it. Because it was hopelessly absurd, she did not resist the satisfaction it made her feel; but because she thought this satisfaction degenerate, she quit following the speech. Without the words, the noise of the loudspeakers swarmed all over her mind like hysteria. She clutched with her eyes at the people near at hand.

A young man in the nearest row was contemplatively eating grapes and spitting the seeds at a post. A mother clapped her hand over the mouth of a child who had leaned against her to ask something; the child did not squirm. Betty realized she had seen no child running around nor heard any child laugh or cry. Nobody either met her eye or seemed to avoid meeting it. Nobody seemed to want much, except the end of the world.

21

In the press box, which was not half filled, she sat on the first available chair and did not engage by word or glance with any of the others; René was not there. She scrutinized as from an eyrie this field full of those who called themselves the other sheep. After a time she found her eyes sliding across the crowd indifferently and resting on the vacant gazebo of a speaker's stand; she sat back in her chair and closed her eyes.

"You know," one reporter said, "the President's mother is a Witness."

"Poor woman," said another, "her son is a minion of Satan."

147

All bad men are going to kill each other off in Armageddon, which will take place within the life span of many now living. The other sheep will survive and, together with a flock of resurrected sheep, will spend a thousand years cleansing the earth of its ruins and planting the earthly paradise.

Betty thought: They cannot think about last things nor leave them alone. Neither can I. Last things are my murk. Those who think best, the scientists, do not speak about last things. Yet they are the ones who pushed the Last Thing into everybody's mind.

René's smooth voice said in her ear, "You look like you're having a good chiliasm."

She opened her eyes, intending to say something rude, or to glance at him balefully and turn her back on him. Only his lips smiled; his eyes were fearful.

"Come look through the binoculars. I've spotted a couple of beautiful grasshoppers for you. It helps a person forget there's a plague of them."

The high-powered glasses swiveled on a pivot. René carefully focused them and then gave his place to Betty. She saw a girl adorned with vermilion, green, violet, and phosphorescent orange; her coiled bleached hair had glass fruit in it. Beside her leaned a man in a short-sleeved Hawaiian shirt, whose right arm was only slightly longer than its sleeve; from the stump grew three processes with which he was stroking her arm. He nudged her nigh breast with the stump. Frowning coquettishly, she batted her eyes, lifted his arm, and rubbed the processes against her cheek.

Betty looked here, then there.

The speech was naming Jehovah-God's enemies. The most important were the Communist party, the Protestant and Catholic clergy, and every government of any kind.

"*Illegitimati non carborundum*," said René.

"What does that mean?"

"Don't let the grasshoppers eat you down." He trained the binoculars on a spot above first base. "Here's another one for you."

It was Julia beside her mother. Betty felt the blood rush to her heart. Her ears rang. She dimly resented René for prying into her so deviously, but he had found Julia for her. Resentment of him, like the rest of her turmoil, was blotted out by a surge of desire to be with Julia. A touch of dizziness closed her eyes for a moment. Watching again, she saw Julia say something to her mother, and then pass down the row to the aisle and go down the steps toward the nearest exit.

"What's the matter?" said René.

Betty avoided his eyes. "I've got to go to the john." She was aware, as she hurried out, that he was looking for Julia through the binoculars. On the stairs she heard him call after her.

22

Just as Betty was going into the women's toilet nearest first base, someone came out of the exit door, and she heard Julia's voice cry, "René!" Betty immediately came back out, and was aware of René's lifted eyebrows when he glanced at her.

"Betty, you too?" said Julia. "It's quite a coincidence, isn't it?" She was flipping the tip of her nose with her forefinger and looking from one to the other.

"Not a bit," said René. "You said you'd be at first base. I'm reporting, Betty's slumming. Didn't you know, sweet stuff, you're the flypaper and we're the flies?"

Julia kept glancing from under raised eyebrows. Betty's throat aborted a word.

There were several people standing around in the large corridor, most of them munching, licking, or drinking. A little squirrel-voiced woman near them was telling an usher she was afraid she would lose her way home.

"So you couldn't stand it?" René said to Julia.

"Well, it's pretty hard to take. All that gobbledygook. I told Mama I'd wait for her down here."

"Now you just listen to me, lady," the usher said in a rough, emotionless voice. He looked like a train conductor. "We'll get you home after the meeting. We'll get you home. You just don't worry."

"The subway scares me, the subway scares me. That's the thing and I'm far away from here. Oh."

Julia took her finger from the tip of her nose and leaned toward René familiarly. "You remember what I told you last night?"

"What did you tell me last night?" He made as though to rub noses.

She let him get close, then with a pulling hand pushed his head to one side. She said something Betty could not hear, and rolled her eyes.

René caught Julia's hand, then looked at Betty. "She said she betted you would remain true to the memory of your husband. That's a rare thing, you know."

Julia ducked her head away. "I just mean."

"It was a tribute," said René.

Betty nodded. Her heart clenched.

"I got the name of the place in my purse, mister," said the little woman. "I'll show it to you."

"Now you don't need to do that, ma'am," said the big man roughly, restraining her arm.

"It's a number," she said. "I was wrong, it isn't a name, it's a number. One of the brothers got it for me. He just buzzed and asked. They're Jews. I prop my chair against the door of my room at night. Isn't that all right? They don't make me pay anything. They don't want the word. They asked me to watch their TV with them. I don't. What do you think?"

"Listen," said the usher sternly. "You just listen."

"I'm to go home tomorrow."

The speakers issued loud, Yankee Stadium applause; fainter applause came down directly from the Polo Grounds above them. Ushers shook hands. The countermen slapped spatulas, lined up paper cups, and wiped counters. The alarmed woman searched her usher's face, smiled, and gave out squirrely chirps. The applause went on much longer than any other had done.

"Do you know why they're so happy?" said René. "Because they are so many. Betty, did you hear how many they claim are in attendance? Two hundred and fifty-three thousand. They won't fight, they won't vote, all they want is to have the earth scorched so they can take over." He was keeping an eye on Julia, who was looking at the first hurriers coming down the tunnel.

René suddenly stepped in front of an elderly couple walking down the corridor. They apologized to him. The man took the woman's arm and guided her around René. René cupped his hands and shouted upward, "You are a plague of locusts!" The woman looked over her shoulder and nodded pleasantly to him. Julia bent with laughter.

"What are you going to do about them?" René said to Betty. "There are nine hundred thousand of them. The sun never sets on them. What are you going to do?"

"Nothing. What are you?"

"Love them of course. I'm not much on churchgoing. I'm just the Golden Rule type. I'm going to love them as I love myself. Okay?"

Betty turned to Julia and asked her the question; but her voice was so urgent that Julia took a half step backward.

"Well," said Julia, addressing herself to René, who took her hand again, "I'm going to go home and work on 'The Trout' tonight—that is, after Mama calms down enough to leave me alone. I'm going to sing the best I can and have me a ball once in a while, that's what I'm going to do about it."

Betty told herself many things. She had as much right to touch Julia as René did, but at the moment she ought not to try because she could not do it casually. Another time. There were many little plans she could make to see Julia often, reasonable plans, friendly gestures: a weekend at the Tanglewood Festival of Music, a picnic with Francy, dinner and a play, who could say what all? There was much to hope for. Patience, caution, restraint. Her heart paid no attention to her head and began voiding its desire.

Julia let René not quite rub noses. When he brushed lips, she stretched away to look for her mother among the throng debouching sluggishly through the exit tunnel.

Betty looked at them coldly. This mere flirt who happened to be able to sing well, and this desperate seducer—they both used sex as it were to immunize themselves against trouble. But in the land of the sick, Betty thought, it is shameful to be well; they were carriers, criminally negligent, cowards who dared not face the world unless inoculated with sex.

They became aware of her gaze on them. René raised a finger, then went over to the squirrely woman. Julia, eyes flicking over the emerging crowd, leaned against Betty, shoulder to shoulder, arm along arm, and said something in a friendly voice. Betty did not listen to what she said. The touch she had longed for, Julia's voluntary touch, was making its way into the muscles of her arm and shoulder, and she watched to see if it would spread to her heart. She was so confident it would not she did not even move away.

René led the little woman up to Betty and assured her that Betty was a social worker who knew the city well and would see that she got home safely. The woman said she didn't know and looked at them suspiciously. She said there were so many. She came from Milwaukee but the last forty-five years she had lived in Ontario. Her husband died last winter of blood poisoning; stabbed his foot with a pitchfork.

"There's Mama!" cried Julia and began waving.

With irony, fury, and gratitude, Betty said thank you to René, who winked and followed Julia. Betty took the little woman by the elbow. The woman peered up into Betty's eyes.

"Why, you're crying, miss. It's because it's too much. There's so many. Come along."

Betty dashed the tears from her eyes and let the little woman let her help her. On their way out to a taxi, a middle-aged Texan with pop eyes and a mole on his Adam's apple asked them if they were saved. The little woman chirped that she was. Betty refused the leaflet he was handing out by keeping her head bowed.

A white young man and a black young woman passed hand in hand, gazing into one another's eyes.

23

On the ferry to Staten Island she gazed for a while at the Statue of Liberty, that ugly thing standing for a thing once beautiful. It occurred to her that she had better begin looking for something to want, for there was not much time, though as much as always. Meanwhile, till she found it, she had better do what would keep her conscience clear. She would take at least a part-time job with the Staten Island schools. This was no more what she really wanted than was the end of the world or a love affair with Julia, but it was what she could do and it was worth doing. For the time being she might as well try wanting what she had left.

Sandra

A F E W years ago I inherited a handsome, neo-Spanish house in a good neighborhood in Oakland. It was much too large for a single man, as I knew perfectly well; if I had behaved sensibly I would have sold it and stayed in my bachelor quarters; I could have got a good price for it. But I was not sensible; I liked the house very much; I was tired of my apartment-house life; I didn't need the money. Within a month I had moved in and set about looking for a housekeeper.

From the moment I began looking, everyone assured me that I should get a domestic slave. I was reluctant to get one, not so much because of the expense as because of my own inexperience. No one in my family had ever had one, and among my acquaintances there were not more than three or four who had any. Nevertheless, the arguments in favor of my buying a slave were too great to be ignored. The argument that irritated me most was the one used by the wives of my friends. "When you marry," they would say, "think how happy it will make your wife to have a domestic slave." Then they would offer, zealously, to select one for me. I preferred to do my own selecting. I began watching the classified ads for slaves for sale.

Some days there would be no slaves listed for sale at all; on Sundays there might be as many as ten. There would be a middle-aged Negro woman, twenty-two years' experience, best recommendations, $4,500; or a thirty-five-year-old Oriental, speaks English, excellent cook, recommendations, $5,000; or a middle-aged woman of German descent, very neat, no pets or vices, good cook, recommendations, $4,800. Sensible choices, no doubt, but none of them appealed to me. Somewhere in the back of my mind there was the notion of the slave I wanted. It made me restless, looking; all I knew about it was that I wanted a female. I was hard to satisfy. I took to dropping by the Emeryville stores, near where my plant was located, looking for a slave. What few there were in stock were obviously of inferior quality. I knew that I would have to canvass the large downtown stores to find what I wanted. I saw the ads of Oakland's Own Department Store, announcing their January white sale; by some quirk, they had listed seven white domestic slaves at severely reduced prices. I took off a Wednesday, the first day of the sale, and went to the store at opening time, nine forty-five, to be sure to have the pick of the lot.

Oakland's Own is much the largest department store in the city. It has seven floors and two basements, and its quality runs from $1,498 consoles to factory-reject cotton work socks. It has a good, solid merchandising policy, and it stands behind its good in a re-assuring, old-fashioned way. The wives of my friends were opposed to my shopping in Oakland's Own, because, they said, second-hand slaves were so much better trained than new, and cost so little more. Nevertheless, I went.

I entered the store the moment the doors opened, and went straight up to the sixth floor on the elevator. All the same I found a shapeless little woman in the slave alcove ahead of me picking over the goods— looking at their teeth and hair, telling them to bend over, to speak so she could hear the sound of their voices, stick out their tongue, like an army doctor. I was furious at having been nosed out by the woman, but I could not help admiring the skill and authority with which she inspected her merchandise. She told me something about herself. She maintained a staff of four, but what with bad luck, disease, and her husband's violent temper she was always having trouble. The Federal Slave Board had ruled against her twice—against her husband, really, but the slaves were registered in her name—and she had to watch her step. In fact she was on probation from the FSB now. One more adverse decision and she didn't know what she'd do. Well, she picked a strong, stolid-looking female, ordered two sets of conventional domestic costumes for her, signed the charge slip, and left. The saleswoman came to me.

I had made my decision. I had made it almost the moment I had come in, and I had been in agonies for fear the dumpy little shopper would choose my girl. She was not beautiful exactly, though not plain either, nor did she look especially strong. I did not trouble to read her case-history card; I did not even find out her name. I cannot readily explain what there was about her that attracted me. A certain

154

air of insouciance as she stood waiting to be looked over—the bored way she looked at her fingernails and yet the fearful glance she cast from time to time at us shoppers, the vulgarity of her make-up and the soft charm of her voice—I do not know. Put it down to the line of her hip as she stood waiting, a line girlish and womanly at once, dainty and strong, at ease but not indolent. It's what I remember of her best from that day, the long pure line from her knee to her waist as she stood staring at her nails, cocky and scared and humming to herself.

I knew I should pretend impartiality and indifference about my choice. Even Oakland's Own permits haggling over the price of slaves; I might knock the price down as much as $300, particularly since I was paying for her cash on the line. But it wasn't worth the trouble to me. After three weeks of dreary looking I had found what I wanted, and I didn't feel like waiting to get it. I asked the saleswoman for the card on my slave. She was the sixth child of a carpenter in Chico. Chico is a miserable town in the plains of the San Joaquin Valley; much money is spent each year teaching the people of Chico how to read and write; "chico" means greasewood. Her father had put her up for sale, with her own consent, at the earliest legal age, eighteen, the year of graduation from high school. The wholesaler had taught her the rudiments of cooking, etiquette, and housecleaning. She was listed as above average in cleanliness, intelligence, and personality, superb in copulation, and fair in versatility and sewing. But I had known as much from just looking at her, and I didn't care. Her name was Sandra, and in a way I had known that too. She had been marked down from $3,850 to $3,299. As the saleswoman said, how could I afford to pass up such a bargain? I got her to knock the price down the amount of the sales taxes, wrote out my check, filled out the FSB forms, and took my slave Sandra over to be fitted with clothes.

And right there I had my first trouble as a master, right on the fifth floor of Oakland's Own in the Women's Wear department. As a master, I was supposed to say to Sandra, or even better to the saleswoman about Sandra, "Plain cotton underwear, heavy-weight nylon stockings, two dark-blue maid's uniforms and one street dress of conservative cut," and so on and so on. *The slave submits to the master:* I had read it in the FSB manual for domestic slave owners. Now I find it's all very well dominating slaves in my office or my factory. I am chief engineer for the Jergen Calculating Machine Corporation, and I had had no trouble with my industrial and white-collar slaves. They come into the plant knowing precisely where they are, and I know precisely where I am. It's all cut and dried. I prefer the amenities when dealing with, say, the PBX operator. I prefer to say, "Miss Persons, will you please call Hoskins of McKee Steel?" rather than "Persons, get me Hoskins of McKee." But this is merely a preference of mine, a personal matter, and I know it and Persons knows it. No, all that is well set, but this business of Sandra's clothes quite threw me.

I made the blunder of asking her her opinion. She was quick to use the advantage I gave her, but she was very careful not to go too far. "Would you like a pair of high heels for street wear?" I asked her.

"If it is agreeable with you, sir."

"Well, now, let's see what they have in your size. . . . Those seem sturdy enough and not too expensive. Are they comfortable?"

"Quite comfortable, sir."

"There aren't any others you'd rather have?"

"These are very nice, sir."

"Well, I guess these will do quite well, for the time being at least."

"I agree with you, sir."

I agree with you: that's a very different matter from *I submit to you.* And though I didn't perceive the difference at the moment, still I was anything but easy in my mind by the time I had got Sandra installed in my house. Oh, I had no trouble preserving the proper reserve and distance with her, and I could not in the slightest detail complain of her behavior. It was just that I was not to the manner bred; that I was alone in the house with her, knowing certain external things to do, but supported by no customs and precedents as I was at the plant; that I found it very uncomfortable to order a woman, with whom I would not eat dinner at the same table, to come to my bed for an hour or so after she had finished washing the dishes. Sandra was delighted with the house and with her quarters, with the television set I had had installed for her and with the subscription to *Cosmopolitan* magazine that I had ordered in her name. She was delighted and I was glad she was delighted. That was the bad thing about it— I was glad. I should have provided these facilities only as a heavy industry provides half-hour breaks and free coffee for its workers— to keep her content and to get more work out of her. Instead I was as glad at her pleasure in them as though she were an actual person. She was so delighted that tears came to her eyes and she kissed my feet; then she asked me where the foot basin was kept. I told her I had none. She said that the dishpan would do until we got one. I told her to order a foot basin from Oakland's Own the next day, along with any other utensils or supplies she felt we needed. She thanked me, fetched the dishpan, and washed my feet. It embarrassed me to have her do it; I knew it was often done, I enjoyed the sensuous pleasure of it, I admired the grace and care with which she bent over my feet like a shoeshine, but all the same I was embarrassed. Yet she did it every day when I came home.

I do not think I could describe more economically the earlier stages of my connection to Sandra than by giving an account of the foot washing.

At first, as I have said, I was uneasy about it, though I liked it too. I was not sure that as a slave she had to do it, but she seemed to think she had to and she certainly wanted to. Now this was all wrong of me. It is true that domestic slaves usually wash their master's feet, but this is not in any sense one of the slave's rights. It is a matter about which the master decides, entirely at his own discretion. Yet, by treating it as a set duty, a duty like serving me food in which she had so profound an interest as to amount to a right, Sandra had from the outset made it impossible for me to will not to have her wash my feet. She did it every day when I came home; even when I was irritable and told her to leave me alone, she did it. Of course, I came to depend upon it as one of the pleasures and necessary routines of the day. It was, in fact, very soothing; she spent a long time at it and the water was always just lukewarm, except in cold weather when it was quite warm; as they do in good restaurants, she always floated a slice of lemon in the water. The curve of her back, the gesture with which she would shake the hair out of her eyes, the happy, private smile she wore as she did it, these were beautiful to me. She would always kiss, very lightly, the instep of each foot after she had dried them—always, that is, when we were alone.

If I brought a friend home with me, she would wash our feet all right, but matter-of-factly, efficiently, with no little intimacies as when I was alone. But if it was a woman who came with me, or a man and wife, Sandra would wash none of our feet. Nor did she wash the feet of any callers. I thought this was probably proper etiquette. I had not read my *Etiquette for Slaves* as well as Sandra obviously had. I let it go. During the first few weeks, all my friends, and particularly all my women friends, had to come to observe Sandra. She behaved surely and with complete consistency toward them all. I was proud of her. None of the women told me that Sandra was anything less than perfect, not even Helen, who would have been most likely to, being an old friend and sharp-tongued. After the novelty had worn off, I settled down with her into what seemed to be a fine routine, as one does with a mistress. To be sure, it was not long before I would think twice about bringing someone home for dinner with me; if there was much doubt in my mind about it, the difference in Sandra's foot washing alone would sway me not to bring my friend along, especially if my friend was a woman.

When I would come home late at night she would be waiting for me, with a smile and downcast eyes. I went, in October, to a convention in St. Louis for a week. When I came back, I think she spent an hour washing my feet, asking me to tell her about the physical conditions of my trip, nothing personal or intimate but just what I had eaten and what I had seen and how I had slept; but the voice in which she asked it. One night I came home very late, somewhat high, after a party. I did not want to disturb her, so I tried to go to my room noiselessly. But she heard me and came in in her robe to wash my feet; she helped me to bed, most gently. Not by a glance did she reproach me for having disturbed her sleep. But then, she never reproached me.

I did not realize fully how much I had come to depend on her until she fell sick. She was in the hospital with pneumonia for three days and spent six days convalescing. It was at Thanksgiving time. I declined invitations out to dinner, in order to keep Sandra company—to tend to her, I said to myself, though she tended to herself very nicely. I was so glad to have her well again that the first time she could come to me I kept her in my bed all night—so that she might not chill herself going back to her own bed, I told myself. That was the first time, yet by Christmas we were sleeping together regularly, though she kept her clothes in her own room. She still called me sir, she still washed my feet; according to the bill of sale I owned her; I thought her a perfect slave. I was uneasy no longer.

In fact, of course, I was making a fool of myself, and it took Helen to tell me so.

"Dell," she said over the edge of her cocktail glass, "you're in love with this creature."

"In love with Sandra!" I cried. "What do you mean?"

And I was about to expostulate hotly against the notion, when it occurred to me that too much heat on my part would confirm her in her opinion. Therefore, seeming to study the problem, I relapsed into a brown study—under Helen's watchful eye—and tried to calculate the best out for myself.

I rang for Sandra.

"More Manhattans," I said to her.

She bowed, took the shaker on her tray, and left. She was impeccable.

"No, Helen," I said finally, "she does not make my pulses race. The truth is, I come a lot closer to being in love with you than with Sandra."

"How absurd. You've never even made a pass at me."

"True."

But Sandra returned with the drinks, and after she had left we talked about indifferent matters.

As I was seeing Helen to the door, she said to me, "All the same, Dell, watch out. You'll be marrying this creature next. And who will drop by to see you then?"

"If I ever marry Sandra," I said, "it will not be for love. If I have never made a pass at you, my dear, it has not been for lack of love."

I looked at her rather yearningly, squeezed her hand rather tightly, and with a sudden little push closed the door behind her. I leaned against the wall for a moment and offered up a short prayer that Helen would never lose her present husband and come looking in my part of the world for another. I could have managed to love her all right, but she scared me to death.

I thought about what she had told me. I knew that I was not in love with Sandra—there were a thousand remnants of Chico in her that I could not abide—but I could not deny that I needed her very much. What Helen had made me see clearly was the extent to which I had failed to keep Sandra a slave. I did not know whether it was her scheming that had brought it about, or my slackness, or whether, as I suspected, something of both. Some of the more liberal writers on the subject say, of course, that such development is intrinsic in the situation for anyone in our cultural milieu. It is a problem recognized by the FSB in its handbook. But the handbook advises the master who finds himself in my predicament to trade his slave for another, preferably some stodgy, uninteresting number or one who is deficient in the proper qualities—in my case, as I thought, copulating. The trouble with this sound advice was that I didn't want to get rid of Sandra. She made me comfortable.

In fact, she made me so comfortable that I thought I was happy. I wanted to show my gratitude to her. After she had straightened up the kitchen that evening I called her into the living room where I was sitting over the paper.

"Yes, sir?" she said, standing demurely on the other side of the coffee table.

"Sandra," I began, "I'm very proud of you. I would like to do something for you."

"Yes, sir."

"Sit down."

"Thank you, sir."

As she sat, she took a cigarette from the box, without asking my permission, and lighted it. The way she arched her lips to smoke it, taking care not to spoil her lipstick, annoyed me, and the coy way she batted her eyelids made me regret I had called her in. Still, I thought, the Chico in her can be trained out. She's sound.

"What can I give you, Sandra?"

She did not answer for a moment. Every slave knows the answer to that question, and knows it is the one answer for which he won't be thanked.

"Whatever you wish to give me, sir, would be deeply appreciated."

I couldn't think of a thing to buy for her. Magazines, movies, television, clothes, jewelry, book club books, popular records, a permanent wave every four months, what else could I get her? Yet I had started this offer; I had to follow up with something. In my uneasiness and annoyance with myself, and knowing so well what it was she wanted, I went too far.

"Would you like freedom, Sandra?"

She dropped her eyes and seemed to droop a little. Then tears rolled down her cheeks, real mascara-stained tears of sadness, of profound emotion.

"Oh yes, sir," she said. "Oh my God, yes. Don't tease me about it. Please don't tease me."

So I promised her her freedom. I myself was moved, but I did not want to show it.

"I'm going for a short walk," I said. "You may go to your room." I went for my walk, and when I came back she had prepared my foot bath. She had burned two pine boughs in the fireplace so that the room smelled wonderful. She had put on her loveliest dress, and had brushed her hair down as I liked it best. She did not speak as she washed my feet, nor even look up at my face. All her gratitude she expressed in the tenderness with which she caressed my feet and ankles. When she had finished drying them, she kissed them and then pressed them for a time against her breast. I do not think either of us, during these past few years, has ever been happier than at that moment.

Well, I had my lawyer draw up a writ of substantial manumission, and Sandra took the brass ring out of her left ear, and that was that. And that was about all of that, so far as I could see. She was free to go as she wanted, but she didn't want. She got wages now, it is true, but all she did with them was to buy clothes and gewgaws. She continued to take care of the house and me, to sleep in my bed and keep her own personal possessions in her own room, and to wash my feet as before. The manumission was nothing in itself, only a signpost that there had been some changes made. Continually and slowly changes kept being made.

For one thing, we began to eat together, unless I had guests in to dinner. For another, she began to call me Mr. Oakes. It seemed strange to have her go where she wanted, without asking me about it, on her nights out. I became so curious about what she could be doing that finally I asked her where she went. To night school, she said, learning how to type. I was delighted to hear that she had not been waisting her time at public dances, but I could not imagine why she wanted to learn typing. She had even bought a portable typewriter which she practiced on in her room when I was away. "Why?" she said. "My mother always said to me, 'Sandra, they can't fire slaves.' Well, I'm not a slave any longer. That was one nice thing about it, I wasn't ever afraid you'd fire me."

"But, my darling," I cried, "I'm never going to fire you. I couldn't possibly get along without you."

"I know it," she replied, "and I never want to leave either. All the same, I'm going to learn how to type." She had her own friends in to visit her; she even gave a bridge party one evening when I was not at home. But she never called me by my first name, she never checked up on me, she never asked me the sort of intrusive, prying question which a man hates answering. She kept her place.

Then she discovered she was pregnant. I immediately said I would assume all the financial responsibilities of her pregnancy and of rearing the child. She thanked me, and did not mention the subject again. But she took to sleeping in her own bed most of the time. She would serve breakfast while still in her robe and slippers. Her eyes were often red and swollen, though she always kept some sort of smile on her face. She mentioned something about going back to Chico. She began serving me canned soup at dinner. I drove her off to Reno and married her.

Helen had been right, I had married Sandra; but I had been right too, it wasn't for love. Oh, I loved her, some way or other, I don't know just how. But I married her simply because it was the next thing to do; it was just another milestone.

Nothing much happened for a while after we were married except that she called me Dell and didn't even take the curlers out of her hair at breakfast. But she hadn't got to be free and equal overnight. That was to take some months of doing.

First of all, as a wife, she was much frailer than she had been as a slave. I had to buy all sorts of things for her, automatic machines to wash the clothes and the dishes, a cooking stove with nine dials and two clocks, an electric ironer that could iron a shirt in two minutes, a vacuum cleaner, one machine to grind the garbage up and another to mix pancake batter, a thermostatic furnace, an electric floor waxer, and a town coupe for her to drive about to do her errands in. She had to get other people to wash her hair now, and shave her legs and armpits, and polish her toenails and fingernails for her. She took out subscriptions to five ladies' magazines, which printed among them half a million words a month for her to read, and she had her very bathrobe designed in Paris. She moved the television set into the living room and had a tear-drop chandelier hung from the center of the ceiling. When she had a miscarriage in her sixth month, she had a daily bouquet of blue orchids brought to her room; she had to rest, and pale blue orchids are so restful. She became allergic to the substance of which my mattress and pillows were composed, and I had to get a foam rubber mattress and foam rubber pillow, which stank. She finally insisted that we go to visit her family in Chico, so we finally did, and that we go to visit my family in Boston, so we finally did. The visits were equally painful. We began to go to musical comedies and night clubs. Helen had been right: my friends did not drop by to see us, and they were apt to be sick when I invited them to dinner. Still we weren't all the way.

One night I came home late from work, tired and hungry. Dinner was not yet started, because Sandra had been delayed by her hairdresser. She fixed pork chops, frozen green beans, and bread and butter, with canned apricots for dessert. I had done better myself. After dinner, after the machine had washed the dishes, I asked her if she would bathe my feet. I was so tired, I told her, my feet were so tired; it would be very soothing to me. But she said, in an annoyed voice, that she was feeling nervous herself. She was going to go to bed early. Besides, the silence she left behind her said, besides I am your wife now. She went to bed and I went to bed. She was restless; she twisted and turned. Every time I would shift my position or start to snore a little, she would sigh or poke me. Finally she woke me clear up and said it was impossible for her to sleep like this. Why didn't I go sleep in her former room? She couldn't because of her allergy, she had to stay in the foam rubber bed. So I moved into her room. And then I knew that she was my equal, for most of the equal wives of my friends lived like this.

Another night, I came home wanting very much to make love to her. She had avoided my embrace for a long while. She was always too nervous, or too tired, for the less she worked the tireder she became; or she was busy, or simply not in the mood. But tonight I would admit of no evasion. She was beautiful and desirable, and I knew how well she had once made love to me. Finally, I held her in my arms. She knew I wanted her, and in a way as odd as mine she loved me too. But there was no sensuous pressure of her body against mine, no passion in her kiss. She put her arms about my neck not to caress me but to hang like an albatross against me. She pressed her head against my shoulder not for amorous affection but to hide her face, to shelter it, in loneliness and fear and doubt. She did not resist me, or yield to me, or respond to me, or try to avoid me. She only went away and left me her body to do with as I pleased. And then I knew that she was free, for most of the free wives of my friends were like this with their husbands.

I had four choices, as I saw it: divorce her, have her psychoanalyzed, kill her, or return her to slavery. I was strongly tempted to kill her, but I was an optimist, I thought she was salvageable. Besides, who would do my housework for me? I made her a slave again.

It is a wise provision of the law that says no slave may be completely manumitted. Even substantial manumission provides for a five-year probationary period. Sandra had not passed probation. I had the necessary papers drawn up, told her, an hour before the men came, what was happening, and had her sent to the FSB Rehabilitation School in Colorado for a month.

She came back with the ring in her ear, saying sir to me, and the very first night she washed my feet. Furthermore, she made love better than she had done for a year. I thought we were to be happy again, and for a week we seemed to be. But the machines are still there to do most of the work, and she still has her allergy. She does what a slave is supposed to do, but it is an effort, she has to will it; it exhausts her.

One evening six months ago, I came home to find no dinner cooking, no foot bath waiting for me, no sign of Sandra in her room. I found her lying on my bed reading *McCall's* and smoking with a jewel-studded holder I had given her when she was my wife. She flicked an ash onto the rug when I entered the room, waved a languorous Hi! at me, and kept on reading. I had my choice; she had clearly set it up for me. I hesitated only a moment. I went down to the basement where I had stowed away the three-thonged lash which had been provided along with the manual of instructions when I first bought her, and I beat her on the bed where she lay.

I think I was more upset by the beating than Sandra was. But I knew I had had to do it. I knew I had neglected my duty as a master not to have done it long ago. I think now that all this trouble could have been averted if formerly I had only kept a firm hand, that is to say, had beaten her when she had risen too presumptuously. For the truth is, Sandra is happiest as a slave. That beating did her good, it kept her in place, and she knew where she stood. It is no doubt all right to free exceptional slaves, but not one like Sandra who is happiest when hoping, when wheedling and pleasing, when held to her place.

But the beatings I should have given her formerly would simply have hurt; she would simply have avoided getting them. Now, I am not so sure.

For she repeated the offense, exactly, within a month, and I repeated the punishment. It wasn't so bad for me the second time. She began seeing just how far she could go before I would bring out the lash. She cooked more and more badly till I gave her a warning one evening. When I had finished speaking, she sank to the floor, pressed her forehead against my foot, looked at me, and said, "Your wish is my command." The irony was all in the act and words, if irony there was, for there was none in the voice or face. The truth was, as she discovered the next evening when she served me corned beef hash and raw carrots for dinner, my lash is her command. She seems happier, in a way, after these distasteful blow-ups, comes to my bed voluntarily and with the welts still on her back, does her work well, hums sometimes. Yet she falls back into her old stubborn mood, again and again. There seems to be nothing else for me to do but beat her. The FSB manual supports me. Yet I find it repugnant, and it cannot be good for Sandra's skin. I had to lash her a week ago, and already, from the dirt she is allowing to collect on the living room rug, it looks as though I'll have to do it again. This was not what I had wanted. Of course, I have learned how to make the lash perform for me, how to make it sting without really damaging, how to make nine blows lighter than three. But it seems a pity to have to resort to this, when it was all quite unnecessary. It's my own fault of course; I lacked the training, the matter-of-fact experience of being a master, and I did not set about my duties as a master so conscientiously as I should have. I know all this, but knowing it doesn't help matters a bit. Sometimes I think I should have killed her, it would have been better for both of us; but then she will do some little act of spontaneous love, as now bringing me a cup of hot chocolate and kissing me lightly on the back of the neck, which makes me glad to have her around. Yet tomorrow I shall have to beat her again. This is not what I had wanted, and it cannot be what she wants, not really. We were uneasy and felt something lacking when she was a slave before, though we were happy too. We were altogether miserable when she was free. Yet this is not what either of us had ever wanted, though we are both of us doing what we must.

Rilla

O N E   O F   T H E reasons I went back to driving a cab was to steer clear of the fair sex. Driving a cab, you don't have to come any closer to women than "Thanks for the tip"—unless you want to. However, as my wife used to say, "Bert, you were born in the wrong house." She was talking about Scorpio and Gemini and the planets and such like, but you could get her meaning without too much trouble. That was before she was put away. Well, the main person I had to deal with in the Spee-Dee Taxicab Service was the expediter of course, and the swing-shift expediter was Rilla.

The afternoon I went on the job I didn't really pay too much attention to her. Emory introduced me to her, naturally, but the main contact I had with her was, she came out when I was wiping off my cab and gave me my record sheet.

"Here you are, Bert," she said as friendly as you please. "Did Mr. Emory tell you the clutch is bad on this Plymouth? Don't get stuck on a steep hill. You'll have to back down."

"Thanks, kid," I said. "The way the old man talked, the governor of California would be honored to ride in a limousine like this."

She had a nice laugh, a real nice laugh. In fact, she was well fleshed and I liked the way she dressed and I liked her coloring, so it's surprising she didn't make more of a first impression on me. I think it was the way she batted her eyes. She had nice eyes, shiny as a squirrel's, and long dark eyelashes. But she used them too much. She batted them at me when she wished me luck, and she looked at me up from under, sort of. Anyhow, when I got down to my stand at Twenty-second and Broadway, I didn't give her a second thought. I honestly didn't anticipate any more trouble from that quarter than I would from a waitress in a cafeteria.

When I was driving cab during the war they didn't have these two-way radios, so it was three or four days before I discovered I could listen in when the other drivers were gassing with Rilla. Mostly, she hadn't talked to me much. "Bert," she'd say, "go to Bonita Avenue," or some such place; and I'd say, "Okay." You don't get much of an idea from scraps like that. But one night about quarter to seven when everybody was holed in for dinner and not ready to step out any place yet, I snapped on the radio to tell her I was going to cruise for a while, I was sick and tired of the blinking neons, and I heard this conversation going on.

"Hey, Chester," Rilla was saying, "have you had a fare yet tonight?"

"Yes, from the Leamington to the SP station. It came to a dollar even. He didn't tip me a thing."

"Well, here's a woman that wants to be down to the San Francisco airport by eight forty."

"Hot dog!" Chester said. "I get a break. Where is she?"

Rilla told him the address, and then I heard another voice, I didn't know whose it was.

"Hey, Rilla, I just had me a customer."

"Mm-hmm," she said, very nonchalant, the way a person will when they think you mean more than you're saying.

"He was sloppy drunk and he kept saying he had a broken heart."

"Who was it?" said somebody else, but Rilla didn't say anything.

"He was wall-eyed and he had a mustache," says this same voice.

Then everybody else that's listening in, four or five, yell in chorus, "Percy Glasscock!" And Rilla makes a funny noise and clicks off the radio. She can click anybody and everybody off the radio any time she feels like it.

Well, naturally I didn't know all the ins and outs of the matter, but it seemed pretty rough to me to have the whole bunch of them jump on her at the same time. So she had broken Percy Glasscock's heart maybe; so she probably felt bad enough about it already without everybody jumping on her. That's the way I was figuring it, but still I didn't want to get mixed up in anything.

What I did was, when I clicked back on, I told her in a nice way I was going cruising, and when she said okay in a dispirited way, I asked her would she like a milk shake. Her voice perked up a lot at that, and she said she sure would, vanilla, and it was really lonely there in the garage by herself from four thirty till one. So I took one by for her and gassed awhile as she drank it. She was friendly as could be and I noticed how well built she was, and she kept tucking her blouse in more than I could see any call for, and she kept batting her eyes, which wasn't so good, and I went back onto the streets.

I went down to the Twelfth and Broadway stand and it was empty. Now mostly the other drivers hadn't been too talkative with me, which is what I wanted as much as anything else, so this time I just sat there having a good time watching the people walk by and playing my imaginary trombone. That was a habit I got into, left over from the days when I played in big bands, till the drink and my wife's trouble got me and I never went back to playing. So I was really surprised to see another Spee-Dee cab pull up behind me and this human ape step out with a forehead so low his cap sits on his eyebrows.

"Hello," he says, leaning in the window, "you're the new man."

This was the joker with the Percy Glasscock story. I recognized his voice, and I didn't like him already.

"Yep," I said, "Bert's the moniker." I got out to be sociable.

We shook hands, only he's got a grip like a vice.

"Ormie's mine," he said. "Pleased to meet you."

"Sure, Ormie," I said. I was feeling better. A guy like that, it would be a pleasure to call him Ormie ten times a minute.

"Well, how do you like the job?" he says.

Well, what does anybody in my situation say to a lead like that? You like it fine, Ormie, fine. Only I like to appear good-natured and peppy, as I appreciate such features in others; so what I did now was, I sort of tipped my hat and bowed a little and I said with such a fleet of cars and such fellow workers I was honored to be a member of the Spee-Dee Taxicab Service. Maybe I laid it on too thick, because he just stood there and hitched up his pants and looked at me sour. His little black eyes were so far apart you were surprised to see them work together.

"Say, Ormie," I said, "those are really nice socks you got there."

That was a little better. He hitched up his pants again to look at them and he puffed up like a kid. That's what they were, kid socks, red and yellow diamonds of that neon color they have nowadays that glows like it was alive. He looked like a pig that somebody had painted his ankles so they could catch him in the dark.

"Sure," he said, "I like 'em . . Rilla gave 'em to me."

"Is that so?" I said. I couldn't feature it. Besides, if she really did give them to him, I couldn't see the way he'd laughed at her on the radio.

"Yes, that's so," he said, tough. "Rilla's a nice kid, only you got to know how to handle her."

"Like you?" I said, really pleasant.

"What do you mean?" he said, suspicious as all hell.

When one of those guys begins pawing the dirt, what you've got to be is fast on your feet.

"Who's Percy Glasscock?" I asks, so he won't get up too much momentum.

"Percy Glasscock was a driver, see?" Ormie pokes one of those chopped-off cigars he wears for a finger against my chest. "He thought he could make some time with Rilla but he didn't get nowhere, see?" He keeps punching at the same place, very painful, only he's five inches taller. "There ain't nobody gets nowhere with Rilla so you'd might as well not try, see?"

"Sure," I said. He had me up against the window of the cigar store, and I don't mind saying it, his breath was not of the best. "Sure, she's a nice girl. That's what I always thought."

"I just don't want you to forget it, that's all. You and your milk shakes. She's poison."

Frankly, right then I'd just as soon I'd never met either one of them, so I just stood there. I won't say I wasn't sore, inside and outside. Ormie goes into the cigar shop, and from the way the guy waited on him it was clear to the naked eye it was just for the business and not for the friendship. Ormie cracks a couple of jokes, but the guy doesn't even crack a smile. I like the cigar man better from that minute on, even if he does wear a toupee.

The next afternoon when I came to work, who should be laughing and kidding in the office with Rilla but my old pal Ormie. You'd have thought they were bosom friends from the way they were laughing and pushing each other, and I can't deny it, she was as set up as he was.

"Hey, Ormie," I says behind my hand, only out loud, "ask Rilla if I can have my stuff."

"What's the matter, Bert?" she says.

"Yeh," he says, "what's the matter?" Little Sir Echo.

"You told me last night it'd be just as well if I didn't speak to her any more."

I winked at Rilla when I said that, so she'd be sure to see it was just a joke. Only nobody took it as a joke. Ormie got so mad he wanted to push me through the floor. He couldn't because Rilla was there, so he just went out to clean up his cab. And Rilla was mad at him too, but she was sweet as pie with me.

There were a couple of things I wanted to find out about her, how sweet was she really with me, and who wasn't she sweet with? You can have too much of a good thing.

"Say," I said, "those are sure loud socks Ormie's got on."

"Yes?" she said, and she put on lipstick, only she didn't need any more lipstick that I could see.

"Did you give them to him?" I said. "He said you did."

"Sure," she said, "don't you think they're cute?"

"No," I said, real mournful. "I've got to be honest with you. I don't think they're cute. The least I can say is, they're not cute."

"Well, Ormie likes them," she says, and she straightens a shoulder strap. One thing about Rilla, if you're around her she sees to it you have a hard time looking at anything but Rilla. Of course she's got something to look at. "Ormie likes them and he's the one that's wearing them." She was as pert as you please and I liked her for it.

"When's your nights off, kid?" I said.

"Wednesday and Thursday."

"How about going out with me Thursday?"

She didn't even pause a second, and the way she said, "I'd love it," I really thought she meant it. In fact it worried me a little how much she meant it, me being practically a stranger as you might say. About that time Chester came in, and she was as friendly with him, batting her eyes and all, as with anybody else. The truth is, I didn't have her figured out.

This Chester now, he was a good enough fellow, but nothing out of the ordinary that I could see. He wasn't any taller than I am, which isn't tall enough, but he was thin and sort of frail looking. He had a big voice which he was always using real deep; in fact, it sounded flat most of the time it was so deep, like a kid playing grown-up. Now what would a woman see in a flat-chested little guy like that?

That same day I was just telling about, I found Chester standing in front of a pawnshop with his hands in his pockets and staring at the guns. He was such a sad sack I couldn't keep from trying to buck him up a little. It was a slow day, so I thought I'd tell him about some of my experiences as a hunter. But by the time he'd said a few things like "I've never gone to Trinity County" or "Me, I never even shot a thirty-thirty," I was dragged down so far I couldn't even finish the story I was on. That man just made me *tired*.

It was a good story too. My father and I went up on the Trinity Alps the summer I was fifteen, deer hunting. The first five or six days we didn't see more than half a dozen doe and not a buck, so the last day we lit out from camp early for a little valley my father had heard of, where practically nobody ever went; it wasn't too far from the Oregon border. Well, the long and the short of it is, we scared up as big a nine-point buck as I've ever seen and cornered him in a pocket of that valley where he couldn't get out. The way he came at us when he saw how we had him at bay, you wouldn't believe a deer had it in him if you didn't see it. My father told me I should never trust a deer at bay no matter how they act, and I believe him. I went back to that valley by myself once, a few years later, and I cornered me a doe in the same spot. Only I let her go. In fact I think even if I could have shot her legally I'd have let her go. She was a nice fat doe, scared to death, but she was game. The feeling it give a man to let a creature go like that, it's worth it.

Well, how could I tell a story like that to a character that probably never even saw a damned deer outside of a zoo?

"Say," I said, "Chester, I just remembered I promised to take something over to Rilla. I'll see you later."

He quit whistling. He'd been whistling between his teeth, "Do not forsake me, O my darling," and naturally I hadn't been too overjoyed talking to a whistler.

"Rilla," he says, "Rilla." He sort of snorted. "Just watch your step."

I was downright sorry for him, and it occurred to me that that was the way Rilla felt about him too. All the same it isn't pleasant to see a man be so hypocritical, talking with a woman and laughing real friendly with her but then speaking against her behind her back. So I didn't even answer him. I just drove away. I didn't even go to see Rilla. I thought I'd let it ride till Thursday and then we'd see what we'd see.

So that Saturday afternoon I'm lying on my bed reading a mystery and I hear the landlady showing a guy the next room and he takes it. There's a locked door between my room and his, but you can hear through it pretty well, if you're so inclined. I go out about four and who should be walking down the hall ahead of me but Chester himself. You can just imagine how my pulses began racing at the sight of him.

"Hey, Chester!"

He sort of jerks and looks around at me. "Where'd you come from, Bert?"

"I live here, next door."

"Well, by golly, let's go have something to eat before we clock in."

"Those were my sentiments exactly. Do you like chow mein?"

He liked chow mein. While we were shoveling six-bits' worth of it into our mouths, he said to me, "Have a good time Thursday night?"

"Sure," I said, looking at him sharp. "What were you thinking of?"

"Rilla. Ormie seen you coming out of Sweet's Ballroom with her."

"So what?"

"So nothing. Don't get sore at the drop of a hat. I just thought I'd let you know Ormie saw you."

"How do you know he did?"

"He was mentioning the fact."

"I suppose I've got to make an account of myself to Ormie every time I want to take Rilla to a damned dance and buy her a drink. Well, by God."

"Don't get so excited," he said, with a sort of little grin on one side of his face. "He's got nothing to go on."

"So he hasn't. What difference does it make? And how does he know he hasn't?"

"Look, Bert," he said and reached for his wallet. "Here's a ten-dollar bill. I'll lay it against a one-spot that you can't make any time with Rilla between now and Monday night."

I had a sneaking feeling I was being suckered into something, but by the time I saw his money I was so mad I didn't give a damn. I laid a dollar beside his ten. "Will you take my word for it?" I asked him.

"Oh, I'm next door to you," he said. "Get her into your room. I'll hear."

The way he grinned at me I felt like a heel, but I didn't back out. Still, when I was alone in my cab and had time to cool off, I began to think it would be the decentest thing to Rilla to not go through with it. For one thing, we'd had a good time all right Thursday night, but that wasn't all there was to it. When I was driving her home after the dance, she kept holding hands passionately. Can you imagine a man like me that's been married once for four years wanting to hold hands passionately? Anyway, she did, and she got me pretty well steamed up. I stopped the car and put my arm around her to kiss her but she ducked. I kept on trying and she kept on ducking, till finally I brought my other hand into play and she gave me a left jab in the ribs I could still feel Saturday night. So we didn't part on the best of terms, but I still wasn't mad enough at her to want to hurt her reputation. I just wanted to keep out of trouble, but here I was sucked into it. Besides I wasn't sure I could make the grade with her.

Still and all, I like to get along with people, so when she clicked me on about eight thirty and told me in that low-pitched, friendly voice of hers that I had a pickup, I couldn't be anything but friendly back with her. When a person likes you and likes to laugh a lot, there's no point in trying to do anything but like them back. At least when you're with them.

The address she gave me turned out to be an ice-cream joint, so I knew what she wanted. I decided to make peace and I took her up a milk shake.

Ormie's cab was parked out in front of the garage and when I opened the door to the office there he was coming out looking like the wrath of the Lord, with the finger marks on his cheek where Rilla had slapped him. I held the door open for him and took off my hat and bowed. He grunted like a hog and hit the milk shake up so it splattered in my face. If Rilla hadn't been there he wouldn't have stopped with a little tap like that.

She was crying, and by the time we'd got me mopped up and her calmed down we were pretty good friends again, and when she kissed me on the cheek good-bye I'd really decided to let Chester have my buck.

But just as I was going out she flips on Chester's radio to give him an order and there's Ormie's voice.

". . . *any* where you see him."

"What do you mean?" says Chester.

They'd obviously been having a conversation with the microphone left on.

173

"Look," says Ormie and you can just see that King Kong scowl on his face from the way he's roaring, "all you've got to do is find him and trail him. Let me know where he is, get it? Leave the rest up to me."

"Okay, Ormie," says Chester quick as he can. "Okay, anything you say."

Rilla snaps them off again and comes running over and grabs me by the arm.

"I'm scared of him," she says. "He's mean. Don't go out there, Bert. Go home. He'll calm down."

Those were my sentiments exactly, and if she'd let me alone I'd have done just that. But here I was put on my mettle by a woman.

"No," I said. What else could I say? "It would take a better man than that moron to scare me out." By God, for a minute I felt up to my own words.

I pulled her up against me and kissed her. It wasn't the best kiss in the world, I guess she was too upset to put her heart into it, but at least she didn't stop me. It's a good thing she wasn't too reciprocal with me right then because if she had been I think I'd probably have begun falling in love with her and that would have been a hell of a note.

I cruised up and down Foothill Boulevard, where nobody would be likely to look for me for the good and sufficient reason there isn't any business out here. They're not rich enough to not mind the money for a cab, and they're not poor enough to get a big boot out of riding in one. But about midnight a colored sailor hails me on the corner of Seminary; he's been up to Oak Knoll hospital where a friend of his was dying, and he wants to go to a place down on Fifteenth Street. Okay.

I avoid the main arteries as much as possible getting him there, but I hadn't any sooner than dropped the sailor and driven up a couple of blocks than I see a Spee-Dee cab leaning around the corner and heading straight down the block at me. Of course it may be one of a dozen but then it may be Ormie, and this is a damned dark street, Sixteenth or so down near Cypress, where the cops walk in pairs. He's coming like a bat out of hell, that's for sure, and I don't know his intentions. I would have had my radio on, only Rilla told me she was keeping me off the air so no one could find me. What I figured was, if this was Ormie he was going to block the street and try to grab me before I could back away. So just before he got to me I ducked up a double driveway onto the sidewalk. There wasn't anybody on it so I gunned her down to the corner, bumping on the driveways and walks and running over a toy that went pop, and dropped off the curb and got away without any trouble. But Ormie was trying so hard to catch me he swerved to hit me; he swerved too sharp and caught the rear fender of a parked car with the left corner of his front bumper; it tipped his cab over onto its right side. I laughed fit to kill as I drove away.

I didn't laugh long. As soon as the sirens began verging down there toward Ormie on his side, I began to get riled. When I passed a prowl car with its red lights winking I really got mad. It could have been for me. In fact it had been supposed to be for me. By God, thinks I to myself, that Ormie and his stooge Chester, who do they think they are? They think they can scare me off, do they?

It was twelve thirty and Rilla quit at one. I was supposed to stay on till two, but I drove straight to the garage and told Rilla to close up for the night. She didn't even argue a minute. She just said Ormie wasn't hurt bad and came along. When I told her what he was trying to do when he got hurt, she got so worried and upset that I had to quit being mad and try to kid her out of it. Besides, it had its humorous side all right, and I like to laugh as a rule. So by the time we'd had a couple of drinks in a place called the Bar None, she was over being scared and I was over being mad and we were both laughing, all keyed up like.

Rilla had such a throaty, hearty laugh it was a pleasure to watch her throw her head back and let her rip. In fact, in about fifteen minutes with her, she was so friendly and sexy and full of fun it just slipped out of my mind the run-around she'd given me two nights before. I kept her laughing. I told her about my grandmother that used to hear angels sing, and used to hit me on the head with her ear trumpet when she got mad, and died at ninety-seven. I told her how my brother and I ran away from home when we were about ten and a bull chased us to the top of a haystack where we had to sleep all night till the farmer came and rescued us. I had plenty of stories for her and she liked them. When she began wanting to hold hands again, I began to get real wrought up. I couldn't believe, holding her hand under the table and listening to her laugh and feeling her roll over against me once in a while, that she was only flirting with me. All the same, I avoided the direct approach.

I told her a story that happened to me when I was playing with Charlie Shaw's Chanticleers. It was a slow evening in a night club, and I'd tickled the vocalist with my trombone slide in the middle of a number so she'd jumped and taken a pratfall. She'd gotten so mad she'd started a free-for-all and Charlie had fired me.

Rilla laughed, but not too much. "You're kidding me," she said. "You never played with Charlie Shaw, did you?"

"You're darned tootin'," I said. "For two years. I made 'Smoke Gets in Your Eyes' with his outfit. Best record he ever made."

"Don't kid me," she said.

"Who's kidding who?"

"Why did you quit?"

"It's a rough life." I shrugged and spread my hands out. "The war came along. Look, I'll get that record on the juke box."

They had one of those machines in the Bar None where you put in a coin and tell a woman, who has hundreds of records to choose from, which one you want. I'd had her play Shaw's rendition of "Smoke" before, but this time she said she didn't have it any longer. She had five other recordings of it though, wouldn't one of them do?

I was pretty sad. But I didn't want to show it. If I looked hard enough I could find a copy of it in some secondhand store in town, but I wanted it right now for Rilla. That was bum luck.

"Too bad," I said when I sat down in the booth beside her, "they broke the record. It's a collector's item."

"Oh," she said, really sympathetic, "that's a dirty shame."

"That's the way the ball bounces," I said and laughed, sort of.

Then, by God, she did something I couldn't figure out. She took me and pulled my head down on her shoulder and patted me like I was a baby. I can't say I didn't like it.

"Say," I said, "Rilla, I've got that record. You want to hear it?"

"Where?" she said.

"Not too far," I said. "I just live a few blocks away."

I don't know what came over her to fall for a gag as old as that. I figured she'd changed her mind about me, or else she was drunker than I thought.

"Sure," she said, only not sexy any more, "sure, Bert." Not sexy at all; in fact, she sounded like she was talking to a baby.

She kept patting my leg while I was driving to my place. When I stopped the car, I guess I was drunk because I sort of flopped over with my head in her lap. She took advantage of me, and rubbed my head and kept calling me Bertie in such away that I couldn't tear myself away, but I really resented it, lying there enjoying myself like that. You give a woman an inch and she'll take all you've got.

When I had her in my room with the door closed behind her, and turned on the light so she could see I didn't have a record player or a record even, or nothing but a chair and a bed, I really felt good for a minute. If Chester's home yet, thinks I to myself, I've won my ten bucks. So I kissed her first thing, which was like kissing a corpse.

"Where's the record, Bertie?" she said.

I started to laugh, but I saw tears in her eyes and it wasn't funny. "I don't have it any more."

So what does she do? Does she yell at me or hit me or run out or laugh at me or freeze up and order me to take her home or anything you'd expect? No. She lies down on my bed with her face to the wall and doesn't make a sound. Here she is, at bay like, and she doesn't fight or anything. She just lies down as much to say, Kill me if you want to. What satisfaction is there in that, I ask you? She wasn't even going to let me leave her go in peace. In fact, her dress was riding up above her stockings in one place, and I was so embarrassed for her I pulled it down. She was so helpless that I couldn't do a thing, and naturally I thought she couldn't be dangerous. I thought she'd given up. I went over to make some coffee on the hot plate.

I was quite a while at it because I wanted to give her a chance to pull herself together. I heard her stirring a little on the bed and I felt better. But when I turned around with the cups in my hands, there she was reading something. I got close enough to see it was a letter, and then I recognized the handwriting. It was a letter from my wife I had left under the pillow. She didn't write often, and I'd just got it the day before. She always signed them upside down.

Dear Bert,
Yesterday the candy came that you sent and it was all eaten up in an hour everybody liked it so much I only had three pieces to myself

but two of them had cherries. I felt so good I fixed myself up a little when we went to the movies last night and Dr. Smardon said I was looking very attractive. I didn't know where to look when he said that and after the show Winnie Stuart told me I was better looking than the movie star herself even, that was Ava Gardner. She meant it too because she told somebody else and they told me she told them. Of course she's a Capricorn.

I just thought you might like to know.

Your wife,
Celia L.

Well, when I saw Rilla had read it, I was so mad I spilled the coffee putting it down. I grabbed the letter from her hand so hard it tore. I really hated her then. "Get out," I said. "God damn you, get out." I could have hit her too. I hadn't looked at her I hated her so much, but when she didn't even stir I looked at her face. She was crying and looking at me.

"I'm sorry," she said. "I wouldn't have done it if I'd known. I wouldn't have done it for worlds."

"But you've done it," I said. "I don't want to see you any more."

"I was just evening things up," she said.

"Now they're even—so get."

"You had no right to trick me to come here."

"So I didn't," I said, "so get going."

I'll say this for her, she had a lot of poise. She sat up and fixed her face so she'd look presentable and adjusted her clothes, not sexily but just put them in place, and then she said in a very dignified way, "You will drive me home, Bert."

Two minutes before if she'd said that I'd have felt like kicking her downstairs, but now she'd won me over again, and I said okay, I'd drive her home.

She hadn't any more than got her hand on the knob than we could hear somebody climbing the stairs and whistling in a special way, "Do not forsake me, O my darling."

"Wait a minute," she whispered.

He let himself into his room, next door of course, still whistling. Rilla looked at me puzzled.

"It's Chester," I whispered. I thought it was only a grim joke so I wasn't in the least prepared for what she did next. She turned white as a ghost.

"He could have heard me," she whispered. She looked at me. I nodded. "He would have told Ormie." Her eyes got big. She really looked betrayed, and I never felt like such a heel in my life. "You knew it too."

She didn't say a word all the way home, and she wouldn't let me walk her from the car up to her door. I waited a good minute for her to let herself in the apartment house, but she seemed to just be standing there all hunched over. I went up to find out what was the matter, and when I saw she was crying and her hand was trembling so hard she couldn't fit the key into the lock, I just plain loved her.

"Rilla," I said, "Rilla—goddamn it all, honey."

So I hugged her and kissed her tears away, and she shivered for a while up against me. This time when I kissed her it was a real kiss— a real, real kiss, and the way she leaned back and looked at me I thought probably she loved me too. I was afraid for a minute she was going to talk, which would have been a mistake at a time like that, but she didn't.

The only time I've seen her since was in a restaurant where I heard her laugh in a booth toward the rear. It warmed me up to hear her, and I started to go back to say hello. It had been a couple of months and there didn't seem to be anything she'd done which was particularly unforgivable any more. But then I saw her batting her eyes up at some zootie character with a goatee, and I changed my mind and went back by my lonesome to my hamburger steak.

POEM

Fever and Chills

A man desired his wife's best friend,
His best friend's heavy-shouldered wife.

They sat late after a sunny day,
Four best friends, eating figs and cream,
Children in bed. She twined her arms
Forward across the table, shook,
And yawned. "When I became a mother,
I dreamt that I became my mother."
She arched, tossed up her head, and yawned
Skinning her patched and off-white teeth;
Then she collapsed onto herself.
"I feel so happy. Don't you love figs?"
They said they did. He said he did.
She glanced at him affectionately,
And it seemed to him: if his head
Lay in a lap, cheek to belly,
These were the eyes that should look down,
These the shoulders his hand should reach.
"The night I became a father,
I cried. I forget my dream."
Folded, resting on the table,
Her skin still flushed from the day's sun,
She cuddled. He wondered whether
Her breasts and haunches glowed so brown
Or paled in patches; and desired her.

All night his darkness blazed with pale
Auroras of silent desire,
And his skin cursed the usual sheet
Shucking him in. The next morning,
Knowing she would be home alone
(Her husband worked by day, he by night),
He found her squatting in the shed,
Painting an old chair. When he spoke,
She lost her balance in surprise,

Half sprawling back, propped on one arm.
He helped her, and for a moment
His hands felt her give him her weight.
She left the paint can uncovered,
But zipped off her smock, shook her hair
Free from its kerchief, and led him
In the house for coffee. All he knew
Became silent and spectacular.
Waiting for the water to boil,
She leaned back against the sinkboard
Chittering tight of voice. He kissed her.
In blind avarice, they clashed teeth.
He had neither supposed nor doubted
The readiness of her desire.
She did not grant, he did not take;
They were both there at the same time.

Since they took care not to give it
Its social name nor to let it
Ever make a child, their desire
Justified their indifference
To all consequence—merely friends
Whose fortune was to make love well.
He praised her body with his eyes,
His endearments were her name: "Susan.
I love you, Sue." When they were not
Mumbling with desire, they talked like friends
Just as they talked in the presence
Of the friends they were married to,
Coasting among habited islands.
But when they made their arrangements
To meet again, they scarcely touched,
Their voices thinned, chilled, and fell,
Neither of them had a name.
He did not think this a stiff price;
Only a minute or so each time;

Nothing really. It was nothing.
Quick chills with nothing in them.

They were twilight riding home, full
From a picnic, in the back seat
Among heaps of blankets and baskets,
Her child in his lap, his in hers,
His puppy nestling her bare feet,
In the front seat their best friends,
All six singing "Old MacDonald
Had a farm, he I, he I, Oh"—
and the muscles in his shoulder,
Arm, thigh less than an inch from hers,
Shoved to fall toward her, till he burned
All over from the not falling.
He did not come to hate his wife
But cared for her much as before;
For his friend, who was suffering
No bed-loss, his affection held.
He resented these bonds, but was
So ashamed of his resentment
He did not know most of the time
That it was there, never what it was.
He did not study the monsters
His dreams dredged, but took witty snapshots
Of them to laugh at with his friends;
Who liked to show their own familiars.

This man, who loved his countryside,
Whose country's ways were part of him,
Loathed the State he had been reared in.
With each vote, he had pronounced
Of his own will: *Let the State be,*
And the State (already) was.
It had used his will, like a wrench,
Proudly to bring forth two new things

Which it had swaddled from cradling
Parachutes and eased through summer air,
Annihilating two cities
He did not hate as much as that.
He ceased to vote, so withholding
His will, but did not rise against,
Half declining and half holding
The citizenship his birthright.
The State, indifferent to him,
Had wills enough to wrench together
All the sleek offspring it wanted
And to do with them as it pleased.
Not only in the State did this
Man's will not rule as he would like,
But in his own home and in himself.
His will's perfection lay with her
Consummate perfection in acts
Done secretly, in such darkness
He could not see what they meant or
What it meant that he had done them.
Half dreaming, outspread, he performed
A safe fantasy of danger:
Himself was a person of the sky;
Stars were his atoms; his form was
An incarnation of vacancy
Made visible by casual stars;
Through this so-imagined void, sped
Cold no-things of macrocosm
Which had such energy that, if one
Should hit one planet of one star,
The person should no longer be,
For re-explosion of the stars.
So, half awake on his friend's bed,
He imagined his pleased body—
Which microphysics conceived as
Matterless and nearly empty—
Streaked vagrantly by cosmic rays

So potent: if one bombed into
One least moon of his least hangnail
Solar system . . . But it would not,
Ten to the *n*th . . . But it could . . .
His hand stirred onto her. His eyes turned.
She lay facing the wall, sleeping.
He saw no stars in her moist skin.
She had the smooth, abrupt shoulders
Of a medieval statue queen,
And a mole in the small of her back.
Her body was entirely sunned.
Sleep, from which he had surfaced lank,
Left a thought gasping in his mind:
Though he was half there socially,
And physically was scarcely there
At all, yet he was penetrant
To the dense, destructible heart.
He aroused her into his arms.
Her vagrant, reginal flutter
Profoundly gratified his glance;
Yet his hankering plunged him on,
To make love that would not stay made.
He conceived nothing, stark awake.

In the second summer of this,
They parked one noon by a locked gate
Which all six climbed through, and they packed
The furniture of the outing
Through a field of bearded grasses
And down a gully in the sea cliff.
The smooth gray gravel of the beach
Rattled when the surf scratched at it.
They pitched their blankets end to end
Under a flowering overhang,
Sunned, drank red wine, dozed in the shade;
Nearby in a safe lagoon, naked
The children bathed, screaming like gulls.

The other two poked up the straight beach
In search of well-wrought driftwood,
Leaving them in pretended sleep.
Just before it was safe, one eye cocked,
He inched up till they could burlesque
At snatching kisses, nose to chin.
He did it for the filch itself;
But she, when he stroked her shoulders
Secretively, shook with desire,
And slapped her arm over her head
Against his body on the side
Away from the children, just the back
Of her arm, all she could, writhing it.
He was relieved when the children
Careened back visiting, for them
To make much of. She walked apart,
Sat on the crest of the gray bank,
And stared, chin on hands, at the waves—
At the endlessly sudden heaves
Lunging against the abrupt shore
Which broke them. He knelt by her.
He could not tell whether the drops
On her still cheeks were spray or tears,
But he knew she felt that he should
Have done something he had not done,
Something he did not want to do
But might do for her, if only
To avoid uneasiness like this.
He yearned to soothe with his new skill,
Turn tenderness of compassion
Into delicacies of desire:
But they were sitting in full view,
And the truceless sea prevented him
From rubbing her even with his voice.
He wanted to leave her stranded;
Instead, he scrutinized her face
Like an artifact, he the numb

Keeper of a wild museum
Inspecting her in her sadness
As though she were the squat statue
Of some name-forgotten goddess.
By the time the others returned,
The afternoon breeze had stiffened.
The men arranged some large flat stones,
Dragged up driftwood planks and branches,
And built much too big a campfire.
The women were preparing food,
The children began a sand fight,
The pup reveled in the bustle.
The sun set red. Spume in the air.
A leaf of flame fluttered away.
The fire became a bed of coals.
The salad was made, the chicken
Was floured and ready to fry.
And Susan, carrying the full
Skillet, stumbled on the puppy,
At once got grit in the salad,
Knocked over her husband's wine mug,
And spilled the chicken on the coals.
"Stupid!" she cried. Then kicked the dog.
Neither man said, "It's all right, Sue."
Neither helped her define her blame
By scolding her. She went on working
With head bent, a smile frozen on her lips.
After the meal, the children wanted
To be rolled in blankets and laid
As far toward their known lagoon
As they dared go from the campfire;
They said the ocean stamped too hard.
Coffee, and oatmeal cookies. A full moon.
He watched her husband watching her,
And watched him tell the deft tale
Of her clumsy stupidities
That day, and watched her face crumple:

Even the way she drank from her mug
Became a clumsiness to tell.
He demurred a little, sorry
For the ugliness of her tears.
When she scuffed down the obscure beach,
Shoulders broken, it occurred to him
He might go with her and hold her:
They were friends too. But he wanted
Not to do what he ought to do,
And watched his wife do it. The men,
Intent on finishing the wine
Before the reproachful women
Should draggle back wanting to go home,
Only half watched the moon set
Oblong at the blurred horizon—
Though he had meant reverence for it
While he'd still had speech with the surf.
When the women returned, he put
The fire out by kicking the coals
Cold-eyed at their silent reproof;
He hawed; he guffawed; he would not
Make an extra trip to carry
His sleep-laden son up the hill,
That was a job for squaws. Yet,
Once they were home and Sue snatched him
Into a crevice in the stir,
Whispering moistly in his ear with the
Cunning lingo of stalled lovers,
She made him feel behind her lips
The rank need. He would come to her.

This man had been raised without names
For the plain female things of sex;
It seemed they ought to have no names;
Possibly they were not even there.
For his own body there had been
Pet names for the facts of voiding

Spoken with sprightliness of tone
As though they were not nasty, really,
And gutter names that really were:
Which nomenclatures of disgust
Occasioned and diffused in him
Their special guilt. Later, he learned
To cross-word some medical names,
But they had nothing much to do
With what took place.—Early next day
He found her alone, vacuuming
Her child's room, and he approached her
Cautiously, expecting to be
Accused, to apologize, to hurt
Till they should soothe each other's wounds
In ways unnamed or named hardly.
Instead, at the first clash of kiss
She writhed her shoulders against him
Wordless and passionate, nor could
She pull her clothes off fast enough,
Even wrenched at his. He, rather than
Wrestle her down till he could stand
Up against her, fell sex-appalled
On the child's bed, ignorant. She
Like a witch bestrid him and rode,
Mouth stretched against the gale swirling her,
Until she gasped up without him
To a blind solitary moan.
With divorced and rational eyes,
He watched her resume her own face.
He had supposed that every kind
Of sexual experience
Which the gutter way of knowing
Did not guess nor reason describe,
Whose sufficient rationale was
Just to take place, which was its own
Meaning for little whiles, no name,
Although it also entwined both with love

And with the job of generation
Inextricably, could yet be
Itself wholly, could redeem sex
Of nastiness, and was proved sure
By their reciprocal pleasure.
But this that they had just done, proved
He did not know what; it had rocked
To impulses he would not want
Names for; *love* felt strange on his tongue,
And *generation* had been mocked . . .
He did not look long at these thoughts.
Propped on his elbow beside her,
He brushed her moist neck free of hair
And nuzzled tenderly; he warmed
His mind with the hope this had been
Some stitch of sex with an odd name,
Which might of itself go away.
He wanted to ask her some safe,
Worried, uxorious question:
"What did I do wrong, dear?" Instead,
He spelled out with a fingernail
On her still back DO YOU LOVE ME?
She rolled over, studied whether
He had been playing, and told him
She loved him as much as he loved her.
So they spent ten minutes rubbing
Cosmetic endearments on each
Other, till desire swelled robust
Over these puzzles and clasped them
In affection consummately.
She wept in his arms a little;
He soothed her to sleep, watchfully.

Their mutual affection endured,
Their scrupulously childless love;
But sometimes the same thrust of sex
Clenched them again unspeakably,

So cold the coldness burned them,
Then tossed them back onto the sheets
Treasonous and together—things.
This he thought a stiff price to pay,
But he paid it. Though he believed
Each action meant its consequence
Whether he looked at it or not,
He turned from their divisive deeds
Broomstick and witch, reasoning:
Sex is natural, I love her,
The natural is right, love is good:
A false child sucking a dry teat.
He went fishing, in the vague hope
Things would straighten out in his mind
If he were alone. They did not.
A mare of the sea, her neck arched,
Her gray tail switching, stamped the shore,
And bared her huge, yellowing teeth,
Neighing that he should mount her.
But he was as small as a pea
And he knew what ought to ensue.
"Friend," said one like him, "my best friend,
She needs a pear."—"Isn't she yours?"
He said. "Besides, *we* are a pair."—
"You pea, pea! She eats squirts like us.
Get out!"—He woke in frightful tears.
And analyzed this to mean that
He'd kept Freud's promise by having
Once upon desired his mother;
By which masking of a danger
Present in a past archetype
He declined to be the wiser.

One hot night, Sue and her sister,
While their parents were away, gave
A party in their family house
For five couples of married friends.

He gave himself over to jazz,
Liquor, the raucous intention.
Once in a while, he pranced with Sue's
Flirtatious sister in a gross
Gallop of their own invention;
At the bow finishing each round,
Dimpling she leaned back on his arm,
And he amorously kissed her
Adam's apple in general fun.
His wife was busily making
Her own fun; they smiled in passing.
He enjoyed another woman
In scrupulously knee-deep talk
About prejudice, elections, the Law.
With thwarted gestures, the laugh in time,
An insistence in their glances,
Her serious accommodation
To odd steps in his argument,
His leaning toward her, licking his lips,
They embraced as near as dancers,
In a party way of sex;
When he left her, she was breathing fast.
He came on Susan in the pantry
Munching olives, her eyes watchful
And imprudent. He had scarcely
Spoken to her, not danced with her,
Not responded when their eyes caught.
Now, he would have said Hi and passed,
But she stroked his chest with soft claws,
And forced an olive in his mouth.
He made desecration a game:
Cold eyes melting, he leaned toward her,
Cheek to cheek whispered, "My darling,"
Then slid his hand under her blouse,
Which was stained, half-tucked, and twisted,
Squeezed her breast and tweaked the nipple.
Her body, not with the insult,

Shook, but her eyes did not like him.
Along roved one of the husbands,
A lean one who had praised her strong
Feet for being so earth-goddessy
And who now sniffed at her armpits
And proclaimed them divine; she laughed
Unravishably, let herself be
Carried to the main room, enthroned
Upon the crotch of the piano,
And goatishly worshiped—her knees,
Her ankles, and her wild wild toes—
Queening it over her lover
With scornful glances at the doorway
Where he lounged. He watched her husband's
Restless prowling and side looking.
Himself he saw freed for a while
From female hungering. And yet,
When a buxom and rigid wife
Beckoned him beside her, he went.
With the hand not holding her glass,
She padlocked him to her. Coolly
He got her to swallow so much
Flattery neat that she came unhinged
To the very eyelids, which he kissed.
They fumbled up to the attic
And found a chaise longue silk to touch;
She perched on it. He slid her back,
Amply unstayed her to the waist,
Kissed her lips unlocked, and suppled her
Till her arms forgot to instruct
But rocked him as he lolled her there.
'Drink till the jug runs dry. Why not?
Why her?' Matter no matter.
Feet on the stairs jerked them apart.
She coughed, "Wait, please." He half hid.
A light clicked, and there stood Susan
Tense to use the whip in her eyes.

No one spoke. There was a sniff.
She turned off the light when she left.
He thought it might be possible
That she hadn't recognized him,
But he did not clutch the thought hard.
By the time he got down the stairs
He reeled drunken. He felt himself
Clearly grinned at by a blurred husband.
He came on a glass of punch, drank,
Groped to a bed, eased onto it,
And throttled his consciousness down
Like a man resisting nausea.
The party stirred into his room;
The mattress quaked; he was tickled;
He emerged enough to mutter,
Through a vacuous grin, something
Obscurely desperate, and belch.
Blank. She stood over him whipping:
"You crouched like a rabbit. You twitched."
"Suey, you don't know what a son
Of a bitch I am." His slow words
Echoed like a fart in a dome.
He could not tell by her corpse gaze
Whether she had understood him.
The next time he opened his eyes,
She'd gone. At the back of his throat,
He tasted the rising vomit,
Forced it back. He slept fitfully
Until daylight. Inside his skull,
Scrabbles of unconceived sensations
Clotted to each other, emitting
Short, very keen, supersonic squeaks.

They spent next afternoon in shorts
With the children on a green slope
Hangover idling, four best friends.
The party they gossiped about

Was not the one he remembered,
And he did not catch Susan's eye.
He began, hopefully, to think
He had not behaved so strangely.
The other two appeared easy;
His friend was drinking too much beer,
But amiably. Prudently
He resolved not to go to her
For a week. But then, he watched her
Settling herself on the bare grass,
And the luxury of her thighs
Throbbed his heart with desire as fresh
As though he had never known her:
He imagined, like a lover
Who has not yet declared himself,
The delights of embracing her.
The others left them a minute;
They gazed in one another's eyes
Until she smiled—not much, but smiled.
He'd not gone too awry last night,
Surely. All the same, he did not now
Lay plans for them to meet, being,
At last, afraid to pay the price.

On the second day he dropped by.
Her eyes were bloodshot. She gave him
A tight Hi for greeting, and turned
From his hand. She sat on the couch
Clenched in the attitude of a girl
Prepared against being seduced,
Offering him bent knees to fondle.
He asked if she had a stiff neck;
She said it was no importance;
He would rub it, but she said no;
He insisted; tears bleared her eyes;
He unzipped her dress in back,
And found a bruise on her shoulder,

Swollen, hot, black and blue; she sobbed.
Her husband, jealous of the lean
Goat-husband's lust at the party,
Had hit her; when she had denied,
He'd pushed so hard she'd fallen,
Striking her shoulder on the stove.
She said that she would tell the truth . . .
If she did, he would tell his wife . . .
He soothed her till she unfolded
Enough to let him wipe her tears.
She averted her face and said
Her husband was due home shortly.
The risk inflaming him, he forced
His impenitent desire on her.
Whatever hardness of reproach
Her tears had not softened in her,
Now became—against her will—part
Of a tumid and responsive
Need groping at him with curled lips.
He thinged her, and she wept again;
Because he could not help it,
He pleased her; then he slipped away.
He was conscious only of being
In a hurry. Yet he was glad
To meet her husband in the drive
And hold him in talk about baseball—
Passing the time of day, friend-like.
He was glad to think, afterwards,
That when they parted they shook hands.

This man meditated sometimes
While driving along by himself
And could benefit, for an hour,
From walking by the sea alone,
But he had no true competence
In the uses of solitude.
Now, in the sparse room he rented

In separation from his wife,
He was alone most of the time:
Not solitude, but loneliness;
Communing with nothing; cut off.
He knew little of confession:
The matter-of-fact confession
He had billeted on his wife
She received with natural blame;
He could no longer see his friend
(Now gone to another city;
Susan perhaps to follow);
He had no priest; it had never
Occurred to him he might confess
To himself, nor would he have known
How to do it. He was cut off.
Susan came to his narrow bed,
But they did not find much to say.
They had debased friendship's small change.
They neither lied about the big thing
Nor wished to find the truth of it.
Obscurely they felt: in measure
As their love failed they should suffer.
Even in the clasp of *What else?*
Their unspeakable success shamed
From their lips all love but kisses.
One day she found her child curled up
In the basket of dirty clothes,
Thumb in mouth, sobbing herself to sleep.
He could not bear to think of that.

On the first night of his fever
It seemed to him he groped for water
So often in order to rid
Himself of his laborious dream.
Once, to balk it, he tried sitting
In a straight chair for half an hour;
But hands and neck combined had not

Strength to support his molten brain.
He was—they were—all mixed up in
A violent charade of hunting
Throughout a large, unsteady ship
For the governor, who was lost.
They did not want to play, they had to.
It seemed to him he woke up just
To escape the strict gaiety,
And that only brain-heaviness
Pulled him back into it. Nor did
He know where the governor was
(Though he kept searching in the head)
Nor even care who he might be.
An almost level shaft of sun
Clarified his room and woke him
From another, shapelier dream.
He did not feel like getting up,
And, once up, he did not feel like
Staying up but lay back down hard.
Well, he deserved a lull. He would
Lounge abed with his window wide
To songs of birds, and watch the wind
Riffle across the poplar leaves
Turning their green a furred green-gray.
His last dream kept pestering him.
In a rough obscure room, he spied
A nude woman on a chaise longue,
Her head bent over a stiff child
And her hair hiding her features.
Her shoulders shook rhythmically.
As he tiptoed nearer, he heard
The child's gluttonous sucks, and saw,
With delight, that she shook because
The child nuzzled like a calf.
Then, with a pang, he recognized
This ramrod child: it was his son.
At that moment, the large woman

Scowled at him, pulled the little one
From the spurting nipple, and tucked
That one, red lips working the air,
Under her arm. He watched that round
Little face pucker and draw in
And disappear in her armpit.
She stood enormous and he ran.
"Stupid!" she cried. "It's your own fault!
Why did you try to hide out here
In plain sight? It's all your own fault."
For several minutes after he
Had awakened, he breathed in spasms,
As though he'd cried too long too hard,
A man ill-acquainted with tears—
Although in fact his eyes were dry.
He could not elude this harsh dream.
When he turned the woman into
His mother, the rest of the dream
Jigsawed together pretty well.
Yet the question would not stay down,
"What have I been doing out here
In plain sight?" He felt it confront
Him now himself, conscious, adult:
It was himself he had betrayed.
Which of course was absurd. His son
Had been, of course, the dream-betrayer,
And besides, in any deep sense,
Betrayal was something one did
Only to others. Nevertheless,
Sense or nonsense, not all his glib
Interpreting could keep him from
Feeling that he'd betrayed himself,
And who was to forgive him that? . . .
Before he had waded out deep
Into this confusion, he dozed;
And wakened with the dreaming
Parched out of him. He had not minded

That scramble up from sanity;
Nor did he resent the great sweat
Fetching him empty-handed down
To that clutch of muscles, the chills,
For it let him sleep imageless.
He drank much but was not hungry.
He fevered, sweated, chilled, and dozed.
He did not worry about it.
That evening, during his third high
Hallucinating, Susan came.
Sometime by daylight, a doctor,
Who gave him pills. Susan rubbed him
With alcohol to cool him off.
He roared incontinently:
With laughter, that she ticked him;
With tears, at her indifference
To stinging his eyeballs. He knew
The extravagance of his noise,
And he could feel her shrink from him
Even as she nursed him. He thought
He could stop whenever he willed;
It was just that he saw no reason
Not to do what he wanted to,
And whatever he did was what
He wanted to do: he was free.
He sweat till the sweat that soaked him
Was without salt, tasteless; and his back
Ached till he howled behind his teeth.
He never complained, for he had
The ease of nothing in his mind
Even when Susan was with him:
In the place of auroras, nothing . . .
On the third day his wife came
And sent him to the hospital.

Before he had quite recovered,
Susan was to join her husband.

The night before she left, they met.
He desired her because he thought
He ought to. For the first time, his
I want you failed to generate
Hers. She lay with face averted
And helped him make what had been love;
She thought he wanted to. Even
Then, their bodies could not quite fail.

His wife, who did not reprove him,
Also did not forgive him, but
She wanted him back, and he went.

ESSAYS

The Novelist as Meddler

T H E   W O R D "novel" has been used to describe almost every sort of long fiction. The *Odyssey*, an epic poem, is sometimes called the first novel. *Tristram Shandy*, a satiric autobiography with no plot whatever, is called a novel, and so is *Alice in Wonderland*. But "novel" has also been used more strictly a good deal of the time, to describe the sort of long prose fiction which has been dominant in Western literature for over two centuries. In this essay, "novel" means this one species and not the larger genus.

Not many novels are formally pure in this restricted use of the term "novel." None of the three books listed above is properly a novel, though *Tristram Shandy* is partly one; neither are *Don Quixote, The Castle,* and *Moby Dick.* T. S. Eliot and André Gide have said that as pure, as "novelistic" a novelist as ever wrote is Georges Simenon. Perhaps they are right; if so, the lack of strength in his pure novels only suggests the necessity to adulterate fiction, as gold or silver must be adulterated, with some baser alloys, to make them strong. Flaubert and James are commonly referred to as formal masters of the novel; an inspection of *Madame Bovary* and *Portrait of a Lady* would disclose the extent to which these books are strengthened with alloys of romance and satire. *War and Peace, Bleak House, The Red and the Black, Huckleberry Finn, The Brothers Karamazov, Remembrance of Things Past, Tom Jones:* all these celebrated books are commonly called novels, and all are by any formal criterion manifestly imperfect. In other words, the novel is odd in this: great representatives of the form are impure and imperfect.

The novel, the realistic species of long prose fiction, is differentiated from realistic drama by far more than the form in which it is printed. James's advice to the novelist to disappear into his material, which he must *render, present, dramatize,* pushes the novel toward drama and away from essay; yet a true novel is not just a realistic play with stage directions spelled out and speakers described rather more fully than is conventional with printed plays. A novel presents the characters' hidden life with an extensiveness, intimacy, and analytic subtlety which drama forbids, and it is a story controlled by a narrative voice.

Here is a formal definition of the (realistic) novel.

In the novel, (1) objects, behavior, and social customs resemble those existing in some actual society at some actual time, and motivation is probable, which is to say that the characters are mostly in the middle range of experience without being altogether consistent and if their behavior is extremely irrational it is presented in the light of convention as criminal or mad; (2) the principle for selecting and arranging the parts derives primarily from concern to reveal and to explore the pattern of relations, both hidden and open, of characters with one another, with social institutions, with ideas, with the natural world, or each with himself and his own beliefs; and (3) the reader's relation to the imagined characters is appreciably modified by the attitude of the narrator (who may or may not also be the author) toward the reader, toward the moral and social values of the world he is describing, and toward the characters as imagined persons, including the narrator's earlier self if that self is one of the characters.

The content of the novel, as here defined, is intercourse among a few credible characters and between them and the reader, who knows them by their public actions, their intimate words, and their unrecognized impulses. But this is also the area of moral concern. Both in fiction and in life, an attitude toward the behavior and motive of individuals related in and to a natural and social world almost necessarily becomes moral as it becomes engaged. The scientific attitude toward behavior and motive is that of detached observation; Balzac, Flaubert, and Zola all announced their intention of assuming this disengaged stance, but in fact neither they nor any other novelist worth reading ever did so consistently. The aesthetic attitude of pure interest is much more congenial to a writer than the scientific one, the novel being, after all, a form of art. "Let us become epicures of experience, valuing it according to its refinement and intensity." Gide is the practicing apologist of this attitude. It is possible to read his *Strait Is the Gate* and *Lafcadio's Adventures* in such a way as to value Alissa's spiritual agony above Lafcadio's zeal for gratuitous malice only because imagining her agony is a more refined and intense pleasure than imagining his malice. Pleasure of this kind is of course a part of the enjoyment afforded by even as nonaesthetic, propagandistic a novel as *Uncle Tom's Cabin*. But Gide's theoretical amorality is in fact extremely rare in fiction; it is also possible to read his finest novel, *Strait Is the Gate*, as a work of moral commitment. The very process of writing a novel and imagining characters engages the spirit, and this engagement almost necessarily assumes a moral quality. Even Gide the aesthete trembles on the verge of *ought;* his position can be imagined as this: "To purify experience to its finest and then to explore it, either actually or imaginatively, is my (the?) highest good." In sum, it is possible for a novelist to take the position of purely aesthetic engagement with matters that are the heart of moral concern, but it is rare for him to do so and the results at best are lacking in strength.

Meanwhile, perfect or imperfect, great or small, whatever the moral stance, novels and part-novels all face certain problems in common. Formally, the most important of these is point of view. The ideal held up by James the theorist and by his critical descendants is of an invisible, inaudible author; preferably there should be no narrator; if he is there he must meddle with the characters and their world only ironically, that is, in such a way as to reveal his own character; to author and reader, a narrator should be only another personage in the story. But since almost all substantial novelists do in fact meddle (including James the novelist) and since such meddling is apt to be not just formal but also moral in nature, this essay will concern itself both with ways in which author-meddling does not damage a novel but instead leaves it pretty much unscathed and also with ways by which such meddling can be turned to a novel's advantage, and then at the end with the one sort of meddling for which there is no forgiveness.

2

A harmless sort of intrusion is for the author to turn from the story to expound his theories on some subject or other directly to the reader. His justification for doing this is that you should understand the true nature of old maids, the gods, social upheaval, storytelling, whatever, in order to appreciate the significance of his characters' acts and thoughts. But what ordinarily happens is that you listen for a while to what the author as a private person has to say, and then you go back into the world of the novel with your own opinions on the subject intact and with your connection with the characters untouched; for as a man of opinions a novelist is no better than his neighbor.

In devotion woman is sublimely superior to man. It is the only superiority she cares to have acknowledged, the only quality which she pardons man for letting her excel him in.

I doubt it; but this disagreement does not interfere with my understanding of Eugénie Grandet, of whom it is said, or with my affection for Balzac, who said it. Tolstoy's long quarrel with the French historians, in *War and Peace,* and his elaborate theory of history have so little to do with what is valuable in the novel that a disagreeing reader takes to skipping those sections. The most to be learned from those chapters is the hardly surprising knowledge that a novelist, who is primarily concerned with individuals, finds the way of a historian, who is primarily concerned with social movements, exasperating and uncongenial. Meanwhile, however, the long asides do not damage the novel proper, because they are presented openly and separately and because an understanding of the characters' behavior does not depend upon them. One can find Tolstoy's notions about how to write a history of the Napoleonic invasion of Russia silly and yet find, while reading the novel proper, that every action and thought of every important character during his account of that invasion rings absolutely true. For the worth of the novel, the truth of this ring is what matters.

So long as an author is saying *This is what I think,* all goes well enough; when he begins to say *This is what you ought to think,* the reader is likely to resist. Even so, if this preaching is open and is separable from the novel proper, it will do no essential harm.

That is the whole history of the search for happiness, whether it be your own or somebody else's that you want to win. It ends, and it always ends, in the ghastly sense of the bottomless nothingness into which you will inevitably fall if you strain any further.

I feel Lawrence pushing me with his rhetoric to accept this as true not only for the character who is dimly supposed to be thinking it, but for the world at large. I not only doubt the truth of this opinion, I also balk at being pushed. Even so, my pleasure in *The Fox* remains unimpaired, and my regard for Lawrence continues only slightly impaired.

When a novelist's comments on experiences strike you as true and good, your pleasure is increased.

There are in the music of the violin—if one does not see the instrument itself, and so cannot relate what one hears to its form, which modifies the fullness of the sound—accents which are so closely akin to those of certain contralto voices, that one has the illusion that a singer has taken her place amid the orchestra. One raises one's eyes; one sees only the wooden case, magical as a Chinese box; but, at moments, one is still tricked by the deceiving appeal of the Siren; at times, too, one believes that one is listening to a captive spirit, struggling in the darkness of its masterful box, a box quivering with enchantment, like a devil immersed in a stoup of holy water; sometimes, again, it is in the air, at large, like a pure and supernatural creature that reveals to the ear, as it passes, its invisible message.

This passage has little or nothing to do with any of the characters in Proust's novel, except as it is one of the opinions of Marcel the narrator, who in such respects is Proust himself. But it and a thousand others of its kind constitute much of the excellence of the book. It has a legitimate if slight tonal function in the section in which it occurs, *Swann in Love;* but its main virtue is to give elegant expression to something true, something with which one cannot disagree and for which one could not possibly have found better words.

To a novelist with the urge to tell the reader what something of the world is like, the best, hopeless advice is: Be subtle, be wise.

3

A description of surroundings is likely to be closer to the heart of a novel than is a general comment on life, because the circumstances in which a character acts modify what he does and our understanding of him. The operative principle here is plain enough: the amount and intensity of the description of anything should be proportionate to the importance of that thing in revealing character but should not be determined by the author's personal interest in the thing described.

Descriptions of nature are notoriously long winded and are com-

monly skipped—for example, those in the romances of Scott and
Cooper. Descriptions of hunting and fishing sometimes go on longer
than necessary, even the famous set pieces of Tolstoy in *War and
Peace* and of Hemingway in many of his fictions. Readers who like
hunting and fishing for their own sake find the passages delightful,
but those who are indifferent to those sports find the descriptions
excessive for presenting character—though they are not very dam-
aging to the novel since they are abridgeable by the impatient reader.
Surely the authors dwelt upon these scenes at such length mostly be-
cause they themselves loved those sports. But here is a description of
nature, from Mary Webb's *Precious Bane,* which is wholly justified.

When I look out of my window and see the plain and the big sky with clouds
standing up on the mountains, I call to mind the thick, blotting woods of
Sarn, and the crying of the mere when the ice was on it, and the way the
water would come into the cupboard under the stairs when it rose at the
time of the snow melting. There was but little sky to see there, saving that
which was reflected in the mere; but the sky that is in the mere is not the
proper heavens. You see it in a glass darkly, and the long shadows of rushes
go thin and sharp across the sliding stars, and even the sun and moon might
be put out down there, for, times, the moon would get lost in lily leaves, and
times, a heron might stand before the sun.

It is a novel of country people who see the world alive with myste-
rious connections, as the narrator in this description does; and none
of the novel's descriptions go on too long.

Closer yet to the heart of fiction are descriptions of man-made
things, for the artifacts a character has made or has chosen to exist
among affect him, reveal him. Here, the usual advice is to let con-
crete things speak for themselves, and Flaubert is the model. Emma
goes with Léon to the house of the wet nurse who is taking care of
her baby.

The ground-floor bedroom—the only bedroom in the house—had a wide
uncurtained bed standing against its rear wall; the window wall (one pane
was mended with a bit of wrapping paper) was taken up by the kneading-
trough. In the corner behind the door was a raised slab for washing, and
under it stood a row of heavy boots with shiny hobnails and a bottle of oil
with a feather in its mouth. A Mathieu Laensberg almanac lay on the dusty
mantelpiece among gun flints, candle ends, and bits of tinder. And as a final
bit of clutter there was a figure of Fame blowing her trumpets—a picture
probably cut out of a perfume advertisement and now fastened to the wall
with six shoe tacks.

The author imposes on the reader no attitude toward this room and the items in it he has chosen to describe; "a final bit of clutter" does not exceed the bounds of reasonable observation. Two sentences later, Léon's attitude is given: "it seemed to him a strange sight, this elegant lady in her nankeen gown here among all this squalor." Indeed, this is about as meticulously hands-off as a novelist can be. But here is a passage from *Our Mutual Friend* which operates on another principle entirely.

Mr. and Mrs. Veneering were bran-new people in a bran-new house in a bran-new quarter of London. Everything about the Veneerings was spick and span new. All their furniture was new, all their friends were new, all their servants were new, their plate was new, their carriage was new, their harness was new, their horses were new, their pictures were new, they themselves were new, they were as newly-married as was lawfully compatible with their having a bran-new baby, and if they had set up a great-grandfather, he would have come home in matting from the Pantechnicon, without a scratch upon him, French-polished to the crown of his head.

For, in the Veneering establishment, from the hall-chairs with the new coat of arms, to the grand pianoforte with the new action, and upstairs again to the new fire-escape, all things were in a state of high varnish and polish. And what was observable in the furniture, was observable in the Veneerings—the surface smelt a little too much of the workshop and was a trifle sticky.

This description is not so concrete as Flaubert's, but surely it is fictionally valuable to learn a little about this house in such a way as to learn far more about what its owners are like; and Dickens's openly satiric view of the Veneerings is surely no less legitimate than Flaubert's professedly objective but, in the whole novel, covertly satiric view of the world of *Madame Bovary*. And here is a passage from *The Ambassadors*. Strether is visiting Miss Gostrey's place in Paris.

Her compact and crowded little chambers, almost dusky, as they at first struck him, with accumulations, represented a supreme general adjustment to opportunities and conditions. Wherever he looked he saw an old ivory or an old brocade, and he scarce knew where to sit for fear of a misappliance. The life of the occupant struck him, of a sudden, as more charged with possession even than Chad's or than Miss Barrace's; wide as his glimpse had lately become of the empire of "things," what was before him still enlarged it; the lust of the eys and the pride of life had indeed thus their temple. It was the innermost nook of the shrine—as brown as a pirate's cave. In the brownness were glints of gold; patches of purple were in the gloom; objects, all, that caught, through the muslin, with their high rarity, the light of the low windows. Nothing was clear about them but that they were precious, and they brushed his ignorance with their contempt as a flower, in a liberty taken with him, might have been whisked under his nose.

This is literary impressionism: there is not a concrete image in the passage; yet, by suggesting the effect the room makes on Strether, James succeeds in creating in the reader's mind a sense of the room, its owner, and its viewer. And though James's own attitude toward the room is as scrupulously absent as was Flaubert's toward the wet-nurse's room, one is in no doubt of James's aesthetic love of it.

In *Laocoön*, Lessing suggests that, in a competition between a visual and a verbal representation of a thing, the visual must win. If he is right, as he probably is even for people with strong image-making faculties, the usual advice about the best way to describe things in a novel needs qualifying. It is no more valuable to let the things in the room speak for themselves as Flaubert does than it is to give the impression of a room as James does or to give both that and also the narrator's opinion of the room and its inhabitants as Dickens does. Words can carry a thing-in-itself not at all and an image of the thing vividly but imperfectly; but they can, marvelously if less vividly, carry someone's impression of it and relation to it.

4

Because a point of view is, literally, geographically fixed, there is a kind of assumption that the metaphorical "point of view" of fiction should be fixed too. To a writer who feels bound to maintain one consistent point of view and to keep the same distance from events and people, all sorts of special benefits come from his restricting himself to one clearly defined consciousness, which ordinarily means using *I*. The most obvious benefit of *I* is the increase of credibility: "I was there, I saw it." That the body of *Wuthering Heights* is narrated by Nelly Dean, the respectable housekeeper, to Lockwood, the respectable lawyer, gives the book a credibility and solidity it could not possibly have had if told in the free manner of a Gothic horror story. Another benefit of *I* is that certain of the actual author's narrative or stylistic peculiarities can be put to use by being so disposed as to reflect upon and reveal the character of *I*. Conrad's fondness for generalizing was never put to better use than when it became part of Marlow's character as he tells *Heart of Darkness*, nor James's famous ambiguity than as it opened depths in the story within a story of *The Turn of the Screw.*

But it is only theoretically that lack of consistency in point of view matters very much. Critical prescriptions are to be reached inductively: if many good novels violate a formal prescription, then that prescription must be modified or discarded; and many do violate the one about consistent point of view. *The Possessed* is told by an *I* most of the time, but when it is inconvenient for the *I* to be present at a scene, he simply disappears from the book and the scene is told by Dostoevsky from the unspecified point of view conventional in narratives of all sorts; nor does the book suffer from it. And in *Crime and Punishment*—which is surely one of the greatest novels—Dostoevsky begins one chapter:

It would be difficult to describe the exact reasons which gave Mrs. Marmeladov the idea of the absurd funeral meal.

For the rest of the paragraph, Dostoevsky speculates on her possible motives. But during the course of the chapter he gets more and more involved with her—presenting her, to be sure, by external description and by objective reporting of what she says—until early in the next chapter he is close enough to say:

Mrs. Marmeladov remained standing in the same place, as though thunderstruck. She could not understand how Mr. Luzhin could have disavowed her father's hospitality, for by now she believed in it blindly.

Only a narrow theory would object to such a shift in how much the novelist should allow himself to reveal of what is going on in a character's mind. Fielding is sometimes reproved for his intrusions and shifts, even though *Tom Jones* is as much satire as realistic novel.

[Jones] returned the fellow his empty pistol, advised him to think of honester means of relieving his distress, and gave him a couple of guineas for the immediate support of his wife and his family; adding, "he wished he had more for his sake, for the hundred pound that had been mentioned was not his own."

Our readers will probably be divided in their opinions concerning this action; some may applaud it perhaps as an act of extraordinary humanity, while those of a more saturnine temper will consider it as a want of regard to that justice which every man owes his country. Partridge certainly saw it in that light; for he testified much dissatisfaction on the occasion, quoted

an old proverb, and said, he should not wonder if the rogue attacked them again before they reached London.
The highwayman was full of expressions of thankfulness and gratitude. He actually dropped tears, or pretended so to do.

Here Fielding moves from a rather distant reporting of action, to an author-comment which would break any illusion, back to an even cooler reporting. But the shift is open, the author's voice is clear, and the story and characters have vigor enough to survive the comments of writer and reader alike. *Here is the way to look at my characters:* this is bad only if the author's way of looking is stupid and the characters but half-alive.

The theory that the Dostoevsky-Fielding-Balzac method is so inferior to the Conrad-Joyce-Flaubert method as to render their novels inferior as works of art makes one huge assumption: that the reader of a novel should not feel himself in the hands of an artificer or storyteller and that the novelist's true art is to create an illusory actuality, appearing to have no art. But this assumption goes too far. It is the equivalent of that theatrical assumption that the audience can be looking through a fourth wall into an actual room. Just as a spectator never really forgets that he is in a theater watching actors, so the reader of a novel does not really forget he is being told a story. When the narrator is open about his role as storyteller, as most have been in every sort of fiction, the reader happily allows him all sorts of liberties of point of view: everyone recognizes the artifice and enjoys it. Only when consistency is promised must inconsistency disturb.

As for fixity of remove—the steady distance which "point of view" metaphorically promises—it is made nothing by the example of the best, Tolstoy. He moves at will from the most panoramic aloofness above a battlefield to an account of the inmost feelings of a man at the moment before his death, and he moves anywhere between when and as it pleases him; and it is hard to imagine this lordly freedom troubling a reader for any reason but a narrow literary theory or his own private and uninteresting pathology. There is a great peace in delivering oneself into the hands of a writer who *knows:* "Tell us what you know, any way you will."

5

In fiction the point of view that matters most, and is least like the geographical one, is the author's set of values, what he considers important, especially morally; for this gets at the heart of the novel, the character's being and doing. The subject is so important, and so tricky, that I am looking at it under two aspects: first, the relation of the author's values to the reader, and then the author's relation to the characters he is creating.

Before going on, I must spell out an assumption: that everyone concerned with a novel, reader, writer, and character, has a set of attitudes, preferences, judgments, or values about human conduct, and that, whether these values are conscious or unconscious, articulated with logical coherence or only manifest in sometimes contradictory acts, they must finally be considered, if the word moral is to mean anything, moral values. This is no more than an *ad hoc* definition, much too loose to satisfy any ethical philosopher. Its justification in this essay is to insist that everyone says, or at least implies, "good" or "bad" when he looks at human conduct or when he himself acts: the hyperconscious aesthete for whom the high good is savoring refined experience; the self-indulgent reader who seems to ask no more than that a novel remove him from moral concern but who is also asking for the author and the story to assure him, at least temporarily, that self-indulgence and sloth are all right; even Faulkner's feebleminded Ike Snopes, whose great good is to love, though he knows that the world thinks he should not love, a cow. These are extreme cases. Typically, people accept the code of conduct of their society, class, religion, province, whatever, without much distinguishing between convention and morality. It is a considerable part of the novelist's art both to let the reader understand the code of the imagined world and also to define the characters as they conform to, modify, rebel against, ignore, affirm, use this code.

The novelist's understanding of the imagined society's code of manners and values is essential to the reader's understanding of the characters, but the novelist's own code need not be and seldom is identical with the imagined code. Even where there is a substantial agreement, as with Jane Austen, the excellent novelist yet has a moral vision which much of the time perceives in the characters, including the narrator if there is one, a disparity between official reason and private motive, between society's requirements and the heart's need, that delights the reader and rings true to what he knows. One may say that a novelist will be interested in manners and convention, if only because he needs them to portray his people, and that his code of moral values may greatly differ from that code of manners but cannot utterly deny it. Any sort of writer who, like a mystic, says that social mores are of no importance or who, like a nihilist, says that all actual societies deserve destruction will have little interest in writing novels. Tolstoy the radical prophet necessarily rejected the works of Tolstoy the novelist. To this extent a true novelist is conservative: he says that the society he is writing about is worth at least our attention, for within it and of it are people worth noticing, worthy of our concern. The coherence of a novel depends in part upon the coherence of its characters and of their society. No doubt the society which every novel presents could or should be improved; meanwhile, something has been presented worthy of improvement. Nobody who can be considered an adequate reader of fiction requires that the code of conduct in the novel's world be the "right" code, if only because a part of what a novel can do is to bring news of strange parts, news of people with unfamiliar customs or with different attitudes toward familiar customs. Similarly, no reader asks that the novelist's own moral code be the "right" one; for those who think they know exactly what the right code is and how to apply it to a given occasion are happier with sermons than with a form so relative, so much a network of relationships and opinions, as the novel.

Nevertheless, since the narrator, whether the novelist himself or a character, is in fact going to have his own personal and moral opinions about the characters, his expressing them openly need not interfere with the reader but may very well please and help him. Both Dickens the novelist and David Copperfield the narrator dislike and disapprove of Uriah Heep, and any reasonable reader so fully shares this attitude that the expression of it adds to his pleasure. But in *Bleak House* Esther Summerson's view of herself is not likely to be identical with a reader's view of her; her humility is too conscious and she is too keen to report the praise of others for her to be accepted at her own evaluation, or, for that matter, at that of the other characters; and in this very disparity Dickens's own estimation of her reveals itself—to the reader's pleasure—as being not identical with any of those in the book. When the expressed view of a character is neither acceptable in itself nor dramatically acceptable as being a character's but is eccentrically the author's own, trouble may enter in but it need not be very serious. Fielding's excessive affection for and approval of Sophia in *Tom Jones* need interfere only slightly with a reader's somewhat reserved fondness for her; and Richardson's almost commercial equating of virtue and virginity in *Pamela* impairs the book but does not prevent one from seeing Pamela's holding out for marriage as a matter of some moral interest and complexity. In both these cases, the authors have created characters and situations of sufficient vitality to flourish apart from their creators' opinions of them. Bad trouble comes when the characters lack this vitality—in which case the author's opinion of them will not help or hurt much anyway. Worst of all is for the characters and actions to exist chiefly to demonstrate the author's views—whether Dostoevsky's anemic saints or Genet's evil-be-thou-my-good satanists or Katherine Mansfield's only-to-be-pitied victims. For in such cases the author's opinions come to be what matters, not the characters, and the reader has experience of polemic in the guise of fiction.

The relation of reader to writer is like that of two acquaintances talking about a mutual friend (in this case a character in a novel). The writer may express his opinions and the reader may share those opinions or allow himself to be persuaded by them; but finally the reader wants to make up his own mind on the evidence of the character's actions and thoughts. The trouble is, he can't. The analogy to the friends and their mutual acquaintance breaks down, because all the reader can know of the character is what the writer tells, shows, arranges, and comments on. The reader may think he is free to make his own connection with a character but in fact he is controlled.

Flaubert's ambition in *Madame Bovary* was to do nothing but present the evidence. However, what reader is (or should be) allowed to admire Homais? Every novelist, even if he does not overtly develop his personal and moral opinions as such, has those opinions and they will manifest themselves whether he intends them to or not. "In a corner of every notary's heart lie the moldy remains of a poet," Flaubert opines like any Balzac and then ducks back into the story out of sight. But whether it shows itself overtly, the author's moral judgment will—must—inform the very structure of action and delineation of character. That Emma Bovary should kill herself at the end of the book is right and inevitable in every way, including that of reflecting the author's moral views; but that the details of her dying are reported so extensively and with such vividness mainly reflects Flaubert's punishing cruelty, just as the hideous blind man's improbable appearance outside Emma's window at the moment of her death singing a love ditty reflects very little more than Flaubert's weakness for romantic irony.

If a novelist is wise enough, he need manifest his moral views only in the actions and contours of his characters and in little cues along the way; if he is not wise enough for that, at least he will do no harm by telling the reader his opinions openly so the reader can estimate how much the novelist's opinions are affecting the presentation of characters and his response to them.

6

The reader prefers not to trouble himself over the writer's attitude to the character, though he will keep an eye on the narrator when the story is told in the first person. When he agrees with the writer, as he agrees with Dickens about Uriah Heep, or when the writer is so powerful and wise as to give the ultimate illusion "life is really like that," as Tolstoy often does, then the reader happily pays attention only to the characters and actions. But the novelist can never afford to neglect the reader. He must never forget that his connection with a character does not exist for its own sake only but exists partly to create the reader's connection with the character.

In this the most intimate and crucial of novelistic relationships— the writer creating character—there is, finally, the necessity on the novelist not to meddle. He may like the character as a person, and say so; he may disapprove and say so; he may develop all sorts of general theories about the type of person the character is or the social institutions he belongs to; he may be close to the character sometimes and far off at others; he may do all he can to control and direct the reader's response to the character when the character's acts or thoughts are not the instant focus of attention. But at the moment of action, of speaking, of thinking, of choice, he must not interfere; for it at that moment anything whatever gets between the character and the reader, nothing good will be created. Dickens notoriously could not let a dying child alone. Here is the death of Jo in *Bleak House*. The trouble is not with Dickens's comment at the end but with what Jo is represented as saying:

"Jo, my poor fellow!"
"I hear you, sir, in the dark, but I'm a-gropin—a-gropin—let me catch hold of your hand."
"Jo, can you say what I say?"
"I'll say anything as you say, sir, for I knows it's good."

"Our Father."

" 'Our Father!'—yes, that's wery good, sir."

"Which art in Heaven."

" 'Art in Heaven'—is the light a-comin, sir?"

"It is close at hand. Hallowed be thy name!"

" 'Hallowed be—thy—' "

The light is come upon the dark benighted way. Dead!

Dead, your Majesty. Dead, my lords and gentlemen. Dead, Right Reverends and Wrong Reverends of every order. Dead, men and women, born with Heavenly compassion in your hearts. And dying thus around us every day.

Plato loved Socrates, Boswell loved Dr. Johnson, in *Heart of Darkness* Marlow had strong and complicated feelings about Kurtz; yet the deaths of those three subjects affect us far more than Jo's does because their telling is clean. Tolstoy himself sometimes falters even in his greatest fictions. At the moment of the death of Ivan Ilych, Tolstoy does not just report what was going on in the character's mind but makes his wish Ivan's.

"And the pain?" he asked himself. "What has become of it? Where are you, pain?"

He turned his attention to it.

"Yes, here it is. Well, what of it? Let the pain be."

"And death . . . where is it?"

He sought his former accustomed fear of death and did not find it. "Where is it? What death?" There was no fear because there was no death.

In place of death there was light.

"So that's what it is!" he suddenly exclaimed aloud. "What joy!"

The reader knows he is no longer seeing Ivan's experience plain and responding to that, as he feels he has been doing up to this passage of the story; he also sees this as Tolstoy's wish and must shove Tolstoy aside in order to get cleanly to Ivan.

Here, ultimately, technical advice to a novelist becomes moral advice to any man. Grant others their otherness. "Justice," says Socrates in *The Republic*, "means minding one's own business and not meddling with other men's concerns"—which concern, for a novelist, is the intercourse of reader and character. At the moment of greatest intimacy, of creation, do not judge, or you will be judged for having judged. Like a god, grant your creatures their free will. Like a father, give your children their independence. Like a friend, love them and leave them alone.

Against Pornography

So much has changed in attitudes toward pornography, as toward sexual matters generally, since this essay first appeared in 1965 that I thought of updating it, even though my opinions on the subject have not changed in any major respect. But who knows what further shifts the seventies have in store? The only thing one can be sure of is that there will be plenty of them. Built-in obsolescence is not for cars alone. This is the original version, polished a bit and with a note appended.

P O R N O G R A P H Y is like a squalid, unnecessary little country which owes its independence to a vagary of history. But, though pornography is seldom of much importance, it may be of considerable interest, for to talk about it is unavoidably to talk about the Great Powers adjacent to it. Pornography speaks the language of Art; in recent centuries it has come within the sphere of influence of the Law; Psychology and Morals have vested interests in it. Moreover, occasionally pornography becomes genuinely important—when it is used as a seat of operations by the erotic nihilists who would like to destroy every sort of social and moral law and who devote their effective energies to subverting society as such. One who undertakes to discuss pornography finds himself, willy-nilly, falling back upon some of his ultimate positions in matters aesthetic, social, psychological, ethical. If a reader agrees with these opinions, he is likely to view them as principles; if he disagrees, prejudices. Here are some of mine.

Before plunging ahead, I had better indicate two mutually antagonistic dispositions, one liberal, the other conservative, in my opinions on pornography. On the one hand, I favor the liberal view that the less power the state and the police have over us private citizens the better, that the less the state concerns itself with the individual's thoughts, entertainments, and private sexual actions the better, and that we should do what we can to counter the drift toward totalitarianism.

In other words, let us have no censorship because it strengthens the state, which is already too strong. Also let us have none because most of the things that in fact get censored are less harmful than some of the things that do not—for example, large circulation newspapers and magazines. Society is harmed far less by the free circulation of a book like *Fanny Hill* than it is by routine and accepted practices of the daily sensationalist press: let a man inherit ten million dollars, pour acid on his wife, or win a Nobel Prize, and reporter and photographer are made to intrude upon him and his family and then to exhibit to public view in as gross a manner as possible his follies, shames, or just plain private affairs. Such invasions of privacy are not only allowed, they are allowed for the purpose of letting the public enjoy these same invasions vicariously, all in the name of freedom of the press. I believe that this accepted practice has done more damage to society as a whole and to its citizens individually than massive doses of the most depraved pornography could ever do. So much for my liberal views.

On the other hand, I favor the conservative view that pornography exists among us and is a social evil, though a small one. That is, in a good society of any sort I can imagine—not some daydream utopia where man is impossibly restored to sexual innocence but a society populated with recognizable, imperfectible men—in a good society there would be active opposition to pornography, which is to say, considerable firmness in the drawing of lines beyond which actions, words, and images are regarded as indecent. Furthermore, the opinion that pornography should not be restrained I regard as being commonly a symptom of doctrinaire liberalism and occasionally an evidence of destructive nihilism.

A liberal suspicion of censorship and a conservative dislike of pornography are not very compatible. Some sort of compromise is necessary if they are to live together. Their marriage, being of the earthly sort, will never be without tensions, but maybe the quarrel between them can be patched up well enough for practical purposes.

Originally the word pornography meant a sort of low erotic art, the writing of and about whores with the intention of arousing a man's lust so that he would go to a whore. But some centuries ago, the word, like the practice itself, came to include considerably more than aesthetic pandering. It has come to overlap with obscenity, which originally meant nothing more than the filthy. Obscenity still means that primarily, but notions about what is filthy have changed. Defecating and urinating, instead of being just low and uninteresting, came to be viewed as filthy, obscene, taboo. Apparently, down in the underworld of taboo, things and functions easily become tinged with sexuality, especially functions as near the genitals as urinating and defecating. In any case, since in common practice no clear distinction is made between pornography and obscenity, I am offering, for the sake of convenience, a definition in which the single word pornography is stretched to include most of obscenity. The definition is mine, but not just mine; it also reflects the usage and attitudes of my society.

Pornography is the representation of directly or indirectly erotic acts with an intrusive vividness which offends decency without aesthetic justification.

Obviously this definition does not just describe but also judges; quite as obviously it contains terms that need pinning down—decency, for example. But pornography is not at all a matter for scientific treatment. Like various other areas of sexual behavior in which society takes an unsteady, wary interest—homosexuality, for example, fornication, or nudity—pornography is relative, an ambiguous matter of personal taste the consensus of opinion. The grounds for this definition are psychological, aesthetic, and political.

Psychologically, pornography is not offensive because it excites sexual desire; desire as such is a fine thing, and there are happy times and places when desire should be excited and gratified freely and fully; moreover, even in inappropriate times and places there is plenty of free-floating desire abroad in the world; it doesn't take pornography to excite excesses of desire among young men and women. Nor is pornography offensive because, in its perverted and scatological versions, it excites disgust; in the proper context disgust serves the useful function of turning us from the harmful. Psychologically the trouble with pornography is that, in our culture at least, it offends the sense of separateness, of individuality, of privacy; it intrudes upon the rights of others. We have a certain sense of specialness about those voluntary bodily functions each must perform for himself—bathing, eating, defecating, urinating, copulating, performing the sexual perversions from heavy petting to necrophilia. Take eating, for example. There are few strong taboos around the act of eating; yet most people feel uneasy about being the only one at table who is, or who is not, eating, and there is an absolute difference between eating a rare steak washed down with plenty of red wine and watching a close-up movie of someone doing so. One wishes to draw back when one is actually or imaginatively too close to the mouth of a man enjoying his dinner; in exactly the same way one wishes to remove oneself from the presence of a man and woman enjoying sexual intercourse. Not to withdraw is to peep, to pervert looking so that it becomes a sexual end in itself. As for a close-up of a private act which is also revolting, a man's vomiting, say, the avoidance principle is the same as for a close-up of steak-eating, except that the additional unpleasantness makes one wish to keep an even greater distance from the subject.

Pornography also raises aesthetic questions, since it exists only in art—in painting, literature, sculpture, photography, theater—and my definition implies that it is offensive aesthetically. The central aesthetic issue is not whether certain subjects and words should be taboo, but what distance should be maintained between spectator and subject. Because of our desire to withdraw from a man performing private acts and our doubly strong desire to withdraw from a man performing acts which are not only private but also disagreeable or perverted, we wish aesthetically to remain at a certain distance from such acts when they are represented in art. Nothing whatever in human experience should, as such, be excluded from consideration in a work of art: not Judas betraying Christ nor naked starved Jews crowded by Nazi soldiers into a gas chamber nor a child locked by his parents in a dark closet for months till he goes mad nor a man paying a whore to lash him with barbed wire for his sexual relief nor even husband and wife making love. Nothing human is alien to art. The question is only, how close? But the criterion of distance is an extremely tricky one. Aesthetically, one good way to keep a spectator at a distance from the experience represented by an image is to make the image artificial, stylized, not like us. If it is sufficiently stylized, it may be vivid and detailed and still keep a proper distance from the viewer. One would normally feel uneasy at being with a lot of men, women, and children engaged in every imaginable form of pleasurable erotic activity. Yet the vivid throngs of erotic statues on certain Indian temples create in the viewer no uneasiness but are simply delightful to look at. The viewer is kept at a considerable remove by the impossible poses and expressions of the statues; he cannot identify with the persons performing the acts. For the statues do not represent lustful, passionate, guilty, self-conscious, confused people like you and me, but pure beings to whom all things are pure, paradisal folk who are expressing their joy in generation and the body by erotic acts: these are stylized artifices of blessedness. Another way of keeping the spectator at a proper distance from a private experience is to give very little of it—make the image small, sketch it in with few details. One does not want to be close to a man while he is defecating nor to have a close-up picture of him in that natural, innocent act—not at all because defecating is reprehensible, only because it is displeasing to intrude upon. One would much rather have a detailed picture of a thief stealing the last loaf of bread from a starving widow with three children than one of Albert Schweitzer at stool. However, Bruegel's painting *The Netherlandish Proverbs* represents two bare rear ends sticking out of a window, presumably of people defecating into the river below, and one quite enjoys the sight—because it is a small part of a large and pleasant picture of the world and because the two figures are tiny, sketched in, far away.

To be sure, a satiric work of art may purposely arouse disgust in its audience. Even the breast of a healthy woman is revolting when inspected too closely, as Swift knew when he had tiny Gulliver revolted by every blemish on the breast of the Brobdingnagian wet nurse suckling a baby. Our revulsion at the description of her teat sticking out a good six feet, with a nipple half the size of a man's head, is necessary to Swift's satiric purposes, and it is kept within bounds by his reminding us that if proportions had been normal— if Gulliver and she had been about the same size—both he and we would have been pleased by the sight of her breast. When the artist's purpose goes to the limit of satire and he intends, as Swift does in the fourth book of *Gulliver's Travels,* to disgust us with man as such, then he will force us right into the unpleasantly private, as Swift gets us to contemplate the Yahoos copulating promiscuously and lovelessly, besmeared with their own excrement. The aesthetic danger of such powerful evocations of disgust is that the audience may and often does turn not only against the object of the artist's hatred but also against the artist and work of art for having aroused such unpleasant emotions. Swift, just because he succeeds so powerfully, is often reviled for his misanthropy in the voyage to the Houyhnhnms; the fourth book of *Gulliver's Travels* is even called a product and proof of madness—which is convenient and safe, for of course the fantasies of a madman may be pathetic and scary but they don't apply to us; *we* are sane. There is a special problem raised by realism, because it aims to present people as they actually are. How can a realistic artist be true to his subject if he is forbidden direct access to an area of human behavior which is of considerable importance? The aesthetic problem is for the realistic artist to represent these actions in such a way as to lead to understanding of the characters without arousing disgust against them or a prurient interest in their activities. When he can accomplish this very difficult feat, then he is justified in including in a realistic work of art representations that would otherwise be pornographic. Here are two instances of intimate erotic acts realistically represented, one of a kiss which is pornographic, the other of a copulation which is aesthetically justified and hence is not pornographic.

In the movie *Baby Doll,* made by Elia Kazan, a healthy young man and woman who desire one another embrace. By this point in the movie the spectator is convinced that their lust is powerful but banal, and a brief and somewhat distant shot of their embracing would adequately suggest to him how intensely they wanted to consummate their desire. Instead, he is subject to a prolonged series of images, especially auditory images, the effect of which is to arouse his own lust and/or disgust, to no aesthetic end. The kiss becomes so severed from characters and plot that the spectator does not care how the couple are related, but cares only that they are given over to desire, and he is encouraged by the very depersonalization of that desire to give himself over to a lust of his own. He may be excited to want some sort of sexual activity with the next available person, but, more probably, observing and sharing in that movie embrace becomes a kind of substitute sexual activity on the part of the spectator. For, just because the scene in *Baby Doll* arouses its spectator vicariously and in a theater, the chief appetite it whets is not for casual fornicationbut for more voyeurism—which is good at least for the movie business. Even if *Baby Doll* were a good work of art, as it surely is not, this episode in itself would remain aesthetically unjustified and therefore pornographic, and would merit censoring.

The other example of an intimately presented erotic act is from the novel *Pretty Leslie* by R. V. Cassill. The reader is given an emotionally intense account of a young man and woman copulating in an abnormal way; the man hurts the woman, and the reader understands how he does it and why she lets him do it. This would seem to be essentially pornographic, yet it is not. The art of this novel redeems its ugliness. The reader is not encouraged to use this episode as an incitement to casual fornication or voyeurism. Instead, what is aroused in him is a profound understanding of the characters themselves, of a kind he could have got in no other way. To understand what these people were like, how they were connected, and why they did what they did to each other, the reader must be close to them as they make love, and because he knows this is necessary for his understanding, he will not use either the episode or the whole novel for pornographic ends, unless he himself is already perverted. In *Baby Doll* a natural private act, by being brought close for no legitimate reason, excites an uneasy desire whose satisfaction can only be indiscriminate or perverse. In *Pretty Leslie* the account of an unnatural private act is not so close as to create disgust but is close enough to lead toward moral understanding and aesthetic satisfaction: there is no other possible way for the novelist to accomplish this legitimate end, and the emphasis he gives the episode is in proportion to its contribution to the whole novel.

The aesthetic problem has been stated succinctly by Jean Genet. As a professed immoralist and enemy of society, he has no compunction about using pornography. But as a writer, he has this to say about his art (in an interview in *Playboy* magazine for April 1964): "I now think that if my books arouse readers sexually, they're badly written, because the poetic emotion should be so strong that no reader is moved sexually. Insofar as my books are pornographic, I don't reject them. I simply say that I lacked grace."

Nothing said thus far would justify legal suppression, official censorship, for, though the effect of pornography in a work of art is aesthetically bad, it is no business of the state to suppress bad art. The effect of pornography on an individual psyche is that of an assault, ranging in severity from the equivalent of a mere pinch to that of an open cut; but in the normal course of things one can avoid such assaults without much trouble, and besides the wounds they make are seldom very severe one by one, though they may be cumulatively. To be sure, there are people who want and need pornography, just as there are those who want and need heroin, but such a secret indulgence is not in itself socially dangerous. Here again, the state has no business intruding: a man's soul is his own to pollute if he wishes, and it is not for the state to say "Be thou clean, be thou healthy, close the bathroom door behind you." It is only when pornography becomes public that, like dope, it takes on a sufficiently political cast for censorship even to be considered. It is unlike dope in that it sometimes acquires political overtones by being used ideologically, when put in the service of nihilism. But in one important respect it is like dope: it usually becomes public by being offered for sale, especially to the young.

The classic example of pornography is a filthy picture: it is ugly; it is sold and displayed surreptitiously; it allows the viewer to intrude vicariously upon the privacy of others; it shows two or more men and women posing for money in front of a camera, in attitudes which sexual desire alone would lead them to assume in private if at all. An adult looking at such a picture is roused to an excitement which may lead either to revulsion or to satisfaction, but whatever his reaction, he should be left alone to decide for himself whether he wants to repeat the experience. The state has no legitimate political concern with his private vices. But the effect on young people of such a picture, and especially of a steady diet of such pictures, is another matter. A common argument against allowing young people to have unrestricted access to pornography runs somewhat as follows:

About sex the young are curious and uncertain and have very powerful feelings. A filthy picture associates sexual acts with ugly, vicarious, and surreptitious pleasure, and helps to cut sex off from love and free joy. At the most, one experience of pornography may have a salutary effect on the curious, uncertain mind of an adolescent. To be shown what has been forbidden might provide him a considerable relief, and if he has feared that he is warped because of his fantasies, he can see how really warped are those who act on such fantasies. Moreover, by his own experience he can learn why pornography is forbidden: experience of it is at once fascinating, displeasing, and an end in itself, that is to say, perverse. However, too many experiences with pornography may encourage the young to turn their fantasies into actions ("in dreams begin responsibilities") or to substitute fantasies for actions, and so may confirm them in bad habits.

Whatever the validity of this argument, it or something like it is the rationale by which our society justifies its strong taboo against exposing children to pornography. For my own part, I would accept the argument as mostly valid. The state has no business legislating virtue; indeed, one of the symptoms of totalitarianism is the persistent attempt of the state not just to punish its citizens for wrongdoing, but to change their nature, to make them what its rulers conceive to be good. But patently the state has the obligation to protect the young against the public acts of the vicious.

This means that, in the matter of the sale and display of pornography, the state, the apparatus of the law, should have two effective policies. It should strictly forbid making pornography accessible to the young: "No One Under 18 Admitted." But as for pornography for adults, the law should rest content with a decent hypocrisy: "Keep it out of the marketplace, sell it under the counter, and the law won't bother you."

An assumption underlying such policies is that a certain amount of official hypocrisy is one of the operative principles of a good society. It is hard to imagine that any tolerable society would not disapprove of adultery, for the maintenance of the family as an institution is one of the prime concerns of society, and adultery threatens the family. Yet, on the other hand, imagine living in a country in which the laws against adultery were strictly enforced—the informing that such enforcement would entail, the spying, breaking in upon, denouncing, the regiment of self-righteous teetotalers. What is obviously needed here is what we have: unenforced laws. It is only an all-or-none zealot who cannot tell the difference between the deplorable hypocrisy of a man deceiving his neighbor for his own gain and the salutory hypocrisy of a government recognizing the limits beyond which it should not encroach upon its individual citizens. Another assumption underlying these recommendations is that the censorship of simple pornography for adults will never be very effective. There is a steady demand for it, and it is not important enough to prosecute at much expense. The main function of laws against adult pornography is to express disapproval of it.

A by-product of society's official disapproval is worth mentioning: it is a kindness to those who enjoy pornography. Just as a criminal's status depends upon a line beyond which he has transgressed, the law for him to be outside, so the pleasure of one who enjoys pornography depends upon his act's being thought shameful. It is a pity that some people can enjoy sex only or most when they think that what they are doing is shameful, but since there are such people, it is cruel to deprive them of their shame, just as it is cruel of a parent to withhold from a disobedient child the punishment he has courted. Indeed, it might be socially imprudent so to deprive those who enjoy pornography. Their indulgence in that vice does not demonstrably lead to other antisocial behavior, for they are inturned people whose unpleasant sexual tensions are more or less adequately relieved through pornography. If society has any respect for them, it will sternly assure them that what they are doing is nasty by passing a law against it, and then will pretty much leave them alone.

Clearly the logic of this argument leads to prohibiting certain books and works of art that are now legally available in some parts of the country. For example, in some localities the courts have refused to prohibit the sale of *Fanny Hill*. This refusal seems to me quite irresponsible on any grounds other than a general refusal to censor pornography, for by any meaningful definition *Fanny Hill* is pornographic. Such story as there is in the novel exists for no other purpose than to provide occasions for detailed accounts of sexual encounters, and these accounts are the only passages in the book with power to stir the reader's emotions. The characters are very simple types without intrinsic interest, and Fanny herself is little more than a man's fantasy of female complaisance and sexual competence. The one literary quality which has made the book celebrated is a certain elegance of style; compared to most simple pornography it reads like a masterpiece, but to anyone familiar with eighteenth-century English prose it reads like several other third-rate novels. Surely the world is not in such need of third-rate eighteenth-century English fictional prose as to allow this consideration alone to justify the public sale of a work of sheer pornography. What else would justify its sale is hard to imagine. To deny that the book is pornographic, or to say that its literary value redeems its pornography, is to blur distinctions, and for an august court of law to do so is for the state to abrogate one of its functions. An essential and conservative function of the state is to say "Thou Shalt Not," to formulate society's taboos. Unless I am seriously mistaken, in this instance the court, speaking for the state, has refused to draw a clear line which corresponds to society's actual customs. In our culture the place for nudists is in a nudist colony, not on the city streets, and the way to sell books like

Fanny Hill is under the counter, not over it. In the name of enlighten-ment and sexual permissiveness the state is violating an actual taboo, and the counterreaction to many such violations may very well be a resurgence of that savage fanaticism which burns books and closes theaters.

I am going to defer a consideration of the nihilistic use of por-nography, which would logically come next, and instead look at certain borderline questions of enforcing censorship. The censorship of unquestionable pornography is of little interest; it pretty directly reflects what decent society considers indecent at a given time; it is custom in action. But the censorship of borderline pornography demands discrimination and philosophy, without which censorship can degenerate into puritanical repressiveness of the kind there has been quite enough of during the past two or three centuries.

Thus far my argument on what to censor and why has led to a legal position which is at least within hailing distance of common prac-tice in the United States now. To purveyors of raw pornography our practice says in effect: Bother your neighbors, especially children, and you will be punished; leave others untroubled by your vice and you will be viewed with disapproval by the law but left alone. This attitude is fine until one gets down to cases, but once it is a matter of wording and enforcing a law, the question must be answered: How is one to distinguish between pornographic and decent art? Still, such lines must be drawn if there are to be laws at all, and they must, in the nature of things, be arbitrary. As I see it, a more manageable form of the question is this: Who should do the censoring? How should the board of censors be constituted? Whatever the answer to this question may be, whatever the best method of censoring, one thing is clear—our present method is unsatisfactory.

As things stand, an object is banned as pornographic on the judg-ment of some official in customs or the postal service or else by some police officer prodded by a local zealot. In most cases this judg-ment presents little difficulty: even civil liberty extremists who are opposed to all censorship on principle are apt to blanch when they are confronted with genuine hard-core pornography, the unarguably warped stuff, the bulk of the trade. But sometimes there is the ques-tion of assessing the value of a work of art, and for this task the bureaucrats and policemen who are presently empowered to make the day-to-day decisions are unqualified.

Should *Fanny Hill* be offered to the public freely? When society has said No for generations and when judges and literary critics cannot agree, it is wrong to allow a police sergeant to decide the matter. If a duly constituted public authority says *"Fanny Hill* shall not be sold in this state," then the policeman's duty is clear: arrest the man who displays it for sale. But to leave to bureaucrats and policemen the task of making all the delicate discriminations necessary in deciding whether the novel should be censored in the first place, is genuinely irresponsible of society at large and of legislators in particular. To be sure, cases are brought to court, where judge or jury decide. But the laws offer such vague guidance that far too much depends on the quirks of the judge or jury at hand. No censorship might be preferable to what we have now.

In fact, a strong case can be made for removing all censorship of pornography. Here are six arguments for abolishing censorship. The first three seem to me valid. No law can be framed so as to provide a clear and sure guide to bureaucrat, policeman, judge, and jury. It is very hard to demonstrate that pornography does in fact injure many people severely, even adolescents, for if the desire to break taboos is satisfied imaginatively, it is less likely to issue in antisocial acts. The less power the state and the police have the better. There are three further arguments against censorship which are commonly used but which I find less persuasive. Decent citizens can by their very disapproval segregate pornography without assistance from the state. But, in an age as troubled as ours and with so much private indiscipline and theoretical permissiveness in sexual matters, there is little reason to suppose that the moral disapproval of decent citizens would actually limit the public distribution of pornography. It is arguable that some people are rendered socially less dangerous by having their sexual tensions more or less satisfied by pornography, tensions which unrelieved might well lead to much more antisocial acts. But pornography if it is to be of help to those who use it, must be outside the law, must be clearly labeled *shameful*, as a weakly enforced censorship labels it. In the past, censorship has not succeeded in keeping books of literary value from being read but has only attached an unfortunate prurience to the reading of them. But the prurience attached to reading pornography derives less from breaking a law than from violating the taboo which caused the law to come into existence.

There is another argument, more important and more erroneous than these six, which is commonly advanced in favor of abolishing censorship. It hinges on a mistaken liberal doctrine about the nature of sexual taboos. According to this doctrine, sexual taboos, like fashions in dress, are determined by local custom and have as little to do with morality as the kinds of clothes we wear. However—the argument goes—people frequently mistake these sexual taboos for ethical rules, and pass and enforce laws punishing those who violate taboos. The result is a reduction of pleasure in sex and an increase of guilt, with an attendant host of psychological and social ills. The obvious solution is to abolish the taboos and so liberate the human spirit from its chief source of oppression and guilt. At the moment in America, this doctrine finds extensive elaboration in the writings of Paul Goodman and is present to some degree in the writings of many other intellectuals.

It presents a considerable difficulty: by supposing that the potent and obscure emotions surrounding sexual matters derive from unenlightened customs, it holds out the hope that enlightened views can liberate us from those customs so that sex in every form can become healthy and fun for all. This is a cheery, optimistic view, not unlike the sweet hopefulness of the old-fashioned anarchists who thought that all we have to do, in order to attain happiness, is to get rid of governments so we may all express our essentially good nature unrestrained. Such ideas would show to advantage in a museum of charming notions, along with phlogiston and the quarrel about how many angels can dance on the head of a pin, but turned loose in the world they sometimes cause a bit of trouble. Sexual anarchism, like political anarchism before it, is a lovely daydream and does no harm so long as it is recognized as a daydream. But it has come to be a part of fundamental liberalism, and so a part of the body of doctrines accepted by more and more of the rulers of the nation. Conceivably the First Amendment will be taken literally ("Congress shall make no law . . . abridging the freedom of speech or of the press") and many or all legal restraints against pornography may in fact be removed. But I believe that so far from eliminating sexual taboos, such an official undermining of them would only arouse the puritans to strengthen the bulwarks; the taboos would be made more repressive than ever; and many of the goods of liberalism would be wiped out along with and partly because of this Utopian folly. Decent people had better learn how to censor moderately, or the licentiousness released by liberal zealots may arouse their brothers the puritan zealots to censorship by fire.

A civilized method of censoring is feasible. One does not have to imagine a Utopian system of extirpating pornography through some sexual revolution, an Eden of erotic innocence in which prohibitions will be unnecessary because social relations will be as they should be. In our actual, historical United States, in which perversions and pornography flourish, one can imagine a better method of restraining pornography, which is yet within the framework of our customs and procedures. It would operate somewhat as follows:

All decisions about what is legally pornographic in any of the arts is in the custody of boards of censors. Such a board is elected or appointed from each of three general categories of citizens: for example, a judge or lawyer of good repute, a professor of art, literature, or one of the humanities, and a social worker, psychologist, or clergyman. These are not exciting categories; but in them, if anywhere, are likely to be found citizens whose own opinions will reflect decent social opinion and who are also capable of making the various discriminations the task calls for. Obviously it is necessary to keep sexual anarchists off the board; just as a person is, or used to be, disqualified from serving as a juror in a murder case if he were against capital punishment, so one would be disqualified from serving on a board of censors if he were against censoring pornography. A board of censors must never look to a set of rules of thumb for guidance—not, for instance, to the quantity of an actress's body that must be covered. Is a burlesque's dancer's breast indecent from the nipple down or is it the nipple itself that offends? That way foolishness lies. Rather, the censors must look only to their own personal experience with a given work of art for only in such experience can art be judged. For this reason, the censors should be people for whom society's taboos are part of themselves, not something in a code external to them. No photograph, drawing, book, stage show, or moving picture is banned by the police except at the instructions of this board. Its decisions, like those of every quasi-official public agency, are subject to appeal to the courts, but the Supreme Court would do all it could to dodge such cases. The banning is deliberately hypocritical: out of sight out of mind, so long as children are not molested. The aesthetic and moral principles guiding the board are roughly these: distance and effect. At the distance of a movie close-up, a kiss between husband and wife can be pornographic. If a child and an adult were sitting side by side watching a stage performance of a witty Restoration comedy of adultery, they are at altogether different distances from the play, the adult closer than the child; but at a marionette performance of a fairy-tale melodrama they reverse distances, the child closer this time and the adult farther away. As for effect on the spectator, this consideration is only slightly less tricky than distance. The question to be asked is whether a story intrudes on the privacy of its characters in order to give the reader vicarious and perverse sexual excitement or in order to provide him with a sympathetic understanding which he could have got in no other way. These criteria of distance and effect—these rubber yardsticks— apply to the parts as well as to the whole, so that a novel or movie of some aesthetic merit may be judged as censorable in part. In a movie the part is excisable with more or less aesthetic harm to the movie as a whole; with a book, if the board decides the gravity of the offense outweighs such literary excellence as the whole book may possess, the book is banned—not burned, just no longer offered for public sale.

This system is scarcely watertight; it presents plenty of opportunity for contradictions and revisions; it has tensions built into it. But it would not be likely to become troublesome politically; for, without strengthening the state appreciably, it provides a better way than the present one for our society to enforce certain inevitable taboos. Civilization behaves as though men were decent, in full knowledge that they are not.

The last aspect of the subject I am going to deal with is the use of pornography as a weapon of nihilistic destruction, especially by a writer important for so using it, Henry Miller. The term nihilism here signifies a great deal more than it did originally. In Turgenev's *Fathers and Sons,* where the word was given political currency, nihilism was quite idealistic; it held that a given society (Russia, in that case) was so corrupt or wicked that it should be destroyed, but destroyed so that a better society could emerge from its ruins. However, there is a nihilism which is not against this or that unjust society or social injustice but against society as such; its rage is not just political but metaphysical as well; and pornography is one of its weapons.

Of nihilistic fictions, Henry Miller's *Tropic of Cancer* is one of the most widely read and best spoken of. Miller is not only a fairly good writer, but the personality he projects in his book is attractive. When he stands stripped of his civilization—stripped down to his language, that is—the savage that is left is not exactly noble but he is at least honest about himself, self-indulgent, energetic, beauty loving, and interested in the world, not a cold-hearted, torturing pervert. The one overwhelming moral virtue Miller embodies in his book is self-honesty; if you're going to be a whore, he says, be a whore all the way. This honesty is doubtless what most attracted Orwell in Miller's writing, though Orwell was a most fastidious man otherwise. Miller's prose is usually vigorous and sometimes splendid, and he is the best writer of "the character" since Sir Thomas Overbury. Should *Tropic of Cancer* be censored or not? According to the standards for censorship advanced earlier in my argument, it should not be censored for its pornography: as a work of art, it has considerable merit, and it could not achieve its ends without the use of intrinsically pornographic episodes and images. But the conflict of interests in judging this book is acute, for the purpose of Miller's novel is not just aesthetic, it is nihilistic as well. The literary value of the book is enough to redeem its pornography but not enough to make one ignore its destructive intention. *Tropic of Cancer* has no structure and is very verbose; it is, like Miller's other books, an anatomy and a segment of his imaginary autobiography, a string of images and actions. But it does have an unmistakable message: society is intrinsically vile, let us return to the natural man. In effect, this return to nature means as little work as possible and lots of loveless sex. Miller has often been mispraised, for example by Karl Shapiro, for a supposedly pagan rejoicing in sex. Miller himself is honest about his intention. Again and again he represents the sexual antics of his characters as evidence of desperation, lurking behind which is the total despair of meaninglessness. He is what he says he is: an enemy not just of the badness of our society, not just of our specific society, but of society as such. To do what he can to get his readers also to become enemies of society, he assaults with persuasive force taboos, especially sexual taboos, which are intrinsic to social order.

Yet a whole new set of justifications are needed if *Tropic of Cancer* is to be banned, justifications having to do with pornography as a destructive social act. As an act against society, to write, publish, and distribute a book like *Tropic of Cancer* is more serious than to write, publish, and distribute a pamphlet which intellectually advocates the forcible overthrow of the government but less serious than to take arms against the government—about on a par with inciting to rebellion, an act which a secure, free government will watch carefully and disapprove of strongly, but not forbid and punish. In other words, the only plausible argument for suppressing *Tropic of Cancer* would be that its publication is a dangerous political act and not that the book is pornographic, even though its pornography is the main instrument of the book's nihilistic force.

If you want to destroy society—not just write about a character who wants to, but if you want to make your book an instrument for destroying, a weapon—then you need pornography. For since society, at least Western society, is founded on the family as an essential social unit, nihilists and totalitarians must always attack the family as their enemy: conversely those who attack the family as an institution are enemies of our kind of society. The totalitarians would substitute the state for the family; the nihilists would dissolve both the state and the family in the name of unrestricted gratification of natural appetite. To effect this dissolution, nihilists assault taboos, both because taboos restrain appetite and because they are an integral part of civilized order, of society as such. And since of all taboos the sexual ones are much the most important, pornography becomes for the nihilists (as it does not for the totalitarians, who need taboos) important as an instrument of dissolution; obviously a nihilistic representation of people violating taboos will be effective only if the representation itself also violates taboos. The reverse does not hold: pornography is not intrinsically nihilistic; conventional pornography recognizes and needs the rules it disobeys.

Because most pornography is not terribly harmful, and also because of the prevalence of liberal permissiveness in sexual matters, our society is falling down on one of its lesser jobs—the drawing of firm lines about what is decent. Furthermore, it has not sufficiently recognized that indecency can be and sometimes is put to politically dangerous uses. Society should oppose those who proclaim themselves its enemies and who subvert it by every means they know, not least of which is pornography. But violent repressiveness is not the best way for it to oppose them.

If one is for civilization, for being civilized, for even our warped but still possible society in preference to the anarchy that threatens from one side or the totalitarianism from the other, then one must be willing to take a middle way and to pay the price for responsibility. As things stand now, so liberal are we that a professor whose salary is paid by the state can speak out more easily in favor of *Tropic of Cancer* than against it, applauding not just its literary merits but also what he calls its celebration of sensuality and antisocial individualism. These are his honest opinions, and he, no more than the book, should be censored for advancing them. But his colleagues should not allow themselves to be cowed by his scorn of what he calls their bourgeois respectability but should rise in opposition to those opinions. In Miller's own presentation, his sensuality, intended to guard against despair, becomes a way to despair; his individualism is a frenzied endeavor to compose a self in the vacuum of alienation, an alienation which he childishly blames the absolute villain, society, for imposing on him, the absolute victim; he intends his book to be an instrument for persuading his readers to abandon society, abrogate responsibility to their fellowmen, and revert to a parasitic life. He claims that this sensual life is more joyous and fulfilling than any other possible in civilization; but what he describes is not a sensuality which is indeed a fulfillment for adult persons, so much as a would-be consolation for those who aspire to the condition of babies as a remedy to their grown-up woe.

To be civilized, to accept authority, to rule with order, costs deep in the soul, and not least of what it costs is likely to be some of the sensuality of the irresponsible. (In this respect the politically repressed are irresponsibly being denied responsibility. This would help account for the apparently greater sensuality among American Negroes than among American whites, for as a group Negroes have only recently been allowed to assume much social responsibility.) But we Americans, black and white, must be civilized now whether we want to be or not. Perhaps before civilization savages were noble, but, if there is anything we have learned in this vile century, it is that those who regress from civilization become ignoble beyond all toleration. They may aspire to an innocent savagery, but what they achieve is brutality.

At the end of *Tropic of Cancer*, Henry Miller says: "Human beings make a strange flora and fauna. From a distance they appear negligible; close up they are apt to appear ugly and malicious." What Miller says is right enough, but he leaves out what matters most. There is a middle distance from which to look at a man, the flexible distance of decency and art, of civilized society, which defines both a man looking and a man looked at; and from this distance human beings can look pretty good, important, even beautiful sometimes, worthy of respect.

AFTERNOTE

I once published a piece on Page 2 of the Sunday *Times Book Review* which began by taking off on Auden's famous line "poetry makes nothing happen." In the piece I called Auden "our wisdom poet," and for this Seymour Krim later accused me of "genocidal pride," even though the second half of the piece elaborated on Shelley's "poets are the unacknowledged legislators of the world." I had made the mistake of having two ideas on the same page, and he had selected only the one he wanted to hate.

I thought that in this essay the doubleness of my opinions on pornography and on censorship would be obvious to anyone who did not have a closed mind. But the first reactions to the appearance of the essay in *Harper's* pretty well set the pattern of response it has since elicited. Nine or so letters supported my general position, a couple of them preparing me for the onslaught to come, and ninety or so attacked me. A few of these said one must not be against pornography since there was no such thing or since it existed only in the eye of a dirty-minded beholder or since anything promoting sex in any way was good. Most, however, censured me for advocating censorship. "That's not what I said! It's not that simple!" I said that I disliked censorship and that by and large it is badly handled, and that the censorship I conceived as possible for pornography would be erratic, inconsistent, hypocritical, and weak. But they did not notice. From these responses I learned, what I had not adequately appreciated before, how belligerently single of mind liberals are on certain subjects, censorship being high on the list (they can also be bigoted about how open-minded they are). Lawyers seem to have less difficulty in detecting my ambivalence than do literary intellectuals. There being very few reputable intellectuals who have spoken against pornography in public, I am asked every so often to appear on panel discussions and such like, but never—thank the lord—to appear as a witness, on either side, in a porno trial.

In one important respect, events have clearly proved me wrong. I assumed a greater coherence of standards about sexual customs and general attitudes toward pornography than apparently existed in 1964, when I wrote the essay, or certainly obtains now in 1971.

On one small point I have changed my opinion, that laws prohibiting pornography are a kindness to those who need it by reassuring them it is nasty. Sigurd Burckhardt, who read the essay in typescript and pretty much agreed with the argument, thought I was being too fancy in using this rather shaky notion to lend support to even a conjectured censorship, and he was right.

Seemingly, I feared too much a resurgence of reactionary oppression, to which the removal of censorship of pornography would make an emotional contribution greater than its actual social importance. The courts have in fact relaxed the old restraints—though the Supreme Court was still uneasy in the Ginzburg trial over the way pornography is offered to the public for sale. As books, magazines, plays and happenings, movies, and works of plastic art have gotten dirtier, the reactionaries have muttered and threatened impeachments and formed societies for the prevention of—but not much more. In this matter, I hope I will continue to be proved wrong, and I hope further that the Danish experiment of removing all censorship whatever proves demonstrably uninjurious and unthreatening, so that we can follow suit. Pornography itself rapidly gets boring, and so does talking about it. But the case is by no means closed as yet. Seventh-grade teacher: "Here, what's the fuss back there?" Chloë: "Jerry took my porno comic, teacher. Make him give it back to me." Jerry: "Here, stupid, it's nothing but another old Hotbox Fergusson, anyway. Take it." Maybe the reason I cannot imagine such a scene's taking place in reality is that I think it shouldn't. Can you? Should it?

To my mind, the most interesting aspect of the controversy is aesthetic, insofar as I can make a distinction between the aesthetic and the moral, especially in fiction. My approach, treating literary and sexual matters as being also within the moral realm, is, whatever else, not *with it*. However, from many little asides picked up along the way, I suspect that my views, old-fashioned though they are, are more widely held than expressed. But they obviously are not very *interesting*—one of the prime categories of Zeitgeist. This was brought home to me vividly, not long ago, after I had been on a program with Leslie Fiedler, who by any criterion is interesting. A woman I had never seen before bustled up, eyes sparkling, and told me she agreed with me completely but she was writing her master's thesis on Mr. Fiedler's criticism—"I just think his ideas are *terrible!*"—and did I have any influence with him, could I get her an interview with him. It's tempting, after a few like that, to decide you'd rather be read than right, especially when you aren't always all that sure how right you are.

The aesthetic issue that interests me here is not the one I have proposed in "Against Pornography." I have not come across any direct challenge to the thesis that "distance" is the key aesthetic question in determining pornography. The issue is a cluster of arguments advanced by Leslie Fiedler, John Barth, and Susan Sontag, among others.

Fiedler's is the most innocent. In his energetic speculations on the myths buried in pop culture, he is indifferent to the moral dimensions of pornography, as to those of the Western, the gangster movie, sci-fi, or popular song lyrics; what people *think* those dimensions are, *that* can be interesting. One cannot fault him for this approach, which does in fact turn up some notions worth considering, illuminates some odd corners. Its dangers are twofold. First, zestful for the interesting, one can shunt aside the disturbing effect too much pornography may have on adolescents. Second, one can overvalue the aesthetic importance of a myth or archetype which one finds in a pop work; *Tarzan of the Apes,* for example, or *The Wizard of Oz* are aesthetically trivial, whatever interest they may have to a theorist of American culture with a thesis to ride. Enthusiasm for pop of all sorts, not just pornography, produces some astounding judgments; I do not know what else explains how a poet as fastidious as Adrienne Rich could claim that Bob Dylan's pop lyrics vie with John Berryman's dream songs in range and richness of language, above all other contemporary poetic language in the colloquial mode.

Barth's attitude is that fiction as an art is moribund, a mass of work not to be added to or enriched by writers now but for them to pillage and cannibalize. With all traditions discarded, that which tradition despised becomes useful just because it was so despised, and its being offensive, like pornography, is a bonus. Barth also explores, like other postmodernists who turn to pop, the uses of bad taste, boredom ("creative boredom" is his phrase for it), blasphemy, and so on. I had thought Cioran was the ultimate nihilist, but there is a sense in which Barth outdoes him; Cioran still cares that there is Nothing there to connect with, whereas Barth is the disengaged aesthete of nihilism. His endeavor seems merely perverse to me, no more than fun and games—he is the best parodist around. I am willing to be shown, but he has not showed me yet.

Sontag's essay "The Pornographic Imagination" makes the best case I can imagine for the aesthetic possibilities of pornographic fiction. She is contemptuous of most pornography, and she is distressed by its mass availability to the young; she knows what it is. But she makes a valid argument for the perverse seriousness of three pornographic novels; I have read one of them, *The Story of O,* but not the others, both by Georges Bataille. I abominate *The Story of O,* but I cannot dismiss it literarily as I can nearly all the other pornography I have read; it is a novel of some stylistic and structural merit, and to some extent it puts its pornography to the service of an end other than sexual arousal or disgust, as Sade does also, though much more crudely; *The Story of O* is not heavily didactic as Sade's novels are, nor does it try to develop character as novels usually do—pornography is intransigently depersonalizing. It moves, Sontag argues and I think her perception is right, toward a quasi-religious revelation, toward O's transcendence of personality through perverse eroticism, her loss of self through degradation. But there is no gain achieved by this loss of self; O is removed from everyone; nothing but meaningless death can await her now. In my view, this is the erotic nihilism, like Cioran's terrifying theological nihilism, of a balked Christian mystic. I must take on faith Miss Sontag's higher ranking of Bataille's two books, for I shall never read them. In respect of pornography and nihilism, my consciousness has expanded enough. There are things I want not to know.

Never *Nothing*

THE NOTHING to which nihilism aspires is a pure idea—like absolute zero, a limit which can never be attained. All particles, as they approach absolute zero, quit moving; cease to be knowable; lie as they were, like twigs in ice, mutually disconnected. Yet, even in that region of the negligible, they continue to exist, at least potentially; they continue to be related, at least in the eye of one who has observed where they stop moving. Nihilism is a philosophy of rage, for it can never attain what it wants, can be neither fulfilled nor permanently relieved. Its fulfillment would be to have all things cease to exist, the Void; failing that, its relief would be total lack of order in the motions of things, Chaos. But no matter what nihilism does, almost all things keep on moving describably almost all the time. It must substitute a relief which is occasional, fragile, and only sometimes permanent: disconnection.

To one like me, who has felt his own person pulled toward nihilism as a usable ideal, as a dissolver of doubt and a fixed point in shifting worlds, disconnection does not dwindle into familiarity, but retains its own full dreadfulness; and I see in nihilism the sufficient contour of the adversary. Potent as he is, some of his show turns out to be brag and threat: not he but we effect our disconnections. But he can make disconnection seem desirable; he encourages us to it; he can arrange things so that cold hatred seems good and moving love impossible, so that falling out of communion takes no more than indifference but entering into communion is difficult and risky. He tempts me, and I fear him.

The summer I was thirteen, I contained the ingredients needful to become a nihilist, except for a deficiency of rage. First of all, I had an absolutist cast to my Protestant mind; moreover, I could think abstractly, which is to say that my emotions could be as excited by the idea of a word as by its sound or by the image it evoked. I felt a metaphysical certitude that there was a right order hidden in things, not to be tampered with. Take the heavens.

We lived in the Southern California desert twelve miles west of March Field, a military air base. In those days airplanes were few, slow, and small, and even when one came fairly close overhead I was able to compare it to something I had seen in nature, as I cannot a supersonic jet. Most evenings the sky was clear, and often as the family would sit out in front of the house after supper, we would chat about the stars. One evening, to our amazement, great poles of light appeared on the eastern horizon and began tilting about the sky, now one, now another, sometimes three or four at a time, nine in all. We hadn't the vaguest notion what they were for. When they disappeared, the stars seemed brighter.

The lights appeared every evening. A neighbor who could afford to buy a paper on Sundays told us he'd read that war games were being held at March Field. War games? As long as they were games, Mother could ignore their purpose. As long as it was war, Father doubted what games they could be. We kept watching. Sometimes in one of the poles of light a spot brighter than any star would leap into being. Another pole would lean over to it then, and they would keep that bright spot in their intersection, following it. "Isn't it pretty!" cried Mother, and all of us except Father agreed. He had the habit, when he thought of something extremely disgusting, of dislodging both his upper and lower false teeth, pushing them forward between his lips, and clacking them, at the same time making an unvoiced *chrrr* in his throat. He did it now, and I listened attentively to whatever he would say, hoping he could make sense of that actual fantasy in the eastern sky. But all I heard him grumble was "a travesty," a word which I feared the dictionary would not help me understand.

"Daddy," I said, "did God make airplanes and searchlights?"

"I should say not," he answered. "The devil, more likely."

"Oh now," said Mother, "they make them in factories like so many other things."

"Well," I said, "did God want them to be made?"

Dad snorted. "The last thing in the world He wanted."

"Oh goodness," said Mother, "He can't do anything bad, and when anybody does do a bad thing, He won't let them go too far with it. There isn't anything *so* bad about airplanes. It's war's that's bad, and people've always made war. So."

Dad spat.

Among the preconditions of nihilism, one of the most important is to be sure not only that there is a preordained order to things but that this order is worthwhile and means something and that what it means is Christian. The philosophical and emotional ingredients of nihilism are universal enough; but the special configuration of ideas and feelings which produced the word, and the need for the word, "nihilism" did not occur until late in the eighteenth century, after rationalism's full-scale assault on Christian belief. Zen Buddhism, as I understand it, is in one respect exactly the opposite of Christianity; the satori which is the goal of its stern discipline is sudden enlightenment, an essential part of which is realization of the ultimate nothingness of the world; after and only after such awareness, according to Zen teachers, can one return to one's ordinary self there to live in peace, as it were blest.

Even for a Christian writer, direct experience of the void does not have to drive toward nihilism but may seek a purely aesthetic expression; Mallarmé is the laureate of such experience. Nihilism, as I conceive the matter, is an ethical impulse: it is fed by, expresses, justifies the rage of some whom rationalism has unchristianed. It is the dark side of the Enlightenment. When science secularized the universe, some could not get over a sense of having been betrayed: divinity had been the meaning of things, Christ had been love and hope, limit and vengeance had been God's, there was something to die into. Hume shook them, and Voltaire laughed at them in their shaking. They took vengeance to themselves. Nihilistic writers are less interested in expressing their views, aesthetically, than in impressing these views on their readers, morally. They do not cringe in apathy from the tempter's logical whisper, "There is no meaning to the world, so nothing matters." Nor do they give the Zen answer, "Nothing doesn't matter at all." They cry in response, "Oh, nothing matters in the highest, nothing matters more than anything." But they are unsure, being absolutists, whether what they are saying makes good sense; so they shout louder and louder, to cover up their doubt.

The winter before the war games, on the school bus, I had made friends with my first atheists, the Babcock brothers. When I told my parents this, they did not outright forbid me to see the Babcocks. Mother gave me to understand that they were not nice people. But I had been to their house for supper, and the Babcocks were a whole lot better mannered, more thoughtful, and more fun to play with than any of the lunks I'd met in Sunday school. Mother was wrong, but maybe Father was right. He said you couldn't trust appearances. But if the Babcocks had not gravely told me they believed there was no God, I would never have guessed it. How could anybody, especially a family as nice as the Babcocks, not believe in Him? Father was wrong too: I could not distrust their appearance of sincerity. I was especially perplexed by their calmness about it; but the very conception of third- and fourth-generation atheists was beyond me then. I quit stopping by their house on the way home from school, but I also quit going to Sunday school, unless Mother made an issue of it.

In my disturbance, I actually read the poem on a faded old sampler that had been on the kitchen wall as long as I could remember. "Things are not what they seem," one line read.

"Mother," I said, "why is that there?"

"Great-Aunt Hattie made it and gave it to Mama before I was born," said Mother beaming. "Isn't it pretty?"

"Yes, but look at what it says."

"Such a sweet little poem. Longfellow." She chose another line: " 'Life is real, life is earnest.' "

"Yes, but," I quoted meekly, " 'Life is but an empty dream.' "

That made her dig in her ear with her little finger. She gave me a somewhat haughty glance and told me to quit picking at myself all the time. I smiled inwardly, a surreptitious rebel congratulating himself for striking a blow for freedom when all he's done is to give the rug under Mama a little jerk.

My confusion became quite desperate, and I yearned to be rescued. Here I was with a John Bunyan farmer for a father and a Queen Victoria housewife for a mother. But this was the 1930s! Surely something marvelous must be right around the corner waiting to rescue me. But what was it? I began having again the recurrent dream I'd not had for three or four years, about the end of the world. Trouble swarmed me.

There was sex. I was thirteen, and for some time I had been churned to a helpless and buried alarm by unexplained alterations in my body; they had set me rummaging through dictionaries and encyclopedias, from which I'd got a new word at least, puberty. I was ready to be got at by sexology, whose zeal it is to divorce sex from love, leaving it up to you to remarry them if you can.

And there was success. That year, I read a popular book called *The Psychology of Success,* and I watched my father. Success was of the spirit, I had no doubt, certainly not of material goods; it was sort of the way you knew you were tuned in right on Progress; above all, it was not of money. Father scornfully referred to money as "the Almighty dollar," though sometimes he would talk glowingly about what he was going to do when his ship came in. Meanwhile, we did not have enough to live on—this was the depth of Depression—and his face would contort when he had to appeal to an old maid cousin of my mother for money. There were two terrible days when he lay on what he announced must be his deathbed, sometimes moaning, out of his head, "A failure, I'm a failure." Thirty-five years later when he actually died, he didn't have a dollar to his name—he was that kind of failure. But he was attended by his children, who mourned for him—not that other kind. Though I am not likely to doubt my failure if it comes, I could never be certain of my success: having lost every shred of faith in Progress, I don't know what success is if it is.

But of all the qualities which contribute to a man's driving toward nil, I was perhaps best provided with ignorance and impotence. I was so ignorant of the stars, for example, that I knew almost none of their names, much less what astronomy said they really were; knew almost none of the ways in which they moved, much less the laws of their motions. I knew enough, however, to realize that my ignorance was greater than it seemed, for most stars, I had heard, were invisible to the naked eye and even of those I could see most had no names. In my political ignorance, I held in disrespect any customs or laws which had not been commanded by God, that is to say, most of them. I recognized God-and-me and you-and-me. But the network of connections which I now call society and the state was a vague, troubling thing in Washington called the Government; it had been ordained for the good of us all by our Founding Fathers, yet somehow it was also a fraud. Increasingly, as time went on, it got between God and me and between you and me. As for my impotence, it was massive. What could I do to set things straight? War games, the hard times that were making my father miserable, atheism, fraud, puberty— there was only one thing I could do much about, my own ignorance.

But such was my frame of mind that every step forward made me realize not how far I had come in knowledge, but how very far I had yet to go in order to get there, and finally to realize there was no *there* to get to, learning was a way without end. The awareness that there is no end to learning did not fill me with joy at the prospect of inexhaustible riches ahead, but with a heavy sense of inadequacy. What kept me going was pleasure in the going—I just liked to learn.

Ignorance, yes; impotence, yes; but raging hatred, not so much. In part I lacked it because in my half-Quaker, half-Methodist family no taboo was stronger than the prohibition against anger and I had not been endowed with more of it than I could contain. However, the younger of my two brothers, when he was two, occasionally took to crying so hard that he held his breath till his body arched taut as a bow and he turned white about the mouth, then passed out. He did not perform this alarming action for any obvious reason; only once or twice, for example, did he do it after being punished for disobedience. Mother attributed it to green apricots, Father to an ornery streak in his character, but they agreed on calling it a seizure. Cats had *fits,* and *seizure* vaguely implied that he had been invaded—I must say his strumming body looked seized, possessed, by something outside himself. *Temper tantrum,* which they rejected, allowed for the notion of an anger so great you might obliterate yourself with it. Why should, *how could,* their baby be that angry? As for myself, it is only now in my post-Quaker, post-Methodist, relativized middle age that enough rage has been released in me to stain my vision from time to time. But in part my rage then continued deficient for lack of food; helpless as a cave man surrounded by mastodons, it was starved by the very enormity of my complaints. What I saw as wrong was so vast there could be no one worth blaming for it but God. How blame God? Perhaps if someone had tempted me to, I would have tried to blame Him. In fact, as close as I came to it was during the winter after the war games. I was standing one day in an aisle in the public library, thumbing through a fat, blue book entitled *Adolescence,* extending my ignorance of sex. A fellow came up whom I had been avoiding on the school bus because once he had nagged at me all the way to my stop that the Bible said the earth was flat so why did I think it was round. Now, staring at a cross section of the female organs of reproduction—the diagram, for all it meant to me, had as well been of the *begats* from Abraham to Noah—when that fellow accosted me in the library I felt caught in a surreptitious act; but he did not so much as glance at *Adolescence*. He was five years older than I, he had borrowed a nickel from me once and never paid me back, he belonged to the Epworth League, he was a born used-car salesman. He asked me, his fat eyes puckering, his voice sticking so that he had to clear his throat, whether God existed. I half turned, said yes of course, and put the book back on the shelf. He asked me what made me think so. I said I didn't know. My discomfort was so intense that my responses dribbled off into mutters, and he went away. What right did he have to ask me that question? Who was I to say whether the earth was round and God existed? I could not imagine that the world could exist without God to make it and keep it going; that prank of pure reason, "maybe the world isn't," illusion without reality, had not occurred to me yet. It had also not occurred to me yet that God might not be good—evil was our doing, that seemed clear enough. God could not not be, God could not not be good, so why did He let half-baked used-car salesmen who weren't dry behind the ears yet ask me whether He existed? Without knowing it, I was ready to hate Him and even to cry He did not exist. Instead, there chancing to be no nihilists about to tempt me, to authorize rage for me, I neither looked straight at the whole confusion I was in nor went away from it, but messed around, avoiding.

A Christian's cry *There is no God* reaches back to the baby's ultimate horror: not of dying, which is beyond his imagining, but of his parents' abandoning him, which he can imagine every night when he is put to bed. But the crier is also an older child brooding: What evil made them do it? What is wrong with me that they can get along without me? Now suppose a child of heroic aggressiveness, vitality, and imagination, who fantasies every leave-taking as an abandonment. He does not rest content, like a normal child, with giving his parents when they return a few punishing, safe blows; he wants to beat them savagely for having refused to fulfill his fantasies by really abandoning him. It comes to seem to him that the pain of actual abandonment would be a relief from the horror of fantasied abandonment, that the absolute knowledge of their vileness would not be as agonizing as the unconfirmed suspicion of it. Wanting most what he most dreads, he dare not hurt them directly, for then he would have to admit that he *cannot* make them abandon him. Instead, he blurs things over by saying how vile they are and how vile he is, and he becomes obsessed with vengeful fantasies. Contorted by horror and guilt, cancerous with unacknowledged wishes, almost the only relief, even temporary, he can find from this fearful tangle is to deny connection: these cannot be my true parents, I must be a foundling. *There is no God,* the nihilist howls, *there never has been One, and anyway He is dead.*

Nihilists are a missionary sect. Believing in nothing, doubting everything except their own doubt, they also want you to believe in nothing, at least to doubt everything. There are a few, to be sure, who do not proselytize, solipsists like Kirilov in Dostoevsky's *The Possessed.* Believing that the only reality was what he knew, he was able to cause everything to cease to exist by ceasing to know. He shot himself. But few go that far out on the scale of solipsism—another approach to absolute zero. Most nihilists and all nihilistic writers, ground in the jaws of contradiction, believe in nothingness and disconnection but need company. They are so offended by your existence, to say nothing of any sign you may show of conscious and moving love, that they set out to do what they can to pollute you; but to do that, they have to connect with you at least a little. If they get you to undermine and subvert as they are doing, you may not have joined them exactly, but you will at least be disconnected in the same region with them, close enough so that there are others to be torn apart from.

Most of my life I have earned my living teaching college English. It is a cardinal point of the profession that we must stir up the students, especially the freshmen, ask them provocative questions, challenge their assumptions. When I was forty and had thoroughly mastered the pedagogy of undercutting, I was teaching at Barnard (the girls' college of Columbia where intellectual subversion is even more orthodox than it had been at Berkeley where I got my degree). One day in midterm, a girl in a freshman class, tossing her head in evident pain, asked me, "What are you trying to do to us?" "Shake you up." "Well, you're not shaking me up," she said, "you're break- ing me down." Her hands were trembling, her eyes looked askew, when she lowered her head, her hair straggled over her face unkempt. The word had become flesh—my words, her flesh—in a way I had not foreseen. I began wondering what other words of mine had been doing, invisibly to me, once they got into young people, and I have taken greater care with them since that day.

"A nihilist," said Arkady in *Fathers and Sons,* and he ought to know since the word came into circulation chiefly as Turgenev's name for him and Bazarov his mentor, "a nihilist is a man who does not bow down before any authority, who does not take any principle on faith, whatever reverence that principle may be inshrined in." Stephen Dedalus in *Portrait of the Artist as a Young Man* held as a secret motto Lucifer's formula of defiance: *Non serviam.* Back in the days when the West was still in the process of declining, sentiments like Arkady's and Stephen's looked pretty horrific, established a kind of ultimate, a limit. But, to us who come after Stalin and Hitler, those romantic nihilists seem high-minded dandies: like Satanists at a black mass, they strike attitudes which are never quite free of the ludicrous. You won't serve, eh. What will you do then? "Forge on the smithy of my soul," said Stephen, "the uncreated conscience of my race." How gorgeous! And how empty. And how very dangerous: the moment you convince yourself that your race has not already created its own conscience, for better or worse, you are free to impose your will on it like an ideological despot. Joyce doubted himself into a palsy. Shaking with uncertainty, marching under gorgeous, blank banners, he sought relief by destroying and by imposing his will on you through words: the Lenin of literature. *Because nothing matters, only I matter; because words matter to me most, I shall tear out their meat and make handsome designs of their shells. To read me at all you must submit to me.* He made of art a reversed religion, and his greatest accomplishment was to make of himself a travesty of a saint, make of his own life a parodic work of great art. For my part, I value Richard Ellmann's unimposing biography of Joyce above any of his own imposing books.

Romantic nihilists generally, not being of Joyce's heroic proportions, were not steadfast in what they wanted; often they wobbled into the simplicity of merely hating. The trouble was, they could not help hating many things worthy of hatred—injustice, hypocrisy, abuse of power, false ideals. So, which side were they on? Both sides; a dilemma. They desired to heal the social wounds, but saw these as so extensive that they despaired of accomplishing this desire. To escape the dilemma, they would bring injustices to an end, not by establishing a better order, but by wrecking the social order which created the injustices—by every means, from political murder to intellectual subversion. All the same, to us who have seen in Germany a great nation parody-ruled by a sect of fundamentalist nihilists denying the good and loving everything vile, romantic nihilists seem archaic and almost congenial: somehow, they dream, somehow, if we just destroy zealously enough, somehow love and community and the good will manifest themselves in history. Myself, I no longer believe in that phoenix much, but I feel a certain kinship to those who do. In a world whose chairmen are ready, for so stunted a reason as national rivalry, to reduce the earth to polluted ashes from which no phoenix could rise, thereby parodying nihilism itself, malice putrefied into slobbery, evil as stupidity—to us, in such a world, even the most assertive nihilism repays looking at, it is majestic, it has character, definition. I would rather contemplate the king of hell than the pro tem committee to homogenize the world. He is my adversary, whom I shall not become; mediocrity dissolves me.

In this America we have made where it is hard to love, if you love anything bigger than the house on your back you very likely also hate our society—unjust, ugly, violent, more hypocritical than it need be, disturbed by lying dreams, using money to measure worth, all the time measuring worth, distracted and addicted to distraction. Indeed, so strong is the revulsion against the world we have made (not only in America but throughout the West) that literary nihilism can and does justify itself as being able to express this emotion. Our world is disordered? Very well, a true expression of this experience of disorder must itself be disordered; some novelists allow chance to enter into or even control the sequence in which their pages are assembled for publication. Our world is vile? Only vile words, chant The Fugs, among many, can express its vileness adequately. Senseless? Let the poem be one word printed as many times as the page will hold—a device first used by a dadaist and since adopted by advertisers.

There is a certain force to this line of argument, and it helps explain why nihilism has become chic in recent years. If you can't understand a play, for example, *Tiny Alice,* in which playwright and producers show every sign of confidence that they know what they're up to, then your confusion itself must be the end they are after. If the play seems to mean something and finally denies meaning both within itself and in its subject, that is because the world only seems to mean but really doesn't. Relax and enjoy. Confusion, false promises, sleaziness, and blasphemy can be quite charming when nothing is at stake. Albee accommodates himself to fashion: he muffles the play's nastiest insult in argot, a snigger for the *in* crowd ("tiny alice" is buggerese for "tight asshole"). Genet is a rougher type entirely; but though he openly sets himself against the audience, fashion has nevertheless been able to accommodate to him. Do the characters in *The Blacks* seem to assault the audience? Not really, says fashion, what they are really doing is expressing their hostility—and how deliciously they do it. Myself, I share serious nihilism's respect for the power of art: I find genuinely nihilistic art troubling and dangerous and in no way delicious. At a tense moment of Genet's play, in the performance I attended, a black actor pointed his accusing finger at my white face; I felt the anger at him and at Genet which, I believe, Genet intended me to feel, and I did not enjoy feeling it, as Genet intended me not to. Expressing is only part of what art does; arson may be the firebug's mode of expressing himself, but that's the least of my concerns when I find my house on fire.

If the chic aesthetes identify expression with communication, the moral bigots, the book-burners, go to the other extreme by identifying impression with communication. In my view, things are more complicated than this either/or allows for. A play well performed expresses something of its playwright and its age, and if it is great enough it will express something important in actors and audience of any age; but it is also a new thing in the world with power to impress itself on its audience, to affect them, to change for a while the way they see, or even what they see. Attitudes control actions to some degree, and ideas can modify attitudes in those who are vulnerable to ideas. I have seen a student's pupils dilate to a new idea as to belladonna. What about those who are vulnerable to poetry, as I am? How can I not believe it has power to modify my attitudes when I have known it to change me directly? While taking a deep, unsteady breath after reading *The Rime of the Ancient Mariner* the winter I was twelve, I realized that what I was going to do in life was to write stories and poems. Coleridge, not intending anything of the kind, expressing who cares what?, altered the way I breathed and moved. So, a few years later, did Kafka in *The Castle*—that unfinishable tale of incomplete connections. What about writers who intend to use their force to alter the way I see, love, shall die? How can I not take their intention seriously?

Recently a good deal of favorable attention has been paid to some fictions which jerk themselves up to a certain vigor whenever they describe acts of sex or violence, or best of all sexual violence. The most substantial such book I have read is *Naked Lunch* by William Burroughs. By breaking down narrative coherence and syntax, he aims both to disgust and to confuse his reader. He pushes the rhetorical disintegration so far that only an effort of will could slog me from one sentence—one word-clump—to the next. It is a very modern book: in the democratized West generally and in America especially, the idea of subordination as a good has been so spoken against that even the elemental authority, that of parents over children, has been shaken, and no book assaults subordination more vigorously than this one, narratively, ethically, grammatically. Presumably, Burroughs does this as a form of insubordinate rebellion, but so wholesale is he that, there being no sense of subordination left, insubordination has no meaning either; having leveled authority, he rebels against difference; blur is left. There are people, worthy of respect both literally and morally, who think this shattered fiction expresses the age profoundly. Though I think otherwise—what appalls me about our age is the grinding clashes of monstrous superorders— I can sympathize with that position. Burroughs's destructiveness, disgust, and confusion are embodied in shards of images, broken rhythms, felicitous phrases, and spasmodic actions, so powerfully that I can see how some, having in themselves similar feelings, are grateful to him for finding ways to express those feelings. But to call the book's chaotic vividness high moral order, great satire, is like saying that, because plants must be fertilized, mulch is as fine as flowers. Satire addresses itself morally to the understanding, whereas *Naked Lunch* subverts understanding. When a would-be satirist immerses himself for too long in the ugliness he loathes, that ugliness will become part of him; as in a prurient censor at a dirty movie, behind his zeal to destroy ugliness lurks avidity for it; the satire which he intends to be cleansing, instead adds to the world's ugliness. Such a book does not just express the author's disgust and confusion; even more important, whatever he may announce elsewhere about his intentions, the book releases disgust and confusion in the reader, without containing it within the forms of art. When I read with such revulsion, the fellow feeling is blurred from my pity till all that is left is that sense of superiority which makes pity so tricky an emotion at best. "At least I'm nowhere near as bad off as they are."

Literarily, the only nihilists of our age that amount to much are Beckett in his plays and Genet in his autobiographical writings.

Beckett's fiction inverts toward solipsism, carrying parody as far as it will go on its own power, to its deadest end. *How It Is* consists of the ruminations of a consciousness, presumably human, crawling blindly through mud. Beyond that is parody pure, words selected and arranged by a computer programmed to a table of random numbers. Then comes the antibook itself, a boxful of blank pages. But there is a contradiction built into any finally nihilistic parody of art—a concert or play consisting of a half hour of silence on an empty stage, a black rectangle hung on a museum wall, a lump of ice melting on a pedestal. Since they don't communicate anything in themselves, you have to have explained to you how they are supposed to communicate nothing. What they get across is the extraneous meaning which their makers or exegetes tack onto them. They are vacuous icons; pretending to be images of nothingness, they are signs pointing toward a concept of nothingness. An extreme parodist is really a metaphysician using his work of antiart as a club to beat you with.

But Beckett's plays, especially *Waiting for Godot*, which is no parody, must surely be the handsomest work of literature making a nihilistic statement. The very handsomeness subverts the message. "The world is without meaning and hope." Really? Then why does saying it elegantly matter so much? Besides, the characters in his plays are marvelously connected with each other and with us. Maybe we are abandoned in a world that doesn't mean anything ultimately, but Beckett has made a bit of it mean something to a good many of us. I can think of more nihilistic things to do than that.

I believe that Nazism, by figuring nihilism forth so brutally *out there*, altered the nature of subsequent nihilistic writing. Once a fantasy has been realized in inescapable fact, it cannot thereafter be written about seriously in the same way. After the Nazis, either nihilistic writers descend into and stay in the muck like Burroughs—worse, into the chic like Albee—or else they must be honest writers when they put pen to paper, like Beckett and Genet.

Genet's fiction and drama, though powerful, fail to satisfy formally, but his autobiographies, especially *The Thief's Journal*, do not have to offer structural satisfaction, since a flaw of the part does not much weaken the whole; they chronicle the spiritual life of a nihilist superbly. What Genet found as he approached the dead center of his self was what Dante found as he approached his moral center, fraud in its purest form, betrayal. But whatever Genet the man in history may have done and aspired to do, the character in this confession knows when he lies, and the writer of it tries not to lie. Maybe he does it out of Satanlike pride, as he claims. "It is perhaps their moral solitude—to which I aspire—that makes me admire traitors and love them—this taste for solitude being the sign of my pride, and pride the manifestation of my strength, the employment and proof of this strength. For I shall have broken the stoutest of bonds, the bonds of love." But he is not totally given over to solitary pride. "And I so need love from which to draw vigor enough to destroy it!" Evil yearns to parody love to extinction—knowing that this cannot be done. Genet refers to his book as the "pursuit of the impossible Nothingness," and he is right. For by its very excellence the book denies nothingness. For a poet, whatever has a name exists: never *nothing*. As a literary nihilist Genet has two fatal flaws—he loves the beautiful, finding it especially in perverse forms but also in undisguised openness, and he is usually as honest as he can be. (His grandiloquence and glittery paradox can be mostly attributed to French prose. "I shall impose a candid vision of evil, even though I lose my life, my honor and my glory in this quest." Every competent proseur flashes out sentences like this by the gross.) But literary honesty, being a form of communion, threatens that solitude, that disconnection, of which Genet boasts. "By the gravity of the means and the splendor of the materials which the poet used to draw near to me, I measure the distance that separated him from them. . . . If the work is of great beauty, requiring the vigor of the deepest despair, the poet had to love men to undertake such an effort. And he had to succeed. It is right for men to shun a profound work if it is the cry of a man monstrously engulfed within himself." Genet as writer did not stay at the dead center which he says he strove for as character. (The tension between Genet-writer and Genet-character is the strangest I know, stranger even than that in Boswell.) Genet betrayed his betrayal by writing a book which is at once against and with us. It lays bare the moral nature of a nihilist without itself being an instrument of nihilism. Why? Because he went to Germany in the thirties. At first he was "excited at being free amidst an entire people that had been placed on the index." Then he thought to himself, "If I steal here, I perform no singular deed that might fulfill me. I obey the customary order; I do not destroy it." And before long what he "desired above all was to return to a country where the laws of ordinary morality were revered, were laws on which life was based." After that, he knew that he was defined by disobeying our law as certainly as we are by obeying it, that criminal and citizen are bound together by the law which separates them and which both of them need. After that, moreover, he knew that he needed moral words, the language of Christianity in which he had been reared. When he says "evil" he does not mean something else as Sade sometimes does, nor does he try to confuse you into thinking "evil" has no meaning, nor does he mean by it something personified by the devil. He is an intellectual: he does not worship a person, Satan; he loves an idea, evil; and when he says he loves evil, he means what he says as exactly as Milton's Satan, who was also an intellectual of sorts, meant it when he said "Evil, be thou my good." His experience of Germany in the thirties marked the moment after which nihilism could no longer be as it had been: thereafter, because the bad dream had been incarnated in an actual society, because the madness had been everted into totalitarianism, because, for one whose need is to disobey, having no legitimate authority to disobey is to lose all shape, thereafter whenever a nihilistic writer who could think well enough to write well enough to be worth reading sat down to write as authentically as he could, he would have to go straight and by just so much cease to be nihilistic.

Even in college I did not get into nihilism over my knees. We Berkeley radicals just before the war were all for manning barricades which we knew would almost certainly not be raised, all for no state and no war; but as soon as the Nazis began conquering, we were also all for strengthening our state in order to fight this war. A few months after Pearl Harbor, I was doing war work for the government. I made acquaintance with criminals, and dabbled in felony a couple of times. I declared there was no God. Yet I wouldn't take the whole plunge.

I continued to be deficient in anger. It did not occur to me to rage against God, since He did not exist; and though I was as adept as the next man at blaming society for people's ills, I could never quite get it out of my head that, even if the state was evil, it was people who made it evil—not just a conspiracy of Wall Street capitalists, Kremlin commissars, or Nazi gangsters, but the rest of us taxpayers too. There had not been planted in me early enough that root of permanent rage, contempt for authority, the set of disobedience. In the pre-Enlightenment of my childhood, obedience was an unquestioned good. We children usually obeyed: our mother because we should and our father also because he had a personal authority that made us want to obey him. In this world still, there is nothing I want more than to have over me authority I can respect and to exercise such authority over those beneath me. It is hard to have the one without the other. Under the presidents and congresses and governors of my life, I have learned contempt for most authorities, all right, but, because of my father, I have not learned to enjoy it as a good nihilist must.

More secretly, I suffered the shame of inadequacy: I could conceive more than I could imagine; for example, the end of the world. My father believed that the Bible prophesied it for the year 2000. My childhood dreams of the end of the world had been nightmares with power to wake me up crying, but their climaxes had always been an image—roiling clouds, a clap of thunder, a stump upside down in the sky inscribed with the words *The End*. The dream-image would represent the moment just before the end. Once I came to realize that I never, even in a dream, reached the end beyond images, I feared and knew I feared to go farther. Suppose that at the end there really was nothing? It was thinkable but unimaginable. The closest I have come to imagining nothing is to build on a childhood memory of shutting myself in a dark closet and squatting among the galoshes, wishing that the Old Hag of the House (my great-grandmother) would die horribly; I dared put the wish into words only in a place where I could not be seen, but not even there did I dare say the words aloud for they could be heard, by myself. By subtracting the wish and the galoshes and then adding the cold silence of a cave I once stayed still in for a few minutes, I lean as far into Nothing as I can reach. But this image, being so negative, so subtractive, provides a less satisfactory metaphor for Nothing than does one of physics' stark concepts: an antineutrino in the vacuum of furthermost space, an almost no-thing under normal circumstances, but, there in the unimaginable void, an almost no-thing lacking even energy, unlocatable, negligible.

But that is rather grand. Maybe it is just that I have always been too impatient to be a good nihilist. When I spoiled other people's pleasure or tranquility, I wanted to be there to get the good of it. Sometimes, I would provoke my next younger brother into wrestling with me, so that I could get him down and lie spread-eagle on him till he beat his head on the ground in frustration. Once I wrote bad words on the wall of the school outhouse, in the clumsy block letters of the school bully. I never told anybody I had done this, but I was there when he was punished for what he had not done, there congratulating myself for having rectified an injustice—think of all the bad things he had done without being caught. I lacked the pure nihilistic zeal to spoil for the sake of spoiling. I once chanced to see a boy urinate on a box of apples which he had just picked and which were about to be taken to town for sale. He did not know I saw him; he would never know who bought the apples; those who ate them would not know the apples had been polluted; he would never know, in all likelihood, how or even whether the eaters would be damaged by what he had done. As I watched him, the expression on his face was serious, gloomy; his eyes did not dart about anxiously; he was not gleeful with naughtiness. I was outclassed, and slunk away.

I had a zeal for connection, and I was lucky in that there were no theories working against my need for friendship. Sexological instruction was viewed in those days, at least in the world I inhabited, as a form of pornography, titillating and shameful. There seems to me even less to be said for sexology than for the blind prudery that came before it. In sexology's glare, mystery shrivels, but for us it at least had dirt to survive in, the teeming filth of prurience. What do the young do now, for whom sex has been not only klieg-lighted but sterilized, who are so clear about the sixty-nine positions of sex that the infinite ways of love seem to them a fearsome labyrinth? Imagine being a young person skilled in operating your sexual feedback system, usually but not necessarily in adjunction to a self-regulating servomechanism of the opposite sex—all this before you are experienced in, much less committed to, that dark other-fucking by which and in which but not for which love is made. I would sooner kill someone with my bare hands, in that intense connection which

natural fury drives us to, than fall into the habit of performing sex-
ology's bright clear travesty of love which divorces body from spirit
as cruelly as puritanism ever did. Believing that man is by nature
a maker of taboos, I see the obscure, ambiguous sexual energies as
being so powerful that they must surely generate in us some taboos,
and when these taboos are detached from sex till it becomes simply
pleasure, they do not just disappear but attach instead to love—
post coitum nihil. I see the sleek body of aesthetic sex as encapsu-
lating the spirit within it in a furious stasis, a tense, septic passivity
like riding in a jet bomber seven miles off the earth where it's 80°
below zero even on a summer day, an antiemotion with death in it,
button-pushing remote-controlled unsurvivable death.

There are those from whom not even death has been able to dis-
connect me, especially my father. He was eighty when he lay dying,
and he had suffered heart trouble for a long time; I was forty-eight
by then and had been father in my own family for a long time. His
left foot died two or three days before his heart stopped beating; it
was hot summer, and the nurses left the sheet off him; we watched
the dark-purple death mount his left leg and begin to mottle his right
foot and leg; then his hands; then his arms. His toenails were long
untrimmed, and the horny nail on his right big toe had scraped an
oozing wound on the side of his left foot—perhaps it had itched as
it was dying. The last time I stood by his bed, I held his purpling
hand; it was cold and did not respond to my touch. For several weeks
afterward, I could not readily fall asleep, as I had usually done, and
I hardly trimmed my toenails. I do not know how long my father's
dying would have continued to live in me had chance not exorcised it
by bringing three events together late that fall. In the same week, two
old friends of mine killed themselves; once, we had all three been
very close; I dreaded what might happen if those self-destructions
got down into me where my father's death still lived. But shortly
before those suicides, it happened that I, the oldest of four children,
had been appointed head of a committee of four to search for a new
chairman of our English department. Never in my life have I under-
taken an ordinary task in the line of duty with such intensity—an
intensity which from here looks mildly comic—for it was more than
a department chairman I needed to find. Before long, my left foot
ceased to be so cold when I went to bed, and I ceased to be occupied
by the insomniac fear that if I dropped off I might scrape my left foot

with my right big toenail, which I took to keeping trimmed short. What survives in me now of my father was him alive, for in that appointed search and finding his death died in me.

At the bottom of hell, walking through murk toward the center of all things, Dante and Virgil cross a frozen plain, and here in the innermost region of windy cold, they find traitors totally immersed in ice haphazard as they fell, "like straws in glass," immobile, cut off from God and from one another. Here is disconnection pure. But in the murk at the center of the moral universe it is not nothing Dante finds; it is the huge, gloomy figure of traitorous Satan, the perfect rebel who dared refuse the perfect authority, the ultimately proud one who does not submit even in defeat but rears in ceaseless torment, weeping, raging, slavering, in his three mouths chewing the three greatest of human betrayers.

Nihilism has a comparable human figure, the Marquis de Sade, that three-faced absolutist. A need for coherence and honesty does not redeem his writing up into valuable literature. His books are like the hideous wings of Dante's Satan beating forth a freezing wind: their only virtue is power. With one of his faces Sade rages against God for having permitted evil in the universe, for having granted him the freedom to disobey. With another face he denies: denies that men have a common nature (which is vile in any case), denies that God exists (Who is to blame for everything wrong), contemns all custom as not being a sure reflection of the moral law (which does not exist either), asserts that we can be certain of nothing beyond our sensations and our egoes (thereby reducing value to *what I want,* for which there are two fundamental satisfactions, the orgasm and the imposition of will, me over you). But with his third face, Sade— the man more than the writer—shows melancholy vestiges of a love so strong that not even he could wholly pervert it: for example, as a functionary during the First Republic, he was imprisoned for lack of zeal in accusing and turning in for execution victims suspected by the Terror. Perhaps he was not moved to that action by love so much as by one of love's facsimiles, hatred of injustice—a risky passion for a nihilist, being easily mistaken for love and indeed sometimes engendering love. However that may be, it seems clear enough that the freedom sought by the cruel, powerful criminals of Sade's novels has nothing to do with justice, only with force; it is for themselves only. They have the bodies of men and the brains of *philosophes,* but they are conscienceless, being, emotionally, devouring babies.

But how is a writer to make his books into instruments of nihilism? Practically, how can a philosophical storyteller be compared to a bloody tyrant, Sade to Marat? What can even that most noxious of books, *The 120 Days of Sodom,* boast of comparable to the harm done by one of Stalin's secret police in the performance of one day's duties? What is a war game beside war itself? Perhaps doubt of this kind provided food for Sade's rage; perhaps overcoming that doubt, having to substitute mental defilement for physical destruction, increased his missionary fervor to insatiable frenzy. In any case, by the world at large these books are not considered symptoms of a mental disease so much as carriers of a moral one; it matters less that they can be considered expressions of a disordered mind than that they are intended to, and can, disrupt the mind on which they make their impression. To be sure, there are no corpses to point to which would demonstrate the power of Sade's novels to produce direct results. But their being banned in nearly every civilized country except ours, at least in the language of the country, attests to the power they are usually thought to have to shape people's attitudes.

The force of Sade's fiction is both general and specific. Generally, I believe, he and his descendants have made two radical contributions to the unfinished revolution that began with the *philosophes* his fathers. The *Sadistes*—not the sexual perverts but the adherents to the philosophy of *Sadisme*—have encouraged men to distrust experience (not your testimony about your experience, but my own experience in my own thoughts) and to deny community as a lying dream (not such and such an unjust nation in history, but the very idea of society, institutions, customs, laws). These radical distrusts are so devious and obscure that the vitiation they have caused cannot be demonstrated: all the same, I believe it has been far from negligible. An instance of the specific force of Sade's writing is the unbelievable inflation of the philosphical, scientific, and literary merit accorded his books by some who do not resist their power—his biographer Lely, Geoffrey Gorer, Simone de Beauvoir, among many. They compare him, seriously, to Nietzsche, Freud, and Shakespeare. They count the boredom of his books as a virtue, as being a part of his literary strategy. There are even those so chic they can say they enjoy his scourging fiction ("Epatez us again, Daddy-O, we love it")—which reduction, I think, would have enraged him yet more, for he intended his lashings to wound you morally, not titillate you fashionably. For other specific instances I must point to experience. I know a sophisticated literary critic of mature years, a professor at Yale opposed to censorship, who bought a copy of *The 120 Days* in English some years ago when he was in Italy and found himself, once he'd read it, uneasy at having it in the house. He lent it to a friend, who tried to return it as soon as he found out what it was like, but the owner did not want it back. They wound up destroying the copy, they burned a book. Edmund Wilson, who likes to read at breakfast, has said *The 120 Days* is the only book he has been unable to read while eating, and he had to make himself finish it even in his study at night. For my own part, having spent a couple of hours reading around in it, I know that I *cannot* read that book.

For Sade knew how to spoil things in the reader's mind. He did not do it by violating narrative and syntax, making his books themselves confused in the manner of Burroughs; his prose is moderately elegant and his stories, though feeble, are shaped enough to provide occasions for the passages for whose sake they exist. It is in these many passages that his books accomplish their intention. Blasphemy, parody of moral structure as well as some straight literary parody, repetition, boredom in toxic but not quite lethal doses (Sade is the only writer who both bores and fascinates me), a slick gloss over mental blur, unresolvable paradox, dissolve of values from one end of the story to the other—all these are aids, they make their useful contributions, but they are not the main elements. The main things are confusion and defilement, that is, pseudo philosphy and massive pornography.

The philosophy, abstracted from the novels, is a sort of Humean parody of Rousseausism. Intellectually, Hume's skepticism is far better formulated and more devastating, but Sade's philosophizing, as it appears in the novels, hits harder imaginatively. (None of his ideas is original, only the way they are combined and used.) Philosophically, *Justine* is his central fiction, for not just the preaching author but the fable itself vilifies and ridicules and assaults the ideal of virtue in the person of the goody-goody heroine, who, abandoned by every lawful authority, is vilified, ridiculed, and assaulted by criminal force. As a character, Justine is as vapid as Pollyana, there's not enough to her to feel about one way or the other. But that very vapidity, though it is a reason the novel is without merit fictionally, helps one understand Sade because it makes Justine invulnerable to us emotionally; for the ideal which she incarnates could not be polluted by even Sade's hatred. Still, he knew it; he is at least that honest.

As I interpret the matter, it is his intention, in the name of unshackling us, setting us free, to undercut and confuse every hope of our ever knowing, much less attaining, the good—by assaulting religion and the religious, by sophistic reasoning, by the argument from comparative customs, by attributing to every action the lowest and most hypocritical motive. Of *Sadisme*'s entire arsenal of ideas, none is so damaging as its contempt for limits; it holds that to accept, much less to want, limits is mere atavism, a relic of our troglodyte ancestors who made taboos out of their fear and moral principles out of their taboos. We who are enlightened are beyond all that. But true *Sadistes* are not content with intellectual liberation alone; they want to be liberated morally as well, and, fired with apostolic zeal, they set about liberating others wholesale.

I hope this configuration of notions sounds familiar and current; for once an unchristianed Westerner grants, as very many do, that value comes only from one's own nature, *Sadisme* is hard to crack. In the ferocity with which it pushes toward its extremest statement, it is the most disquieting possible travesty of liberal, progressive attitudes. *If there are no moral limits, why not?* To this argument decent liberals have no adequate reply, only sentiments. *I don't want to. I wish you didn't want to. You must be sick.*

As for Sade's pornography, it is intentionally revolting. For him, love is a never-resting enemy that cannot be obliterated. Remember Genet: "I so need love from which to draw vigor enough to destroy it!" Sade knows that, if he is to impose himself sufficiently upon his reader, he must spoil love as best he can. The most intense form of love known to most of mankind is erotic communion, in which for a time things are what they seem and Another is not strange. Sexual intercourse can both make and be a symbol of making love; and love's perfection is what in more ceremonious days was called rapture or bliss (sexology teaches us to settle for simultaneous orgasm). It is this true dream of connection which Sade sets out to, and does, pollute—robbing love to pervert it. But his account of what he is up to is not, like Genet's, detached and lucid that we may understand, but steamy, blurred, turgid, that we may be uncoupled. A cartoon image that appears over and over in Sade's fiction in one form or another is of a hideous old man, rich, of high station, outside the law achieving a solitary sexual spasm while he is devouring the excrement of a beautiful young victim whom he watches being tortured to death by his brutal slaves. So put, such an image seems merely grotesque, but in the novels' detailed and exciting prose it has a certain force (and at least it is not death-sterile but full of filthy life). Still, that cartoon is nearly as far from my experience as an antineutrino in empty space. Pornography defeats philosophy: it is too ingenious, too pat.

I can more nearly reach the extremes of *Sadisme*, I can follow better the convolutions of its psychology, by remembering my little brother holding his breath. I imagine that the paroxysm bending his body taut as a strung bow ended in an obliteration more nearly total than orgasm even, that by annihilating his solipsist consciousness he annihilated all of us too and thereby imposed his will on his parents more cruelly than by any other act open to him—he was too young to know how to kill himself. In that little boy ashen with a fury the cause of which none of us understood but the potency of which was measured by its violation of our strongest taboo, hurting all he could, eyes rolled up till only the whites showed, froth at the corners of his mouth, I see Sade plain. That unappeasable baby is what a disappointed Christian absolutist had better have in him if he is to dedicate himself to taking vengeance on the world.

Genet, the whore's bastard, is luckier than Sade, the privileged nobleman. Because the world hurt Genet so cruelly when he was a child, because he was actually abandoned by his parents, he could hurt back at it with a free conscience, and out of simple fear that it, being so much stronger than he, would kill him, he dared try to please it by the very way he provoked it: his extremest fantasy is to be a saint—of evil. But Sade, who was not actually abandoned as a child, was unable to forgive the world for having pampered him; he interpreted every kindness as a sign of weakness, every mercy as a failure to stop him in time; and he dedicated his manhood to provoking the world to insult him relentlessly, that his fury might never dwindle into propitiatory gestures; almost nothing he wrote was meant to please the world, or did please it. By the common meaning of the word, the world has seen far worse sadists than the

Marquis himself, but never a writer so devoted to polluting the wells of truth and love. Yet, since such malice exists in the world, and in myself, I am not sorry to have read a good deal of Sade's fiction: to confront an adversary as majestic as this is to learn something ultimately important about the nature of things and of oneself.

But I could never have confronted him by myself; to do that, I needed and got much help. At Christmastime when I was four or five, my father sang Herod in a nativity play at the Quaker church. I had not been to a play before, I did not know who Herod was, I sat beside my mother, the church was full of Friends. Father's robe and crown made him appear very tall, and the makeup, especially the heavy eyebrows, made him cruel and strong; everyone looked up to him, bowed before him. When the wise men told him what the bright star meant, he shouted that all the firstborn men-children in his kingdom must be killed. I was sheltered by my mother's arm, the room was full of tranquil-seeming people, that very afternoon he had kissed my elbow where I'd fallen on the ice and bumped it. But for these, I would surely have given way to the hysteria that swelled to bursting in me, for all that my emotions knew at that moment was that he wanted to kill me. For an hour that night he sat by my bed holding my hand till I dared to go to sleep.

Dante has helped me, too, even as I am sure he has helped unnumbered thousands of others, even as Virgil helped him. When the two of them had crossed that desolate lake, they came to Satan. Dante looked at him and understood what he saw—"if he were once as handsome as he is ugly now." But they did not stay long in that frigid "air of lost connections" (in Robert Lowell's phrase). Dante took hold of Virgil, who "caught hold of the shaggy sides," clinging to Satan for a while because there was no other way to go beyond him, and when they had passed through dead center in a kind of parody of birth, they turned around so that what had been down now became up, what left now right. Then, right side up, they went away, leaving that dark cave, which will always be there and which they could do nothing about, their ears no longer ringing with the howls of those whom God had abandoned, of those travesty-babies in that dead womb, and they climbed back up to the world of light, where the sun and the other stars shine unobscured, where communion is possible.

The Sky and a Goat

I NO LONGER regret having spent most of my youth in a desert, though at the time I thought it hard not to be living among that Nature described by the poets I loved. Of course, I knew in a general way that lizards and rocks and dry weather were Nature too, but they weren't what I had in mind; and our striking events—earthquakes, dust storms, cloudbursts gullying the fields, three-day north winds—were acts less of Nature than of God. Nature was skylarks, nightingales, daisies pied, wild thyme, storms at sea, rustic maids, meads; when melancholy, one could wander cloudlike among Nature or, if it was evening, weep against her bosom. Nature flourished in England, Greece, and Italy, and generally around the Mediterranean; there was a good deal in the Rhine Valley and more in the Alps, some in Arabia and New England, and scarcely any in such places as Brazil or Australia. In southern California, crouched behind Mount San Jacinto from a really deadly desert, we had tumbleweeds instead of broom, buzzards instead of ravens, greasewood instead of lilies, nothing fell in the fall, it did not snow in the winter, we had to irrigate even in the spring, and the only Nature I recognized was the sky and the heavenly bodies.

Shelley, my most adored, sent me to Plato, and from *The Symposium* I learned about the ladder of love, which I resolved to climb. But I found most of the rungs missing, the rungs that should have been provided by Nature.

We had no lawn; my mother's synecdoche of a garden was a line of geraniums on the shady side of the kitchen. Our house was at one corner of a carob plantation. Like a lion farm, an ostrich farm, an alligator ranch, a stucco Chinese temple movie house, a town near Hollywood named Tarzana, this plantation was a creature of southern California fantasy. The carob, native to the eastern Mediterranean, produced a brown, dry pod which had been (so we were spieled) the locust which John the Baptist ate in the wilderness, and which furthermore was so highly nutritious that it would be prized as a health food; for reasons such as these carob was sure to have a booming future in California. But the taproot of our imported carobs, long before it got down to water, hit the granite hardpan lying just below the surface of our desert and curled up like a pig's tail, so that our trees were a scrubby five feet tall instead of a luxuriant thirty-five; nor did the health-food addicts acquire the carob habit. But the most desolate thing about the plantation was that the trees had been planted in rows twenty feet apart east and west and thirty feet apart north and south; years of staring down these rows, or squinting fanwise across them to seek out or fabricate all manner of diagonal rows, have left me with the tic of lining things up, a spot on the windowpane with a plane in the distance, a pencil point with the tip of your nose. It was an imbecile geometer's version of perfection.

The desert did not like us. Sometimes, especially at sunset, it was beautiful, but its beauty was not responsive in any way; it was just there; sometimes after supper we would sit on the front porch and awe at it. Yet, neither did the desert *dis*like us. The beasts of the desert were not congenial: jackrabbits, roadrunners, gopher snakes and gophers, horned toads like suede models of dinosaurs, scorpions and centipedes and black widow spiders, tarantulas, gila monsters, stink bugs. They could not be taken as responsive to a man as a man: rattlesnakes did not strike nor coyotes slink away because you were human but because you were a thing that threatened. The pathetic fallacy, which had so enriched poetry's pastures in Europe, was wholly absent here and it transplanted badly. I tried personification on a raggedy, misanthropic sheepherder once—we did not have shepherds but sheepherders—but when I learned he had piles he ceased to be the Spirit of the Desert roaming the hills in self-elected solitude and became a Portugee named Lou. The sky was there, the perfect sky in which the clouds, when they appeared, were far too huge to be friendly or laughing; the sky was *there*, not here. (As it still is; up in a plane thirty thousand feet above the ground, I do not feel myself to be in the sky, for I can't get it to stick in my head that the air around me is pantheistically One with the vast Inane.) And lord of it all was the sun, surely the very source and power of Nature; but the desert sun gave not just abundantly of its heat and light, but superabundantly, indifferent to what we needed or wanted, gave endlessly of itself with harsh force and strange love, witheringly; gave, gave and would not take in return.

I substituted poetry for Plato's ladder, and got so I could run up it like a monkey up a palm tree and jump off the top step into a Palgrave posy of perfection.

Hail to thee, Bright Star, half-angel and half-bird!
Who, to the last point of vision, and beyond,
Mounted with full-throated ease! Thou was not born for death;
When old age shall this generation waste,
Thou shalt remain upon the sole Arabian tree,
The goblet of thy beaded-bubble song
Staining the white radiance of eternity.

Would I were steadfast as thou, Blithe Spirit,
Who in broad daylight shin'st unseen. Yet hark—
Heard melodies are sweet, but those unheard
Are sweeter; wherefore, sweet Thames, run gently
That all the woods may answer and the echo ring.

Bright effluence of bright essence increate,
Art thou a vision or a waking dream?
Sophocles long ago heard thee on the Aegean,
Singing of Mount Abora. Do I wake or sleep?

It seemed to me at the time that all that really mattered was the realm where Truth was Beauty, God was the spirit of the Universe, and the quality of Mercy was not strained, and that my family and I alike were clayey beyond redemption. I might in fact have grown toward Manicheism—that desert-born heresy—shoving the Will for Good up among those sky-blue abstract nouns and concentrating the Will for Evil down in the carob plantation. But fortunately I did not much like the sun, which was the embodiment of the unattainable: it was just a ball of gas doing what it had to, and it made the climate dry, and dry air hurt my nose. More fortunately yet, the clay of my family was yeastened not just with affection, which I dismissed as an analgesic, but also with a whiff of *agape,* about which my poets had not instructed me.

We had a two-holer. Often after supper when the kids were in bed and I was ensconced with a romance by the coal-oil lamp, my parents, wanting a quarter-hour's sociability alone and fearing to stroll far in the snake-infested twilight, would take the Sears Roe-buck catalogue and go up to the outhouse together. One evening I crept behind it with a stick in hand; my prank was to poke it through a knothole behind the inner seat and to prod whoever was sitting there between the shoulder blades. It was Mother; I could hear her talking against Vick's salve for my brother's croup, and Dad grumbling for it. The outhouse at the moment was attached to the back of the aviary, which was housing some guinea hens—restless birds. Under cover of their stirrings I managed to get my stick through the knothole without being detected. My parents were Protestants fresh from Indiana, so that their natural newcomer fear of such outlandish creatures as scorpions had been heightened by Isaiah: prophecies fulfilled. The door to the outhouse was not wide and the latch wouldn't work if you were pressing against the door. As soon as my mother felt something on her back, she let out a yell that startled the stick from my hand. "On my back!" she screamed. "What is it? Scorpions!" Father, seeing in the gloaming that something dangled from the knothole, hollered, "Rattlesnake!" Mother pressed for the door, shrieking, and father bellowed to her not to push. I was paralyzed by the consequences of my harmless practical joke; my father cursed, as I had almost never heard him do, cursed at his pants for hobbling him and shouted rudely at my mother to quit jamming him in the doorway; I ran. I hid under the guest bed. From there I could hear Father calm Mother down, get the lantern and shotgun, return presently with an oath about the stick in the hole, and call my name. In half an hour or so they found me. They scolded me roundly and lectured me on cruel teasing and asked me what in the world I'd thought I was up to and told me never to do a tom-fool thing like that again: they gave me a chance to repent. Mother and I both cried a bit, and Father sat smoking his cigar, looking out the window and shaking his head. Then Mother began to giggle, and nudged Father, who barked; and by the time she had got in the middle of telling over again everything that had happened, all three of us were helpless with laughter.

When I went to college, matriculating up into literary criticism, Coleridge was my man. It was about that time that I first saw a Shakespeare play decently performed and began to realize what all the shouting had been for; but *Macbeth* is by no means about perfection or the ideal, and not much about Nature, and Macbeth himself is both admirable and wicked in a way which nothing but actual life could have prepared me for. Troubled by all that life, imperfect life, in so great a poem, I was immensely grateful for Coleridge's luminous guidance: by his light I saw that the play itself was a part of Nature (*organic* unity) and that, being Shakespeare's, it itself was perfect (the Hell-Porter scene, so low, must have been added by some low tamperer). With this general view of things I remained content for years: instead of having perfection and Nature for subjects (indeed I got fed up with them about this time), I would ask only that the primary, esemplastic Imagination work through the poet to fashion out of intrinsically valueless materials a perfect work of art; a poem must *be* perfection. If there was anything the New Critics agreed on it was this, and I loved them all; and furthermore they confirmed my chronic disposition toward short poems, for most of the well-wrought Urns in literature turn out to be short poems. Yvor Winters put the case as strikingly as it could be put, but on the whole I preferred such critics as Cleanth Brooks, who would sneak in a sizable excerpt from *Paradise Regained* or trace a theme throughout a play and would even give honorable mention to novelists, though usually to such U writers as Flaubert or Joyce who did not permit love of their characters to interfere with the exercise of their craft.

Though it had occurred to me that hankering after Platonic ideals might very likely be a form of escapism, much to be censured, it was not for years that I suspected I was doing something of the sort when studying the perfection of Urn shapes without Platonic contents. Yet, even during my most esemplastic period, there were forces working against my U tendencies. Partly, to be sure, there was the clay-cum-love of which my family was compounded; partly there was my irrepressible fondness for writers such as Dickens and Hardy who were blatantly imperfect; but I also gave credit to the subversive influences of the only urn I'd come across in daily life.

It belonged to Lois's mother. Lois lived up the road a couple of miles, and her father drank too much. Lois herself was a chasmal couple of years older than I, and I remember of her best an Arabian Nights belly, "like a heap of wheat" (my secondary imagination was convinced her wheat was golden under her dress and very likely smelled of nard), and in her navel one "could put an ounce of ointment" (a dalliance which still has power to bemuse my fancy). When Lois's father died, her mother, who had abused him publicly in a shocking way when he was living, had his body cremated and the ashes put in an urn. This urn was of yellowish cream color and encrusted with purple lumps representing grapes; it was thick-necked and heavy-based; it was kept on the mantel in the parlor and flanked by very tall white candles. On the anniversary of his death the candles burned all day, and for the hour before and after the hour of his death Lois and her mother sat in the room, reading the Bible because one should, and "The Shooting of Dan McGrew" because it had been his favorite poem.

As for well-wrought Grecian Urns, I've looked pretty closely at the amphorae and lekythoi in the Metropolitan Museum, but I can't say I've been as impressed as I'd hoped I'd be. The Greeks made them to contain olive oil or wine, but there in their cases they stand choked to their necks with solemn, museum air. I would rather have a bucket full of goat's milk.

Wyatt's poems, for example—I liked them from the first lines I came upon, all the way through the collected poems.

> They flee from me that sometimes did me seek,
> With naked foot stalking in my chamber.

Maybe a New Critic could make a case for this poem's perfection— for all I know one of them may have tried to. But though I have read it a hundred times with never-failing pleasure I have always felt the last couplet (like the couplet concluding nearly any of Shakespeare's sonnets) to be a decided letdown from the rest of the poem, especially rhythmically, and not the sort of letdown that is *really,* if you just get the right point of view on it, a good thing, intentional, justifiable, crafty:

> But since that I so kindely am served,
> I fain would know what she hath deserved.

And one of the things I especially like about the poem is its content: I delight in imagining myself a nobleman into whose chamber women have stalked with naked feet (one in especial with arms long and small), who through his gentleness is forsaken by her in favor of newfangledness, and who perceives and withstands this with elegant irony. This delight, so far as I can see, is non-esthetic: I would have

273

done it if I'd had the chance, and by *it* I mean the part that does not
be but *means*, the part that would have had much the same effect if
I had read it in prose instead of in verse.

I think *The Rime of the Ancient Mariner* is the best narrative poem
in English since Chaucer, but not all the king's men can convince
me that everything in it is justifiable. I share Coleridge's posterior,
table-talk opinion that the moralizing at the end is too blessed heavy-
handed.

> He prayeth best, who loveth best
>   All things both great and small;
> For the dear God who loveth us,
>   He made and loveth all.

It sounds like a Sunday-school song for kindergartners. Pope thought
several of Donne's satires needed purifying, and turned them into
heroic couplets. Ben Jonson thought Donne, "for not keeping of
accent, deserved hanging," and wished Shakespeare had blotted a
thousand of his lines. While Coleridge the perfectionist held me with
his glittering eye, I used to agree with sentiments like these. But I am
like the wedding guest:

> He went like one that hath been stunned,
>   And is of sense forlorn:
> A sadder and a wiser man,
>   He rose the morrow morn.

Only I'm not sadder for no longer pretending that God's speeches in
Paradise Lost are much better than the big-talk suitable to the Father
Divine who used to operate out of Philadelphia or that the slaughter
at the end of *Hamlet* is other than meathouse melodrama.

Of all the non-U poems I know of by contemporary poets, there
is none I like better than Winfield Townley Scott's "The U. S. Sailor
with the Japanese Skull."

> Bald-bare, bone-bare, and ivory yellow: skull
> Carried by a thus two-headed U. S. sailor
> Who got it from a Japanese soldier killed
> At Guadalcanal in the ever-present war: our
>
> Bluejacket, I mean, aged twenty, in August strolled
> Among the little bodies on the sand and hunted
> Souvenirs: teeth, tags, diaries, boots; but bolder still
> Hacked off this head and under a leopard tree skinned it;

I see no good reason to separate "our" from "Bluejacket" as the poet has done, and "ever-present" is rather less than distinguished.

> Peeled with a lifting knife the jaw and cheeks, bared
> The nose, ripped off the black-haired scalp and gutted
> The dead eyes to these thoughtful hollows: a scarred
> But bloodless job, unless it be said brains bleed.

The last clause seems to mean more than it does.

> Then, his ship underway, dragged this aft in a net
> Many days and nights—the cold bone tumbling
> Beneath the foaming wake, weed-worn and salt-cut
> Rolling safe among fish and washed with Pacific;
>
> Till on a warm and level-keeled day hauled in
> Held to the sun and the sailor, back to a gun-rest,
> Scrubbed the cured skull with lye, perfecting this:
> Not foreign as he saw it first: death's familiar cast.

The "foaming" wake is uninspired. The syntax or punctuation of the first two lines of this fifth stanza is, if not impenetrable, at least needlessly tough.

> Bodiless, fleshless, nameless, it and the sun
> Offend each other in strange fascination
> As though one of the two were mocked; but nothing is in
> This head, or it fills with what another imagines
>
> As: here were love and hate and the will to deal
> Death or to kneel before it, death emperor,
> Recorded orders without reasons, bomb-blast, still
> A child's morning, remembering moonlight on Fujiyama:
>
> All scoured out now by the keeper of this skull
> Made elemental, historic, parentless by our
> Sailor boy who thinks of home, voyages laden, will
> Not say, 'Alas! I did not know him at all.'

I get into a fuzz of logic, in the first three lines of the last stanza, and I do not know why one line ends with "in," another with "our," another with "will," syntactical wrenches without much formal cause. But these are about as important as Einstein's sweatshirts and uncombed hair. There are charges of intensity leaping from stanza to stanza that seem to me splendid, and the last line once stood the hair up on the back of my neck and still can moisten my eyes. In other words, my experience in reading this poem is not just esthetic: not the least of the reasons I like it is that it has shown me a truth about something that matters. In the image of the U. S. sailor cleaning the skull of the beheaded Japanese, and in the last line of the poem, are contained a horror at the sailor's indifference and a pity for his alienation from his enemy whom he has dehumanized, that have not only moved me but have taught me to see something about the attitude of Americans towards their enemies generally. An expression such as "heightened awareness" does not explain what I take from the poem. It is a message, an old-fashioned message, of the sort that has been added to what I know, that might have been and can be said in other words but never has been, to my knowledge, said as well as here, that derives from the poet's experience of life and adds to mine. No more than telling a story is this something that all poems do, nor is it what is proper to poetry as poetry, this incarnating of an idea; but when a poem does this, I think it churlish to hold that the idea (which is of course *also* one of the ingredients of the poem) has value *only* as an ingredient. Scott, I am convinced, embodied this idea in this poem, not just because he liked it and thought it useful but because he thought it was true. And the experiences about which the poem is concerned—both the sailor's dealing with the skull and the poet's reflections on this—are important apart from the poem: I would have enjoyed reading about the sailor's act in the *Times,* and I would have enjoyed hearing the poet talking about it in conversation. The poem doesn't create the values of this act and this meditation but clarifies and orders these values; to be sure, this process itself magnifies the values and holds them together (not quite inextricably) with its own special power; it is this wonderful binding and shaping power, which of course itself has a value of a high kind, that some critics, in extremities, maintain is the sole true value of any poem. But for my own part, when on certain occasions I have repeated to myself, "Who will not say, 'Alas! I did not know him at all,' " I have done it less because it is beautiful inside the poem than because it is true outside as well.

Sometimes I am amused to consider how far I have backslid from estheticism, and I while away my apostasy by such reflections as this: Would Chartres cathedral have been esthetically more pleasing if the architects had only known they were creating an outsize Urn instead of thinking they were just building an edifice for the benefit of men and the greater glory of God?

I have, as befits one of my generation, tried to untranquilize my recollections of childhood in hope of flushing a trauma which would explain my tolerance—indeed, my partiality—toward imperfect poems that contain a message. Traumas I seem to be short on, but a decisive influence I am satisfied that I have found—Eva, our three-titted goat, whom I used to milk.

My brother needed goat's milk for his health, and we were fortunate to get, in Eva, a nanny that not only was a good milker but also had a sweet disposition. She did not stink as goats are said to; when she was chewing alfalfa hay her breath was sweet and moist. As I would tear off a slab of hay from the bale with a pitchfork and loosen it for her, she liked to butt me with her head; she had back-arching horns, but she never tried to use them against any of us. I liked to watch her head jerk at the hay and her quick jaws chew it. She sometimes turned as I was milking her and nibbled at my hair with her lips. I cannot say that her baa was as melodious as a cow's moo, yet it was more expressive—affectionate, anxious, demanding. One of her eyes was pure brown and the other brown flecked with hazel; I found it fascinating that their pupils were rectangles, the sides of which were slightly convex arcs. I saw her give birth to her twins, their white hair as soft as down, their bleating and hers enough to bring tears to your eyes, their bones as soft as butter. A cow's tits hang from her udder like four fingers, but a goat's two tits are continuous, conical extensions of her udder. Some sportive gene had misfired in Eva, so that instead of one large right tit she had two, a middle-sized one and a small one. When her bag was swollen with milk, her left tit jutted forward and out as it was supposed to, but on the right side the middle-sized one pointed straight down and the small one stuck a bit backward. I always milked her from the right side because I liked it better; the two smaller tits were easier to hold in the hand and definitely gave more milk than the large left one. I would lay my head against her soft-haired belly, in the hollow in front of her hip and below her backbone, sort of nudge her so she would half-baa peaceably once in a while as she chewed, and squirt the rich milk into the foaming pail.

Eva helped form me, split-titted Eva; for she taught me that love, any sort of love, even of poetry, no matter what beautiful-true perfection it gets up to, forgets at its peril the nuzzling, butting, pie-eyed clay in which the foot of its ladder had better be secured.

Getting Away from the Chickens

L A S T   S U M M E R   I picked up *The Princess Casamassima*.
Reading and talking about what I read is my living now; I have
to know about James and I'm supposed to like him. Thirty-five or
forty years ago I would have had to know about, and try to like,
George Meredith, not Henry James. But nowadays Percy Lubbock
says James is the man, and so do F. R. Leavis, Lionel Trilling, articles
in all the literary journals, Auden in a poem, and the Old Possum
himself; Graham Greene, a formidable witness, not only refers to
James as the Master but calls him the Shakespeare of fiction: Well.
After all this pressure *ex auctoritatibus,* I'd consider myself lucky
that I liked even one James story, "The Turn of the Screw"; those
ghosts may be dense with meanings, whether Wilson's neurotic pro-
jections or Heilman's symbols from theology; I find it charming to
see how the critics have adorned it with theories like an Easter egg;
but meanings or no meanings it's the best ghost story I ever read,
and a ghost story is what *James* said it was. Once I make my way
into any novel of his I usually get all wound up in it; and further-
more, he's relevant, significant, seminal, morally serious, and a lot
of other adjectives of literary praise; I respect him, which clears my
conscience. I'd put off *The Princess* for a long time, though I'd been
guilty of the perversion of reading two critical articles about it, be-
cause it concerns an anarchist named Hyacinth; now any hyacinthine
anarchist I've ever known or can imagine would have changed his
name to Bill at the age of five; I did not believe James knew whom
he was writing about.

The volume fell open to chapter thirteen. The Princess asks Hya-
cinth about his family.

> "I have no family."
> "None at all?"

278

"None at all."

"But the French blood you speak of and which I see perfectly in your face—you haven't the English expression or want of expression—that must have come to you through someone."

"Yes, through my mother."

"And she's dead?"

"Long ago."

Anarchism? literary classic? the Master? If you wish; but a proud orphan whose blood showed in his face—such a one was Tarzan. Hopefully I turned back to the first chapter of *The Princess* and settled down to cut the cackle.

But, oh, density of significance and subtlety began to weigh on me. The book had good ingredients—high life and low life, intrigue, love, the illegitimate son of a French whore and a British nobleman, self-sacrifice, danger—and James knows how to spin a good tale; but he'd gone and freighted the rifts with ore, just as the critics said he had. Still, I'm glad to report there's a lot more Tarzan to Hyacinth Robinson than they led me to believe. ("The Influence of Henry James on Edgar Rice Burroughs"? or, better, "*The Princess Casamassima* as *Tarzan of the Apes*"?) In fact there was so much Tarzan that after a couple of hundred pages of *The Princess* I went to the Columbia University library and got out *Tarzan of the Apes* (the only Burroughs book it lists).

The first sentence encouraged me:

I had this story from one who had no business to tell it to me, or to any other. I may credit the seductive influence of an old vintage upon the narrator for the beginning of it, and my own skeptical incredulity during the days that followed for the balance of the strange tale.

Not James, maybe, but a sort of bare-bones Conrad, and Conrad was (of course) a great disciple of James. In five minutes I was right back into it.

The summer I was sixteen, in the slough of the Depression, I left home for the first time, for my first job, tending chickens. I fed, watered, and cleaned up after twenty-five hundred White Leghorn hens, five hundred pullets, and enough roosters to keep things perking; on Sunday I worked only three or four hours, but on weekdays nine or ten; for this I was paid twenty-five dollars a month and found. Since I was saving to go to college that fall, I spent no money, except on one movie, *A Midsummer Night's Dream*. (Shakespeare's reputation and the title got me there, but Bottom the Weaver made me ache with laughter and the fairies had stars in their hair.) I had only one friend in town whom it wouldn't cost me money to see. He came over once in a while and we would lounge around the back porch debating capital punishment, pacifism, the differences between socialism and capitalism, the Middle Ages, and the existence of God; his mother and brother were Holy Rollers, and his brother sometimes spoke in tongues. I admired my friend's fervor for distant causes, and when I was with him I was a pacifist, a socialist, and a rational atheist. But most of my free time I spent getting away from the chickens.

Tarzan, Mars, Pellucidar, Fu Manchu, Poictesme, the Faerie Queene, Gay Paree: they did the job well. Now that I'm a professor of English, I wish that I could say that I liked *The Faerie Queene* best, but in truth what kept me going past the first book or so was the knowledge that, if I read it all, William Lyon Phelps would admit me to his Faerie Queene Club, in his column "As I Like It" in *Scribner's:* I did, he did. It wasn't that I didn't like the dragons and bowers, Britomart the lady-knight, the twins who committed incest in their mother's womb, the jousts; but the poem was too long, the stanzas were lovely but too lulling (they still are), and there were too many serious meanings swarming about, so many that I had to put out a bit of energy to keep from trying to guess what they were. Still, by August I could dream in Spenserian, and I wrote James Branch Cabell a fan letter in five gorgeous *Faerie Queene* stanzas. My stern friend tried to bring me down to brass tacks with *The Outline of History, Merchants of Death* and Spinoza's *Ethics,* and he gave me a sermon once on a candy egg his brother was fond of. It was one of those frosty-sugar eggs with a hole in the end, through which one peeped at a Swiss chalet set among delicately pink mountains; this, said my friend, had absolutely nothing to do with reality and it was very likely immoral to enjoy anything so *pretty*. Once, to my shame, I substituted *Gay Paree* for Stuart Chase, an act of rampant magic-carpetism which I did not confess to my friend, for I dared not challenge his scorn; the biggest defense I put up for myself was that Cabell was highly respected and Spenser was a great literary classic; he was impressed, and told me I ought to read John Stuart Mill's *On Liberty,* which was a classic too. I said sure.

The hens were kept in rows of wooden sheds with small yards to dust in, maybe a hundred to a shed; the pullets had a large shed and a huge yard to themselves, with trees. Prepare the mash and slop it in the troughs; scatter the grain; clean the water jars and keep them filled; clean the nests; scrape the stinking roosts. Gather the eggs, clean them, candle them, pack them. Collect the dead chickens, put them in a large garbage can, and pour gasoline on them to keep them from stinking too much, till there should be enough of them to bother burying. Rescue any that showed blood, for the others would not stop picking till they'd killed it; watch for sticktights sucking the hens' vitality, and dust against them; return the escapees, and clip the wings of the high fliers; beware the one-eyed rooster, whose peck hurt. We buried once or twice a week, at dawn for the neighbors' sake, but it spoiled my breakfast. When my boss was not home, I had to sell friers to people who came to the place to buy them. I had shot rabbits and killed snakes with stones, but I had never been *holding* a creature at the time I was killing it. I would catch the bird's legs in my left hand, flop it onto the chopping block, smooth its neck out with the flat of the hatchet till it stayed put, then chop; the neck is gristly, and tough to a dull hatchet; if I chopped too high up, the neck squawked; I stuffed the convulsing body into a slot to keep it from splattering blood on me, but before I could get it in there, the legs strove in the palm of my hand. One day in July the temperature rose to 123°; the hens in their panic huddled together; I went from house to house scattering them and sprinkling them with a hose; the rancher's wife—he happened to be out of town that day—came out to help me but the heat prostrated her; she worried about me, and when I slumped into the kitchen to rest she made me take a tablespoon of salt, the sting of which clung to my tongue; I thought the pullets, being thin, would not need my care, but as it turned out they piled up under their roost so that two hundred of them suffocated; the hens' fat melted, so I was told, and ran inside their skins; in any case, three hundred of them died. In August disease started; I collected the forty or fifty afflicted chickens into cages and trundled them down by the death cans; I would reach one out to the boss; if it was too far gone, he would slit its throat and toss it in a can; if it was in the early stages, he would press a feather dipped in kerosene up through its mouth and out its ear, and hand it back to me to return it to its cage; if it had large sores, he cut the sores open with a knife, swabbed them with iodine, did the kerosened-feather job, and gave me the bird to take to the sick house. After fifteen minutes of this I fainted.

Tarzan—there was a man! His dreadful wounds left no scars; he ate his meat raw; he threw his woman over his shoulder; he killed a lioness with a full-Nelson. Yet he was at the top of the scale of evolution, white and British (it was an Englishman, after all, who invented evolution). He was so savage he was an ape, though even then he was saved from cannibalism by hereditary instinct, and he was so noble he was Lord Greystoke, though even in Jane Porter's own house he was restrained from killing an obnoxious suitor of hers only by her pleas for clemency. O noble savage! He taught himself to read and write English. He could run through the trees at night with a man on his shoulders as easily as an ordinary man might walk down a London street at high noon. Kipling? In plenty, and lots of Defoe and Cooper too. Stevenson? Mutineers, buried treasure, treachery, murder. Homer? Bloodshed in every chapter, epic epithets, and a hero guided and protected by the great gods Instinct, Reason, and Progress. The villains look like rats; the professor's name is Archimedes Q. Porter; Kala's mother-instinct (she was an ape) is as sterling as any woman's. The Africans are childish blacks, natives, whom the whites must treat with understanding and severity, for their own good. Danger? The prelude and condition of victory! Contradictions? Who cares? . . . At every moment Edgar Rice Burroughs, that middle-aged, middle-classed, middle-Western unsuccessful business man, believed in the fantasies and prejudices he compounded his stories of. A hero above the law, brought within the law by a woman's love, the tale told with plenty of suspense— you can't beat it, especially when you are adolescent, which is to say an as yet unsuccessful man.

It didn't mean a thing and you couldn't make it mean a thing if you tried. As for *A Midsummer Night's Dream*, it means a lot, I'm sure, but I went to it hoping to get fun from it and fun I got, unpolluted fun. After all, they had plenty of chickens in the old days too, as Shakespeare knew well enough—armadas of them. And James, to get away from the Plymouth Rock variety, spent most of his life in Europe.

In Tarzan's veins "flowed the blood of the best of a race of mighty fighters"—i.e., British aristocrats. But of course! He was an epic hero (wasn't he?) fighting and killing a gorilla, armed only with a knife, when a mere ten years of age. Now Hyacinth Robinson, though "it is a remarkable fact that at the age of ten he was ironic," was not powerful enough to be a warrior of any kind, even if he'd tried, and was far too subtle to be a hero. "But all the same he was happy to feel he had blood in his veins that would account for the finest sensibilities," the blood of "his long-descended, supercivilized sire." (*My* veins and arteries flow with corpuscles and antibodies and various other of the modern products which have supplanted the blood of belted earls; it is type O and free from such noxious qualities as leukemia, so that I helped put myself through junior college by selling it for twenty-five dollars a pint in hospitals.)

As for being *civilisé*, Hyacinth, when the Princess vaguely extends an invitation to him, might make "a silent inclination of his utmost stature." (I tried that one, in the privacy of my own living room, with dismal results.) But Tarzan has qualities even James would not disdain. He "manipulated the knife and fork as exquisitely as did the polished D'Arnot," *only a month* after he first used table instruments! And he drove an automobile with complete aplomb *less than three weeks* after he left Africa! (You can't home experiment with Tarzan's feats and stunts.)

Which do you think this is, Tarzan and Jane or Hyacinth and the Princess?

The pure, high dignity with which she had just spoken and which appeared to cover a suppressed tremor of passion set his pulses throbbing, and her tone, her voice, her wonderful face showed she had a generous soul.

In the above passage I have cut a few phrases whose reference would have betrayed the book, but this that follows is the old boy (which old boy?) word for word, with a single adjective omitted.

It was a stately and gallant little compliment performed with the grace and dignity of utter unconsciousness of self. It was the hallmark of his aristocratic birth, the natural outcropping of many generations of fine breeding, an hereditary instinct of graciousness which a lifetime of uncouth training and environment could not eradicate.

Inimitable, no?

I haven't done anything to chickens for the past twenty-five years but eat them; all the same, they crowd me now and again; I've been keeping an eye peeled for up-to-date magic carpets. *Hercules, My Shipmate* is fun and probably doesn't mean anything, though I wouldn't swear to it; Graves is tricky. About the best I've found is *The Golden Strangers* by Henry Treece: invasion, magic, prodigies, killing, malice, passion, war, primitives—it's terrific. But Treece is so reasonable and unprejudiced that every once in a while I get the feeling he is headed toward making a Comment on Life. His people are primitives, not savages, and his heroes are superior not because of the blood in their veins but because of the anthropological psyches in their heads; in the end they are gorily defeated. His stories keep the chickens at bay, all right, but only just.

For a few years there, beginning when my friend was sentenced to a camp for conscientious objectors, I set my gaze sternly toward realism. In practice this involved driving a taxicab and reading *Studs Lonigan,* neither of which I enjoyed. Gradually it occurred to me that pimps and drunks and hot jazz addicts were no more real than anybody else and that books about The People, who grimly did not think, were like bad dreams. Scratch a realist and find a reformer: no wonder; the world he sees is only half there. The last I heard of my conscientious friend he had just returned from a peace mission to Russia and was doing public relations work for an organization whose aim is immediate, universal disarmament—beside which a sugar chalet in a hollow egg seems to me eminently practical—at least you can eat it.

A great thing about Burroughs was that his fantasy seemed pure. He thought his prejudices were truths; all the *Golden Bough,* White Goddess sort of thing which has been enlightening us nowadays, he neither knew nor wanted to know nor would he have believed had he known. That White Man's Burden, for example, with which he larded his Tarzan books—when reading them I believe (and believed) in it about as much as I believed that, in order to save Jane, Monsieur Tarzan flew through the treetops of a Wisconsin forest on fire—it's one of the ingredients with which Burroughs makes a good story. His prejudices are so gross that no one bothers to analyze them out or to attack them. They are also out-of-date: the three branches of the New York Public Library I went to listed no Burroughs at all; I had to go to four secondhand bookstores down on Fourth Avenue to find a few Tarzan books, and the sellers said most were long out of print; in eight stores I could find not one of his Mars series; maybe, I was told, Sears Roebuck still lists some of them for the Midwestern trade. . . . But they were clear-eyed, well-thewed prejudices arrayed only in a loin cloth; you can take them or leave them, unless *your* big prejudice happens to be anti-prejudice. What matters is the story, which tastes good.

And the great thing about *The Princess* seemed to be this: it's Burroughs for sophisticates. Not that James didn't add sprigs of reality to his blooming prejudices, but it is the charm of the arrangement that *really* matters most.

Or is it, *really?* Did I, a white American of British ancestry, like Tarzan just for the story? And as for James, consider some of the ingredients of his concoction.

He likes religiose metaphors, and religiosity flourishes nowadays: for example, he often speaks of sacrifices where none exist; Hyacinth's father is said to be the "sacrificed Lord Frederick," when in fact he was murdered by a cast-off mistress—Hyacinth's mother. You may object that James is being ironic here, intending the idea of sacrifice to be Hyacinth's, not the author's; I suppose this is the eighth type of ambiguity, and I'm sure it's one of James's specialties, but in cruder circles fancy irony like this is known as eating your cake and having it too. Like every taleteller, he makes his characters extraordinary: Hyacinth is highly attractive to lovely ladies and to upstanding men of all sorts; the Princess is (repeatedly) "the most remarkable woman in Europe"; Hoffendahl, the conspirator to whom Hyacinth "gave his life away," was "the right man," "the real thing," "the Master indeed." As for glamour, the Princess is scarcely discernible beneath its shimmer—

Purity of line and form, of cheek and chin and lip and brow, a colour that seemed to live and glow, a radiance of grace and eminence and success—these things were seated in triumph in the face of the Princess, and her visitor, as he held himself in his chair trembling with the revelation, questioned if she were really of the same substance with the humanity he had hitherto known.

Even the Prince, a sad sack of a fellow, is after all a nobleman; perhaps he had

much of the complexion which in late-coming members of long-descended races we qualify today as effete; but his tone might have served for the battle-cry of some deep-chested fighting ancestor.

(Tarzan was both a member of the House of Lords and his own deep-chested fighting ancestor: crude, but effective.) And oh, those revolutionaries! Lionel Trilling in the introduction to the book thinks James had a remarkable grasp of such as them, and it's true that Trilling was an old acquaintance of Whittaker Chambers; but George Woodcock, who is an anarchist himself as well as a writer, refuted this contention in an essay a few years ago; and for my part, I, who have known a few home-grown Hyacinths in California, find James's revolutionaries about as probable as the half-men half-apes that guard the jewels of Opar for their High-Priestess La: Hollywood wouldn't have to touch a hair of their pointy little heads.

One of the chief, essential facts about both James and Burroughs is this: they were blatant snobs. (By the way, the first of the two test passages was by James, the second by Burroughs.) Their heroines are swooningly beautiful and high-born, and the prose describing them glitters and shimmers; James, being complicated, makes his princess *also* destructive and tormented. Their ignoble characters, whether good or bad, are patronized indulgently; Burroughs, being simple, makes them *also* ugly. In a word, a title gets you preferential treatment. With a title Hyacinth would never have been called by the author "a little bastard bookbinder." If Millicent Henning had been Lady Millicent, James would never have put her in these sentences:

> They had taken possession of a couple of chairs placed there to the convenience of that superior part of the public for which a penny is not prohibitive, and Millicent, of whom such speculations were highly characteristic, had devoted considerable conjecture to the question of whether the functionary charged with collecting the penny would omit to come and demand his fee. Miss Henning liked to enjoy her pleasures gratis.

A lot of us like all this not only because the stories are adequate to suspend disbelief for a while, but also because one of the essential facts about us who enjoy either James or Burroughs, or both, is this: we are secret snobs. Maybe not the genuine article like the two Masters themselves, not the pure sort "that dearly loves a lord" (in submaster Maugham's phrase); but we respond to this snobbism, however obliquely and shamefacedly—we sons of St. Louis businessmen, provincial headmasters, New York tailors, or Indiana farmers. Because we think we're better than other people in some essential respect, we dearly love good improbable stories told by snobs with easy

consciences. Because we know we oughtn't to think so, and because
we know that in some even more essential respect we aren't better,
we are especially fond of James: his dazzling, enchanting, incredible
Princess is in the end revealed to be morally vile and weak, for which
she is punished dreadfully—and most gratifyingly. Moreover, it is
clear enough what James thinks of our sort; we are people only a
low-lifer like Dickens would take seriously. In *Notes on Novelists*
James writes:

> Save under the immense pressure of Dickens we have never done anything
> so dreadful as to recognise the vulgar. . . . When his people are not funny
> who shall dare to say what they are? . . . They belong to a walk of life that
> we may be ridiculous but never at all serious about.

This, by the way, was published six years after *Tess of the d'Urber-*
villes, that novel about a humble girl whom Hardy, fortunately for
some of us, took to be worthy of tragedy.

"The poet is one who consents to dream about reality." Good
enough; no fantasy is pure, alas, not even Burroughs'. But it seems
to me that reality was only a portion of what James was dreaming
about in *The Princess Casamassima,* to such an extent that he was
not always sure which was which, and that the least a commentator
can do is to point out this fact. However, this is not the line, not part
of the profounder significance, of the figuring forth to be found in
the book, as you can see by reading the introduction. All this is, is
an unambiguous, wry-necked cock of a fact.

I am willing to admit that I may be crotchety. But I plead bad
luck to interpretation. For example, the egg which a hen laid in my
mouth one night that summer I was sixteen.

At the time, when eggs were eggs to me, it was a disquieting
and startling event, but the pleasure I remembered from seeing that
handsome egg, and feeling it slip into my mouth, so dominated my
memory of the experience that nothing else about it mattered. A few
years later, however, I read *The Interpretation of Dreams,* that anti-
escape book, that book for re-imprisoning escapees, and I learned to
hate that egg. First I took it as an anal-erotic symbol; the hen was
a nice big fluffy motherly old bird (*motherly,* get it?) and I was, at
the time I was reading, convinced that I'd been stuffed with a lot
of wasteful attitudes by my mother. Presently it occurred to me that

the egg was really a symbol of something from either the oral or the genital stage of my infantile eroticism or even, for all I knew, from the latency period; but trying to thread my way among the perversions which this notion entangled me in depressed me off and on for years.

Then came *The White Goddess* and I was immensely set up, for a while. The hen (a *she*) had been a *White* Leghorn and had sort of been levitating a few inches above me in a supernatural way. So maybe that egg had also been a fructifying sperm of inspiration egg-planted by the Goddess upon my eager lips (*inspire*, from the Latin "to breathe in"). This was a whole lot better than Freud, but the catch was that I couldn't see any results of this divine fecundating. In fact, there *aren't* any results, except this essay.

No more interpretation: let the egg be the given, my lopsided, indecent, absurd, yet incredibly marvelous donnée (as James would so elegantly have put it). However, even as an Easter egg is dyed, hidden and found again, so my egg must endure being decorated with my fantasies; I hide it in my mind for long periods and am pleased to come across it again as now, to metaphysically dye it again, being, as I have been *ab ovo*, a fantast. For the egg, the irreducible brute egg, the egg *an sich,* a double-yolker I bet by the size of it, the egg's the thing. Laid by a clucking hen with spotless tail feathers, accepted by my pursed lips, yet that egg remains in my memory perfect in mid-air between, as in a still from a movie, neither hovering nor falling nor dropped, just there, a great big clean egg, dyed or undyed signifying egg.

Photographs and Photographers

F O R convenience, this essay will divide the art of photography into two categories, the compositional and the referential.

Compositional photography is that sort which is largely or entirely a matter of the lines, shapes, and gradations of shade (and occasionally of color), and very little of the *subject* of the photograph. Two eminent artists of this sort are Edward Weston and Ansel Adams. One of Weston's well-known pictures of a nude will illustrate the point. The viewer of the picture cares almost nothing for the actual woman who posed for the photograph, though her body and limbs are evidently smooth, full-fleshed, and well-proportioned. At first glance he is not even sure the subject is a woman, for her arms and legs are so involved among themselves and so contained within the single outline of the image—not an outline familiar in life—as to suggest nothing in ordinary experience. He does not see her face, for her head is bent towards the camera. She is not located; that is, there is no background. The composition that Weston arranged and then registered in two dimensions on his film has far less in common with any actual woman, including the model herself, than with certain other compositions which Weston arranged and photographed using for his subject a shell, a green pepper, or a bare toilet bowl seen prow-on from a vantage point just above floor level. In all four of these, the dominant image is of a central, gleaming, irregular, vertical oblong (in the nude's case her folded, erect right leg) protruding from a larger, similarly shaped bulk and related to it by a complexity of curved forms and shaded volutes.

Referential photography, by far the more popular of the two forms, is that sort which depends for its effect primarily (though never entirely) upon its fidelity to the visual impression which the subject might have made on the viewer if he had actually seen it.

The forms on the page in front of him are intended to be recognizable and the image is supposed to be true to what was actually there. Portraits are of this sort, and the success of portrait photography is demonstrated by the inroads it has made on portrait painting during the past century. Like the greatest painters a good photographer gives the viewer an image which can allow him to imagine the actual person portrayed. Carjat's portrait of Baudelaire (reproduced in Beaumont Newhall's *The History of Photography*) is admirable partly because the artist posed and lighted the subject well, but mostly because Baudelaire's face powerfully expressed a powerful soul; Nadar's portrait of Sarah Bernhardt on the facing page is quite as good technically, and the subject is glamorous, but the picture is less interesting because Bernhardt's face far less interestingly expresses her soul than does Baudelaire's—or else because, as one suspects, her soul was itself far less interesting than Baudelaire's. One can imagine the person of Carjat's portrait, quite apart from knowing anything about Baudelaire, at least as well as one can imagine the anonymous subject of Titian's "Man with Grey Eyes," Holbein's "Erasmus," or Rembrandt in one of his self-portraits. Obviously Carjat's photograph is not comparable to any of these paintings as a work of art, as an esthetic object; but, though this representational power is not the whole of any work of visual art, neither is it necessarily as unimportant as current theory and practice in painting suggest. It is a Laputan state of affairs that nowadays referential photography can be scorned esthetically *because* it is about actual life and that non-representational painting can be highly regarded *because* it is about nothing outside itself.

The term *documentary* is commonly applied to that sort of referential photography which is intended to show ordinary people and their artifacts in their customary surroundings. A certain unpleasant odor still clings to the term because so much of the original documentary photography (such as Jacob Riis's work) was a mere collection of social injustices, pressing the viewer too hard with its liberal message: "Aren't you ashamed that you let fellow Americans live like this?" Any photograph or collection which exists for the sake of this message stinks like all propaganda, but the best such collections, of which Walker Evans' *American Photographs* is clearly one, are quite exempt from the charge. An admirable example from the book is on page 40: "Child in Back Yard, 1932." We see a ragamuffin's head and the upper half of her body. She is standing against an old shed, of which we see two boards with a large gap between them. On the board to the left, just behind her, there happens to be a hinge, out of focus. On the board to the right there is, in focus, a child's crude sketch of a girl, suggesting a certain modishness of hair and dress, a Monkey Ward catalogue modishness. The actual little girl, freckled, hair disarrayed, dress ragged at sleeve and neck, is glancing slyly to her left, and from the expression on her wide, thin, stained lips one suspects that she is contemplating lively mischief. The photograph would be called documentary partly because it is in a book of pictures of similar intent, but mostly because we are given, both in the title and in the picture itself, the sort of circumstantial details about the girl which comment on her sociologically—or, more accurately, which could be thought of as commenting on her sociologically. Moreover, in this picture Evans has been successful, as he nearly always is, in the special craft of referential photography, a craft never more important than in documentary work: he gives the illusion that this is what the viewer would have seen had he been there and looked for himself. Documentary photography, like realism in fiction, is a servant art: it aims to create in the viewer the naive illusion, "That's what things are really like." Just how illusory this naive impression is every thick-thumbed amateur knows when after looking at a book such as this, he goes around seeing some of the things of the world with fresh eyes for a while.

This compositional-referential, or form-content, division clearly has little meaning when one comes to talk about the very best photographs. Take #101 in Cartier-Bresson's *The Decisive Moment*. It is captioned: "Sumatra, Indonesia, 1950. Rice fields in the Menangkabau country." But one would do as great a violation to one's experience of it by talking primarily about modern-day peasants still working their flooded rice fields by hand, as one would do by talking primarily about how the visual tension created in the systems of curves made by the dikes between the flooded fields is resolved by the inverted ogive low in the center of the picture. One's experience of this photograph is of neither form nor content but of both together as a part of something strange and indivisible. The broad image in hues of gray is as beautiful as the scene itself must have been, but in a wholly different way: simpler, purified of sensory distractions, ordered; yet the two sorts of beauty are harmonious with one another. In the picture, the relationship of the human figures to the world they have modified is so easy, and likewise the modifications they have made look so lovely, that ultimately the picture sustains the ineradicable wish that a true image of human life lived in accord with the natural world is sheerly beautiful.

This is an impression superbly sustained by #87, of robed Moslem women in Kashmir praying toward the sun rising behind the Himalayas (1948); they are in the postures one feels human beings have used ever since they first raised their hearts and hands to mountains. Precisely the reverse of this impression is given by #49, of a filthy street under an elevated in Chicago (1947) with a tall brick wall running beside it, a rigid pattern of structures and shadows; in the foreground is the only figure, of a crouching, anxious-looking boy gripping an erect baseball bat like a club. This picture says— though not quite so potently as the other two, for Cartier-Bresson loves harder than he hates—that a true image of life lived in violation of the natural world also violates our own nature, is ugly and pathetic. The elegance of the visual structure which relates the boy's shape to the patterns made by the elevated and the wall exists only in the picture and not at all in the scene referred to; this very elegance, which turns back on the picture ironically, is an esthetic twist of the knife.

Walker Evans' *American Photographs,* first issued in 1938 and reissued in 1962 by the Museum of Modern Art, contains eighty-seven photographs taken in the years 1929 to 1937. They record faces, towns, streets, houses, interiors, fields, and signs mostly in the South and in New York City, but also in New England, New York State, Pennsylvania, and New Jersey; two are of men in Havana, presumably made when Evans was in Cuba taking the photographs for Carleton Beals' *The Crime of Cuba* (1933). The locale of thirteen of the photographs is not given; two of these are of minstrel-show posters of a kind which in the Thirties were pretty well localized in the South; eleven are American shards of the sort that could turn up anywhere in the country: "Main Street Faces, 1935"; "American Legionnaire, 1936." The volume also retains an unnecessary but harmless essay by Lincoln Kirstein on photography in general and on Evans in particular.

Thirty-six of the American Photographs were taken in 1935–37 for the Farm Security Administration (or its predecessor). Three of these and one other not for FSA were taken in 1936, when Evans was in the South with James Agee, collecting the material out of which they made *Let Us Now Praise Famous Men* (1941). The photographs in that book serve as reminders of the irreducible brute facts about which Agee's prose describes its impassioned arabesques.

Evans has not published another book. Since the war he has worked for *Fortune,* of which he has for the last several years been an associate editor, and he has published his photographs almost entirely in that magazine. On the evidence of these frequently good but always lesser photographs, especially of some of old resort buildings ("Summer North of Boston," published in the August 1949 issue), it seems clear that the body of documentary photographs of American architecture which he has made, but not yet gathered in a comprehensive volume, is important.

The photographic unit of the FSA was organized by Roy Stryker, and among the dozen photographers under his direction were Ben Shahn, Russell Lee, Jack Delano, and Arthur Rothstein, and—by far the most illustrious as photographers—Evans and Dorothea Lange. Both of them seemed to have been stimulated more by their FSA assignments to make excellent pictures than by anything before or since; at least they both owe their most celebrated pictures and also their books to that stimulus. (Lange's thirty-three photographs in MacLeish's *Land of the Free,* 1938, and those in her own book, *An American Exodus,* 1939, were taken for the FSA.) They remain the two foremost American documentary photographers.

Both Evans and Lange have demonstrated themselves capable of photographs to which none of the odium of "documentary" clings. The one by Evans described above, of the child in the back yard, is delightful as revealing the girl herself but uninteresting as displaying—much less preaching about—something about social conditions in the United States during the Depression. It does not make "a social comment" but allows the child's immediate circumstances to enrich our seeing her; it is as little about social injustice as is *Tom Sawyer.* Nevertheless, to some extent Evans' book, like Lange's, is tainted with the social protest common among artists of the Thirties. When nearly all the pictures in a collection are of the depressed, even though no single one of them is propagandistic, the viewer nevertheless begins to feel a bit propagandized. The thesis obtrudes, and indignation at injustice is surely not as inexhaustible esthetically as it seems to be morally. "The victim" is one of realistic art's riskiest subjects.

Lange's temptation is to sentimentalize the subjects with whom she so evidently sympathizes. She generally takes pictures of people, and usually the center of interest is a face expressing a troubled emotion. Again and again she redeems these pictures from sentimentality by the honesty and clarity of her seeing. The eighth picture in *Land of the Free*, "Pea-pickers in California," centers on a manifestly decent woman whose face is ravaged by immediate worry; her right hand plucks at her cheek, pulling down the right corner of her mouth, which looks as though it wants to be humorous. She is poor, and we assume that her poverty and the uncertainty of the future is the cause of her worry. But the viewer is less concerned with her poverty as such, and far far less with the social conditions that imposed poverty upon her, than he is with the profounder, the humanly universal, results of that poverty. For the picture is a sort of anti-Madonna and Child. One sees the back of a child's head pressed to each of her shoulders, and down in the lower left corner of the picture one sees on her lap part of a sleeping, dirty baby; but the mother, who, we feel without reservation, wants to love and cherish her children, even as they lean on her, is severed from them by her anxiety. The second picture in the book, of a "Missouri farmer now a migratory farm laborer in California" crouched at the wheel of a Model-T Ford, is rescued from the too simple, too easy feelings which the spectacle of a trapped victim inspires, by his eyes; they gleam from that weak, fearful, narrow, pitiable face, mindless and heartless as a weasel's.

Evans is not in the least tempted by an excess of sympathy for his subjects. Indeed, more than half the pictures in *American Photographs* have no people in them, and nearly all those in which a face is the central or dominant image are unmistakably of people conscious of "having their picture taken." If they appear sullen, suspicious, truculent, resentful, like the two young men in "Main Street Faces, 1935," or worldly overwise and weary like the befurred woman in "42nd St., 1929," that is because they want to appear so or do not mind appearing so, not because they were caught at it. One never feels with Evans, as frequently with Weegee, that he is keyhole-peeping or outright invading people's privacy. Moreover, Evans' photographic technique mitigates against much sympathizing on the reader's part. He commonly stands in the middle distance from his subject, the snapshot distance; one is seldom aware of effects of light or shadow; it seems always to be a bright, lightly overcast day; he shoots from no special-effects angle; he usually stands square in front of a house or detail of a house; he does not tamper with his negatives. The result of all this is a severe honesty.

Evans' temptation is toward a perverse delight in the hideous. Sometimes this leads him to a certain obviousness. In "Houses and Billboards, Atlanta, 1936," he takes a broadside shot of two long, low billboards advertising movies, one with a picture of Anne Shirley in a dynamic pose, the other of black-eyed Carole Lombard vamping you over her shoulder, the billboards plastered in front of and below two identical, squalid, and spectacularly ugly houses. Despite this propensity, Evans nearly always redeems his pictures. A few are plain beautiful. "Maine Pump, 1933," is an elegant image of a domestic detail which itself is elegant. Some are made complex by a comment which rescues them from the merely ugly or ordinary. "Wooden Gothic House, Massachusetts, 1930," is of a house which is neither handsome nor hideous nor so constructed as to make a compositionally strong picture, but referentially the photograph has the power to stick in the mind. The facade of the house has five Greek columns, of which the two to the left are obscured from view by a tree; on the center column is a large FOR SALE sign, esthetically as obtrusive in the picture as it was in actuality. We are in no way asked to sympathize with the owner because he needs money; we see an old house casually defaced; we see the past discarded. And in the context of the whole book we see this earlier failed attempt at elegance rejected by a present ugliness which does not even try to be anything else.

The whole book: it is this that constitutes Evans' achievement. The photographs comment on one another. The whole is much greater than the parts added together as separate units. Learning the book, one appreciates how the "yowsa" darkies of the minstrel-show posters are a kind of counterpoint to the lined, experienced face of the Negro coal-dock worker and the melancholy face of the young Arkansas flood refugee. After a while one gains a certain fondness for the curlicue eaves decorations which appear on many of the pictured houses. One begins to imagine the view of things figured forth by the stark, symmetrical rectangles of "Frame Houses in Virginia, 1936."

Finally, despite its diversity and complexity, the book has a dominant tone, and despite the differences between Evans and Lange his tone is not far from hers. He is disengaged where she is unmistakably involved with her subjects; he turns more towards man-made objects and she towards faces; he is sometimes perversely gleeful over ugliness and she sometimes sentimental over victims. Nevertheless, both communicate a sort of nostalgia which one must respect, a sense of valuable things scorned, broken, corrupted, thrown away, badly replaced, gone. An emblem for *American Photographs* could be the photograph with which the first of its two sections concludes, "Louisiana Plantation House, 1935." The viewer is shown two sides of the mansion, each side fronted by square two-story pillars behind which there is a deep porch on both floors. There is no evidence that the house is occupied; there are many indications that it is physically deteriorating. In front of it, breaking up the building's very handsome lines, an uprooted dead tree lies in the yard; from some of its branches dry moss is hanging. The viewer knows well enough what social conditions produced the wealth to build this house originally and what social conditions were allowing it to decay in 1935. Nevertheless, the strong impression the picture leaves in the mind is of a large nostalgia, of a high thing fallen.

What a monster is The Artist—that is, a man who dedicates himself to constructing works of art, and who believes that a great work of art is the highest of all things made and that making one is the highest of all occupations. When The Artist has purged himself of vanity and doubt—like Joyce, like Edward Weston—then he is monstrous indeed, for then he is wholly justified. The religion of art is like Calvinism: in both, the elect are known by their works but are justified by their faith, by their very being.

Let Tolstoy and Van Gogh represent another sort of artist. Both of them elevated *Uncle Tom's Cabin* into the ranks of important art, an error of judgment The Artist would be incapable of making. But they saw true art as efficacious in revealing the unknown or instructing to virtue, and the efficacy of *Uncle Tom's Cabin* had been demonstrated unmistakably. They saw an artist as important, first as any man is important, then as he succeeds in making a work of art which creates a communion among those who admire it. They were concerned to save men, to help men save themselves. They despised The Artist, some of whose works they could not help admiring. Let Poe's tales and poems be the blazon of The Artist. From Baudelaire to Valéry, the theorists of The Artist made him their own. His work was in every way inferior to theirs, yet it was the emblem they reared—an error of judgment Tolstoy or Van Gogh could not have made. Like Poe, they defined themselves against social involvement, religious belief, art as communion. They created a mirror cult; that is, a cult of self-consciousness, a cult in which things are reversed. In that reversed religion, The Artist is a saint: Rimbaud a martyred saint, Picasso an heroic saint. Now that The Scientist has lost his capital letters and is becoming one of the boys, has joined the commissars, generals, executives, and engineers, the world may be in for a bad stretch during which The Artist is worshiped uncontended. What this means in effect is more and more beat bohemians, mescaline mystics, and self-regarding phonies. This very worship, one can hope, may encourage The Artist to leave the mirror cult; any new giant capable of becoming a true Artist-Hero will also be too fastidious to endure being slobbered on by the ready-made cultists, who are now too numerous to escape.

Edward Weston was The Artist as photographer. To be sure, in the advanced regions of art criticism, still photography has no status as an art, though the photography of cinema is deemed worthy of discussion. Unbelievable nonsense, if it is on canvas, is exhibited for sale, discussed seriously, and hung in museums; whereas books or exhibitions of photography are not discussed in the advanced intellectual journals, and only one important museum in the country has a permanent exhibition of even the best photographs by the acknowledged masters.[1] A chic attitude toward photography is that it removed a tiresome burden from painting, the burden of representing the visible world as it appears; such representation being held irrelevant to true art, photography is suspect just because it does suggest the visible world better than any other medium. It is likewise chic to suppose that, because a photograph is the result of a mechanical process, it is not also the result of an artist's creating.

[1] The George Eastman House in Rochester, N.Y., under the direction of Beaumont and Nancy Newhall. Mrs. Newhall has edited the first volume of *The Daybooks of Edward Weston*. She was also appointed by Weston as his official biographer.

One remedy for such snobbery is to look at good photographs. Weston records such a conversion. A woman arranged a meeting between him and a man who, unknown to Weston, hated photography and photographers.

Finally, deadlocked in our differences, I opened the portfolio to prove a point. The first two prints were enough, he retracted everything, he capitulated absolutely. His admiration was deep, enthusiastic, sincere: he proved one of the keenest critics I have met lately, thanking me for having changed his attitude. Once he said, "Anyone seeing that line and recording it could have done great things in any art!"

Another remedy for the notion that photography is an inconsiderable art is to read Weston's *Daybooks,* for in them he reveals himself as being so austerely The Artist, and his intelligence and honesty are so considerable that it is simply not conceivable he would have wasted his time on a mechanical frippery. He was a relentless self-critic, and strove for and sometimes attained perfection. He took, and preserved with formidable consistency, the esthetic view of things; it was the form that counted, no matter what object embodied the form, whether the smooth back of a nude woman on pure sand or a slender, smooth-folded stone on pure sand; when he caught the face of a man in sudden action, he sought the moment of revelation, not because the truth would be revealed so much as because at that moment the face would make the most beautiful image. He was against religion, puritanism, respectability in dress and play; he was indifferent to civic responsibility; he was for free love, primitives, Art. In his life he subordinated everything to his pure dedication to his photography, to himself as image-maker.

Here is a passage which suggests something of his quality.

Morning came clear and brilliant. "I will do some heads of you today, Zinnia." The Mexican sun, I thought, will reveal everything. Some of the tragedy of our present life may be captured, nothing can be hidden under this cloudless cruel sky. She leaned against a whitewashed wall. I drew close . . . and kissed her. A tear rolled down her cheek—and then I captured forever the moment.

Let me see, f. 8—$\frac{1}{10}$ sec. K I filter, panchromatic film—how mechanical and calculated it sounds, yet really how spontaneous and genuine, for I have so overcome the mechanics of my camera that it functions responsive to my desires. My shutter coordinating with my brain is released in a way as natural as I might move my arm.

Is this not The Artist's mirror-world, self-conscious and reversed? His mistress is sad. He kisses her—and then, so perfectly is his camera a part of him, he inserts it between. The photograph he made on that occasion is stunning. To us who look at it only as a picture in a book, its beauty is moving. But a chill seizes me to learn that at the moment when he might have consoled her, have wept with her, he instead took her picture. Why then? Because no model could have generated an expression of woe so genuine, so valuable for his art. Is this not the authentic monster's uncommuning coldness of heart?

A Piece of Lettuce

T H E D A Y I turned three I learned how important it was that I had been born on my mother's birthday. Mother made the fact an occasion for delight, and of course I enjoyed it too. But I was already my father's son and felt this coincidence to be heavy with a significance it nevertheless obscured; somehow I had been destined to be uniquely close to Mother. We spent that day on a train on the way to Oregon, and though I was old enough to expect a big birthday cake and a party, I did not feel cheated at having no more than a piece of dining-car cake with one candle on it and a book of paper-doll cut-outs for my only present. Mother made these seem special just because she and I were wonderfully sharing birthdays on a train. I cannot recall my father's being with us, though in fact he was.

A few months later, in a stormy twilight, I went with my father to feed the chickens. A gust blew my black umbrella inside out and pulled me over. He picked me up, assured me that it didn't matter, and carried me back to the warm kitchen. I hid my face against his shoulder, blinding myself to the umbrella's broken ribs. I was inconsolable, not because I was hurt, as my parents thought, but because this dangerous reversal had happened with my father beside me.

In that same year we were taking a Sunday-afternoon ride in a touring car. Mother was holding me to her side so that I would not interfere with my father. He watched the road with an intent scowl. Later I came to realize that he disliked driving and would fight any car he drove, but at that time I thought he was scowling with ferocious disapproval of something bad about me. I did not try to figure out what I might have done that was bad; it did not occur to me to doubt that I was somehow bad; the reason for the badness did not concern me, only what might come of it. By muddling two Sunday-school stories, I thought it was an angel speaking from a burning bush who had saved Isaac from Abraham's knife; and I had seen my father hang up a shoat by the heels and stick it in the neck with his slaughtering knife. In a field quite a distance from a house and barn, I saw from our touring car a tree on fire, a large tree, perhaps an oak. After I grew up I asked my parents about this recollection of mine; they could recall nothing. Whatever actually was there, my memory brings me to a tree alone in a field of grain stubble, in flames, with no one paying attention to it but me, me sheltering against Mother.

Within a year we returned to Indiana, and on the day I turned four a brother was born. This was no coincidence: it was an intrusion cheating me from sharing birthdays exclusively with my mother. I took refuge on Father's lap. I knew the hymn: God's eye was on the sparrow and I knew he thought of me.

There is an amazement proper to the experience of all great art, but the special amazement which *War and Peace* revives in me while I am reading it is like that of a child. The child does not expect the unexpected; that would already be a preparation against it. He does not for an instant doubt that a certain event had to happen; such doubt obscures. He may even have been told beforehand that it was going to happen; such foreknowledge is as little a part of him as is a label in his cap. He is able to look at the thing itself. The event reaches him radiant with magical causes but not yet trapped in sufficient cause. Tolstoy does not, as many do, achieve this freshness by transporting the reader into a never-never land. On the contrary, his fictional mode is realistic: the people in his novel appear and behave like possible people in the world we daily live in. His achievement is the greater because he uses the mode of realism, for realism suffers a threat to which other literary modes are not subject, the encroachment of mediocrity.

The variety of mediocrity that constitutes this threat grew to importance along with realism and has a social habitation and a name: the bourgeoisie. Bourgeois mediocrity is not only an offense to any writer both as a writer and as a moralist, it is a double offense to a realistic writer because its vast extent makes it all the more difficult for him to enliven his story and to characterize his people with contrasts of customs. Everywhere and always the mediocre man has accepted his society's ways for safety's sake; a bourgeois does it so rigidly that he does not understand how other people *can* do things differently and, worse, he cannot imagine that another way could be better or that other people could *really* believe any other way is better than his. The bourgeois has demonstrated enormous missionary zeal, wanting the whole world to be respectable, profit-seeking, and efficient. He wants the world to be made safe for him by a tyranny of democracy. He has made a theology of science, trying to use it as a shelter against the outrages of chance and fortune—though it has been two generations since the high priests of science have given him much support in this timid endeavor, as he is beginning to realize. His practical religion is technology and machinery. To him, nothing is more troubling than the irrational—whether God, chance, or his own unconscious soul. It is not easy for a man to be bourgeois right to the core; maybe the bourgeois parody of saintliness consists in being a missionary even to oneself. Auden says:

> The dense commuters come,
> Repeating their morning vow,
> "I *will* be true to the wife,
> I'll concentrate more on my work,"
> And helpless governors wake
> To resume their compulsory game:
> Who can release them now,
> Who can reach the deaf,
> Who can speak for the dumb?

Because of the dullness of mediocrity—not just the bourgeois variety, but every kind—most writers ignore or satirize it. It did not bother Dante. There were throngs of those who had not taken sides, the neutrals—"I had not thought death had undone so many"— but of his one hundred cantos he accorded less than a third of one to these pusillanimous ones whom hell would not have. It did not bother Dickens with the Podsnaps, or Faulkner with the Snopeses; the authors contained their characters' deadliness with unrealistic exaggeration, humor, and open loathing. But realism aims to make a well-proportioned image of social, psychological man, of man as he appears to be. What shall it do with the inhabitants of Middlemarch, of Winesburg, Ohio, of all those provincial towns in Chekhov's work, of Bloom's Dublin, of Emma Bovary's Yonville, with just folks, those who neither sin mightily nor love God greatly but are for themselves only? In any sort of aristocratic system—political, ethical, esthetic—they are spurned contemptuously. But for a century or

two liberalism has given importance to their sheer bulk by finding
the Social Will in the majority of votes cast; and material nations for
their material good have elevated to the ranks of duty and honor the
special ugliness of trimmers, of those who would be fully insured—
avarice, mere industry, the unearthing of riches and turning them
not into art or acts of mercy, but into comfort and force. Thus truth
requires that a realistic portrayal of modern civilized man should
accommodate great gray splotches of mediocrity. A good deal of
serious writing, especially naturalism, has been debilitated by the
spreading of the mediocrity which it intended to expose, as Farrell
intended in *Studs Lonigan,* or which it even set out to justify, as the
narrator of Bourjaily's *Confessions of a Spent Youth* announces he
is doing.

A few excellent writers of realistic fiction have dared to make
the mediocrity they see in the world their very subject and yet have
succeeded in writing great stories: Chekhov in *Ward No. 6,* Tolstoy
in *The Death of Ivan Ilych,* Flaubert in *Madame Bovary.* They de-
scribed it in concentrated form, in respectable bourgeois provincial
life, and they found their task painful and bitter. Chekhov loathed
writing *Ward No. 6.* It took Tolstoy as many years to complete *Ivan
Ilych* as *Anna Karenina,* which is fifteen times longer. "How exas-
perated I am by my *Bovary,*" Flaubert said in a letter. "I've never in
my life written anything more difficult than these conversations full
of trivialities." They protected their stories from the effects of the
subject by pushing their detestation of mediocrity to the limit: they
chose central characters who could not know that they were being
damaged, and then ground them to death.

By the spring I was nineteen, in college five hundred miles from
home, real-life wonders were few and far between, and my fondness
for wonderful literature was not unlike my fondness for a two-bit
banana split, called a Banana Wonder, that had four flavors of ice
cream and syrups. I have been told, and suppose it is true, that loss
of wonder is natural to growing up; but to me it seemed dreadful,
and my Swinburnes and Dunsanys were at best feeble substitutes,
even garnished with whipped cream, chopped walnuts, and a mara-
schino cherry. For some years I had been seeing more and more medi-
ocrity—in my family, in the people I knew at school, in "life," in "the
world"—and at Berkeley I acquired the notion that everything was

subject to the rule of rigid and subtle law, especially society and the individual's psyche (no longer a soul). I accepted this as a dogma liberating me from religion; everywhere I looked I was seeing squads of unalterable law; physics was metaphysics was truth; I knew all about the God I realistically did not believe in. On the other hand I saw the mediocrity of things as determined: the irrational was only the coincidental or the pathological, both of which could be accounted for rationally; all things were rationally ordered and hence were without wonder because wonder depends on the mystery of irrationality. The logic by which I demonstrated the mediocrity of things does not bear close inspection, but my feelings were sometimes potent.

One day as I was sitting in a hamburger joint near campus, a newsboy came in waving headlines. Hitler had invaded Austria. First my guts felt hollow. But the course of international politics was determined by historical necessity! Then they griped.

A few weeks later I was hitchhiking home for summer vacation. The day before, a hitchhiker on this highway had killed and robbed the man who had given him a lift. There were sixteen thumbs ahead of me on the highway at the edge of the city. Normally by nightfall I would have been on the last leg home, but that day dusk found me less than a hundred miles along—near a crossroad fifteen miles from the nearest town. Some of the trucks already had their riding lights on. Occasionally I picked up my suitcase and walked awhile. My smile had worn out but I kept my forehead unfurrowed so as not to put a driver off. I had been there for four hours and no one had slowed up at sight of me, not even a couple of buses I tried to flag down; perhaps my flagging had lacked conviction because I knew I could afford to buy a ticket only to the next town. I had not been able to line up a job for the summer; I would probably have to live off my father. A dusty old Model-A pick-up came chugging along with two barefoot girls sitting in the truck bed dangling their feet over the end; they waved till I waved, then they thumbed their noses at me. A big semi going my way met a big semi headed the other way. They must have been going sixty-five or seventy, and when they passed, the concussion of their air-bulks colliding shook me. I stood looking at my feet undecided whether to walk on. A cigarette butt scuttled on the edge of the road toward a grimy clump of dandelion and came to rest on it.

Like a gas the suspicion began to seep into me that nothing in this

law-abiding scene was interesting and that this scene was the world.
I did not recognize this suspicion so much as sniff it. I knew that if
the suspicion really became a part of me, that if I came to believe
that nothing was interesting, nothing wonderful, I would no longer
want to live.

Conscious of no feeling, I thought I had no feeling. I did not know
that I was numb from freezing dread. Even if I had known this, I
would not have recognized what I dreaded most—that I too, an un-
exceptional young man without accomplishments, promise, money,
or the love of desirable girls, might myself be infected with wonder-
less mediocrity.

Tolstoy put the matter in the fewest words. "Ivan Ilych's life had
been most simple and most ordinary and therefore most terrible."
Indeed, his mediocrity encases him so strongly that it is cracked only
by his mortal sickness. The doctor in Chekhov's story learns from
a madman such glints of truth as he finds, but his own descent into
madness is no ironic plunge toward truth; it is the extinguishing of
light. Emma Bovary is so caged by her society's mediocrity, which
she wants to escape, and by her own, which she does not recognize,
that her dreams are false and her loves are lies; Homais, the con-
gealed essence of lukewarm mediocrity, survives to gloat over her
dead death.

Ivan, Chekhov's doctor, Emma—their authors forced them into
postures which appall and which are therefore worthy of Tolstoy's
hope for redemption, of Chekhov's compassion, of Flaubert's intense
bitterness. Perhaps Chekhov contemplated mediocrity in its social,
bourgeois aspect till it appeared to be morally even more threatening
than it is. Surely Flaubert did. The world's mediocrity is as gray and
as dense as they feared, and it may be as vast. Tolstoy too, even in
War and Peace, saw it dense and vast when his interest flagged. At
the end of the novel, his once-lively characters—Pierre and Natasha,
Nikolai and Marya—are shown as settling into the gray repetitions
of middle-aged respectability which, we are made to feel, is the des-
tiny threatening everyone in our bourgeois culture: "most ordinary
and therefore most terrible." But fortunately for us all—as Tolstoy
showed when he was at his best—the mediocrity of things, even of
bourgeois things, is not impenetrable. It is riddled with holes.

The summer I was thirteen I first suspected that my father might be mediocre. The word was his, not Mother's; I had been noticing for some time that he used it in a way which the dictionary did not help me with much. The liberal spirit of the age had started getting to me through H. G. Wells's *Outline of History,* and I was beginning to see in my father the superstitiousness of religion, the illusions of Christianity; Mother was exempt from my suspicion because I saw that religious belief was the least of the reasons she went to church—as it was the greatest of the reasons Father stayed away. But though I was beginning to look sideways at him sometimes, I never doubted his use of moral words. When I heard him say that a barley farmer up beyond the schoolhouse was a mediocre husband, I could neither mistake the scorn in the bark of laughter with which Father punctuated the statement nor challenge his right to that scorn.

That bark of my father's was a complicated laugh. I would think about it. It seemed to mean both that the kind of safety which mediocrity offered against the world's dangers was loathesome and that there was no escape from it. Gorki in his reminiscences of Chekhov puts the matter succinctly.

His enemy was banality; he fought it all his life long; he ridiculed it, drawing it with a pointed and unimpassioned pen, finding the mustiness of banality even where at the first glance everything seemed to be arranged very nicely, comfortably, and even brilliantly—and banality revenged itself upon him by a nasty prank, for it saw that his corpse, the corpse of a poet, was put into a railway truck "For the Conveyance of Oysters."

If no one was exempt, what about Father? One day I rode to town with him to buy grain for the goats; the feed-store owner, a swag-bellied man with big pores on his big nose, started boasting about a sharp deal he had pulled on a Portuguese farmer by playing on the Portugee's bad English. My father, who owed the feed man money, chuckled appreciatively. Not till he was in the truck going out the driveway did he look sour, click his bad teeth, and spit in disgust. For a long time I had wanted to be more like my father. But this pusillanimity of his—was it mediocre?

Father had taught me that God said the world, and Mother had the gift of interest. My tenth birthday also we had spent on a train—going to southern California—Mother and I and my interloper of a brother, to whom I had grown accustomed. Father had gone ahead and built us a house in the desert. That day I learned a troubling truth: I had been born fifteen minutes after midnight of the day following Mother's birthday. Mother said it was because Indiana had been on daylight saving time, which threw everything out of kilter; by God's time, we had all three been born on the same day, so let's sing "Happy Birthday" to one another and hold hands. Well, all right. Still, my brother had been born on her birthday even by daylight saving time. It did not occur to me that Mother was doctoring the truth a bit; nor could I imagine that the truth could ever be flexible, especially about anything so important as my birthday.

Our paucity of neighbors in the desert quite agreed with Father, but it stimulated Mother to overcome her dislike of driving; she went seven miles each Wednesday afternoon to a woman's club, of which before long she became an active spirit. The desert is a good place to seek the truth, but hard on one whose passionate interest is in other people. It was a long time before I realized that, though my parent's qualities underlay my life like strata—emerging here, disappearing there—they did not often blend.

One evening we were seated at table: Father, Mother, my two younger brothers, and I. The meal consisted of pink beans boiled with sowbelly, a salad of cottage cheese on lettuce, bread, and water, milk for the little ones. My youngest brother, going on three, was the most winning child in the world, spontaneously affectionate and never sullen; the family nickname for him was Sunny Jim. There was usually something wrong with him; when there was nothing else, there was his turned-in eye to worry about. A week before, Sunny Jim had fallen off the lath house and bitten a hole through his tongue. He had made a game of teasing Mother by suddenly sticking his tongue out and waggling it at her. He did it now and she quickly yelped with horror and hid her face in her hands. Everybody enjoyed it, and we turned back to our plates. Mother put a dollop of salad dressing on her cottage cheese with a flourish as though it were a treat, cut into the lettuce, and took a good big bite.

Sunny Jim began whimpering and mumbling. His head was bent over and he began fussing at his eyes with his fists. Mother shook him a little and ordered him to behave. He kept on whimpering. Sighing, she put down her fork, pulled his fist away and tilted his head back to see what he'd got in his eye. She screamed so loud we all jumped. She turned to Father. "His good eye! His good eye's turned clear in!

He's blind!" She clasped her baby to her bosom, and he started up like a siren. Father scowled at her and told her not to get the boy stirred up. Her effort to control herself could not prevent her sobbing in little quick snatches. Father pried him from her, told me to hold his arms at his side, and ordered him to quit crying. Astonished, confused, he obeyed and did not even squirm on Father's lap. I heard Mother take a deep unsteady breath; she was biting her knuckles. Father's left hand held my brother's head still, and the hard fingers of his right hand held the boy's eye open so that he could not blink. Motionless, we all stared. His left eyeball was white. Then Father snorted, shook his head, took out a handkerchief and took a swipe at my brother's eye. The color appeared again. "Let your eye roll," said Father, and the eye rolled. A white piece of lettuce had flipped up and cupped itself so neatly over the cornea that the lid had blinked right over it.

Mother clasped him to her again, and cried that it was wonderful, just wonderful. Sunny Jim was still somewhat befuddled; he'd just had a funny feeling in his eye but everybody had acted as though he'd been in great danger. When he could pull free of her, he laughed and crowed, and Mother talked over every little detail of what had happened. My next younger brother, the one who had cheated me and doubly cheated me of my fourth birthday celebration, asked why the piece of lettuce had done that, and she told him it was just the way things happen. He was perfectly satisfied with this, for she said it in the tone of voice with which one says everything's going to be fine and dandy.

But I was satisfied with neither her words nor her tone of voice. I glanced at Father. He had not joined in the babble over the astounding event; he had chucked Sunny Jim under the chin a time or two and then reared back in his chair. When I glanced, his head was tilted back at a cool, surmising angle—I sometimes feel my own head finding that angle—and he was gazing at Mother.

I caught his eye. "Did God mean things to happen that way, Daddy?"

He did not say a word. He drew the corners of his mouth down and raised his eyebrows.

"What a question!" said Mother. "Pooh. It was just a little accident with a happy ending, so let's enjoy it."

So we did.

I did not forget my father's riddling eye.

The first time I tried to read *War and Peace*, I abandoned it in boredom after a hundred pages. It was not realistic enough for me. That party with which the novel opens, Count Bezuhov's dying, the whole Rostov family: Tolstoy seemed to me cheating by making his characters rich and high born, for actually they were just the mediocre walking dead I daily bumped into. Realism should not be about my neighbors in fancy dress. Realism was about a pigeon-chested little janitor, drunk because he was unemployed because of his race, scraping some dog shit off his shoe at a curb on a side street in Chicago. You could tell the truest truth because it was the ugliest. This was a year of the Great Depression. It was shortly before World War II, when foreign policies were more and more often being called realistic; at first realistic seemed to mean facing the facts honestly, but I soon discovered that all along it had meant facing the ugliest facts and creating more like them; this became unmistakably clear when everyone learned how the Germans were exterminating peoples, the Americans saturation-bombing cities, the Russians enslaving nations. The war in Tolstoy's book looked pretty run-of-the-mill, and his peace was plain old family life. Moreover, his world was by no means reliable, in the way I demanded of realism. Unexpected events and irrational impulses were constantly disturbing both Tolstoy's characters and me the reader. Of course, if I had persisted long enough in the novel I would have got to Tolstoy's philosophizing about history, which I would no doubt have found as congenial as I now find it irrelevant. It is as though Tolstoy himself could not endure the ceaseless shiftings in the world he was creating and tried to defend himself against his own disturbance by a rigid theory of historical necessity. "What *seems* to be irrational and coincidental is *really* determined by profound and hidden laws." Had I known that the master was flatulent with this wisdom, I would very likely have allowed the story to entertain me. I would have noticed no more than he apparently did how the art of his novel contradicted its author's preaching. As things were, I guarded myself from what the art said by denying that the art was good.

The dread that was freezing me the summer of that same year, as I squatted by the cigarette butt which had been blown onto the clump of dandelion, was a buried dread, and its logic went something like this. All things are determined. The best literary demonstration of this is realistic fiction. A great deal of the world shown in realistic fiction is mediocre. Moreover, when I see the world about me as though I were a character in a realistic novel, then it looks mediocre. This is the world that made me. Therefore, I must be mediocre. . . . I leapt out of that dread in the only direction I could go, toward the irrational. But I did not make a Kierkegaardian leap of faith; at any rate I did not land with both feet solidly in the Absolute.

It was a short flattened butt brown at the tip. The dandelion stalk was yellowish green and broken off. I heard a car approach but I did not look up as it passed; then a rattletrap with yellowish highlights; then a car with whining tires. I folded my arms on my knees, rested my chin on my forearm, and stared. I felt a thin, authentic terror pierce me. The stub had come into being for sufficient human and physical reasons, and its motions had been wholly law-abiding. The dandelion had done what biological forces and physical circumstances made it do. But that this butt came to be on this dandelion at this time obeyed nothing; disobeyed nothing; meant nothing; caused nothing. Then the wind of a truck's passing blew the butt off into the ditch by the road. An event without value had been brought into and taken out of being by coincidence; at the same time, each several element of the event had obeyed its laws. The tight fabric of things had holes in it. My relief was greater than my terror. I looked up, seeing the same dreary roadside in the gloom. I did not think that *anything* could happen—law had not been suspended—but I did think that on every side things were taking place inside the law and yet at the same time outside it. Normally I would have surrounded coincidence like this with a nimbus of significance in my mind—with that shimmering fogginess which had succeeded Providence when I had replaced the one omnipotent God with rational universal law. But this event was so trivial that it generated no fog to protect my looking at it. It was not nothing, though it came from nothing and went toward nothing. It was not meaningless so much as it was apart from meaning, had no necessary connection with any system that could give it a meaning. I brought it into meaning by thinking about it. But I did not know what to think. It squatted in my mind like a toad in a hole, staring at me. I took a deep, unsteady breath, and stood up.

When I got home, Mother was washing the breakfast dishes. She hugged me and cried a little; she cooked for me and sat with me while I ate; she wanted me to tell and hear everything that had happened since my last visit at Christmas vacation. I knew I had looked so hard at the butt on the dandelion partly because I had inherited Mother's zest for experiences, but this experience was too metaphysical to trouble her with. My father and I had always done our talking about God outside the house. Mother put her faith in going to church. To please her I would tell her that I often went to the University Methodist Church (in fact I had gone only once); I would tell her this in such a way as to imply that I attended just to please her. I suspect she saw through my double lie, though she pretended to believe it. She would probably have liked me to tell the truth and go to church; she certainly liked very much that I showed I cared for her. She did not know that the fabric of things was riddled with holes, but she knew that something was wrong with it.

Fear of death is the cruelest of bands, but I do not think it constrains me more than fear of chance, of sheer conjunction. Fear of chance is far more dreadful than fear of those spirits which used to inhabit the world. Then, each several event happened because some being willed it. Under that dispensation, I think with some wistfulness, a man might be able to pray to the arbitrary, malicious gods so that they might want to do some things his way. Prayer is a form of intercourse, and intercourse holds things together. The myths are full of comforting stories of divine rape. I was raised in that Christian theology according to which chance was really the wide, benign Providence of all-powerful God—this even though He was far less accessible to human understanding than the pagan gods had been, especially since He was good. (A baby was born with a third leg growing out of his neck, and died in lethargy in six days. God, Who willed this sport, is good, is only good. . . .) Under Providence, for a man to be as safe as he could be, he needed to perform just the one act of believing in God, of making himself the bride of Christ— a permanent act, a marriage. I also found a certain security from chance in a wholly natural world so long as it did nothing but obey the laws like a machine. In that world, it was man who wanted things other than the way they were, who moved to change. But that world, because it did not satisfy his spirit, did not contain it, and the contests which politics and science have come to engage in are boundless. Unconstrained, our spirit has lost its shape and identity like a gas, and we are in danger of unmaking one another into vapor entirely at a temperature of three hundred and fifty million degrees. Bands of steel are better.

A recent refuge from fear of chance is psychoanalysis—not the teaching of Freud as such but the magic many of his true believers have made out of it, encouraged by concepts such as the death wish and being accident prone. I would no doubt have tried this refuge too, had not I been made leery of the system before I rightly understood its tenets. When a friend died of polio—a healthy young woman, well married, mother of a child she loved, possessed of a self-less cause—another friend said she must have unconsciously wanted to die. She died, didn't she? Q.E.D. Getting involved in the death-wish argument is like blowing your nose on a hoop. Then there is accident proneness: anyone who gets killed in an accident must have collaborated in his death. He got himself killed, didn't he? But beyond these are coincidences which occur entirely apart from us. Here the True Believers leave the Master far behind. I have known some of them to take toward a random physical event an attitude like Freud's toward a slip of the tongue: a coincidence is a sort of eruption of the world's unconscious, as though the cosmos had a psychopathology like ours. Well, it may be a silly position intellectually, but at least you can *think* about it. At least it keeps you out of a world where some facts are brute, where some phenomena are unthinkable.

"The material world is, morally, a cloud chamber; when a sentence is shot through it, it becomes morally structured." This idea of Sigurd Burckhardt's is so beautiful it should be true. But how can I accept it? In the first place the material world obviously behaves according to schemes which operate apart from our formulation of them into systems of laws. Moreover, the chaotic events in the material world—coincidences—resist all formulation. Only a solipsist could think that they pay attention to sentences shot through them. Still, the beauty of Burckhardt's sentence shakes me. If it were true, an ultimate confidence would be possible—difficult, unresting, dangerous, yet a genuine confidence. For then, despite the risk and effort it demands, we could devote ourselves with grave gaiety to shooting sentences through the world.

Law, will, and chance: they mingle in Tolstoy's world. Pierre wanders unscathed for hours among bullets in a furious battle. Petya is shot through the head in the first skirmish he rides into. You may say that Petya was killed because some French soldier aimed well and that Pierre was untouched because they all aimed badly. Tolstoy does not say that, not *just* that. Those willed and law-abiding bullets were also wandering in the wilderness of probability, and one of them happened at a certain moment to shoot through a boy's sentence-making head, turning it into a clouded chamber.

What Tolstoy's art tells me is that if you look at the law-obeying, mediocre world with enough interest, it will also be seen to be full of wonder-making power, for irrationals emerge into it ceaselessly. For many years that was too much for me to take in. Wonderless mediocrity *and* wonderful irrationality—I could not contain both at once even though by that roadside I had caught a glimpse of this unholy two-in-one. For a moment there, chance had seemed to release me from mediocrity, but then it had merely added itself on— as Tolstoy added chance onto mediocrity in his novel. And if there was one thing I dreaded even more than being mediocre, it was the absurd inversion of the absolute; the absolutely relative; chance.

When I think about coincidence, randomness; about the diverse, incurable paradox, *something which is nothing;* about the discrete, the irreferent, the unintended—then I feel at the core of my mind a tearing sensation which blinds me and which I can stop only by thinking of anything else, even death. The last intellectual umbrella against fear of chance is studying "the laws of chance." "The laws of chance" is no sheltering paradox; it is a tissue-paper parasol stretched on ribs of straw. Nothing is less convincing than a man treating like a valentine from the wide world a table of probability statistics.

Things contain both a pre-established harmony which makes possible for our minds a sublime intercourse, and an endlessly erupting discontinuity by which we are uncoupled. Not one now and the other then: both continually.

In the spring of his eighth year the son of close friends and a playmate of my daughter was given his first pair of roller skates. After he could skate fairly well, his mother permitted him to go on the sidewalk around the block but not to cross the street. There was a slight slope to the sidewalk on the back side of the block and he learned to go down the entire slope without falling, though for a couple of weeks he boasted of the scabs on his knees. I saw him perform his feat once; he went stiff-legged and thrashed his arms about, hooting softly as he rolled.

One morning when he was going down the slope as fast as he could—not really very fast—an old lady with a little dog on a leash was coming up the sidewalk. The dog barked and jumped at the boy. He swerved, stumbled on a piece of wood, clutched at a painter's ladder, jarring it, and then sprawled out on the sidewalk.

The ladder was one of two leaning against the side of a three-story building, with a plank extended between them. At the moment the child jarred the ladder, the painter, taking a break for a smoke, was kneeling on the plank, about to strike a match on the underside of his thigh. Though the ladder was well-chocked and the jar was not great, he lost his balance and toppled over towards the bucket of paint. To avoid hitting it with his hand, he clutched for the edge of the plank, but missed. His chest hit the bucket and knocked it off. He half-rolled off the board, but caught himself before falling.

The child was sprawled prone, the left side of his face against the pavement, not hurt so much as peeved. The lady with the dog reported that she thought he had been scowling as he lay there. The bucket hit his head, the heavy flange by which the handle was attached to the bucket striking him behind the right ear. A moment earlier or later; a slightly different angle of shove; an inch to one side or the other. . . . If the scrap of two-by-four had not been left just where it was (this had not been the painter's doing) or if the old lady had taken her morning walk on the other side of the street as she usually did. . . . Once or twice that evening the child's lips moved and he whimpered. The disconnection was beyond repair. Shortly after noon the next day he died.

Every few seconds a couple, doing what gives them ease, and sperm, egg, genes, doing exactly the possible, law uninterrupted by will's occasioning, so dispose things as to enjoin a miracle. From the lawful will of these dear friends came a son, brown-eyed and thin-voiced like his mother, his head flat in back like his father's, his self his own. The continuation of the miracle is the boy's unforeseeable self. I had grown so accustomed to him that I thought I knew what to expect. Expectation closes the wounds of strangeness for a while.

Out of being the boy went as inexplicably as he came in. No law was tinkered with that he might come, stay a while, go. It has no name. The name is the namer's, and words mean. It sheers meaning. Love is a being's spring toward another, and when that un-being for which there cannot be a word makes the heart's spring fail, falling we must hold on. We now would have to lie to cure our pain, for we have nothing to consent to but our heart's knowledge. Let us stand fast on our truth, which cannot remedy this death but will outlast our pain. Meanwhile let us roar.

The world and the people of *War and Peace* are always recognizable; yet at any moment something unexpected may emerge from them or emerge among them out of nowhere. These unexpected events are never fictionally arbitrary, are neither the whims of fantasy nor the astonishments of artful suspense. When I join again the carrion crows clustering about Count Behuzov's deathbed waiting for him to die, I regain so completely the world's ways that I accept as completely the unlikelihood that Pierre will be favored. My consciousness is divided, as it is when I am in a theater seat, having gouged out my eyes with brooches from the costume of my mother-wife who has just hanged herself offstage. Neither *Oedipus Rex* nor Freud and his congregations could accustom me to desiring my mother. I cannot live by such dark rules, just as I do not live by them in *War and Peace*. Yet they exist surely enough, within us and about us. They will emerge in events and behavior which cannot have been foreseen—though we spend vast energies trying to foresee them afterward, to safen things down again.

Tolstoy provides the best simile to reading his book. It is like being on a battlefield, where you know the unforeseeable is likely to happen. Whether it will be a Dolohov plunging among the bullets, an Anatole mortally wounded, a Platon captured, one cannot be sure, but one can be sure that something of the sort will take place. Despite this expectation, when the event emerges, the person involved (the character on the battlefield, the reader with the book in hand) discovers that foresight does not provide for dealing with the actual experience, and the unexpected swarms him. We are like the brave Nikolai Rostov in his first battle.

"Who are these men?" thought Rostov, unable to believe his own eyes. "Can they be the French?" He looked at the approaching Frenchmen, and in spite of the fact that only a moment before he had been dashing forward solely for the purpose of getting at these same Frenchmen to hack them to pieces, their proximity now seemed so awful that he could not believe his own eyes. "Who are they? Are they coming at me? Can they be running at me? And why? To kill me? *Me* whom everyone is so fond of?" He thought of his mother's love for him, of his family's and his friends', and the enemy's intention of killing him seemed impossible. "But perhaps they will!"

Tolstoy does not look at an event expecting it to fulfill the law. He looks with absolute interest at it itself. Mostly it abides by the laws— but also mostly it doesn't. Pierre made rich by the fillip of an old man's free will; wounded André filling with pity and love at the sight of his most hated enemy, also wounded—whatever it is, if we look with anything like Tolstoy's interest we will be thrown back for a moment, like Nikolai under fire, to a child's way of responding. But not so completely as a child, for the reader's consciousness is divided; he is also sitting in a chair because he wants to, he is also obeying the law.

Not even a mediocre trimmer is buried from Tolstoy's interest. We have seen Anna Mihalovna, for instance, cawing at Bezuhov's deathbed, hoping to get money to advance the career of her trimmer little son Boris. There is no one we less expect to sympathize with than Anna Mihalovna. But Tolstoy did not put her in the novel to prove anything. He is not dedicated to hatred of mediocrity as was Flaubert, or corroded with it as was the narrator of Bernanos' *Diary of a Country Priest*. Usually, to be sure, he presents Anna Mihalovna in a way of which Flaubert or the country priest would have approved. She goes to see her old friend Countess Rostov, who is family-centered and soft-hearted, and we see her working on her friend's mild goodness. The countess offers money and we watch Anna Mihalovna's response.

Anna Mihalovna instantly guessed what was coming and stooped to be ready to embrace the countess gracefully at the appropriate moment.

Of course; the calculation in this embrace was no more than to be expected. But then the countess repeats her offer in the most ordinary words—"This is for Boris from me, for his equipment"—and everything somehow shifts. Something wonderful shoots through, redeeming the ordinary.

Anna Mihalovna was already embracing her and weeping. The countess wept too. They wept because they were friends, and because they were warm-hearted, and because they—friends from childhood—should have to think about anything so sordid as money, and because their youth was over. . . . But the tears of both were sweet to them.

Our moment of sympathy will not save Anna Mihalovna, any more than our contempt had forever damned her. She continues to be out for number one; but not always, not only. After this scene we do not forget that once when we looked with intense interest at this trimmer herself, we saw a person emerge.

The most satisfying event in the book is also one of the most irrational: the reuniting of Natasha and André. The lovers are rich, noble, beautiful, estranged, and young, and there is nothing we yearn for more than their joining. Tolstoy has so majestically deployed the severed parties that their approach to the meeting seems inevitable. The turmoil of war reduces the improbability of the coincidence. Once it has happened, the lovers accept the chance as though it were ordained. They are so perfectly one that to the reader it seems that André's suffering atones for Natasha's guilt. That which fulfills both their desire and ours, so moves us that we need not bother ourselves about the desperations of chance: the event was not empty and did not terrify. Nevertheless, we know very well that they have come together by unexpectable coincidence.

It is the consolation of art that, in its realm, everything is meant to be the way it is. Of all the important kinds of experience there is none like it; in that world, at least, everything was created. The special satisfaction afforded by a performing art comes in good part from the spectator's knowledge that the irrational of real life is working in the performers at the unique moment of that work of art's existence; when they come through successfully, not only has something been created but the Other has been quelled for a while too. *War and Peace* gives as powerful a suggestion of the living as a fixed art can do, and we know that any chance which entered into its creation is subject to its author's control. In that imagined world, which seems to be the daily world revealed and redeemed, the irrational ceaselessly appears: as an intrusion of the subconscious, as a creation of human will, or as an inrushing of the unnamable. Even when it is this last—the unsymbolizable, the irrelevant, the voiding force, an intolerable anti-epiphany on the part of that which cannot be felt toward because it cannot be defined or named and but dimly approached through metaphors for nothing, the most dreadful, the altogether Other—even then we do not freeze with fear, we do not cease feeling. For we know that the lovers rejoin, just as the bullet shot through Petya's head, because Tolstoy's hand wrote the words, because his shaping imagination aimed the sentences. The love of André and Natasha, our love for them, our yearning for their coming back together, everyone's joy at their union: all are created by his chanceless words, and we rest secure in this knowledge.

It is no more a god than it is the unconscious mind of the cosmos that brings into and takes out of being random events—the rolling of a cigarette butt onto a clump of dandelion, the accidental killing of a child, the flipping of a piece of lettuce into a baby's eye—or works of art, or moral acts. These are not many of the things in the universe but they include most of what matters to me, to every me. Perhaps a god causes them, the unnamed, unnamable god, but I have no way of knowing that he does or of imagining why; the effect on me is exactly the same as if they resulted from irregular mixtures of men's will, chance, and natural law. Either way, not having landed on the Absolute when I leaped, I live in the modern world: we create some of reality and some of the beautiful; holiness and virtue are nowhere but in us. No wonder that among us many who earlier would have been exegetes of the Word of God are now literary critics justifying the words of a writer. Of the supreme writers Tolstoy has been justified the least. He leaves little for an exegete to say. His words are so plain that they seem not to have been chosen and placed but to be a transparent medium through which we look at the world they say; and in the body of the novel his immanent will is sure as was God's will when His eye was on the sparrow and I knew he thought of me.

Snarls of Beauty

I W A S teaching in a Catholic men's college run by brothers for whom it was also a monastery, and my best student in freshman English was an acolyte who said little, wrote well, and kept his gaze lowered in chastity of the eyes. Since each class opened with a prayer and I was not a Catholic, I asked him to serve as prayer-leader and he did so with a voice that was never perfunctory; his vows might not be binding yet, but he was bound by them. I had known student brothers, and even a lay student or two, who were as conscientious and intelligent as he, perhaps even as devout; what was remarkable about Brother Charles was his beauty—not virile handsomeness, not serene spirituality, but an inward, unassertive, sensual delicacy of face and composure of gesture about which not even envy had anything to say beyond the comment of a glance or two.

This was in the early 1950s, long before the days when good manners became suspect as a form of hypocrisy, long before encounter sessions and letting it all hang out and the like had hit the country. Then, the place for a hang-up was at home in the closet with your pajamas. Then, the standard brands of exhibitionism and voyeurism, those of the flesh, were shameful, not even barber-shop respectable, and the far graver sorts, those of the spirit, were tolerated only in chic, kinky circles—the TV self-exposure shows were just getting started. This was also a few years before there was a fad of party games which had more than a little in common with the deceitful sort of psychological experiments and were really devices to get you to reveal yourself unwittingly. For such reasons, and doubtless for one or two others as well, it was with a clear conscience that I assigned this topic to my freshmen: Look in the mirror and describe what you see. Good. Here was a new topic to replace all those houses, sunsets, grandmothers, and uncles I was so fed up with; each paper would describe something different, and I would be able to check the description against the thing described. What could be better?

My Most Unforgettable Teacher, that's what.

Every one of those young men liked his face, one of them spectacularly. He was a solid fellow with a round head, butch cut, pug nose, and orthodontured teeth; in the Old World his ancestors had been peasants at least since the Flood, but America was making him into a second-generation Buick salesman with a wall-to-wall wife. The face I saw was Great Plains, but his prose was Hawaiian traveloguese onto which he had sloshed that freshman brand of irony which evaporates in seconds after it is applied. He dwelt for a whole purpurescent sentence on the dimple in his manly chin; he described firming his jaw, flaring his nostrils, narrowing his eyes, half-turning his back to the mirror in order to observe the ripple of his shoulder muscles and powerful biceps; finally he rhapsodized his lips, and he found them so voluptuously kissable that he wound up the theme with a one-sentence last paragraph in which he pressed his lips to themselves in the mirror exclamation point ha ha period.

Brother Charles was absent the day those papers were due, but two days later I found his on my desk, with a covering note apologizing for the tardiness. He had been so distressed by the assignment that he had eaten and slept badly and had gone to his superior for permission to ask me for another topic; but the superior had said his vow of obedience applied to his lay teachers as well as to his religious advisers, so do the assignment, it would be a good humiliation. The face which that paper described was one nobody else had ever seen; it was not only not beautiful, not even an attractive mask for secret evil, it was positively and beyond shame repulsive; yet he did not apply the word "ugly" to it. You would have thought, if you had never seen him, that a couple of acne pimples on his forehead and the stomach sore he had everted his lower lip to get a good look at were leper spots; he said his ears lay flat to his head like a scared dog's. Only his eyes even halfway survived this assault, for at least he allowed "pleading" to appear in the same sentence with them, though there was no indication what the eyes were pleading for and though his freshman irony had branded the word with quotation marks.

I resolved never to assign that topic again.

But a few years later I was teaching in a secular college for women, and the temptation to compare was more than I could resist. These girls were far more sophisticated than the boys had been, and of course the reader they were writing for was of the opposite sex; moreover, the self-betrayal party games were in circulation by then. Even so, I do not think the reason their papers were one and all boring was that the girls were unduly wary; they were only seventeen or eighteen, they could and did say absolutely blanching things at other times in other papers. On guard or not, they described their faces in a matter-of-fact way, like unambitious dancers talking about their legs—"I can do thus and so with them, and maybe if I work hard I'll be able to do that, but they'll simply never have the strength to do the other." The pretty girls, who were only pretty, showed no signs of aspiring to be ballerinas of beauty and the plain ones no signs of trying out even for the corps de ballet, and that was that. I picked up from a twitch here and a sniff there that they thought the assignment had verged on bad taste; the place for a woman to study her features was alone in her room or in a beauty parlor.

The Greeks knew a thing or two; Narcissus was a youth, not a maiden.

II

How could that glass-kisser have been so good to himself, seeing in his mirror what was not there? How could Brother Charles have been so hard on himself, not seeing in his mirror what was there? There are some appropriate psychological labels to slide onto those young men, identity, self-image, projection, and so on—a decalcomania which can be a lot of fun but which is often, as here, not very useful. Beauty is more entangling than that.

For example, look what a tangle beauty has got me into already in this essay. Platonists are jabbing at me from one side, and relativists from the other, and the truth is that I have trouble defending myself against either of them. In the matter of beauty, I seldom know where I am for long, I keep shifting. I wish the jabbers would go away and leave me alone—though they won't because they are in me too.

Against relativism, I believe that Brother Charles's beauty was *there*, not in the eye of the beholder, me, and that he was wrong not to see it, as anyone would be wrong not to see the beauty of Sophia Loren, Mt. Fuji, or Man o' War in his prime. But, against Platonic absolutism, I do not believe that there is some divorced realm of Idea wherein Beauty dwells and that Brother Charles's face somehow adumbrated, was connected to, partook of true Beauty. Few things rile me more than to hear a blockhead Platonist produce such a bromide as "This book has greatness"—as though greatness were a detachable essence injected into the book like tallness into a red-wood tree or wartiness into a toad or beauty into a face. Against such idiocy, laughter is the best antidote. Mark Twain had a joke that went something like this: the greatest general who ever lived was Jedidiah Mitford, a blacksmith in Storrs, Connecticut, but since there weren't any wars during his lifetime no one ever knew he was the greatest general who ever lived. . . . And yet, and yet . . . I find it congenial to imagine, and would not be surprised to learn it was true, that a species of fish of dazzling beauty both of shape and of color evolved eons ago and still lives miles down in an ocean trench where no one and nothing has ever seen them, though maybe some day a probe will bring up a colored movie of them. Great, warty, daz-zling—by and large, adjectives, even beautiful, I get and give without inspecting them closely; but when I use the noun beauty, I scarcely know what I am talking about. More, I am leery of those who talk as though they do.

The physicists conceive of light sometimes as waves, sometimes as particles, though it is impossible for anything to be simultaneously wave and particle; in other words, they know what light is, but when they talk about what it is, they use and know that they use in-consistent, mutually contradictory metaphors. Friends! Einstein said that, of certain mathematical apprehensions of the ultimate nature of energy and motion, he preferred one because it was the most beau-tiful. I have not a glimmer what he was talking about but I believe him, and it exalts me to know that there is a realm other than poetry where truth and beauty are interchangeable and that one mind at least has been there.

III

To be talked about, a thing must be known. To be known, some-one must know it. Man is the measure not of all things but of all things which can be talked about.

Man is not even the measure of all he knows. I may know—I do know—that the great Buddha of Nara is more beautiful than any flower, bird, animal, landscape, but I should not say it is unless I pref-ace the statement with "in my opinion." My humanness is increased by the humanness of that Buddha's great beauty, and his humanness would not magnify me as it does without that beauty. I can best talk about the part of my experience of this statue which is inextricably human, and though I know that this beauty transcends humanness, I can only chatter about that transcendence. Hence, "in my opinion," as a way of acknowledging that the intense, incomputable certitude which constitutes knowledge for me constitutes only my opinion for those who do not share that certitude.

A poem is a way of connecting with things which can be known better than they can be talked about. My purpose in writing this poem is only incidentally to talk about what I know of beauty but mostly to connect with it.

For anyone who conceives of knowledge as information to be exchanged between the computer in my head and the computer in his (I derive this metaphor from a freshman), a poem is an imprecise printout which, as poem, as a playing with words whose purpose is to connect you with a felt knowledge that cannot be verified objectively, has no interest for him beyond a possible amusement value. In this, he is right enough. What positive utility has information which does not retrieve exactly as it was stored? For him, ideas of beauty are best nibbled at cocktail parties. When I tell him that my reason for going on making useless connections like this poem is that I wouldn't live without them, he nods, munches it a few times, spits out the seeds, and if offered another says, "No, thanks, I've had enough." On an exclusive diet of his kind of communication, I would suffer a malnutrition as debilitating as the ulcers he would suffer on my kind.

If Plato had only talked about how experience is related to idea, his theories would have mattered less than they did and still do. But his great dialogues are also beautiful poems which make possible an ever-engendering connection between his readers and what he knew; he is more than other philosophers. It is a good thing his Socrates had the face of a jolly old satyr. Had Socrates been beautiful on the outside too, the dramatic dialogues of which he is the daimon would have been much too tidy and Plato only a Platonist.

If you go around chanting "Elbows are beautiful," you may be a put-on artist, you may be a Sherpa of the spirit living in a realm so high that all things are beautiful there, even elbows, you may be a nut, but one thing is likely: back down here in the plains and valleys where nearly everybody lives nearly all the time, you won't get much of an audience. However, in modern times quite a few prophets have been going around chanting, "Sex is beautiful," meaning not just the pleasure and love generated by sex but the things and acts of sex too. So I roll up my sleeves and inspect. Elbows: good old functional wrinkled elbows; glad they're there, hate to do without them; but beautiful they aren't. Those prophets don't look like Sherpas to me, yet multitudes listen and sway. "Om. Hare. To the pure all things are pure. Hare. Sex is beautiful. Om." What is going on?

For one thing, without acknowledging it, many people are superstitious about ugliness. Ugly has force of its own and often has moral overtones: ugly is a word with which people commonly repudiate an impenetrable evil. Hearing of a mother who has beaten her crippled son to death with his crutch, people are likely to go blank, to shudder and say through taut lips "how ugly." But suppose I am repelled by an ugliness about which there is nothing intrinsically moral. The very intensity of my revulsion is likely to summon a justification, to make me feel and act as though that thing were contaminated with some sort of evil. Somehow, a lot of the time ugly is bad luck. I have heard sophisticated people gaze across the room at a buck-toothed, almost chinless, somewhat hunchbacked woman of sixty-five and say how beautiful she is. "And those eyes," they say. "And her smile changes everything." Because she is charming, subtle, kind, humorous, and wise, they lie from the heart.

The emotional logic of "Sex is beautiful," no less distorted than the puritan syllogism that concludes "Sex is ugly," goes something like this. 1. The beautiful draws us. 2. Genitals draw us by drawing one another; they are an integral part of a beautiful nude statue, painting, or person; they can be, have been, still sometimes are, worshipped; they are the source of much joy. 3. Therefore, they are beautiful.

It is *therefore* that pushes that sequence of statements into nonsense, by trying to wrench things together logically. A relaxed, neighborly, unsyllogizing *and* would have accommodated the truth with a humorous shrug. "And they are ugly." *Therefore* is a copula that needs to be firmly restrained, for it is a great one for cause-and-effecting things for no better reason than that they are in the same vicinity. Moreover, an out-of-place *therefore* can generate in such people as the beautiful-genitalia cult a kind of benign hysteria: an ugly image is lifted off the retina of the eye and its ugliness converted to beauty before it is admitted to consciousness. To put a logic-crazed, phobic *therefore* where only *and* should be takes a right-wrong zeal as fervent as Brother Charles's.

IV

In the fall of Brother Charles's senior year, his particular friend, Brother Austin, dropped by my office one afternoon late when nobody else was likely to come around and asked if he might tell me what had happened during his summer vacation. Brother Austin was a rangy, eager young man with a sometimes raucous laugh and a way of ducking his head at you for emphasis, and over the past two years he had, undiscourageably, showed me his doggerel. Some verses the spring before had given me a glimpse of an acolyte's inner struggle. One was a prayer to his mother by an unspecified speaker begging her to come rescue him from the wilderness he had strayed into: I could not help remembering that St. Augustine's mother St. Monica had saved him from heresy and that "Austin" is a contraction of "Augustine." The other, "Riddles," ended with these lines.

> Why does a heretic burn his bridge?
> Because that's all he's got.
> Why do apostates pick their nose?
> Because they're full of snot.

Making a face, I flipped the page back at Brother Austin. "Isn't it hideous?" he guffawed. "Boy oh boy, what a fellow won't do for a rhyme. Just think, I'm a nose-picker myself!" "Just think," I said.

This is the story he came to tell me.

That summer the student brothers had gone for two weeks to a camp in the woods half a mile from a secluded beach. Except for meals and prayers, they were free most of the day to do what they wanted, and he had gone to the beach, every day the weather permitted, to swim and sun-bathe for hours. There was frequently no one else there—with one exception. Every time he was there, without fail, a hundred yards or so up the beach, there was a girl about Brother Austin's age. He would swim out beyond the breakers: she swam out as far. She would body-surf on the breakers into shore: he tried it, and in a couple of days he could do it as well as she. They laughed, they raced, they watched each other, her dog came barking down to visit him, they never once spoke. ("She was not a come-on artist," he assured me. Frowning, he slowed up for a moment. "Not that I ever saw a come-on artist in action." But then he ducked his head at me and picked up momentum again. "But I know she wasn't one.") By the sixth day he hardly knew where he was. He was debating whether to get out of the order; something must have happened to his vocation. That day he missed dinner—he never missed meals—and did not join in the evening volleyball game. If only the girl would go away. If only there was some way to let her know he was going to be a monk, so she would leave him alone. He stayed off by himself in the woods till darkness and a foggy breeze drove him back to camp.

Brother Charles was waiting for him outside the little tent they shared, and asked him what was the matter. "Nothing." There was a long silence, which Brother Austin broke with a snort. "I'm losing my faith, that's all." Brother Charles crossed himself. Then Brother Austin told his friend everything.

Without a word, Brother Charles disappeared among the trees. Brother Austin slept fitfully; every time he woke up, the other sleeping bag was empty.

At dawn, Brother Charles came back, shivering, his face drawn. He had trouble taking off his shoes, getting into his sleeping bag; his legs were stiff; his knees didn't seem to work right. Brother Austin asked him where he had been. "Down by the creek, praying." "All night?" Brother Charles did not answer. "For me, Charles?" "Yes, for you, for strength for you."

"Of course," said Brother Austin to me, slapping his thighs and shaking his head, "I never went back to the beach again. No sir, I got over that hump all right. The worst is behind me now, I hope. With a friend like that on your side, a fellow just can't lose."

A year later he left the order.

v

I find the ugly hard to think about, partly because, according to its nature, it makes me want to turn away from it but more because it stupefies me, and the purer it is the stupider it makes me. My parents gave me no help in thinking about the ugly, about human ugliness, at least; as close as they ever came to mentioning another person's ugliness was to call a mean-spirited, rich recluse of a warty miser on the other side of town unfortunate. Perhaps they did this out of embarrassed charity, but I think that rather it was one of the many important things, including sex and death, they not-thought about as best they could and that in respect of not-thinking about ugliness they were more than good, they were superb, they could let it alone as I cannot. I am grateful for the impurities with which ugliness is usually mixed; they give me something to laugh about, think about, forgive, something I don't have to be stupid about.

The first time I was in London, I was riding in a bus one morning eavesdropping on a couple of working women in the seat in front of me—they were straight out of Dickens—when suddenly off to the left there loomed up the ugliest thing I had ever seen. More accurately, no other ugly thing I had ever seen had been powerful enough, as this thing was, to sink me into blank stupidity. I didn't even recognize it. To be sure, I had come across pictures of the Albert Memorial, but they had no more embodied the ugliness of that edifice which Victoria had commissioned in honor of her dead husband than pictures had prepared me, in any way that mattered, for what I was to see in Chartres Cathedral a month later. I was as open to the exalting beauty of the one as to the stupefying ugliness of the other. The women in front of me also were gazing at the Memorial in silence. After the bus had lumbered past it, the less pinch-faced of the two said to the other, "Coo, she must have loved him." Good for her: she had found something nice to think about instead. Good for me too: I began making connections again, pleasantly ironic ones about taste, and that ugly thing ceased to be a black hole in my mind.

A tree may be beautiful and so may a rock; but to say of a tree that it is ugly is to say little more than that it is deformed, and to say a rock is ugly is to say only that you don't like it—how can a rock be deformed? That is, beauty and ugliness are not complementary; to lack beauty is not necessarily to have ugliness; indeed, there is a French expression, *une belle-laide,* to describe a woman who is at once beautiful and ugly. Our apprehension of the ugly is even more anthropocentric than of the beautiful. The ugliest natural things I have ever seen are a male orangutan in a zoo and an eel in an aquarium, the orangutan because I saw it as a self-indulgent imbecile abandoning himself to gluttony, lust, and sloth, the eel as a turd with teeth. But, because I knew I was attributing to both of these innocent creatures qualities that were not inherent in them but came from my imagination, I was as amused as repelled. The more purely ugly a thing, the more human. A friend of mine avoids going down a certain block near her home, because of three large diamond-shaped protuberances one above the other on the façade of a three-story apartment house. She had passed that building many times without much noticing, but one day she was so unfortunate as to see those diamonds, to see the non-relationship of their size, shape, color, placement to anything else on that weak-yellow, stucco façade, and that sudden seeing plunged her into a blind tunnel. Now, even a glimpse of that purely man-made ugliness sinks her each time anew into the same blank incomprehension. Some ugliness is a mistake, or at least we can think so; some is intended to inflict esthetic pain, so that you can hate the artist. But the ugliness of that diamond-studded façade is pure; no one could say "coo" to it; it isn't about anything; my friend's sadness, each time she sees that thing, is to strive to imagine what went on in the mind that made it, but to fail. Ugliness opens a way into but no way out of a lightless snarl of the mind.

In the past couple of decades there has come to be a fashion of esthetic coprophilia, of applauding art which is ugly in itself and which often is about human ugliness. Just how metaphorical the phrase "esthetic coprophilia" is here, I am not sure; perhaps love of the ugly is no more than like the perversion which sexualizes ordure, perhaps it is a sublimated manifestation of that perversion. You wouldn't have to be very Freudianized to make a plausible case for the sublimating theory. When I read the novel entitled *Naked Lunch,* I consumed something, all right, but "naked" is not the word I would have chosen to describe that "lunch." But whether love of the ugly is literally or figuratively a variety of coprophilia, it can always cop the plea of psychopathology: poor fellow, he's sick.

The moral forms of ugliness are at once fascinating and baffling, and, of these, the one with not a trace of beauty in it is envy. Maybe those who set out to make evil their good, as Genet says he did and as Milton says Satan did, are able to love envy; but I know of no one, including Genet and Satan, who has *said* he loves envy, and I quite literally cannot imagine how anyone could love it.

To see envy as clearly as it can be seen when it has metastasized throughout a soul, one can do no better than to contemplate Iago. And one can contemplate him, for the unrelieved ugliness of his envy is inextricable from the beauty of the play; it is not added onto

Othello like a gargoyle on a cathedral but is essential to its structure yet somehow without contaminating it.

The actor playing Richard III must give a strong impression of physical ugliness, for we must see that the deformity of his body is connected with his wickedness. But, though the actor playing Iago need not be handsome, he must not be ugly, for we must know Iago's wickedness as purely moral, no more mitigated by malformation of body than by poverty or a stroke of bad luck, by anything whatever outside his own soul—speculating on his childhood is about as useful as speculating on the condition of his pancreas. In the first scene we learn that Iago is full of vengeful hatred because Othello has promoted Cassio over him when he was next in line. This is the seed of his envy, just as Richard's deformity is the seed of his malice, but in neither case can I believe the seed adequately accounts for the monstrous growths. Finally, Iago's malignity becomes, as Coleridge said, motiveless, that is, beyond comprehension. Iago could have said as appropriately of Desdemona or Othello what he says of Cassio: "He has a daily beauty in his life which makes me ugly." Nothing extenuates Iago's moral ugliness in our mind; its integration into the elegant structure of the play and the rightness of the words Shakespeare gives him do not mitigate that ugliness but permit us to look at it steadily. When its full extent is revealed to the other characters, shock confuses them, and they turn to him—*why?* We the audience are not shocked at that point because we already know about his moral tumor, we have watched it grow; nevertheless, we too turn to him—*why?* He responds, "From this time forth I never will speak word," nor does he. Shakespeare does not let us off the hook by making us shudder with horror or nod with understanding or mutter "Poor fellow, he's sick." We too are struck dumb. We come out of the play alive again only because Othello's death-speech floods us with emotions—emotions which would be fearfully painful in life but which we are glad to feel fully while immersed in the play because of the perfection of the rhetoric and the magnificence of the poetry and the exact placement of that speech, for only by letting emotion flood us can we escape from the blind hole Iago traps us in.

VI

The self in relation to beauty has something in common with the observer in relation to a rainbow; whether or not anybody sees the

rainbow, everything about it is *out there* except the word; there is
no way to locate any rainbow more than approximately; where *this*
rainbow is depends on where you are; the only place no rainbow
can be known by you is where you are, for you must be at a cer-
tain distance to see it. Also, the self in relation to beauty has this in
common with an agnostic in relation to death: the more intimate the
connection between them, the more likely it is to snarl. And nothing
snarls the self-lines more than guilt, unworthiness, inadmissible sin.

Their words and glances tell her, "You are beautiful," and she
looks in the mirror and says to herself, "If that were another woman,
I would agree that she is beautiful." Mirrors distance her from her-
self, but how much of her own beauty can a mirror show her un-
distorted? Part of it, but not the whole sweep of the arc we others
can see. Or they move in closer and tell her, in the cant of this age,
"You are a beautiful person, you are a saint." If she is quick, she
side-steps that one with "Thanks, I like you too," and goes about
her business. Otherwise, she might get a permanent crick in the neck
from periscoping the beauty of her own goodness.

As for my connections with beauty, they began as snarled as any
beautiful woman's ever gets, and they are still snarled enough—
and in a way that seems to me quite American. To begin with, I
am Scotch-English by descent, and the British are not one of those
people, like the Javanese, among whom beauty is common; on the
contrary, run-of-the-mill Britishers are as unbeautiful as run-of-the-
mill Russians. A few years ago I went on a tour to Moscow and
Leningrad, and one evening we were complaining about the almost
total dearth of attractive-looking Russians we had seen. "Hrmph,"
said an elderly Scotswoman with a muttony face, "what do you ex-
pect? They killed off their aristocrats, didn't they?" My forebears
were yeomen and artisans as far back as I know, unleavened either
by the natural beauty of race or by that assured, fastidious beauty
which generations of breeding can and sometimes do bring out.

Moreover, my parents were low Protestants: in my family vanity
was an horrendous sin. My mother found beauty galore in babies,
brides, and serene old people, but the further you were from those
exempt conditions—and bridehood lasted about a month on either
side of the wedding—the more whiffy the beauty, if any, my mother
was likely to sniff out in you; and my father scarcely distinguished

330

between the primping vanity of a pretty girl and the preacher's *vanity of vanity all is vanity.* In the Old Testament I read, beautiful was an attribute of holiness, pastures, righteousness, Zion, and, on mountains, of the feet of an angel bringing good tidings. When God looked upon what he had created, he saw not that it was beautiful but that it was very good. Only when Eve was about to yield to the serpent's temptation and pluck the fruit, was it mentioned that she saw the tree was pleasant to the eyes; and a woman's beauty, except the bride's in the Song of Songs, was mentioned only when an occasion for sin— Bathsheba's, for example. The Lord in Isaiah says he "will smite with a scab the crown of the head of the daughters of Zion, and the Lord will discover their secret parts," because they "are haughty, and walk with stretched forth necks, and wanton eyes, walking and mincing as they go, and making a tinkling with their feet. . . . And it shall come to pass that instead of sweet smell there shall be stink; . . . and instead of well-set hair baldness; . . . and burning instead of beauty." In the New Testament, Moses is said to have been fair when he was a small infant, but there are no beautiful men or women at all, not even, despite the artists' later portrayals of her, Mary Magdalen. Nor is it mentioned whether Jesus was beautiful; his attributes are moral or divine; John says of the incarnation: "And the Word was made flesh and dwelt among us . . . full of grace and truth." I was not at all surprised to learn, somewhat later when my father urged me to read *Paradise Lost,* that Satan before he rebelled against God had been the most beautiful of all the angels.

However, though I grew up not questioning the sinfulness of vanity, it remained unreal to me, like the pauper's feast or the millionaire's socialism: no vanity without beauty, and except in my mother's three charmed categories, I saw in the people of my life very little beauty, a pair of eyes here, a hairdo there, a smile occasionally. Hollywood stars were notoriously vain and very remote; their beauty was visible all right. But as for real people, and especially real bodies, I was in high school before I saw the beauty of one. He was a Negro in the gym class I'd been put in, and his long-muscled limbs and torso moved and were shaped marvelously; but I am sure now that, if his body had been about the color of mine, and especially if it had been a girl's, I would have been unable to disentangle my self from that beauty enough to see it at all. The first girl I fell in love with was Tess of the D'Urbervilles, words without flesh. Not till I had left home for the university did I see any beautiful women—that is, did I dare look at women's beauty carnate.

Perhaps the worst ingredient in this not-untypical snarl I was in about beauty, especially a woman's beauty, was that I was so damned moral about it. If a girl was beautiful, she was probably vain and so of course I wouldn't have anything to do with her. Much more serious: because beauty drew me powerfully, I would love a woman only if I were drawn to her by her true self, for loving a beautiful woman for her beauty was as unthinkable as loving a rich woman for her money. I could love a beautiful woman only if she did not allow her soul to be tainted by the slightest contact with her mere physical beauty—though of course I knew she would. In effect, I held her guilty of being beautiful.

Fortunately for me, I was an inconsistent prig.

One day I picked up Fitzgerald's early novel *The Beautiful and Damned*. What wisdom must a book with such a title contain! But the story was sleazy and bored me. Not long afterward, Yeats's poem "For Anne Gregory" outraged me. But I memorized it.

> Never shall a young man,
> Thrown into despair
> By those great honey-coloured
> Ramparts at your ear,
> Love you for yourself alone
> And not your yellow hair.
>
> But I can get a hair-dye
> And set such colour there.
> Brown, or black, or carrot,
> That young men in despair
> May love me for myself alone
> And not my yellow hair.
>
> I heard an old religious man
> But yesternight declare
> That he had found a text to prove
> That only God, my dear,
> Could love you for yourself alone
> And not your yellow hair.

My priggish chatter could not prevent the beauty of that poem from connecting me with what it was about.

Recently I met a good-looking woman who said that when she

had gone to college from her poor country town she had been rushed in her freshman spring by one of the two most popular sororities. Surprised and flattered, she pledged. But the next fall she learned why these false sisters had wanted her: they thought she might enhance the reputation of the sorority house by winning the campus beauty contest. "When I learned that," she said, "I just made myself ugly." I asked her how she had done it—hair, makeup, what? "Oh, I don't know. Mostly I sagged." "But you were so young. Isn't it hard to sag at 19?" "Easiest thing in the world." "But what about boys?" "Right. So I entered the beauty contest so they'd be sure to lose, and the next semester I got out of it and quit sagging."

The old men on the walls of Homer's Troy, watching the glorious Helen pass by, wanted to but could not blame her for the war that would destroy their city. When Phryne was charged with profanation, her defense was to remove her robe before the judges that they might know her beauty: they acquitted her. So far from being guilty of their beauty, these Greek women were guiltless because of it. Their bodies had been entrusted for a while with a divine gift which they could accept with the unsnarled pride of the grateful. "That is great poetry," said blind Milton when his daughter read back some lines of *Paradise Lost* aloud to him, "but I didn't write it." (And if that is an apocryphal story, so much the better for apocryphal stories.) Milton's angel had given that poetry to him, and it was his. Rilke and Yeats, whom I take to be the supreme poets of this century, were visited by angels too and dared accept and use the gifts they were offered.

But Enlightened man generally, that is to say, scientized and democratic man, has no experience of gods or angels, a lack which is filled by mod religions little better than by psychedelia. On the one hand, when you look through the lenses of science at a beautiful person, divinity of any kind is filtered out and such matters as genes, statistical probability, vitamins, photosensitivity are let through instead; "divine," as commonly used in the vicinity of "beauty" nowadays, is as secular as a fashion photographer's camera. On the other hand, there are very few ways in which the democratized self believes it right or safe to excel. Where is the equality in this individual's beauty, or the justice, or the progress? On any advanced campus in the late 1960s and early 70s, you could spot a good many egalitarianized young people by their slovenly hair and shapeless old clothes and pubic blankness, by the women's uglifying make-up and the men's languid gestures, by the way they snuffled and scratched with dirty fingernails and sagged.

When the gods bestowed their favors according to their whims, when God moved in a mysterious way, you did not have to justify your good fortune, just as you were less tempted to blame others for your bad fortune. But now that your beauty is a gift of mindless chance, you are likely to say "Why me?" instead of "Thank you," to substitute corrosive anxiety for gratitude. When most events were divinely willed, I did not have to strain to fit everything together; God knew why this was thus, and I did not expect to. But now the mind's empyrean is a fragile network of probabilities gleaming against the vast darkness of chance; and, because I don't know where your beauty comes from or what it means, and you don't either, suspicious explanation comes snarling in where reverent gaiety sometimes used to be, but now so rarely is, that the very term "reverent gaiety" has a nostalgic, lost, medieval ring to it.

A gift of great value, offered meaninglessly and unfairly, is dangerous to accept; all that inextricable guilt, all that unworthiness. Again and again in modern times, it seems to me, poets do not make as well as they could because they are doing it all by themselves. Even when a poet accepts the proffered gift, he needs help to dare use it fully; fame and the hope of fame are hunchbacked substitutes for the muse, an angel, divine afflatus.

VII

For centuries the Platonists have been tidying Plato and the Aristotelians adulterating him with common sense, but because he wrote so beautifully he has survived them all.

In *The Symposium,* that all-night banquet celebrating Agathon's winning the prize with his first tragedy, Socrates tells a fable of the hierarchy of love, from love of one person up to love of Beauty itself. Very exalted, very ethereal. But the form of Plato's poem humanizes the sublimity of Socrates's eloquence. After the fable is told, Plato does not leave us beating our wings in the vast inane of Love and Beauty like a Shelley, but brings in Alcibiades roaring drunk. We learn that Socrates has been attracted to him for his physical beauty and that he has loved Socrates, whose appearance is as far from the beautiful as Alcibiades's behavior is from the good. Alcibiades speaks.

I say that he is exactly like the busts of Silenus which are set up in the statuaries' shops, holding pipes and flutes in their mouths; and they are made to open in the middle and have images of gods inside them. . . . His outer mask is the carved head of the Silenus; but . . . when I opened him, and looked within at his serious purpose, I saw in him divine and golden images of such fascinating beauty that I was ready to do in a moment whatever Socrates commanded—they may have escaped the observation of others, but I saw them. Now I fancied that he was seriously enamored of my beauty, and I thought that I should therefore have a grand opportunity of hearing him tell what he knew, for I had a wonderful opinion of the attractions of my youth.

He tells how he tried to seduce Socrates and loves him all the more for his kind resistance, and also tells how, on a military expedition,

One morning he was thinking about something which he could not resolve; he would not give it up, but continued thinking from early dawn until noon—there he stood fixed in thought . . . until the following morning; and with the return of light he offered up a prayer to the sun and went his way.

When Alcibiades has finished, Socrates responds to him:

This long story is only an ingenious circumlocution, of which the point comes in by the way at the end; you want to get up a quarrel between me and Agathon, and your notion is that I ought to love you and nobody else, and that you and you only ought to love Agathon. But the plot of this Satyric or Silenic drama has been detected, and you must not allow him, Agathon, to set us at variance.

Plato does not make things neat, but neither does he ensnarl us in complication. Socrates is ugly and he has gods in him, Alcibiades is a reprobate and he is beautiful.

And what a blessed liberation for a democratic, half-scientized, dis-Enlightened Judeo-Christian like me to know how beauty can be a power great as goodness and exalted as truth and necessary to love.

Not *therefore: and.*

UNIVERSITY PRESS OF NEW ENGLAND publishes books under its own imprint and is the publisher for Brandeis University Press, Brown University Press, Clark University Press, University of Connecticut, Dartmouth College, Middlebury College Press, University of New Hampshire, University of Rhode Island, Tufts University, University of Vermont, and Wesleyan University Press.

Library of Congress Cataloging-in-Publication Data

Elliott, George P., 1918–
  [Selections. 1992]
A George P. Elliott reader : selected poetry and prose / George P. Elliott.
  p. cm. — (The Bread Loaf series of contemporary writers)
ISBN 0-87451-577-7
I. Title. II. Series.
PS3555.L58A6 1992
818'.5409—dc20   91-50812